MY CHICAGO
JANE BYRNE

MY CHICAGO

JANE BYRNE

W · W · NORTON & COMPANY   New York   London

Printed in the United States of America

First Edition

The text of this book is composed in Monotype Trump Mediaeval with the
display set in Kabel Bold Condensed.
Composition and Manufacturing by the Haddon Craftsmen, Inc.
Book design by Jack Meserole.

Library of Congress Cataloging-in-Publication Data
Byrne, Jane, 1933–
My Chicago / Jane Byrne.
p. cm.
Includes bibliographical references and index.
1. Byrne, Jane, 1933– . 2. Mayors—Illinois—Chicago-
-Biography. 3. Chicago (Ill.)—Ethnic relations. I. Title.
F548.54.B97A3 1992
352'.00092—dc20
[B]   91-25422
ISBN 0-393-03073-3

W.W. Norton & Company, Inc., 500 Fifth Avenue, New York, N.Y. 10110
W.W. Norton & Company Ltd., 10 Coptic Street, London WC1A 1PU

1 2 3 4 5 6 7 8 9 0

For Steven T. Rosen, M.D.,
Director of the Northwestern University Cancer Center
and his courageous staff who uniquely understand
the importance of hope and grit.
Thank you all.

CONTENTS

ACKNOWLEDGMENTS

I am grateful to many people who helped in the writing of this book. The long list includes Ellen Joseph, my personal editor who also became a personal friend; and Ed Barber, my editor at Norton.

I wish also to recognize Charles Flowers, Ted Johnson, Lawrence Bear, Joe Pecor, and Bill Currie for their special help.

Lee Pitaro deserves special recognition for the hours and hours of historical research she contributed to this book.

Phyllis Miceli and Susan Beider deserve special thanks for their many hours of typing of the manuscript.

I also extend my deepest appreciation to my husband, Jay McMullen, for the many patient hours he gave me in the retelling of the many stories that he recorded as a reporter and columnist covering City Hall and politics for twenty-five years for the *Chicago Daily News*.

I also owe immeasurable thanks to my daughter, Kathy, for her many trips to the Chicago Historical Society, the county clerk's office, and the town of Ballina, Ireland, digging back through generations of our family history.

I acknowledge with the deepest gratitude their many contributions to this book.

MY CHICAGO
JANE BYRNE

The First Meeting

E arly in 1964, my parish gave a party to celebrate the thirtieth anniversary of the founding of its church, Queen of All Saints. My shy father made a charming, urbane master of ceremonies. All of Chicago that mattered seemed to be there, including the nation's most powerful political boss, Mayor Richard J. Daley. Ever since the start of John Kennedy's campaign back in 1960, His Honor and I had been seeing a lot of each other at various functions around town.

When I was introduced to him once again, he asked bluntly, "Why do I see you at so many events? What is it you do when you do it?"

To my acute embarrassment, Monsignor Dolan, the pastor of our church, interjected, "You know Janie, don't you, Dick? Why, she was one of the smartest girls who ever went through our school."

The mayor smiled and said, "Why don't you come in and see me?"

I moved on down the receiving line thinking this was the man's routine way of dismissing unimportant people. So far as I knew, one did not simply appear at City Hall asking to see the mayor.

Within the week, however, one of his secretaries called. Would next Tuesday at one o'clock be convenient? And then I chuckled, remembering how many high-powered Kennedy staffers had been barred from Daley's office in 1960.

Just before the appointed hour, I arrived at Room 507, City Hall. Surprisingly, I wasn't nervous. There were two offices I had to pass through. First was the nearly empty reception room, inconspicuously off to the side of the main door; behind its small desk sat a police sergeant, and in two adjacent chairs two more police officers stood guard. The sergeant checked off my name, phoned the mayor's office to announce me, and wrote me a pass. Approved, I proceeded down a long, narrow hallway into the mayor's outer office.

The whole place was eerily quiet. I handed the slip of paper with my name on it to his personal secretary. I was the only one there except for her and two assistants. This office was barren, too, but large. High-backed green leather chairs lined the walls. The silence persisted. None of the three secretaries spoke above a whisper, when they spoke at all. I felt as if I were in church. Obviously, Daley was an adept player of psychological games. The office, I would learn, was nicknamed "the inner sanctum." Suddenly, the secretary intoned, "The mayor will see you now."

I walked in, barely able to notice anything about the room except his presence. He absolutely projected that kind of force. Solemnly rising, he indicated a chair. The City Seal hung on a wall behind his desk, just above a very large picture of his family. We exchanged pleasantries; then there was a sudden switch of gears.

"Why did you go to them and not us?"

I was lost. What *was* he talking about?

"Kennedys," he growled. "The Kennedys." His voice was gruff, his face hard; the lower part looked like a bulldog—two sets of jowls and all.

This was bizarre. Jane Byrne was hardly a household name, to be courted by either a Kennedy or a Daley. I had been a twenty-six-year-old widow with practically no serious political experience.

Before I could respond, Daley barked, "What did *they* do for you? We take care of our people. What did you get out of it?"

Not every word was distinct, because he often turned toward the wall or looked out the window. Only years later would I understand how painfully embarrassed he was about his uncertain command of basic English. But the message got through.

Mockingly, he compared what "they" could have offered versus local perks. "We take care of our people," he repeated.

My Irish began to rise. "Mr. Mayor, I am very aware that you weren't pleased to have a Kennedy headquarters in Chicago. I am also aware that relations were strained during the campaign."

Daley talked right through me and sat down heavily. "We could have put you in *our* speakers bureau. We could have sent you all over. You would have been *known* by now.''

Known for *what?* I wondered.

''We'd have taken care of you. The Kennedy people didn't.''

I was fed up. ''I'm sorry that you feel this way, and sorrier still that you have said these things to me. I never heard anyone at the Kennedy headquarters speak ill of you. That is the truth. The night you put Kennedy over, they were quick to acknowledge and praise you.''

Gathering steam, I blurted out, ''You ask me what I got out of it? I'll tell you. That was a very close election in Illinois, and you certainly produced the necessary votes. But if I brought out even a few votes to help put him over, that's exactly what I got out of it, and exactly what I wanted—Kennedy in the White House!''

Now I was standing, so angry I couldn't stop. ''I've come to the wrong place. I was wrong about you. I had hoped you were behind Kennedy, the man, but you weren't. He was nothing more to you than the spoils of victory. What difference does any of this make? The man is dead, *dead.*''

I was so carried away that I'd failed to observe the mayor's reaction. Suddenly, he pushed his chair back and leaned over, his face out of sight below his desk. His voice was muffled. ''Sit down a minute. My shoelace is untied.''

Obediently, I sat, shocked by my vehemence. A tense minute or so passed. When Mayor Daley sat up again, he turned his head away from me, but I could see that tears lined his face, tears he couldn't acknowledge. Two thoughts went through my head—that I was a chump for losing my temper with the mayor of Chicago, who was grief-stricken in his way, too, and that I wanted like hell to get out of his office lickety-split.

When Daley collected himself, he got back to business. ''Do you have contempt for the Democratic organization, the thing some people call the machine?''

I replied that I knew very little about the machine.

The mayor said, ''Politics is like any big business. We are no different from General Motors. They sell a product; their product is cars. Our product is people. We sell candidates. We are only bad when we sell bad candidates.'' He went on, ''Just as GM has an executive group with a chairman of the board, so do we—that's me—and a sales force and mechanics—that's our organization.''

Chicago's management gathers following a 1975 cabinet meeting with
Mayor Richard J. Daley. COURTESY OF LAZLO KONDOR.

Then he asked, "Are you above working for your ward organization?" I said I didn't think so but admitted I didn't know anything
about my ward organization. He asked which ward I lived in and the
name of my alderman. Sauganash, of course, but I didn't know the
name of my alderman.

The man was stupefied. He looked at me hard, as if I were another
form of life. "Sauganash," he said slowly, syllable by syllable, with
great patience, "is in the 39th Ward, and the alderman is Shapiro. I
can make you anything I want." This was said as simple fact, not
boast.

He shook his head. "You have lost so much time, so many are
ahead of you. You should work for your ward organization and be seen
at it and with it. If you don't do that, no matter what I sponsored you
for, a board or a commission, they'd get you."

I shuddered. Who would want to get me?

Daley continued, "Go introduce yourself to the alderman. Tell
him you want to be active. Don't take anything from him, just go and

be a volunteer. What do you want to be in politics?"

Of course, I had no idea. "I don't even know if I want to be in politics," I answered weakly.

He ignored that. "Member of the House of Representatives—possible. Member of the Senate—possible, but not probable."

Done. He was finished with me. Rising, he said, "Check in once a month."

I left that office weak-kneed and dizzy. No one is going to believe this, I thought. Daley in tears. The House, maybe, but probably not the Senate. Crazy, all of it. I wanted to run out of the building. As I reached the elevator, I doubted I would ever return to Room 507.

My mother agreed. "That place and that man are not for you," she said. But Daley didn't have to be my entire political story. Bobby Kennedy might run for President and try to bring us back to the Golden Age.

What if? I thought to myself. What if?

I could be there to help if Bobby ran, and with that realization, my decision was reached.

CHAPTER 1

A Magic of Its Own

The first time I remember thinking about my city was Holy Thursday of my eighth year. My two brothers and I always looked forward to Holy Thursday Mass, because it marked the end of Lent and the daily rising at the grim hour of six to get to seven-o'clock Mass. It also signaled the fading away of cold dark winter and the first hints of spring, as tulips popped up beneath the evergreens beside our front door in Sauganash, one of Chicago's oldest neighborhoods. The tulips returning to 6242 North Keeler Avenue every year proved to me that the nuns at school were right: Easter really was what they called a "renaissance," a rebirth after tough times.

This Holy Thursday was particularly special to me, because my older brother Billy, then twelve, had been chosen to lead the procession of parish schoolchildren, carrying high the cross that symbolizes Holy Week. Seven-year-old Edward and I marched proudly alongside our schoolmates, each boy paired with a girl in the same class. Dressed in white dresses and matching veils, all of the girls carried white lilies to lay upon the altar at Queen of All Saints Basilica, only six blocks from our house. There, in a ceremony that was both beautiful and filled with promise in my eyes, Billy assisted our pastor, Monsignor Francis J. Dolan, in serving the Mass.

When we raced home afterward, my two brothers and I were greeted by the inviting fragrance of warm hot cross buns and the sweet perfume of bouquets of Easter lilies. We couldn't wait to start dyeing our Easter eggs. Once they dried, we'd place them carefully in a rainbow of colors around the lamb-shaped cake my mother had baked and set out on a pedestal cake stand in the center of our dining-room table. Our whole family loved Easter, but particularly my father, an unusually devout Irish Catholic even in a city famed for the breed. His parents had emigrated to Chicago from Castlebar, County Mayo, and they had retained many of the beliefs, customs, and folkways of the mother country. Two of his brothers, Ed and Joe, had become priests. Ed would cut the larger swath in the ecclesiastical world. A monsignor, he rose to the chancellorship of the Archdiocese of Chicago, at that time the largest of the 155 Catholic dioceses in the United States.

Despite my father's delight in every aspect of Holy Week, a shadow lay in the background of our festivities in 1942. The war that instilled great fear and uncertainty in my generation was blazing fiercely in Europe and the Pacific. On the surface, though, we all joined together in the preparations and good times. After a wonderful family meal, my father sat down at the piano and began to play a song that was new to me—Irving Berlin's great hit "Easter Parade." As always, I enjoyed having him teach me the lyrics of a new song, line by line, but some of these words raised interesting questions. "Down the avenue, Fifth Avenue . . ." Could we parade there? "Oh, no," he laughed, "that's in New York." Well, I thought, what is this "New York" and why do I always hear about it? I knew that it had an East Side, a West Side, and an all-around-the-town, that girls there played Ring-Around-the-Rosie and London Bridges Falling Down, that everybody on the sidewalks of New York seemed to trip the light fantastic. (These, at least, were the messages of popular culture of the day.)

But what about Chicago? *Our* city. It had much more going for it, as I knew from tons of experience and a wealth of family stories. Why didn't Mr. Berlin write a song about us, too?

Such youthful, inchoate stirrings of civic pride had their foundation in the struggles and achievements of both sides of my family, but most of the tales of Chicago's growth and aspirations came from my mother's side, the Cranes. Their past and our present were bound up in the story of this bustling, ever-changing, often self-destructive great metropolis from the day her great-grandparents arrived in 1855, long before the infamous Great Chicago Fire.

Patrick and Margaret Crane and their children, the eight-year-old twins John R. and Bridget Laura, came from the town of Ballina in County Mayo and settled at 107 North Clinton Street in Chicago. John, who would become my mother's grandfather, delighted my

Wolf Point in Chicago's earliest days, dividing point between the north and south branches of the Chicago River. Here a town meeting was held that brought about the incorporation of Chicago. COURTESY OF DAVID R. PHILLIPS.

grandmother and her brother and sisters during their childhood with stories about early Chicago and how he saw it grow. Luckily, he and Bridget could learn their way around Chicago from Patrick's brothers, Thomas and John Crane, who had emigrated in 1844 and 1846 respectively and lived with their families at Kinzie and Wells streets.

I was most proud to be descended from the Cranes, the branch that had come to Chicago so early and that lived with such zest and humor. With their high cheekbones, strong chins, flashing eyes, and tall, slender physiques, they were testimony to Ireland's reputation as a "land of saints and scholars," for they worked hard, respected learning, and helped build their parishes in this new country.

Settling on the northwest side of the north branch of the Chicago River close to Wolf Point, at Clinton and Kinzie streets, my great-great-grandfather Patrick Crane got a job as a blacksmith. He was one of 150 blacksmiths in Chicago—fifty years before the automobile, trade in everything having to do with horses was, of course, brisk. The northwest and north sides then were predominantly German, Irish, Scotch, and Swedish. Each group had its own community and its own church. The Irish worshiped at Holy Name Chapel (later to become the cathedral), the Germans at St. Joseph's Catholic Church or 1st St. Paul's Lutheran Evangelical Church, the German Jews at the north side Hebrew Temple, the Scots at the Westminster Presbyterian Church, and the Swedes at St. Ansagarius. Dearborn Street, north of the river, was then as now the north side's fashionable street for American-born Protestants.

Even a decade earlier, in the days of Chicago's first settlers, Wolf Point had served as Chicago's entryway. It was the place where the north branch of the Chicago River joined the south branch and then flowed as the main stem directly east to the sandbar blocking its path into Lake Michigan. There it turned south and continued to Madison Street before emptying into the lake.

From Chicago's very beginning, the river was its greatest asset, crucial to the city for drinking water and as a potential trade route to the Mississippi Valley and beyond. It would also divide Chicago into its three sides—north, south, and west. These divisions would be not only geographical but also ethnic, regional, and ultimately, racial.

The earliest place of settlement around 1702 was at the bend in the river, recognized today as the intersection of Michigan Avenue and Wacker Drive, and it was here that "the Father of Chicago," Jean Baptiste DuSable, a black man, settled on the north side in Chicago's first permanent residence. DuSable was a fur trader admired for his trading skills and loved for his hospitality. His home, quite lovely for the times, was open to all. There was no indication in Chicago's multiracial beginnings of racial differences to come.

Once the Revolutionary War was over, all America began to look west. In 1795, the Treaty of Greenville, ceding to the United States six square miles of land at the mouth of the Chicago River, was signed by the Potawatomi, Ottawa, Chippewa, Miami, Shawnee, and Delaware tribes and General Anthony Wayne.

In 1803, Fort Dearborn was built to stand at the bend of the Chicago River close to its mouth. This fort promised increased security for those Americans in the East willing to venture to the New Frontier. Slowly, settlers began to arrive and build their houses along the river from its mouth to Wolf Point, where a settlement including a church and hotels sprang up.

During the War of 1812, the soldiers of Fort Dearborn and their families were ordered to move to Fort Wayne, 175 miles away in Indiana. They were not long on their journey when they were am-

The great Chicago River—early trade route between the Great Lakes and the Mississippi River, as well as a divisive boundary separating Chicago's north, south, and west sides. COURTESY OF DAVID R. PHILLIPS.

bushed by hostile Indians, who killed at least two-thirds of these early Chicagoans and left their bodies in the stony sand along the lake. The warring Indians then went west to Fort Dearborn, stole what they wanted, and burned the outpost to the ground. This band of marauding Potawatomi Indians was not from the immediate Chicago area, but from farther west. Disenchanted with their treatment by U.S. government agents, they had joined with the British and, under the leadership of Suna-we-wo-nee, war chief of the prairie bands of Potawatomi, raided several frontier settlements.[1] By contrast, the local Potawatomi took in the Chicago settlers who survived the massacre and tended to their wounded until the rampage ended. Chief Billy Caldwell Sauganash, who was half white and had always got on well with the traders and settlers, personally saved many lives. He would not be repaid—he and his tribe would be pushed off their land.

As children growing up on the far northwest side of Chicago in Sauganash, my brothers and I were bike riding one day and came upon a huge rock bearing a brass plate inscribed "Old Treaty Elm 1835." At this spot Chief Sauganash was forced to sign away the land now known as the Billy Caldwell Reservation. Thrilled by this artifact of

Home of Chicago's first permanent family, the John Kinzies. Located near the Chicago River and Michigan Avenue, in the 1830s. COURTESY OF DAVID R. PHILLIPS.

the romantic Wild West, we rushed home to tell my mother we had found an old Indian treaty spot. Very seriously, she explained to us the true meaning of the plaque. Fort Dearborn had been rebuilt at its original location in 1816, giving new life to burgeoning Chicago, but gradually crowding out the Indians. Finally, Billy Caldwell Sauganash was compelled to trade his ancestral land for unsettled land across the Mississippi River and lead his people there. I asked Mother if he ever came back. "No, he stayed there until he died. By the terms of the treaty, none of the Indians could ever come back across the Mississippi." My mother thought what had been done to the Indians was shameful and often said so.

In the next decade, Chicago grew phenomenally. The federal government spent $25,000 to open the sandbar at the mouth of the river, creating a harbor in its place. Chicago often has very fickle weather, windy with wild gusts, moody with fog, or perhaps brutal with ice and snow. Almost as if to give the workers some help as they dug away at the sandbar, a wild storm blew off the lake; the waves pounded against the sand, beating at the sandbar as the men dug until suddenly the waves broke through, cutting a broad path through the sand. The Chicago River would now flow straight into the lake.

Almost simultaneously with the announcement of the work on the harbor, the Illinois legislature (Illinois had become a state in 1818) set up a commission to lay out a plan for the digging of the Illinois-Michigan Canal and to acquire the lands necessary for the canal to connect the Chicago River to the Mississippi, via the Des Plaines and Illinois rivers. The announcement of the canal hit like a thunderbolt, not only in Chicago but in the East as well. New Yorkers, Bostonians, other Easterners, and Southerners scrambled to speculate in land, not only within the city limits but in the suburbs as well, and more and more families came to settle in Chicago.

By 1830, about fifty families lived along the river. In 1833, a number of them gathered at the Sauganash Hotel, Chicago's first inn, which was built in 1829 on the south bank of the main stem of the Chicago River across from Wolf Point, currently the intersection of Lake Street and North Wacker Drive. There they drafted the charter incorporating Chicago as a town. There were 140 residents, but only twenty-five of them were legally eligible to vote—that is, American-born and non-Indian. Twelve votes were recorded in favor of making Chicago a town. By 1837, Chicago was incorporated as a city of five thousand. This growth did not always occur smoothly, for rivalry sprang up between north siders and south siders, a rivalry that characterizes Chicago to this day.

The building of the Illinois-Michigan Canal created dreams of wealth, dreams that favored the south side in one particular way. From its inception, the Illinois-Michigan Canal planners had set aside residential land for the primarily Irish workers who would build the canal, and their wooden shanties sprang up on the south side overnight. There they built St. Bridget's Catholic Church. First called Hardscrabble, the area later became known as Bridgeport when, deliberately and deviously, a very low bridge was slung across the south branch of the river. The scheme was simplicity itself—barges arriving from downstate Illinois would be forced to stop at the low bridge located at Archer Avenue in Hardscrabble. Merchant seamen had two choices: unload their cargo at the bridge or transport it to the barges waiting on the other side of the bridge. The positioning of that low bridge had literally created a port, making Bridgeport the center of power on the southwest side—commercially, industrially and, ultimately, politically.

Germans soon settled right behind the Irish in Bridgeport. The Irish, Scotch, Germans, and Swedes also moved into the area. On the southwest side, the Germans founded their first Lutheran Church of the Trinity, but most Germans would settle on the north side, most Irish on the south.

Another bridge was the focus of a violent disagreement between south siders and the businessmen of the north side. The small Dearborn Street bridge, the oldest in Chicago, connected the north side to the commercial district south of the main stem of the river. Erected in 1834, it was poorly built and barges were constantly bumping into it, giving the south siders, who wanted total control of all river commerce along the new route, an excuse to ask the city council to tear it down. Great wailing rose from the south siders about how the Dearborn bridge was slowing barge traffic. In 1837, over the protests of the north side businessmen, the council voted to accede to the south siders' request. So heated had been this battle that the south siders, fearing the council might cave in to the storm of protest from the north side and repeal its decision, marched before dawn to the river and smashed the bridge with axes. Thus in 1838 the north siders were left with ferryboats to transport their goods to the commercial district downtown while the south siders had their own bridge at Bridgeport, and the west siders watched their new bridge go up at Randolph Street that same year.

Many Eastern investors considered the north side a logical place to invest. But the large teams of horses—often six and eight strong—pulling the heavy loads of grains and pigs from downstate and central Illinois had a difficult time crossing in ferryboats to the north side. So did raw goods being brought up from the south via the canal to be manufactured, processed, or slaughtered on the north branch. Still, scores of warehouses, grain mills, lumber mills, and factories had been built along the river's north branch, and the wood planking of roads into Chicago was progressing at a fast pace.

As north side rents began to drop, public anger and frustration grew almost out of control. One of Chicago's earliest movers and shakers, Bill Ogden, an Easterner who had invested heavily in the section, stepped in and called a meeting of all the north side businessmen. He unfolded a plan by which they would sell stock for a new bridge to themselves and their friends. Ogden, a native of New York, persuaded some of his business associates back East to subscribe along with the Chicago interests and raised enough money to build a good bridge. But when they petitioned the city council to allow its construction, the battle of the bridges began all over again before a council divided and ruled almost entirely by geography.

Again, Bill Ogden rushed to the rescue. Along with a colleague, Walter Newberry (for whom the Newberry Library is named), he offered the Catholic Church one square block of land on the north side. The church readily accepted the offer of the land, and talk grew of building a cathedral on it. Ogden's political tactic was successful. Catholic council members dared not vote against their church, nor could they deprive the south siders of a bridge to get to the proposed cathedral. The vote was a tie broken by Mayor Benjamin Raymond, Chicago's third mayor (1839–40), and the north siders got a bridge at Clark Street.[2]

Standing north of the river on Ogden's gift of land today, in all its power and ecclesiastical glory, is the Cathedral of the Holy Name. It is the church of the cardinal and the center of power of the Archdiocese of Chicago.

Commercial growth and development of the "infrastructure" were only part of the story, as my great-great-grandfather would discover soon. Whenever Patrick Crane talked to my ancestors about his arrival in Chicago in the mid-1850s, his face reflected his initial shock, for it reminded him of the bogs of Ireland. Yes, Chicago was a substantial city, but it was also a city wallowing in the mire, continually mud-caked. But Patrick would personally witness an astonishing feat of engineering that changed all this.

The city council had tried and failed to force the river back into its banks or to raise some of the lower land. Ditches had been dug, wooden planks laid on the mud. Eventually, several downtown streets had their own sewer systems. But the water problem was too overwhelming to handle in such a scattershot way. The city's engineer, Ellis Chesbrough, devised a comprehensive closed interconnecting sewer system capable of carrying the runoff into the river. But in order to drain the land, the city had to be raised fourteen feet over the sewer system. There were no alternatives. The council did what it had to do—it passed a law that the whole city be raised, over strong objection from the *Chicago Tribune*. The historian A. T. Andreas writes, "The *Tribune* warned that damage to the current structures would be in the millions and that there would never be enough dirt to raise the 1,200 acres of land within the city limits."[3] Nevertheless, the council persisted.

Patrick Crane would tell his grandchildren, wide-eyed, "There

Holy Name Cathedral—seat of power of the Roman Catholic Church in Chicago and symbol of the city's old-time, hard-nose politics. Holy Name is also my parish church, wedding place of my maternal grandfather, home parish of my uncle, Edward Burke, chancellor of the Chicago archdiocese, and scene of worship prior to my taking the oath of office. COURTESY OF LEE BALTERMAN.

were houses, hotels, business establishments being jacked up off the ground, and whole streets of buildings would be moved, perhaps across the street, down the street, up the street. They would be replaced with soil, and then never once disturbing the occupants, they would roll them right back to where they came from. The people may have very well been eating, playing cards, or waving out their window as their house rolled by, but raise the whole damn town they did, God help us!''

The public and its leaders were simply dead set and determined to drain their land. Chicago had already dug its canals on the backs of the immigrant Irish, in order to open its western boundaries to the Mississippi. It had opened its clogged river mouth at the lake, creating a harbor large enough for major vessels to enter. Chicago's power now stretched from the Great Lakes to the Mississippi. It was a city located at the heart of the nation, and what a beating heart it had. Along its banks one could see Sturgis & Buckingham grain elevators, the Chicago Mills grain warehouse, the Hubbard Meat Packing Co., Blogett's Brick Making Co., Dole's slaughterhouse, and the home of the McCormick reaper.

Yet though the river routes had been dominant in early Chicago for water, for commerce, for survival, new factors began to matter more for growth in the 1850s. Booming Chicago was fast becoming a railway center. Within a decade after Patrick Crane's arrival, the population had increased to 180,000, leading to overcrowded living conditions. Cheap wooden houses were constructed for immigrants wherever vacant land could be found.

The largest dry goods store in Chicago at that time (1855–56) was Cooley Wadsworth & Co., which in 1857 hired another newcomer to Chicago, Marshall Field. When I was ten or so, I began to ask my mother about my grandparents—where they all came from and when they came to Chicago. She always used the arrival of Marshall Field as a reference in time. I would, of course, consider that to be antiquity, since Marshall Field's store looked ancient to me. According to Mother, Field was so poor when he arrived that he slept on the counter at Cooley's dry goods store. At least, I would think, my great-great-grandfather had a house on Carrol Street between Des Plaines and Clinton and a bed to sleep in. It crossed my mind to ask why Field, not the Cranes, ended up with a world-famous department store, but I knew such a question would hurt her. She was intensely proud that her Chicago roots ran deep. I would be much older than ten before she told me that Chicago's elite would naturally have high regard for the Massachusetts-born Field but disdain an Irish Catholic immigrant. I was glad she hadn't told me earlier. Nothing in my childhood experience, in fact, had alerted me to prejudice against the Irish in America.

Another newcomer was welcomed by the newspaper industry in 1855. Ohioan Joseph Medill, publisher of the *Cleveland Leader*, came to buy into the *Chicago Tribune*, which had been publishing since 1847. The paper was business-controlled and business-oriented, unlike such earlier newspapers as the *Democrat*, founded in 1833, or the *American*, founded in 1835, which were politically oriented. (In fact, the *Democrat*'s Long John Wentworth so politicized the paper that he could propel himself into the mayor's office in 1857.) The politically ambitious Medill quickly put his autocratic stamp on the *Tribune*, transforming it into one more power block in 1850s Chicago. Some of these same power blocks still influence Chicago more than a century later—the Bridgeport neighborhood, the *Tribune*, and Marshall Field.

While Field and Medill were empire-building, the Crane brothers were raising their growing families. I often wondered why they settled on the north branch of the river off Wolf Point and not on the south branch as most of the Irish had. I suspect it was the love all three brothers felt for the sea and for Ireland's beautiful lakes and glens. Chicago, to be sure, wasn't Ballina in County Mayo, and it wasn't the fresh sea where the Crane brothers had watched their mother wash the "fine linen," but it had a magic of its own. Wolf Point faced the water. In the evening as the lamplighter went from one gas lamp to another, they could stroll down to where the two branches of the river flowed together, or walk straight east toward the masts of the tall ships anchored along the river's stem. When they viewed the *Madeira Pet*, the first ship to arrive in Chicago from Europe, it was probably a link to the past they treasured, and when they watched the *Dean Richard* preparing to set sail for Liverpool, their old home probably didn't seem so far away. As they watched the brig *Sleipner* anchor and viewed the dazed passengers disembarking fresh from Norway, they could empathize and admire the courage it took to do what they had done, to cross the ocean in search of a better life. In December, Patrick would walk the two blocks with his two children, John and Bridget, to board the *Rouse Simmons*, nicknamed the *Christmas Ship*, for its cargo was freshly cut Christmas trees. Chicagoans made their selections right on the deck.

The harbor held a different meaning for William B. Ogden, the Eastern land speculator who had become Chicago's first mayor in 1837. Only two years before, he had come west to take over the real estate holdings of his brother-in-law, 132 acres of prime riverfront land on the north branch of the Chicago River's stem. The two men began to accumulate other acreage. Once, Ogden bought fifty-one acres, then quickly sold one-third of it, recapturing his original purchase price.[4] He explained, "When you're dealing with Chicago property, the proper way to do it is to go in for all you can get . . . and forget all about it. It will take care of itself."[5]

His holdings sat at the prime spot of the water route that would link the Great Lakes via the Chicago River to the Mississippi River, then all the way down to the Gulf of Mexico. Ogden wheeled and dealt with his trove. Sometimes he formed partnerships with other entrepreneurs. One of them, Cyrus McCormick, inventor of the reaper, built his factory on Ogden-controlled land, thus beginning the McCormick dynasty. As the river became more and more important to Chicago's economic development and the lakefront harbor bulged with trading vessels, Ogden snapped up even more property along the north branch of the river at the harbor.

By 1857, the same year that Marshall Field arrived in Chicago, Ogden had decided he wanted his land company (now called Dock and Canal Properties) to be exclusively and legally in control of the harbor. He had made so much money on Chicago real estate speculation that he was in a position to provide the docking facilities necessary to accommodate all of the shipping of that day. Wisely, he retained as his attorney a former member of the Illinois state legislature. By means of legal and lobbying expertise, Abraham Lincoln persuaded the legislature to grant Ogden a special corporate charter giving him the right to "enclose, make and protect wharves, docks and piers for the safety and accommodations of boats and vessels." The Dock and Canal Company could also condemn additional land necessary for harbor improvements. In other words, this extraordinary charter gave Dock and Canal the kind of control over land usually reserved for city and state governments.

Ogden tested his new powers quickly by offering to buy some of the adjacent land. When many of the squatters there refused to vacate, he condemned the land and requested that the local government evict them, a civic responsibility handled with unseemly alacrity. Before long, Ogden had claimed the land from the river's stem east of Michigan Avenue to the lake and north to Grand Avenue. Most of Chicago's best land was now in the hands of a private developer in perpetuity.[6]

I don't know what my forebears thought of these machinations in their new country. Probably neither the Crane brothers nor any other Irish Catholics felt they had a political voice anyway, since the mayor was Levi S. Boone, elected in 1855 on the Know-Nothing ticket.

All across America a political movement termed "nativism" had been developing since the 1840s. Its roots were in the East, where Americans had come to resent the swelling number of immigrants, particularly Irish Catholics, and where the Native American Party evolved from the American Republican Party. In the early 1850s, many secret societies of nativists were organized, and when outsiders asked members about their activities, the stonewalling response was "I know nothing"—hence the nickname of the movement. But their goals were clear: to restrict immigration and to prevent naturalized citizens and Roman Catholics from participating in politics. By the mid-1850s these secret societies had merged into the American Party, which unsuccessfully ran Millard Fillmore for the presidency in 1856.

These attacks against Irish Catholics and immigrants were not new. They had been appearing almost daily in the Chicago papers, notably the *Tribune*, for several years prior to Boone's election. In 1853, the *Tribune* had published an editorial charging that Irish Catholics were the cause of much of the unrest in the city because of their drinking habits. That year, the Know-Nothings, who had enjoyed a good deal of political success around the country, set their sights on the Chicago mayor's chair. Realizing they didn't have enough votes to win, the Know-Nothings allied themselves with the abolitionist movement and the temperance movement. Their candidate, city council member Levi S. Boone, grandson of Daniel Boone, led the entire Know-Nothing ticket to a sweeping victory.

Keeping his campaign promise to the temperance groups, Boone immediately ordered the termination of all liquor licenses at the end of three months and increased the licensing fee for taverns from $50 to $300, in hopes that only Know-Nothing proprietors could afford that sizable an increase. Boone wanted an end to German and Irish Catholic taverns. He also ordered enforcement of the neglected laws on Sunday tavern closings and inspection of licenses and asked the city council to assign the police to his direct command.

At first, the immigrant population did not take Boone's orders seriously, but it was soon obvious that he meant business. Tavern owners who couldn't renew their licenses at the higher fee were arrested and their businesses were closed. As arrests mounted, taverns were shut down on Sundays. The Know-Nothings knew these closings would anger the Irish Catholics, but they were surprised to find the Germans even more furious. Beer gardens were an integral part of the German Sunday.

As Patrick Crane told the story, the Irish sat back and had a good laugh as they watched the German protests mount. Characteristically, the Germans organized well. Every day they marched to City Hall behind their fife-and-drum and bugle corps. Boone remained firm. The arrests continued, and the blue laws were strictly enforced.

Came the trial day of the arrested proprietors, April 21, 1855, and great numbers of Germans assembled in the courthouse, spilling out into the streets. The courthouse became so crowded that the judge ordered it cleared, forcing more people onto the streets, and when the police arrived and tried to move the crowd along, fighting broke out. More police arrived, and more arrests were made until finally the crowd dispersed, returning over the Clark Street bridge to the north side German section.

These arrests and incarcerations incensed the entire German community. Some six hundred of them decided to march back over the bridge to demand that their friends be released. Now, City Hall officials used the Clark Street bridge to their advantage—they raised it, preventing the protesters from crossing to downtown Chicago. After a while the traffic was so backed up that the bridge tender had to lower the bridge, at which point the Germans rushed across and headed straight for the jail. The police and the militia were in battle array. The Germans charged the police line anyway. Fighting erupted and gunshots were fired, but when additional militia were ordered in, the riot ended quickly. The mayor then asked the crowd to disperse. The riot resulted in one known death and scores of injured police and demonstrators.[7]

In reminiscing about the Lager Beer Riot, as it was called, Patrick Crane argued that two good things came of it. For one thing, this was the beginning of the end for the Know-Nothing movement, and that could only be beneficial for Irish Catholics. And, he would say with a smile and a wink, "It gave the Irish a good laugh at it all, for when the militia left, the mayor had to call upon the aid of none other than the Irish Montgomery Guards, to keep the peace in a much-disturbed city."

Meanwhile, as the Irish and the Germans were allowed to return to their kegs and taps, a more essential liquid was under siege in midcentury Chicago. Water was delivered directly by water cart from the lake, or by means of the Chicago Hydraulic Water Works Company with its reservoir at Lake and Michigan; but drinking water presented a growing problem. The spill-off from the slaughterhouses and the glue factories, the chemicals of the commercial manufacturers, and all of Chicago's raw sewage had begun to contaminate the drinking water. Chicagoans had endured the cholera epidemic of 1848, an epidemic caused by polluted water; nearby Lake Michigan was far more contaminated in the 1850s.

Again Chicago turned to engineer Ellis S. Chesbrough, who once again came up with a bold plan. In 1864 he designed a watertight crib, to be floated two miles into the lake off Chicago Avenue, far beyond pollution; there it was sunk to the floor of the lake. Chesbrough had also designed an underwater two-mile-long brick tunnel, wide enough for two mules abreast. The tunnel began at the old and almost obsolete pumping station at Chicago and Michigan avenues. When the tunnel was connected to an opening in the crib, pure fresh lake water rushed into the tunnel back to the pumping station. A state-of-the-art pump drew eighteen million gallons of water a day into the city. To ensure adequate pressure and to stabilize the flow of water into the neighborhoods, a vertical pipe was inserted into the main pipe at the pumping station. Longer underground pipes ran to a standpipe 138 feet high by 3 feet in diameter. Water rested in the old standpipe and flowed into the main pipe when pressure was low, thus producing an even flow of water.

So important to Chicagoans was this machinery that the city hired William Boyington, one of the best architects of the day, to design the two buildings enclosing the pumping apparatus and the standpipe. Boyington chose to use a creamy limestone to build a castellated Gothic design borrowed from medieval English architecture. To Chicagoans of today, these buildings, completed in 1867, are known as Chicago's Water Tower and Pumping Station.[8]

To Patrick Crane's son, John R. Crane, who was about to marry Catherine Howley, the completion of the work was much more than a triumph of engineering. It promised safety for him, his wife, and their children to follow. Death from dysentery and typhoid fever was no longer a threat. John left his parents' home, now at 107 North Clinton, still on the northwest side of the river, to reside with his bride, Catherine, at Huron and Franklin streets. John, feeling all the hopes and dreams of a young bridegroom, was the first of the Cranes to leave the west bank on the north branch of the river and move east. He worked at Young Brothers Wholesale Goods as a teamster-porter, meaning that he had a horse and some kind of cart for transporting wholesale goods.

The 1860s also saw the founding of the first University of Chicago, the rise of a city hall and a courthouse, and construction of excellent schools. A park system was being developed—Jackson and Washington Parks on the south side, Lincoln Park on the north side. The city's first national political convention was held at the Wigwam Convention Center, May 19, 1860, nominating favorite son Abraham Lincoln. The prestigious Historical Society was established, and elegant

The Water Tower—
sturdy survivor of the
Great Chicago Fire,
symbol of survival to
the ravaged people of
Chicago in 1871. The
Water Tower still reigns
as Queen of Chicago's
Magnificent Mile,
Michigan Avenue north
of the river. COURTESY
OF LEE BALTERMAN.

railroad terminals were built. The magnificent Palmer House on State
Street was completed, as was Marshall Field's department store. Carson Pirie Scott opened on Lake Street to compete with Marshall
Field's.

Their rivalry gave Chicagoans wonderful Christmas shopping
days and began the tradition of lavishly decorated holiday windows.
Like many Chicago parents, ours took us children to view the Christmas windows on State Street, and if we went during the day, we'd
stop for lunch "under the huge decorated tree at Marshall Field's," as
the slogan put it. I preferred going at night, when it seemed like
fairyland with all the beautiful Christmas lights adorning State Street,
and we'd always stop for hot chocolate and club sandwiches at Henrici's.

The Chicago of the late 1860s also had its massive Union Stockyards and remained a shipping center. Suburbs were quickly developing along city limits, and transportation systems were under construction to provide public access to the suburbs. Omnibuses (horse-drawn
buses) and horse-drawn streetcars could take you around the town.
Growth and commerce were the heady watchwords of the day.

For all its civic virtues, Chicago lacked one important quality: sensitivity to the plight of the newer immigrants. True, they could find jobs aplenty, at steel mills, steel rail plants, and lumber mills, at slaughter and packing houses, at freight yards, breweries, tool and dye plants, paint and varnish plants, at freight warehouses, shipyards, and grain elevators. But domestic life was hard, and housing was neither planned nor decent. Wooden shanties continued to spring up overnight, clustered and overcrowded amid the commercial, industrial, and retail areas.

Disaster struck on a warm, gusty, dry October night, the kind of autumn night in Chicago when the bright leaves have popped from their branches and briefly make a richly colored carpet under your feet.

To all Chicagoans the night, October 8, 1871, would seem a travesty of nature itself, as a fire driven by the wind grew in only minutes into a force totally out of control. It roared in the wind, moving Northeast from its beginning at 137 DeKoven Street (currently the location of the Chicago Fire Department Academy) and burning to the ground everything in its path. The sidewalks, the streets, the shanties, even the trees were destroyed. How sad I grew as a child when my mother told me of the Great Chicago Fire, and of her great-aunt Bridget's account of the screams of the people as they ran to escape the flames. Some, she said, jumped into the river to escape the heat, and some into the lake, but there was no safety in the water, for the fire, roaring north, jumped the river (it had already destroyed the downtown business and residential area from Harrison Street south), burning bridges and vessels laden with cargo. Once it jumped the river to the north side, the warehouses, plants, houses, churches, schools, and almost everything else burned to the ground. Over two thousand acres of Chicago was reduced to embers, leaving over 17,500 buildings destroyed and 92,000 people homeless. The fire did something like three to four trillion dollars' worth of damage in today's money. The coroner reported three hundred deaths.

When I asked my mother, "What started the fire that burned for almost three days and hurt so many people?" she replied, "Mrs. O'-Leary's cow kicked over a lantern in her barn." How I despised that cow and Mrs. O'Leary, too, when I learned that her shanty still stood intact on DeKoven Street at the end. "What did the poor people who were homeless do?" I asked. "Or the businesses, what did they do?" Mother looked quizzically at me as if to say, "Well, what would you do?'' and in her typically analytical way responded, "They just rebuilt it, and because of the way they rebuilt the city, it can never happen again, and it is why you are safe today."

Chicago, it seems, cannot be burned down. As devastating as the Fort Dearborn massacre was to the thirty or forty families who watched the Indians burn down their only hope of protection out on the lonely frontier, the survivors helped to rebuild the fort. When the entire city was destroyed by fire, the citizens rebuilt it, and made sure that Chicago stood strong and great again on the river.

One hundred and nine years later, when my press secretary asked me if I had a theme for my inaugural address, I answered from somewhere deep inside, "Of course—the theme will be renaissance for Chicago and for *all* its neighborhoods." Chicago is the city of renaissance. So I had learned, literally at my mother's knee, and from all the family stories of new beginnings after challenge and crisis.

CHAPTER 2

The Spirit of Chicago

t is hard to overestimate the devastation of the great fire, yet it damaged none of the key industries, the stockyards, or the freight depots, and few of the plants on the west side of the river. Chicago quickly rebounded. By the time of the fire, it was already a seaport as well as a railway center mid-nation, a manufacturing and processing center, a hub of meat-processing, home of the stockyards, and a major supplier of steel. And Chicago sat near some of the richest farmland in the country, capable of processing and shipping wheat and corn—whether by ship or train—faster than any other city.

The fire and the subsequent reconstruction of Chicago are deeply symbolic to me. In 1970, as commissioner of the Department of Consumer Affairs, I planned an exhibition built around the centennial of the great fire for the city-sponsored Folk Fair, an annual multi-ethnic event held at Navy Pier.

I was new to the department and, in fact, as I will explain later, brand-new to government. In times past, the Department of Consumer Affairs had been known as the Department of Weights and Measures. My mandate, of course, was to protect consumers against crooked butchers and retailers—the department's logo was a scale—but Weights and Measures had a seamy past going back to Commissioner Daniel Serritella, a 1927 appointee of Mayor Big Bill Thompson. Scuttlebutt had it that Serritella was the connection between city government and Al Capone. When I took office, some of my inspectors were so corrupt that Serritella's ghost seemed to loom everywhere.

I became commissioner in 1968, the age of Ralph Nader and the consumer movement. For the Folk Fair that year I wanted our exhibit to represent a complete break with the stereotypes of the past as well as to highlight the consumer movement. Each department of the City of Chicago had a booth to display the services that it performed and competed to have the best display. It was exhilarating to view the flags of all nations over the booths and smell the delicious ethnic foods along the mile-long walk to the end of the enclosed pier.

We used a photo I'd seen at the Chicago Historical Society, showing the burned-out hulk of Chicago as background to two men standing behind a table. Fresh cider, vegetables, and fruit sat on the table and a bushel of apples on the ground. This stand was Shock, Bigford & Co., the "first store opened in the Burnt District."[1] Legend claims the store opened the day after the fire. To me, that photo illustrates the spirit of Chicagoans and the business community as well. We copied the photo exactly, with life-sized wooden figures of the two merchants carved out of plywood and painted in stark black; behind them, twelve feet high and twenty feet across, stood the backdrop of the burned-out city. Our logo high over the scene read simply "One Day After the Fire." We used that exhibit on many other occasions, for Chicagoans responded to its nostalgic and emotional appeal. They recognized that the spirit of Chicago could not be destroyed by the fire.

At the time of the fire, Patrick and Margaret Crane and Patrick's brother, John, were still on the northwest side of the north branch of the river at 102 North Jefferson Street, but my great-grandfather John and his young wife, Catherine, were on the east side of the north branch at 512 Huron Street, directly in the fire's path. As the fire roared, almost everything on the west side of both branches, the north and south, was spared. The fire stopped right at Jefferson Street, where all of the older Cranes resided. John's home on the east side, however, was destroyed. He lost everything.

My great-grandmother Catherine, awaiting her third child, fell ill. Like fifteen thousand other homeless Chicagoans after the fire, the young couple decided to leave Chicago. They were able to stay with relatives in Philadelphia until after the baby was born. I have always been told it was a very sad and fearful departure. They would remain in Philadelphia for eleven years before they finally recuperated financially and could return to Chicago.

If some of Chicago's families were broken by the fire, the wealthy entrepreneurs were not. Bill Ogden, who had left Chicago for New York in 1866, returned to oversee the rebuilding of his properties. Philip Armour, the meat-packer, never left. After starting Armour Meat Packing in 1867, he joined with Nelson Morris, Benjamin Hutchinson, and later Augustus Swift to consolidate the Union Stockyards into the nation's largest livestock-processing facility.

The Stockyards Company had opened its doors on Christmas Day in 1865, showing off a fancy hotel modestly named the Stockyards Inn, with its Saddle and Sirloin Room Restaurant and the Mercantile Exchange. Over 500,000 cattle and 2,500,000 hogs a year were handled at the stockyards in the 1860s and 1870s. The stockyards and their by-products—hairbrushes, buttons, knife handles, fertilizer, soap, glue, leather goods, surgical sutures, gelatin, and oils—attracted other industries to locate there as well. Close by were the saloons and gambling dens. Best known of the saloonkeepers and gamblers was Big Jim O'Leary, Mrs. O'Leary's son, notorious for his alleged payoffs to the police for ignoring the illegal gambling in his saloon.

Montgomery Ward's fledgling mail-order business, wiped out by the fire, also rebuilt in Chicago. Potter Palmer, a wealthy avant-garde Easterner, had bought up three-quarters of State Street before the fire. Palmer, ever the booster, had improved the street, built his elegant Palmer House Hotel, and persuaded the merchants on Lake Street, a few blocks away, to move to State. Even Marshall Field came to one of Palmer's buildings on State Street and, in a sense anchored it. These State Street businessmen would also rebuild. George Pullman, inventor of the jack that had lifted the houses of Chicago when the grade was raised, now manufactured the finest railroad cars in the nation. All were survivors. Having invested so much of themselves in Chicago physically, emotionally, and financially, they were not going to move away. The poor, including the immigrants, might be the last to benefit from this resurrection, but perhaps a rebuilt city would in the long run improve their squalid living conditions.

But who could rebuild the city? Clearly the government had failed its obligations before the fire. Had there been proper planning, or zoning, or an adequate fire department, the fire might not have raged out of control, but there was a vacuum at the top. Most mayors after Bill Ogden had been mere ribbon cutters, wielding little power and always kowtowing to the business community, who were the city's real movers and shakers. Everybody wanted a change.

Business's candidate for mayor in 1871 was Joseph Medill, editor of the *Chicago Tribune* since 1855. Arrogant and demanding, Medill bore the demeanor of one used to having his own way and brought along a complicated political past. In his earliest Chicago days, he had been a Whig, with all that that meant—pro-slavery, pro-business, and anti-immigration. Gradually, the turbulent issues of slavery and immigration had eroded the Whig consensus. Some left the party because of its conservatism; others had become so incensed about the onslaught of immigrants and so suspicious and fearful of Catholics and their presumed loyalty to the Pope that they too had left to form the American Party. A Whig Party so fractured could not accomplish much; the declining success of various Whig candidates in local and national elections confirmed the party's waning power. The Republican Party, formed in 1854, was to be the beneficiary.

The slavery issue was so heated in Illinois that several owners of area newspapers sought to gather a convention of editors and civic leaders opposed to slavery; an organizing meeting held in Decatur in February 1856 resulted three months later in a statewide convention in Bloomington. Cook County sent seventeen delegates. Abraham Lincoln and William H. Herndon sat in the delegation from central Illinois. Herndon, Lincoln's law partner, was later to say that the convention "gave the Republican Party its official christening" nationwide.[2]

Joseph Medill, covering the convention for the *Tribune*, was so impressed that he abandoned the Whig Party to become a Republican. Since Medill was accustomed to urging his views on the public, he would promote the party from that day forward with all the energy and skill he could muster. Indeed, he came to be regarded as a founder of the Republican Party. His arrival on the scene was timely, for the state's leading Democratic Senator, Stephen A. Douglas, had sponsored the Kansas-Nebraska Act of 1854, which allowed states joining the Union to choose for themselves if they would be slave or free. Most of Illinois opposed slavery, but debates were still vigorous across the state in saloons and drawing rooms.

Believing deeply that slavery was wrong and that the powerful Douglas was wrong, Abraham Lincoln began to speak out against both. Douglas faced reelection to the Senate in 1858 as the Democratic candidate. Under these circumstances, Lincoln could not remain a Whig. He switched to the Republican Party, announced for the Senate against Douglas, and immediately challenged him to a series of open-forum debates in 1858. Political campaigns were simpler then.

The Wigwam, Chicago's first convention center and scene of the nomination of Abraham Lincoln. A moving lesson in democracy for my forebears, Patrick and John R. Crane, Irish immigrants. COURTESY OF DAVID R. PHILLIPS.

One cannot imagine a politician of Douglas's stature today facing a rail-splitter, a nobody.

The *Chicago Times* trumpeted Douglas's candidacy; Medill loudly supported Lincoln. He recognized Lincoln's great appeal and began a draft movement almost immediately: Lincoln for President.

Capitalizing on the wide exposure that Lincoln had gained from the debates, Medill discreetly collared Republican friends in the East to invite Lincoln to address their organizations. Each invitation, each speech, was covered glowingly by the *Tribune.* Soon Medill went to Washington to meet with members of the Republican National Committee. He had a double mission—to push Lincoln and to lobby for Chicago as the site of the 1860 Republican Convention.

As John Crane told it to my mother and his other grandchildren, the town went wild at the thought of Chicago hosting a national political convention. A convention center to impress the world had to be built, and so it was—named the Wigwam to reflect Chicago's heritage. While grassroots supporters worked and cheered each other on, Medill quietly made another move—he got himself appointed to the seating committee. No one in opposition to him or his candidate, Lincoln, would occupy any prominent position under the roof of the Wigwam.

The Illinois delegation and William Herndon, Lincoln's campaign manager, stayed at the Tremont Hotel, one of the first luxury hotels in Chicago. The city beat at a fever pitch; everyone had worked so hard to show her off properly. On May 18, 1860, my great-grandfather John joined the twenty thousand people awaiting news of the balloting outside the Wigwam. He recalled the tension and the hoping, and then, on the third ballot, Abraham Lincoln won. A cannon fired to give the crowd the signal. One hundred gunshots rang into the sky from the Tremont. The ships along the river blew their whistles, as did trains down in the railyards. Church bells rang out.[3] John Crane said that he was shocked at first by this tumult, but with cannons and church bells and the total energy of a town exploding exuberantly around him, he realized in a flash what it was to be an American and free. He found himself crying and cheering at the same time. This nomination of the antislavery candidate was a victory for Chicago, too.

When war erupted, Chicago again rose to the occasion. Its trains moved troops across America. When the government issued a call for troops, Chicago filled its quota ahead of schedule. Ethnic pride was on display as one brigade after another took on their native names, the Irish Montgomery Guards and Shields Guards, the Turner Union Guards of the Germans, and the Chicago Zouaves. Hungarians, Bohemians, Slavs, Scandinavians, Belgians, and Swiss all joined in their own brigades. Patrick was too old to enlist, his son John was much too young, but both would talk often in later years about their emotional involvement in this war between brothers. Coming from an island oppressed by the British, the Cranes were astonished to find armies on the move in order to end slavery. This was their first taste of the complex meaning of democracy.

At the war's lowest ebb, Mary Livermore, a manager of the Chicago Sanitary Commission, received a letter from General Ulysses Grant thanking her and all her group for blankets, medicines, and supplies. Could she send more? The Union Army's need was great. Mary had exhausted her usual sources. She had in fact begged from everyone of any means in Chicago. Needing another idea, she and her associate manager, Jane Hoge, decided to hold a fair in the fall of 1863.

The Great Northwestern Fair was truly a happening. The whole Crane family marched in the opening-day parade to Chicago's Bryan Hall, where a band in the balcony played patriotic music. All the booths were decked in red, white, and blue. The Curiosity Shop sold unusual objects of art, plants, and torn Civil War battle standards and American flags that had been carried in battle. In a nearby hall were magnificent works of art on loan from donors all over the Northwest. Chicago had never seen such a fair. Farmers had contributed barrels of crops, potatoes, sorghum, and wheat to be sold to restaurants and to be used for the meals served at the fair. The donated clothing sold out every time the booth was restocked.

President Lincoln provided the greatest treasure, however, sending the original Emancipation Proclamation as a raffle prize. When asked to donate the document by his friend Thomas Bryan (for whom the hall was named), Lincoln replied, "Thomas, I wanted to keep the proclamation to give to my sons as a family keepsake; but my soldier boys are dearer to me than anything else in the world and they shall have it." "There were tears in Lincoln's eyes as he said it," Bryan added.[4] The document wound up, by donation, at the Chicago Historical Society, but was destroyed in the Great Chicago Fire. In all, ninety thousand people attended the fair, which raised $85,000 for the Union troops. Soon New York, Philadelphia, Cleveland, Pittsburgh, and St. Louis copied Mary Livermore's idea.

Jay Robert Nash writes in *Makers and Breakers of Chicago* that Wilbur Storey, of the *Times*, almost caused a Chicago civil war himself by his antics in the middle of the conflict. Pro-states'-rights and anti-Lincoln, Storey wished to embarrass Medill. He realized that with the North committed to victory and his readers likewise, he would have to attack individual military leaders rather than the cause itself. Therefore he singled out various Union Army generals, portraying them as oafs, incompetents, fools, and worse. Chicago was already a hotbed of the so-called Copperheads—Southern sympathizers—so Medill countered by branding the *Times* the Copperhead Press. One evening a group of intoxicated Union soldiers broke into the *Times*, yelling profane abuse at Storey. Unfazed, the editor grabbed one of the men and hurled him out the window. Storey was now in deep trouble with the soldiers' commanding officer, General Ambrose Burnside, who ordered his troops to shut down the *Times* for being unpatriotic. On hearing this, Storey reportedly clapped his hands at the headlines Burnside's folly would provide. Chicagoans, resenting the seizure of a newspaper by the Army, took matters into their own hands. One day in 1863, as my great-grandfather John drove his carriage to town with his father, Patrick, he heard great shouting coming from Courthouse Square at Randolph and Clark streets. Abandoning the carriage in the traffic jam, John joined the protest, though he was a Lincoln Republican. He later told my grandmother that the crowd, mostly Democrats who sympathized with Storey, started shouting, "Shut down the *Tribune*, too." At this point, Joseph Medill armed the *Tribune* staff and surrounded the building with thugs to protect it. The crowds around both buildings grew larger and more unruly. Soon a Republican-versus-Democrat shoving match broke out. Street fighting continued for two days until President Lincoln allowed the *Times* to reopen—unrepentant of its antiwar posturing.[5]

Once the newspaper crisis ended, Medill began to badger Lincoln for a patronage job, specifically the position of Postmaster, for his associate John L. Scripps, part owner and manager of the *Tribune*. Never a timid man, Medill was shameless in his letter: "If John L. Scripps receives the appointment, the county Postmasters of the northwest would work to extend the paper's circulation, which would not only fill the *Tribune*'s coffers, but would 'benefit the party' and promote the legitimate influence of the *Tribune*."[6] Scripps got the appointment, and, of course, the *Tribune* soon increased its circulation in the midwest. This has always amused me, for throughout my political life the *Chicago Tribune* has frequently railed against political patronage and financial gain through politics.

The war was long, and morale would slowly be drained even from Chicagoans. In 1864, Lincoln called for more troops. As the people of Chicago viewed thousands of Southern prisoners at Douglas Camp, they buried thousands of their own men at Calvary and Oakwood and Rosehill cemeteries. It was getting harder to recruit soldiers.

Tiring of the war effort, Medill took a delegation to see President Lincoln, principally to complain about the latest call for troops. According to Chicago historian Bessie Louise Pierce, "The President, war-weary himself, patiently listened, then said, in a voice full of bitterness, 'Gentlemen, after Boston, Chicago has been the chief instrument in bringing this war on the country. The northwest has opposed the south as New England has opposed the south. It is you who are largely responsible for making the blood flow as it has. You called for war until we had it. You called for Emancipation, and I have given it to you. Whatever you have asked, you have had. Now you come here begging to be let off from the call for men which I have made to carry out the war you have demanded. You ought to be ashamed of yourselves. I have a right to expect better things of you. Go home, and raise your 6,000 extra men. And you, Medill, you are acting like a coward. You and your *Tribune* have had more influence than any paper in the northwest in making this war. You can influence great masses, and yet you cry to be spared at a moment when your cause is suffering. Go home and send us those men.'"[7] Medill went home, Chicago made its quota, and a short time later, the Civil War came to its bloody end.

Exuberance over the war's end, however, was soon dashed in April 1865 by the news streaking over every telegraph wire in the country: Lincoln slain by assassin. My great-grandfather, jubilant when Lincoln won the Republican nomination at the Wigwam, now shared the nation's anguish over Lincoln's death. More than 120,000 people came to see Lincoln's body at the courthouse. On May 2, many of them marched behind the casket to the Chicago & Alton railway station. They prayed and wept as they watched the funeral train pull away, carrying Abe Lincoln back home to Springfield. Stories of Lincoln's funeral would always be told when the subject came up at school. As a child, my mother would always get the same surprised yet proud look in her eye when she could add, "My great-grandfather and my grandfather were there!" I, too, felt this intimate connection to history.

The war over, the city needed another rebuilder. If he accepted the draft of the business community, Medill might be the man for the job. The masses of immigrants were too disorganized and divided to nominate a consensus candidate. Language differences and animosities between various groups were barriers. On the southwest side, first- and second-generation Irish had spread farther southwest, as had the Germans. More Irish and Germans came to take their place, but so did Poles, Czechs, and Lithuanians. On the north side, first- and second-generation Irish, Germans, and Swedes moved farther north from the river, as my great-grandfather John Crane had done. The newer immigrants moving in were Irish and Germans and Swedes but also Poles and Italians. On the west side, there were some Germans and Irish, but mostly Bohemians, Greeks, Italians, Eastern European Jews, Poles, and some blacks. Jews had moved to the north side from the beginning of the migrations, but they were German Jews as opposed to the Eastern Jews on the west side. The Irish and Germans were still the dominant nationalities in the city.

Each group was clannish, building its own churches or synagogues, sticking close to home. They often battled one another in the streets; no nationality was welcome in another's place of worship. The Anglo-Saxon Protestants—the great majority of whom had always lived south of the river along Michigan Avenue and Wabash Avenue, not far from the commercial sections of town—did not hide their dislike of the immigrants, particularly the Irish, any more than they had during the Know-Nothing years.

The south end of the commercial district along the river was the red-light district, known as the Levee District, and not far from there was a fast-growing black neighborhood. Blacks had always lived there in larger numbers than on the west side, but after the Civil War, this community grew rapidly.

The lands surrounding Chicago in those days, considered suburbs, had been bought up years before. As explained by Ellen Skerrett and Dominic Pacyga in *Chicago, City of Neighborhoods*, Stephen A. Douglas and others who bought land along the northern and southern lakefronts had great plans for it. In the early 1850s, the Senator had gathered more than seventy acres of land at the lakefront south of the city limits. He dreamed of making it one of the finest residential areas outside of downtown Chicago, an elite community surrounded by two mammoth parks. He deeded some of his land to the Baptist Church, asking that the church build a university, and it became the first home of the University of Chicago. In 1852, Douglas, while affiliated with the Illinois Central Railroad, as well as serving in the U.S. Senate, then persuaded a good friend, Paul Cornell, to purchase another three hundred acres of lakefront land south of Douglas's plot. This acreage Paul Cornell called Hyde Park. Both communities— Douglas and Hyde Park—were laid out beautifully, but development was slow, because travel to the suburbs without proper roads and a good public transport system proved arduous.

Senator Douglas also very much wanted the Illinois Central Railroad to come to Chicago, and he lobbied hard in the U.S. Senate to obtain the federal land grant that would bring in the railway. It would, of course, enter Chicago from the south side; Douglas saw to that, giving his water rights along the lake to the railway and persuading his friend Cornell to throw in sixty acres of his land if the railway would provide service to Hyde Park.[8] A Senate investigating committee today might be suspicious of such behavior, but at least Chicago had the benefit of another railway system.

Meanwhile, Joseph Medill finally made his decision. After refusing the business community at first, he allowed himself to be gradually seduced. A man who enjoyed power, he had quite a bit at the *Tribune*, but he promised his supporters he would consider running, *if* the mayor's office was given detailed powers and more actual governing authority by the legislature. According to the historian David L. Protess, the business community convinced Medill that it would lobby to get legislation passed in Springfield spelling out the authority and power of the office of mayor, and Medill agreed to run. He was also concerned about the credibility of the proposed campaign slogan, "The citizens' Fire-proof Ticket." The *Tribune* had bragged about its fireproof building before the fire, only to see it burn to cinders like every other building.

Medill's philosophy was certainly not the philosophy of Bridgeport, by now an Irish power bloc itself. The Bridgeport Irish, through their control of the official terminal of the Illinois-Michigan Canal, controlled most of the jobs at the stockyards, as well as at the nearby glue factories, the fertilizer and soap works, the leather works along the southwest branch of the river, and the mills and steel plants, which had also located there. They were a force to reckon with. Dire warnings spilled from the taverns in Bridgeport that if Medill's early conviction about freeing the slaves represented his true feelings, then more blacks would move to Chicago and compete for jobs.

Nonetheless, Medill was in the right place at the right time. Campaigning as a reformer, promising to "fireproof" the city, Joseph Medill defeated Alderman Charles Holden of the 10th Ward—the immigrants' candidate—three to one. Medill's coalition was WASP and German, staunch Republicans all.

Medill was very fortunate when he began his term in 1871. So desperate were the conditions in the city that he was given a free rein. There was little available housing. Most people slept in tents or makeshift sheds, their possessions taken by fire. In the late fall, there was no heat to fight off the chill in the air, only small campfires to huddle around. The immigrants were the hardest hit, since they were too poor to obtain credit to rebuild what little they had. Outsiders came into Chicago and looted many of the burned-out homes. Food was scarce, and food lines were long and often violent. Much of Chicago was grim and sad, a city in ruins.

Mayor Medill and the business community moved rapidly, persuading legislators in Springfield to pass the mayor's bill spelling out such new duties and powers of the office as (1) the right to appoint all nonelected city officials with advice and consent of the city council; (2) the right to remove all appointed officials; (3) the right to be the presiding officer of the city council; (4) the right to appoint the council's committees; (5) veto power over the appropriations ordinance (budget), a veto that required two-thirds majority vote of the council to override his veto; and (6) the right to assume special police powers to regulate and maintain order in the city. These rights and duties remain unchanged today.

The bill, so necessary, was going to put Medill on a collision course with the council. Budget-making had been a cherished prerogative of the council members, a great pork barrel of jobs on the city payroll. Medill's new powers put a lid on the council's barrel.

The council members reacted by doing what they've always done, right through to the present day: they went along with the mayor as long as the mayor did not interfere with them.

Rocking the boat was not the new mayor's first priority, however. Consider the new building code. Seeking to avoid another fire, Medill submitted a bill calling for a building code that prohibited the construction of frame houses within the city limits. It was a sensible bill in terms of safety, but shortsighted in view of the housing crisis. Thousands were homeless and couldn't wait for brick or stone housing.[9] Nor would they be able to afford the safer homes even if they had waited. Medill's strict fire code would drive many of the immigrants out of the city to its borders. This exodus was not displeasing to the wealthy, particularly the conservatives who had been the backbone of the Medill campaign.

In fact, many of them were thriving. The city was celebrated around the country for its grit. The business community was riding high. They had their mayor and the bank credit to rebuild. The railroads were stepping back in—the Dearborn Station, the Northwestern Station, and Central Station quickly rose again, grander than ever. The business community commissioned architects of renown. Le Baron Jenney constructed the first skyscraper when he designed a building of structural-steel support instead of concrete and stone for the Home Insurance Building. Louis Sullivan built his Auditorium and Stock Exchange, John Root and Daniel Burnham the Rookery Building, Monadnock, and Montauk. Chicago became the home of high rises, massive structures of concrete, stone, and brick ten to twelve stories above the ground. The wealthy families began to re-build mansions on South Michigan Avenue and Prairie Avenue and South Wabash. Of the three, Prairie Avenue was considered the fanci-est address, boasting residents such as the Marshall Fields, the Ar-mours, and the Pullmans. Homes of great beauty rose on Washington Boulevard on the west side as well. Potter Palmer broke the pattern when he built a mansion on the north side so large that it looked like a castle. Just as he had been the trendsetter for State Street, with his hotel, so he would again be the trendsetter. The north side and its Gold Coast would ultimately become the residential center of Chi-cago's elite families.

Medill seemed to want to govern democratically, but he found it a politically difficult task. After all, he was backed by big business, for the most part American-born. While the Know-Nothing movement was gone, much of the same fear and suspicion of the immigrants remained. On a political tightrope, Medill had to please his backers without alienating the masses. Through no fault of his, a class war was developing. Both groups were pushing Medill to have their way, and pushing with force. His supporters wanted progress and commer-cial growth. The immigrants had such basic needs as temporary hous-ing, mere shelter for their families. Nor did they want to live at the city's border, far from their places of work.

The increasingly powerful immigrant groups wanted something done about the discriminatory fire code. The aldermen, attempting a compromise, agreed with Medill that the code was a fine goal for the future, but why not *temporary* wooden housing until Chicagoans were back on their feet? Medill vetoed their ordinance to that effect. Undaunted, the aldermen revised it three times, and three times Me-dill vetoed it. In the middle of the housing battle, Medill, a liberal on some issues but a fiscal conservative, asked the Chicago Relief and Aid Society to cut off such emergency relief as the food and blankets they were giving to the homeless. This so shocked the poor that hun-dreds of women and children marched on City Hall. Medill was not moved. At this point, the city council sought to help by passing an ordinance that gave it some control over the funds of the Chicago Relief Society. But Medill managed to sabotage this effort as well.

My great-great-aunt Bridget Crane, though unaffected in her home on the west bank, always recalled that Medill and big business had seemed ruthless at the time. It was clear to her that they wanted to drive the immigrants out of Chicago. The Relief and Aid Society, very much under the control of the Medill administration, offered to use some of its funds for one-way railway tickets out of town. Bridget Crane gave Medill credit for some of the governmental improvements, but she despised him nonetheless.

Medill *had* established a centralized library system, and he made good appointments to it and to the school board and the police board. But he could not shake the fire and building codes trouble. Soon his staunch Protestant supporters started pushing on other fronts. They wanted an eleven-o'clock instead of a midnight closing time for the taverns and pubs. When the police superintendent submitted such an ordinance to the council, the council quickly buried it in committee. The superintendent, testing his power, began to enforce the Sunday blue law on taverns, a law even the mayor had never enforced. Once the superintendent revived that law, his days were numbered. The police board—reasonably ethnic in makeup—fired him for insubordination, without even informing the mayor. This so incensed Medill that he fired the uppity board members and reinstated the superintendent.

His authority challenged, Medill's battle royal had begun, and he abandoned any attempt at compromise. When he revoked tavern licenses, the council legally challenged his right to do so. Medill countered by stripping key committee posts from his opposition in the council, and then passed the law on eleven-o'clock tavern closings. The reformers who supported him were delighted, but not his German constituents, who marched once more on City Hall. Chicago's city council has always had the power to tie up any administration. If the mayor doesn't have the votes, all city programs could grind to a halt. In Chicago, and probably elsewhere, political adversaries wait in the shadows for just such an opportunity—then they pounce. Medill was now vulnerable without his German constituency.

Then scandal struck: Medill's administration was accused of investing city money for personal gain through the treasurer's office. The German newspaper, *Stats-Zeitung*, trumpeted the news in front-page headlines. Because the German ethnic bloc was the largest in the city, the headlines did serious damage. There would be no more peace for Medill. The council refused to approve any new mayoral appointments and vetoed his budget. Medill was finished. His health began to deteriorate. In the middle of his second year in office, he advised the city council that he would be leaving for a long vacation. The council happily elected an interim mayor, who served out the term. Medill's administration was later cleared of the investment charges.[10]

Amidst all of the turmoil, few could have realized that a momentous change had taken place, the thing most feared by the wealthy— the immigrants had united to become a political force, a force that would take control of *their* city.

CHAPTER 3

Haymarket Violence

I n the decade following the fire, Chicago mushroomed into a contradictory, booming, miserable, and in some ways elegant place. Tracks went down for trains and streetcars at a greater rate than ever before, both within the city limits and beyond to the suburban communities north, south, and west of the city. The elite of the city moved south to the boulevards of Prairie, Wabash, and Michigan avenues, there to enjoy the luxuries of Jackson Park, focus of elegant tennis clubs, and of the Washington Park racetrack with its "members only" clubhouse. Prairie Avenue would hold its own as the most elegant area of Chicago for much of the mid-1880s and the 1890s. Due south of the downtown area, it was close enough for such leading merchants as Marshall Field to walk to work. The power elite of the business community, a small clique, lunched then at the Chicago Club, as they do today. The north side was just developing around Potter Palmer's mansion on the near north side at 1350 North Lake Shore Drive. The mansions of William Ogden and Walter Newberry on or around Dearborn Street, in addition to the several McCormick mansions, gave testament to their owners' wealth and power. This was the Chicago that visitors saw and boosters touted.

Back at the river, however, and along both branches stood the slums and tenements, interspersed among railroad tracks and factories. This underbelly of the city, running along the two branches of the river, seethed with unrest that was exacerbated by substandard housing and a worsening shortage of jobs. New manufacturing and processing techniques were slowly but surely laying off manual workers of the traditional sort. Even so, the newer immigrants still poured into Chicago. Short of money, speaking different languages, they entered a pattern established forty years before. Each wave found the cheapest housing along the north and south branches of the river sandwiched in among the warehouses and factories. As soon as they could afford to leave, out they'd go, making way for the next wave of new Chicagoans. But not without violence. As the Irish moved farther south and west, earlier immigrant Jews moved west to Lawndale to get away from gangs of Italian and Irish Catholic boys who disrupted their businesses on Maxwell Street by taunting them and throwing stones.

The southwest side, contiguous with the stockyards, brick factories, and lumber mills, was booming. Chicago was now the country's main supplier of beef, shipping from coast to coast. Newer communities near the yards—Canaryville, Back of the Yards, and McKinley Park—housed second- and third-generation Americans in flats or single-family homes.

Until 1875, the *Tribune* ruled Chicago's newspaper business, but in that year, the *Daily News*, a penny daily newspaper, was established by journalist Melvin E. Stone, who sought to publish an "unbiased" newspaper (that is, a more liberal one), a paper not controlled by key business interests. Stone's heart may have been in the right place, but his business sense was nowhere. He had, for instance, determined to take no advertising. Soon the *Daily News* began to sink under its debt. Enter Victor Lawson, owner of a large ethnic paper, the *Skandinavian*, who admired Stone's style and aims and came to the rescue. The two newspapers merged. With Lawson's wealth added to Stone's editorial brilliance and independence, the result was a newspaper that spoke to an increasing number of Chicagoans. The *Daily News* would manage to maintain its political neutrality for most of its subsequent hundred-year history, until its demise in 1978.

Twenty-two miles southwest of the city, a new industrial community, Chicago Heights, was rapidly developing. South Chicago, Lake Calumet, and Pullman Town, and Inland Steel's mills, United States Steel, and Pullman's plant, home of the luxurious Pullman railroad cars, all were located there on the far southeast side. Thousands upon thousands of immigrants were pouring into that part of Chicago seeking jobs in steel factories such as the huge North Chicago Rolling Mills, later called the South Works of United States Steel. Chicago was changing fast, shifting to 80 percent immigrant by the turn of the century.

In this volatile atmosphere Chicago faced the mayoral election of

1879. The city's population had risen to 500,000. The older, established Americans—generally transplants from New York, Boston, and Washington, D.C.—were still mostly Anglo-Saxon Protestant and upper-middle-class. They despised the immigrants and were in turn despised as exploiters, and they were fading. In fact, political control of Chicago had already slipped from the Establishment's grasp with Medill's decline. Ward bosses, often saloonkeepers turned politicians, now doled out patronage and perks, a new chapter in an old story. A step below, the ward heelers took orders from the aldermen without question. Aldermen put them on the payroll or took them off, promoted them or fired them.

Every ward in the city had both a committeeman and an alderman, both elected. These jobs usually reside in the same individual. The alderman attends to the governmental needs of the community—sanitation, street cleaning, the housekeeping duties of the ward—and represents constituents in city council matters. In contrast, the ward committeeman provides political party representation at the precinct level. To combine political patronage and government money in one person obviously favors the machine. Anyone who has secured a city job with the help of an alderman/committeeman has also taken on a second job as a precinct captain. That is as true now as it was in the nineteenth century.

Of course, by 1879, class and economic divisions were blurred. Many of the earliest immigrants, like the Crane family, had already grasped economic opportunity in America. They saw to it that their children worked hard in school and that they had no small plans for the future. By now, the whole Crane family, consisting of my great-great-grandparents Patrick and Margaret and their daughter, Bridget, now married, felt Chicago was a good home. They had been here, after all, for twenty-four years. Patrick was anxious for my great-grandfather John R. Crane to return to Chicago. But in 1879, John and his family were still in Pennsylvania awaiting the birth of their fifth child, my grandmother Margaret Jane Crane. When the Cranes did return to Illinois in 1882, they were a much larger family—great-aunts Mary, Laura, and Kate, great-uncle Patrick, grandmother Margaret Jane, and the newest offspring, my great-aunt Sarah. John Crane opened a small dry goods store at 519 West Chicago Avenue. The family lived above the store, only a few blocks from John and Patrick's house at 350 West Superior Street. John and Catherine remained in Chicago for the rest of their lives. John worked in the offices of the railroads, and the family were members of Holy Name Cathedral parish. My grandmother attended the parish school under the tutelage of the Religious of the Sacred Heart, a tradition that has carried down through the generations to me, my three sisters, and my daughter, Katharine.

The winner of the mayoral election of 1879, Carter Harrison, seemed to be the right man for those times. He would not repeat the divisive mistakes of Joseph Medill or Levi Boone. Although he would have troubles, as we shall see, he succeeded so well in general that he was reelected four consecutive times and then a fifth after leaving office for a term.

Protestant like Medill, Harrison had been raised comfortably on a plantation in Kentucky and spent many of his young adult years abroad in Europe after graduating from Yale. Rather than being a patrician and a journalist/businessman like Medill, however, Harrison was more the populist, having traveled to Chicago with his bride in the 1850s to settle on a large piece of land on the near west side. He had seen Chicago struggle to make something of herself, raising herself literally from the mud and nurturing her industries. He was here when Chicago burned; indeed, the fire had drawn him into politics. He began his political life as a county commissioner determined to help the city rebuild, then became a Congressman.

When Harrison decided to run for mayor, he well realized that his main challenge would be to keep class antagonism from ripping Chicago apart. Sitting in the taverns, Harrison heard the immigrants' tales of terrible ocean crossings on the coffin ships that had brought them to America. He listened carefully. He walked through their slums. He could understand their clannishness, the importance to them of their own churches and taverns. These people had little else for the moment, but Harrison knew that they were the future of Chicago.[1]

(Prime Minister Jack Lynch of Ireland shared a similar appreciation of immigrant grit with me in September 1979. I was a member of the official American delegation to the funeral of Earl Mountbatten, who had been brutally murdered. The day after the ceremony, I visited Lynch in Dublin. Obviously disturbed and saddened, he appeared tired as we talked about the British-Irish situation. As he drew on his pipe, he asked, "Mayor Byrne, do you know why the Irish do so well in America?" Before I could answer, he added, "Only the strong survive! They crawled on their bellies if they had to, to get to the ships.

Dinner reception for Prime Minister Jack Lynch of Ireland, Palmer House, Chicago, 1979. "Do you know Mayor Byrne why the Irish do so well in America? Because only the strong survive?"

Those who survived the human indignities of the crossing, those were survivors, and they became Irish Americans." He puffed again. "Only the strong survive.")

Mayor Harrison's Southern Protestant pedigree made him almost acceptable to the ruling clique, though they thought he should enforce tavern reform, a burning political issue in Chicago for two hundred years. Harrison never did. He recognized that a prairie town on the Western frontier, where fur traders, trappers, explorers, and Indians had once mixed, fought, drunk, and married, could not be a place of patrician temperance.

In this period, labor unrest was growing all across the country, not least in Chicago. Two years before Harrison's election, on July 17, 1877, railroad men had walked off the job in Martinsburg, West Virginia, protesting the third wage cut in ten years and striking the B&O Railroads. A sympathy strike against the Michigan Central Railroad was called in Chicago for July 24.

If a common bond united the businessmen of the Chicago Club, it was hatred of any labor movement. No one was more outspoken on

that score than Marshall Field, merchant prince of Chicago, so it came
as no surprise that when the sympathy strike was called, he lent all of
the Field delivery trucks to the city for use as police vans for the
strike. The state police also joined in the fray. Fights broke out when
ten thousand strikers and sympathizers attempted to stop other railway workers from crossing their picket lines. City and state police
fired into the crowd, killing thirty workers and wounding many more.
But when women and children, mostly Bohemians and Jews from the
near west side tenements, arrived carrying rocks, the police withdrew.
The next day President Rutherford B. Hayes ordered in federal troops
to disperse the strikers. Bridget Crane would later tell my mother,
"Nationally the labor movement was called the Knights of Labor,
there was hope in it, but locally labor had no leaders; the ten thousand
strikers were disorganized and leaderless, and had no programs to
offer. There was just violence and defeat."

Because the strike had failed, railroad management thought it had
won. The *Tribune* dismissed the whole idea of a labor movement and
condemned the strikers as radical immigrant Jews and Bohemians
who preached anarchy.[2]

The *Daily News* took no sides, but it did send reporters into the
crowd to interview the protesters and report the substance of their
grievances. Every edition was quickly snapped up by Chicagoans
eager to know the facts of the strike, which they emphatically did not
get from the *Tribune.* This evenhandedness from the *Daily News*
infuriated the business community, but the paper continued to print
both sides of the dispute, despite pressure from the moguls.

Frustrated and alarmed, the leading businessmen sought to raise
money in order better to supply the state and local police for future
demonstrations. They were determined to destroy this "anarchist"
movement, but the poor of Chicago, its bedrock laboring class, finding
no improvement or hope of improvement after the sympathy strike,
continued to seethe.

One of Chicago's most prominent entrepreneurs, George Pullman,
watched the strike and thought he saw a way to improve the workers'
standard of living and calm the waters. He determined to achieve
labor peace at the Pullman plant by creating a town for his workers,
one fashioned after the company town of Saltive in England and dedicated to Pullman's personal values. The attractive town he built in
the south Chicago area had tree-lined streets and a chain-of-command-
style housing pattern, brought right from the plant. Managers and

skilled labor lived in detached single dwellings, the unskilled in brick row houses. The town boasted a company-owned store, a library with approved books, and a church in which the different religions were assigned hours for worship. No one could own property, of course, and no denomination could build its own place of worship. Taverns were prohibited. Not least, Pullman's company town was a good investment, yielding a solid 6 percent return. Obviously, Pullman expected his workers to dance to his tune, while he turned a profit and led the good life—far away on Prairie Avenue.

For a while, Pullman Town appeared to work; at its peak, as many as eleven thousand people lived there. But George Pullman had made a critical misjudgment—it was the lure of freedom that had brought these Poles, Lithuanians, Swedes, Germans, and Irish to Chicago. They soon railed against his autocratic control. Pullman Town began to fizzle as workers moved on to other neighborhoods. Pullman's benign social experiment would fail.

As labor unrest continued to mushroom across America, Congress held hearings on the causes of the unrest. One clear message emerged—the workers wanted an eight-hour day. The Chicago Establishment geared up against any such concessions.

Meanwhile, as machines replaced men in Chicago, unemployment rose. Why, the workers wondered, couldn't business agree to the eight-hour day? A laborer's work effort would surely improve with a shorter day; more of the unemployed could get jobs to support the economy. The extremely low pay of the laborers, only $5 to $7 a week, compared to the conspicuous luxury of their employers, fueled their anger.

As in many movements, there was within Chicago's labor movement a fringe group of radical extremists. Two of the most prominent were Albert Parsons and August Spies, both anarchists and editors of labor newspapers. Parsons's papers, the *Socialist* and the *Alarm*, were full of incendiary rhetoric like "One pound of dynamite is better than a Bushel of Ballots." August Spies spewed out similar statements of hate and revolution in the German workers' newspaper, *Arbeiter-Zeitung*.[3]

The more inflammatory labor's message became, the more assiduously the business community planned—spending money on the training of police and on building more armories for the State police. The result was predictable. Knowing full well that businessmen were arming the police against them, labor began to arm as well. Conditions were so volatile, polarization so great, that it was only a matter of time before a riot broke out.

On May 3, 1886, Albert Parsons and his allies called a strike on the McCormick Harvester Works. This time the police and state militia stationed at recently constructed armories around the city were ready. Police converged to break up the strike, shots were fired, and three workers fell dead. In response Parsons called for a protest meeting at Chicago's Haymarket Square. Although summoned by the radical element, most of those who came to protest police actions were not looking for trouble.

Gathering on the evening of June 4, 1886, the crowd at Haymarket Square was orderly, as Mayor Harrison could see from a building nearby. True, some speeches were inflammatory, but the thousands of workers gathered in the square were clearly not militant. Harrison, sensing no trouble, left shortly before the meeting ended. Inspector John Bonfield, however, had geared up for this event, aiming to impress business and press with his efficiency and toughness. In the nine long years since the railroad strike, Inspector Bonfield had trained his men to break up demonstrations. He moved in on the crowd, ordering demonstrators to disperse. The crowd grew angry at the charging police and a dynamite bomb was thrown, killing eight police officers and many civilians. The police, unleashed now, arrested seven anarchists, two of whom were nowhere near Haymarket Square when the bomb exploded.

The ensuing Haymarket trial attracted press into Chicago from across the country. Held in the courtroom of Judge Joseph Gray, it was not a model of justice. The jury selection, for instance, took almost half the time of the two-month trial. The bailiff interrogating jurors would not qualify them unless they clearly thought the accused guilty. Businessmen supported this type of trial, and George Pullman, Philip Armour, Marshall Field, and Cyrus McCormick, Jr., who avidly sought conviction, secretly raised over $100,000 to aid the families of the wounded and dead police and aid the prosecution in preparing its case. The trial's foreman was a salesman at Marshall Field's store. The lawyers for the seven defendants fought hard, proving that no one could link any one anarchist to the actual bomb, nor were they in fact even at the rally. Even so, all seven defendants were found guilty. Admitting that no defendant could be linked to the bombing, the judge nevertheless reasoned that if they hadn't incited the crowd by their speeches, no one would have thrown a bomb. On trial here was the issue of whether labor had the right to protest. The Establishment said no and carried the day. The defendants were sentenced to death by hanging.

While great confusion reigned in the minds of many Chicagoans— what *had* happened in Haymarket Square, and who *was* to blame?— many faulted the injustice of the trial. Forty thousand people signed a petition for clemency.

When Governor Richard Oglesby received the petition and reviewed the case, he offered to give clemency if the business community agreed that he should. About fifty leading businessmen met to debate the question. Speaking on behalf of clemency was Lyman Gage, vice president of the 1st National Bank of Chicago. He argued that Chicago did not appear very righteous in the eyes of the world. The socialist movement was martyring the anarchists. Reporters the world over were writing about the miscarriage of justice in Chicago. But as Marshall Field III's biographer Stephen Becker writes, "As Marshall Field's turn came to speak, he yielded to the State's Attorney, Julius S. Grinnell, who argued for the death penalty. The business leaders, believing that Marshall Field had yielded so that Grinnell could speak for him, voted no clemency."[4] Parsons and three others were hanged on November 11, 1887. (Governor John Altgeld later pardoned the remaining three.)

The Haymarket Square trial, so infamous in American history, is marked in Chicago by two separate monuments. In Haymarket Square stands a statue of a policeman, meant to symbolize the eight police who died upholding law and order. The other statue honors the labor movement; it stands in Waldheim Cemetery, where Parsons and the other anarchists are buried. Shortly after the funeral and partly in response to Haymarket, the American Federation of Labor was founded; its first order of business was the eight-hour day.

In the late 1960s the police monument at Haymarket Square was bombed, and some blamed Vietnam War protesters. Badly damaged, the statue was repaired and returned to its spot. Ironically, present at the unveiling of the repaired monument alongside Chicago's police superintendent and his staff was virtually every labor leader in Chicago. As commissioner of consumer affairs, I stood with other cabinet officials, hearing Mayor Daley speak of the good relations between labor and the police and promise, "For as long as I am mayor, there will be law and order on the streets of Chicago." Cheers greeted this pronouncement. At that point, I understood we were not there to admire the repaired police statue or to celebrate amity between an-

Haymarket Monument—symbol of violence of the labor movement in Chicago in 1886 and the violence of the peace movement in Chicago.
COURTESY OF LEE BALTERMAN.

cient enemies. No, we were there to support the Daley style of law and order, to alert dissidents that protests and violent streets would not be tolerated in this town. Chicago and Mayor Daley were still smarting from the negative publicity of 1968, generated by riots in Grant Park during the Democratic Convention. What better place to speak of authority than Haymarket Square? Not so much had changed after all. The ghost of Marshall Field could rest easy.

Dissidents apparently heard Daley's message clearly—a short time later the statue was blown up once more. When I heard about this, I was filled with a sense of dread, a recognition that sometimes American systems fail. Had not the police been abused in both cases—not by the demonstrators but by the Establishment, in order to achieve its own agenda? Hadn't we, the city government, been as obsessively hard-nosed in the 1960s as the business community had been in the 1880s? What differences were there between those in Haymarket Square protesting cruel working conditions and the students protesting a war they didn't believe in?

CHAPTER 4

The White City

In 1888, my paternal grandfather, Michael Burke, then a teenager, emigrated to Chicago from Castlebar, County Mayo, carrying all his possessions in a backpack. His first home was with his brother, Patrick, who had come to Chicago four years earlier, settling in the area aptly called Little Hell. It was a tough place, incessantly torn by turf wars, bounded by Chicago Avenue to the south, Division Street to the north, Wells Street to the east, and the north branch of the river to the west. Grandfather Burke remembered one aspect of his first days in Chicago vividly—his brother's stern admonition to stay away from the gangs. "Don't get mixed up with any of them!" Patrick warned.

Little Hell had been even more violent in years past, when the Irish and Swedes had done battle. Now, as Michael settled in, a gang of young Irish toughs called the Hatch House Gang terrorized the community. Stealing at gunpoint, they would shoot anyone who got in their way. They often victimized Swedes, the established group in town, who had to get more police protection or move from their community. The police ultimately prevailed, but so dangerous had Market Street become that the city council changed its name to Orleans, hoping to erase the memory of so much violence.[1]

Meanwhile, most Swedes had begun to move north to less congested land at Belmont and Sheffield.

Little Hell also had a new gang, the notorious Black Hand, forerunner of today's Mafia. It would last a lot longer than any of the other gangs. The Black Hand victimized everyone indiscriminately—Italian, Swede, or Irish. "Their game," Patrick told Michael, "is extortion." Shopkeepers had to pay them protection money. Any shopkeeper who refused would have his store set afire or bombed. Patrick said that the majority of Italian newcomers weren't criminals, but they had to go along or they'd be killed. "The same thing is going on on the south side," he said. "The Irish gang there is known as Ragen's Colts." As if this wasn't enough unfortunate news for the newcomer to America, Patrick added, "The Protestants over here don't like the Irish any better than their relatives over in England did, so don't expect much fairness from them."

Patrick may have seen the consternation in his brother's eyes, for he continued, "There is hope for us, though, because we have a strong leader in Archbishop Patrick A. Feehan, the head of the archdiocese in Chicago. I'll show you his home tomorrow, a mansion on State Parkway." Feehan knew well the feelings of the Protestants, which had not changed much toward immigrants and Irish Catholics in general, from the days of the Know-Nothing movement. They looked down on both, and Feehan was deliberately building Catholic churches in their neighborhoods. He made certain the Catholic churches were larger and more elegant than the Protestant churches. He was also building schools next to the churches to educate the children.[2]

"You would be surprised, Michael," Patrick continued. "The Irish who came here some time ago are following the churches and moving right into all the Protestant neighborhoods." Because of the continuing influx of Catholics—Poles and other Eastern Europeans, Irish, Germans, and Italians—the Archdiocese was becoming a power in the city. Catholics were growing into a large political bloc. Patrick added, "The Irish have the majority in the Democratic Party's local organization, and many Irish are making it in Chicago through the Irish leadership in the church and in politics."

Whether telling these stories in detail or gently teasing us, my grandfather Michael Burke seemed shy but intelligent, a man who in his youth must have listened carefully to his older brother. Of his three sons, as I've mentioned, Edward and Joseph became priests. As chancellor of the Archdiocese of Chicago, Ed Burke advised the cardinal on all ecclesiastical matters and canon law. The third son, my father, William, went into business. My dad's sister Ethel married and mothered seven children.

Michael first worked at any kind of job he could find, but ultimately became a clerk in Inland Steel's downtown office, a job that left no time for gangs. But he did have time for the Chicago White Stockings, America's first professional baseball team. Every day off when he had the money, Michael would journey to Comiskey Park with the rest of the city to cheer Billy Sunday's uncanny ability to steal home. (Billy Sunday is no doubt best remembered as an evangelical preacher, not as a baseball player. In 1891, Sunday was so moved by a revival meeting he gave up baseball for religion.) Michael Burke also enjoyed visiting Al and J. W. Spalding's Sporting Goods Store. Al Spalding, a Chicago institution, owned the White Stockings, and he and J.W. had received an award at the Paris World's Fair for their exhibit of sports equipment. In 1889, Spalding was showing off his latest invention—a catcher's mitt. Ever the innovator, Spalding once returned from England bearing America's first set of golf clubs and golf balls. My grandfather remembered seeing them on display in Spalding's store at 118 Randolph Street.

Second- and third-generation Americans were a little more tolerant of other nationalities, but they didn't go overboard. By now, Patrick Crane, my maternal great-great-grandfather, had been in America for almost thirty-four years. All of his grandchildren had been born in this country. One of them, my grandmother Margaret Jane Crane, was attending grammar school at Holy Name Cathedral in 1887. Margaret Jane was seven at the time and apparently talking in class when she should not have been, so the school's Mother Schmidt corrected her. There was a rule—still applied when I attended a Sacred Heart college—that when you were corrected, you were to smile, curtsy, and say, "Thank you for the correction." When Mother Schmidt corrected Margaret Jane, she curtsied, smiled, and said her thank you, but evidently not graciously enough, for Mother Schmidt said, "Margaret Jane, give me an example of an imperative sentence." My grandmother, always quick, shot back, "Germans, go back to your country."

Chicago's neighborhoods were always at the mercy of industrial expansion during the late nineteenth century. Railroads, especially, once they had settled on Chicago as the nation's rail center, gobbled up square miles of land. All had built their depots on the south side. Now the Santa Fe bought land for a new freight yard just west of State Street—from Polk all the way to 16th Street—and caused a major upheaval, for this was no ordinary city neighborhood but the Levee District, headquarters for prostitution and gambling at the south end of the central business district. There sin flourished under the aegis of ward bosses Mike "Hinky Dink" Kenna and Bathhouse John Coughlin. Coughlin, of course an Irishman, was alderman of the 1st Ward, much to the embarrassment of the respectable Irish. Mayor Harrison was well aware of social activities in the Levee District, but both Mike Kenna and John Coughlin had supported him, so he looked the other way. And anyway, the Levee gave Chicago a flavor of its earlier frontier days. Now the Santa Fe would push the Levee farther south, into the largest black settlement in Chicago, a fast-growing neighborhood at 22nd and State.[3] The wealthy of Prairie Avenue at 22nd and Prairie saw that these two groups—Levee people and blacks—would soon spread into their fashionable neighborhood. That, and the stench that wafted from the stockyards on a south wind, sent south siders north, to join Potter and Bertha Palmer on the north side's Gold Coast.

While many criticized Carter Harrison for his tolerance of Bathhouse John and Hinky Dink Kenna, he should be remembered also for sponsoring a vital piece of legislation in 1886. Harrison realized that Chicago's huge population and industrial growth were proving the sewer and water systems inadequate. Dysentery and outbreaks of typhoid fever were becoming a problem again. After meeting with the city's venerable chief engineer, Ellis Chesbrough, the mayor made a startling announcement. The only way to stop the Chicago River's flow of contaminants into the lake permanently was to reverse its course. Even for Chicagoans, it was hard to believe that the city's engineers could make a river flow backward. The plan was to follow the course of the old Illinois-Michigan Canal. A deep cut into the adjacent solid rock and concrete earth would make the new canal 110 to 201 feet wide and lower than the Illinois-Michigan by twenty-one feet—thus connecting the once higher Chicago River to the lower Des Plaines River, which flowed into the Mississippi.

The cooperation of the surrounding suburbs was vital, as their communities would be affected by the route of the lower and widened canal. The costs could be shared as well as the benefits. The suburbs affected by this plan were Oak Park, Berwyn, Cicero, and Stickney. To implement the plan, Harrison called for a new form of government—a *metropolitan* government. The name given to it was Metropolitan Sanitary District.

The promise of a permanent method of providing pure water had a wonderful effect on the morale of Chicagoans, as did the prospect of eight thousand new jobs digging and blasting the earth to create the canal. The affected surrounding suburbs were very enthusiastic, but the creation of this district would take the approval of the Illinois legislature. The best of intentions in government do not always produce instant results—Harrison knew he would have to lobby the legislature to establish the district and to create a mechanism by which it would elect its commissioners.

Sad to say, bureaucratic logjams and legislative delays left the project in a state of limbo until the devastating typhoid epidemic of 1891. Bridget Crane summed it up years later: "God help them. They died like flies." In our family, nineteen-year-old Kate Crane was the first to fall ill and die. The family, deep in grief over her loss, had barely returned from her burial in Calvary Cemetery when my great-great-grandfather Patrick Crane was also stricken. He died shortly, and again the Cranes returned to Calvary Cemetery to bury one of their own.

The epidemic aroused such pervasive public dissatisfaction and anger that the government of the Metropolitan Sanitary District got the message and announced that "Shovel Day," when the official digging would begin, would be held September 3, 1891. It is often a frustrating given of government to be party to all the political and bureaucratic delays. It had taken five years and hundreds of dead Chicagoans to bring Harrison's vision to reality. It would take eight more years of backbreaking work to complete the new canal, the Sanitary and Ship Canal.[4]

Other changes were afoot. After the Haymarket Riots, Jane Addams had moved to Chicago, and in 1899 she founded Hull House, where she set about improving the slums of the west side. Chicagoans didn't know what to make of this outsider from Cedarville, Illinois. Here was a young and wealthy woman who with a classmate from Rockford Seminary, Ellen Gates Starr, chose to live in Chicago's worst slum. (Even today, the city's ward leaders view warily any newcomer who makes waves or takes controversial stands. Many potential leaders are turned off by their first meeting with the ward committeeman. They come to offer their services—free legal advice, staffing a legal clinic—and are instead asked to ring doorbells and work a precinct. In fact, committeemen deal only with those they know and can control, whenever possible. Whoever was in charge of Jane Addams's ward must have felt the political ground tremble.)

Many churches and synagogues did not wait for outsiders to help. They made a particular effort to aid their own. Because of a recent wave of Orthodox Jews in the 1890s, there were well over forty synagogues within a few blocks of the Jewish marketplace on Maxwell Street. The old Sacred Heart Convent school would be bought by Julius Rosenwald, philanthropist and president of Sears Roebuck, to build the Chicago Hebrew Institute, which grew into a social and sports center for Jewish newcomers.

Even so, Jane Addams pricked the city's conscience. For most of its citizens, Chicago was a filthy and congested city. The poor lacked adequate sanitation and consequently suffered from horrible diseases. Addams watched children struggling for their lives in the slums, half-naked in winter and so hungry they ate garbage wherever they found it. It was not that fathers failed to find work but that they were paid such scandalously low wages. To supplement a husband's meager salary, mothers worked at home or in garment districts doing piecework or sewing for even more disgraceful pay. Life was equally hard for the older children in the family, who worked from early adolescence.

Jane Addams began by attempting to clothe the children and tend the sick. In this effort, she was able to attract a competent staff of professional women and advisers like Clarence Darrow, the great trial lawyer. Their first endeavor was to establish a kindergarten. Unlike religious institutions, Hull House was open to every ethnic group. She scheduled "ethnic nights" when all immigrants could learn about other cultures through their music, dances, and foods. Crafts were taught, and Addams arranged for the crafts to be sold in various shops around the city. She built a gymnasium to encourage organized sports and a music school to encourage the arts. One of the greatest recitals in the music school was given by the Hull House student Benny Goodman in 1938. He was not the only young and talented immigrant growing up poor on the west side. A. J. Balaban, a Russian immigrant, would one day head a large movie theater chain, and Florenz Ziegfeld would see his name in lights on Broadway.

So furiously did Jane Addams hammer away at the problem of sanitation that she was finally appointed garbage inspector of the 19th Ward, not normally a power position. Addams made it so, however, for every time she gave a speech regarding the living conditions in the slums, the city fathers had to dive through hoops. Jane Addams gained national recognition through her lectures and writings. She urged the poor to enter politics and fight in the council and legislature for social reform. Addams would later become involved in the International Ladies Garment Workers Union, the Amalgamated Clothing Workers Union, and the Consumers League. And gradually her work changed Chicago.

In 1886, the United States Congress nominated a committee to determine if the country should host a World's Fair in 1892—a World's Columbian Exposition, in celebration of the four hundredth anniversary of Columbus's discovery of America. Although that decision would not be made for some time, sparks of interest—and competition—were ignited in Chicago, New York, St. Louis, and Philadelphia.

Chicago's business leaders, of course, wanted to bring the Fair to the shores of Lake Michigan. While many citizens were singing the current hit song "I Love You Truly," written by a local resident, Carrie Jacobs Bond, or clapping their hands to the catchy "Ta Ra Ra Boom De Ray" at church socials or placing bets on the upcoming bout between John L. Sullivan and Gentlemen Jim Corbett, some of the most prominent business and civic leaders were meeting at the Iroquois Club and endorsing the concept of a Chicago World's Fair. They figured New York would be their chief competition. That city's mayor had already established a World's Fair Committee. Members of the Iroquois Club contacted other influential citizens, and a delegation of civic leaders approached Mayor Dewitt C. Creiger for his support. Mayor Creiger, who had followed Carter Harrison's fourth term, requested that the city council vote in a Chicago World's Fair Corporation.

The city council did the mayor's bidding unanimously; however, they made it clear that there would be no change in late tavern closings during the Fair. It was assumed that taverns would do a thriving business, and the aldermen wanted to keep their constituent tavern owners happy. The night after the council's unanimous vote, Bathhouse John and Hinky Dink sat in the Levee District listening to Scott Joplin's ragtime rocking out of the brothels and imagined the enormous sums they would earn if the Fair came to Chicago.

In fact, everyone would benefit from the Fair, and Chicagoans got swept away with enthusiasm. Much of that spirit tapped into their immense pride in their city. (Fierce pride is always evident in polls taken of Chicagoans. In almost every campaign, I have used outside pollsters, and in my 1983 reelection campaign, two were New York pollsters. Both expressed surprise at the depth of pride Chicagoans had in their city.)

The battle lines were drawn between Chicago and New York, and New Yorkers and the East generally were about to be treated to the bombast of Joseph Medill's *Chicago Tribune.* When Medill realized that the Palmers, the Armours, the Marshall Fields, the Lyman Gages, and the Pullmans wanted the Fair, he decided on a no-holds-barred approach in Chicago's behalf. Fair historian R. Reid Badger writes, "On June 28, 1889, the *Tribune* declared, 'New York is not an American city—in its history, in its relations to the nation, in its attitude toward the government during the War of the Revolution and Rebellion, or in its social characteristics. The Fair should be both a world's fair and an all American exposition, and New York is not a patriotic city, not a national city and never was.' "[5]

New York papers responded in kind, labeling Chicago a city with no tradition and little culture, virtually a raw outpost constantly reduced to bragging about grain, lumber, and meat. All the Chicago papers joined the fray, but the *Tribune,* according to Badger, continued to take the lead: "For too long, the American cow had been fed in the west and milked in the east. It was about time to move her hind legs further west, so that some of the milking might be done here."

And for over a year, the debate raged in Congress. So spirited was it that seven ballots were needed in the House of Representatives before Chicago won the majority vote. Michael Burke told his grandchildren many times of the excitement that flashed through the city when the results were announced. Despite turf wars and protection rackets, he had arrived in Chicago at the right time after all. Chicagoans realized they were placing their city in the spotlight to be judged by the world's critics. That same year, 1889, the Paris World's Fair had been acclaimed the greatest in history. Its centerpiece was the unveiling of the Eiffel Tower. Chicago had only three short years to impress the world.

Daniel Burnham, manager of construction for the Fair, worked with the country's top architects, including William Lee Baron Jenney, in supervising and coordinating the Fair's buildings. Jenney, who had designed the first skyscraper and the Home Insurance Building, declared from the outset that the Fair had to celebrate space. So the buildings were laid out with plenty of air and space for moving around at one's leisure. Jackson Park was chosen as the site of the Fair; any land still under water was drained, and the park was raised six feet above the lake. Twelve to fourteen thousand workers were needed to build the fairgrounds, constructing the buildings and landscaping.

All of the buildings would be white—offset by the blue waters of Lake Michigan. Louis Sullivan's Transportation Building was magnificent. Frederick Law Olmsted and his partner, Henry Cadman, designed the gorgeous landscaping. There was plenty of water available, so buildings could go up on islands, surrounded by weeping willows, attractive shrubs, and masses of irises. Augustus Saint-Gaudens, Lorado Taft, and Daniel French were recruited to seek out the most eye-catching sculpture and statuary. The planners, architects, and laborers worked day and night. John Root, Burnham's partner, and even Louis Sullivan slept at the site. Many workers lived on houseboats nearby or slept in tents on the fairgrounds in order to speed along the mammoth project.

October 21, 1892, was dedication day for the buildings of the World's Fair. Michael Burke said often that he had never witnessed such a celebration. When he arrived downtown—all businesses had closed for the day—he saw American flags draped over every building. One hundred thousand people marched to the fairgrounds, led by Vice President of the United States Levi P. Morton, Justices of the Supreme Court, and members of the diplomatic corps. Carriage after carriage of foreign government officials passed by. So did the mayor and thousands upon thousands of cheering Chicagoans. Lunch was served to 75,000 invited guests.

Mrs. Potter Palmer, president of the Fair's Board of Lady Managers, shared the platform and took this unprecedented opportunity, an opportunity rare for a woman, to speak out: "Since it was a woman, Queen Isabella, who transformed Columbus's dream into reality, and since it was the progress of science which had liberated women from their never-ending tasks, woman could now take her rightful place alongside man in education, art, and industry. Even more important than the discovery of Columbus, which we are here to dedicate," she concluded, "is the fact that the general government has just discovered woman."[6]

Mrs. Potter Palmer might have been a WASP Establishment figure, but she spoke true. As early as the New York Fair in 1853, when women petitioned the government to be appointed to the National World's Fair Committee and were denied, Lucy Stone and Susan B. Anthony paraded with their delegation to the fairgrounds, carrying their signs for temperance, women's rights, and emancipation. In Philadelphia in 1876, women tried again in vain to be appointed to the World's Fair Committee. This time they were allowed to set up a women's pavilion, one separate from all the other pavilions. Those wishing to speak were denied access to the speaker's platform. Susan B. Anthony and her suffragettes marched again to the platform, carrying with them their position on women's rights, and attempted to present it to the shocked chairman of the speakers bureau. After they made their point, they marched back out, distributing copies of their position as they left.

By 1892, women had made some progress but not enough. Susan B. Anthony and Jane Addams had lobbied Washington, arranging tea parties for prominent local women interested in women's rights. As Congress took up the question of authorization of the World's Fair Committee, Jane Addams presented a petition requesting that the rights of women be recognized, specifically that a woman be appointed to the Fair's ruling Committee. Several Congressmen, cabinet officials, and Justices were surprised to find the names of their wives and daughters affixed to the Addams petition.

Congress did not agree to name a woman to the all-male committee. But it did instruct the committee to appoint women to the board of managers.

The directors of the Chicago World's Fair Company, a local corporation responsible for the day-to-day operations of the Fair, did agree to to establish a separate Board of Lady Managers in keeping with the will of the Congress. I am not so certain they were persuaded by the merits of the arguments of the women. Bertha Palmer's husband *was* a large stockholder in the Fair. At any rate, the women's pavilion was designed by a woman architect from Boston, Sophia G. Hayden. Exhibits from all over the world were displayed in the women's pavilion, which was visited by thousands of people and stood as a symbol of a struggle yet to be won, for the right of women to vote. To my mind, the Chicago World's Fair of 1893 was instrumental in putting women's issues on the national agenda.

Another social struggle brewed at the same time. Wishing an opportunity to show their achievements since Emancipation, black

Americans had petitioned President William Henry Harrison for representation on the National Committee of the Fair, to no avail. Not only that, black pleas for construction jobs or other meaningful ways of participating in the Fair were made to the local World's Fair Company. The pleas were dismissed. With every building in the Fair painted white, the Fair had been dubbed the White City, a label that held a special meaning for black Chicagoans. In a privately published pamphlet, Ida B. Wells, the Jane Addams of the black community, quoted the words of the highly respected national black civil rights leader Frederick Douglass: "As to the colored people of America, the World's Fair was a 'whited sepulchre.' "[7] What a contrast for Chicago from the days of her founder, DuSable.

Chicagoans' last piece of business before the Fair opened in the spring was another mayoral election, and Carter Harrison was running again. This time the newspapers backed Harrison' rival, Republican Samuel Allerton, in a bitter, hard-fought contest. As always, Harrison was the people's choice. As a representative of the old West and as a populist, he would be the perfect host for the World's Fair. And so he was, winning a close election to stand next to President Grover Cleveland and push the button that officially opened the Fair.

My maternal ancestors, the Cranes, and all their grown grandchildren, Mary, Patrick, Margaret Jane, and Sarah, certainly attended, as did my great-aunt Laura Crane, and her fiancée, John Hogan. They probably never knew such excitement as when they took the hot-air balloon ride fifteen hundred feet into the sky and looked down upon the fairgrounds, indeed over all Chicago. They took in a Paderewski concert. By this time, Michael had met Margaret Mary Burke (no relation), his future wife, also from County Mayo, and he escorted her to the Fair. They walked the length of the Court of Honor. They gazed in the huge reflecting pool and admired the latest mechanical discoveries in Machinery Hall. They looked in wonder at the transportation building, Horticulture Hall, the fine arts building, and Electricity Hall. They rode in a gondola across the pools to other buildings. They rode on moving sidewalks, unheard-of before. They took in all the beauty offered by the Fair as they strolled its garden paths. They walked the Midway and were shocked by the belly dancing in the Egyptian Village. They ate at a sidewalk café and visited every country's exhibit, including the Persian and Indian bazaars. They skipped the scantily-clad dancers in the Algerian theaters, but gazed teary-eyed at the Irish Village. They visited replicas of Sitting Bull's cabin and those of Davy Crockett and Daniel Boone. They watched the reindeer at the Lapland exhibit. They talked endlessly of the thrills of Buffalo Bill's Wild West Show and the boxing demonstrations given by Jim Corbett.

The surprise of this Fair was not a tower but a Ferris wheel, named after its builder, George Washington Ferris, a Pittsburgh builder of structural-steel bridges. Like the Eiffel Tower it was tall and built of steel—but it moved. As the young lovers prepared to leave the Fair at dusk, the final magic occurred. For the first time, incandescent lights, floodlights, and arc lights were displayed. The White City was bathed in white light.

The Fair was an enormous financial and public relations success—it attracted 21 million visitors—but it ended tragically for Mayor Carter Harrison. He sat at home on October 28, 1893, one day before the Fair's closing, reflecting on all that the Fair had meant to Chicago. A knock sounded at his door. Harrison opened it, and a disgruntled political enemy, Patrick Prendergast, shot him. The mayor fell dead. The city mourned the loss of a great public servant. As mayor for eight and a half of the years between 1879 and 1893, he had done much to transform Chicago from a wild frontier town to a cosmopolitan city of world renown. On the heels of an assassination, Chicago was poised to enter the twentieth century.

CHAPTER 5

Coming of Age

Immigrants had always powered Chicago's economic life. In 1893, buoyed by the spirit of the Fair, they were more than ever determined to profit from the city's growth. For a time, they would ignore the crooked politicians who made millions from the brothels and gambling houses in the Levee. They would forgive—if never forget—the insults their parents and grandparents had endured. These immigrants intended to move out of old Chicago and have a role in building the city. My forebears were among them. Laura Crane, my great-aunt, was the first of John Crane's children to leave the old River North neighborhood. When she married William Hogan, they moved to Hudson Street in Lincoln Park, and in keeping with Archbishop Feehan's wishes, they participated in the fund-raising drive to build St. Vincent's parish and a school that became De Paul University. This pattern developed all over Chicago as every ethnic group moved away from the past and into the future.

Mother's family were not the stereotypical slap-on-the-back kind of Irish-Americans, but they were proud of their heritage. They felt they'd seen it all. St. Patrick's Day was very important in our house, of course, but in a fairly solemn way. Mother didn't have much truck with wearing a lot of green. "Just wear a green corsage," she'd say. "When you're Irish, it shows in your face or in your eyes." Our holiday dinner was quite formal, the table set with our best Irish linen and the Havilland china, and all of the bread and rolls were made from scratch. It was a day to respect the struggles and achievements of our forebears.

When I was about nine, it occurred to me to ask my mother why no one in our family was named Patrick if the saint was so important. Since she hadn't known her great-grandfather Patrick Crane, I guess she hadn't told me many stories about him, but she was proud of him as first in our line on these shores. The Cranes, she liked to say, were the dark Irish, with dark curly hair and grayish-blue or green eyes. Strong people, they loved a good time. Mother called them "wild Irish." She felt she had been toned down herself by Nolan blood. Her mother's sister Laura was also different from most of the Cranes, much fairer-skinned, but with the same greenish-gray eyes that my brother Bill and I have. Laura was the oldest, a sergeant major over the youngest kids, and her father's darling. When she married, she was the first to hike up to live in Lincoln Park, and she became very much a leader in the development of the De Paul community.

As a single young woman, Laura had worked as an accountant. Every afternoon, the story went, she and her friends would meet downtown after work at five-fifteen and take the trolley home together. Just as regularly, a man would appear every day at their stop and expose himself. By the time they could get a policeman, the exhibitionist would be long gone. These were the days when big hats were in vogue, attached by very long hatpins. Laura organized her friends. When the man headed toward them one afternoon, ready to show what he had to show, she whipped a twelve-inch-long pin from her hat and led her pack of girlfriends in a charge, all brandishing their own hat pins. There was such brouhaha in the street that the police did catch the man. On the way home, victorious Laura and her crowd had a good laugh. The exhibitionist had enjoyed intimidating these young girls, but they had turned around and frightened him half to death.

Married, Laura was still the leader, and the family followed her up to the De Paul area. They felt no neighborhood was anywhere near as fine as Lincoln Park, with its washdays, baking days, cardplaying days, and picnics in spring and summer. My mother dreaded these all-day picnics as a child. The women competed to bring the most impressive food in their great hampers, and everyone joined in the races, games, golf, tennis, and boating. Mother's problem was that the kids had all stayed in Lincoln Park and knew each other. She'd been sent off to school and felt like an outsider, even at the monthly dances, which she recalled as lovely affairs with a good orchestra hired to play in the park bandstand.

For Laura, who was strong-willed, humorous, and devilishly satiri-cal, life would turn tragic early. When she was about twenty-six or twenty-seven, her husband, a police captain, suffered a ruptured ap-pendix and died, leaving her with two young sons and a baby daugh-ter. About six months after Laura's husband died, her three-year-old daughter died of diptheria. Laura's grief was so severe that she suf-fered a stroke. She would recover, but would limp slightly for the rest of her life. According to Mother, the whole community looked up to Laura all the more, for she compensated for the affliction with great dignity. She worked hard at it, holding her back straight and her chin high, learning to drag the leg a bit, and successfully hid the limp.

Laura was the closest thing I had to a grandmother on my mother's side. That was a significant role in my life, even though I have few actual memories of her. I recall visiting her when I was about five, a short time before she died, in the old graystone on Seminary Avenue in Lincoln Park. Her children and grandchildren lived on the first floor. When we started up the steps to her apartment, I was immedi-ately hit by the most wonderful smell of really good, really strong coffee. Laura was waiting in her wheelchair at the top of the stairs. About seven or eight years before, she'd suffered a second stroke. She was probably paralyzed from the waist down, but everything else seemed fine.

Today, I'm amazed by this woman who had been through so much—the fire, her husband's death, her daughter's death—and tri-umphed. As a child, of course, I just saw her as a very old woman. She was very proud of her long hair, which she wore piled high on her head, and had the nurse brush it every day. This particular day, it was hanging down, which I found a little frightening, for some reason, and I couldn't help staring at her gnarled hands. Yet her eyes twinkled and danced, and she was definitely in charge, wheeling around in her chair bringing coffee and a cake she had baked for us. It was just as my mother had described it from her own childhood, the highest and the lightest I had ever eaten. Even so, I felt uneasy, watching this elderly paralyzed woman.

She suddenly put out her hands and said, "Come here, little one." I was afraid, and my mother knew I was afraid, and I knew that she didn't like it that I was afraid . . . so I went over to Laura. When she put her arms around me, I somehow realized, even then, that though she wasn't really my grandmother, just my great-aunt, she carried the load for all the generations of my family that had gone before. I felt as much respect for her then as a child can feel. It was not long afterward that she died.

The jobs and revenues generated by the Fair cushioned Chicagoan from a depression that gripped the rest of the nation. In fact, some Chicagoans felt no pinch at all. Marshall Field had recently donated $1 million to the newly formed board of the Field Museum to buy the Fair's fine arts building. The board was also trying to keep in Chicago some of the art displayed at the Fair in seventy-four galleries of paintings and sculptures lent from Europe and the United States. Philip Armour's Institute, a school dedicated to educating the young in liberal arts for a nominal tuition fee, opened its doors in 1893. In 1895 another philanthropist, Allen Cleveland Lewis, opened the Lewis Institute. Both served the sons and ultimately the daughters of the working class until they merged in 1940 and became the Illinois Institute of Technology, a college with a current enrollment of over six thousand.

Chicago was growing. With the annexation of much of suburbia in 1889—towns such as Lakeview, Austin, Hyde Park, Kenwood, South Shore, Englewood, and Brighton Park all became part of Chicago—the city's size had quadrupled from 44 square miles to 174 square miles. N. K. Fairbanks, one of Chicago's wealthiest entrepreneurs, was determined to make it even bigger. With other families of the near north side Gold Coast, he purchased landfill from the digging of the Sanitary and Ship Canal and poured it out into the lake, creating some 126 acres of new land east of Michigan Avenue from Grand Avenue to the Oak Street Beach.

About this time, my maternal grandfather, John Nolan, a teenager from Middleton, Ohio, journeyed to Chicago to take a job as a porter at the Palmer House. His pay: room and board, plus tips. One day a railroad executive staying at the hotel took a liking to the lad. "Look me up when you turn eighteen," the executive said, "and you'll have a job with the railroad." Like many young men in those days, my grandfather dreamed of seeing the West, particularly California, and railway jobs were known to be well-paid, secure, and rich with opportunity. The very day he turned eighteen, he looked up that executive and became a railroad man—first a switchman, later a conductor—and he stayed with the Santa Fe Railroad for the next ten years.

John Nolan was handsome and tall, at six feet two, but probably shy in his first encounters with the big city. Anyway, there were plenty of mischief-makers in his family. A slightly older second cousin, Margaret Lane, had come to Chicago before him and happened to be riding the same trolley car one day, carrying her two-year-old in her arms. John was sitting with an attractive young woman he didn't know very well and was obviously trying to impress her by being very proper and gentlemanly. Margaret couldn't resist. The more pompous John became, the more she wanted to create havoc. She stood up, walked over to the pair, and shouted, for the whole car to hear, "Never mind the flirting. Take care of your baby!" Just as the trolley made its next stop, she plunked the child into John's arms and walked off. She knew the baby was in good hands, of course. John told everyone he couldn't manage another word on the long ride home. Margaret followed him on the next trolley and joined the rest of the laughing family. They always had fun in those days, my mother believed, despite the hardships and the prejudice.

Now, all four of my grandparents were Chicagoans. For a city whose politics would be dominated by the Irish, my lineage was just fine. As it happened, we were all north side Irish, although I thought nothing of that in my childhood. To me, Irish was Irish. Not until I entered politics did I learn that there were south side, west side, and north side Irish—and the distinctions were taken seriously by some people. Once in a while, I had heard the phrase "lace-curtain Irish" applied to our neighborhood, but when I asked my mother the meaning of the phrase, she changed the subject. "It isn't very nice. You are Irish-American!" The phrase, it turned out, was a mild slap at hard-working Irish immigrants who tried to better their lives with material comforts, but my mother was not amused. She and my father forbade us to make disparaging remarks about any ethnic groups, including our own.

My parents also felt strongly about equal rights, even feminism. The middle child between two brothers, Billy and Edward, I was treated as their equal in all things. One day the three of us, along with a group of their friends, decided to build a rope swing. We worked on it for two days, also constructing a fort in a hollow of the tree and nailing wooden blocks into the trunk to make steps up to the fort. Billy slid well out on a limb, knotted the rope swing around it, then dropped the other end of the rope within a few feet of the ground. A sturdy loop was made at that end of the rope large enough to slip a foot through. Someone would throw the loop up to where you stood in the fort, then you slipped your foot through the loop, pushed off, and swung out over the lawn below, shouting "Geronimo!"

The first time I started clambering up the steps, I heard someone shout, "This is the guys' fort. No girls allowed."

Already halfway up the tree, I instantly realized that if I didn't go any farther, they couldn't either. Billy must have read my mind. "You guys had better let her swing," he said, "I know her, and she won't budge off that step." The gang finally agreed—I could have one swing.

Riding in the Concorde does not compare to that wonderfully exhilarating swing. On the second arc outward, I shouted "Geronimo!" as the guys had. That did it for Billy—he left.

When I got home, he was plying Mother with every conceivable argument against my being allowed to swing again. His friends did not want to play with a girl. Swinging was not ladylike. On and on. My mother, stone-faced, said that we'd have to settle the matter ourselves. Billy, bless him, was arguing with a woman whose mother had marched the streets of Chicago decades before carrying a banner for "Women's Right to Vote."

The minute our father's car pulled up to the house, Billy ran outside to confront Dad, no doubt assuming a natural ally in the matter. He neglected to mention that I had helped build the rope swing. Desperate, he blurted out, "Well, it's okay with me, Dad, if she swings. If you don't care that every time she swung all the guys could see her underpants, why should I?"

I was mortified. My father didn't blink. He turned to me and said, "The next time you swing, wear long pants."

Half a century earlier, when women were barred from voting booths as well as tree forts, a special election, necessitated by Harrison's assassination, was coming up.

While Carter Harrison had been a good mayor and a charismatic leader, he had ruled with a lot of electoral help from Kenna and Coughlin, the political bosses of the Levee District, winking at their dealings in gambling and prostitution. Chicago was a wide-open town, but its officialdom remained more or less honest.

The special election established quite a contrasting precedent. As in previous contests, the candidates sought the support of individual aldermen, but the election of John Patrick Hopkins represented the first time a coalition of aldermen and committeemen would help secure the mayoralty. Hopkins, part of an Irish faction led by Roger Sullivan, lined up the support of aldermen who shared the Sullivan crowd's interest in government—the money pot. Specifically, they eyed city franchises. The council had always granted franchises for the use of city streets—to the gas company to lay underground mains, to transit companies to put down tracks. The politicians' inspiration was one of the most notorious tycoons in Chicago, Francis Tyson Yerkes, a streetcar robber baron who had bought up smaller transportation lines and their franchises. Through payoffs to city council members, Yerkes was well on his way to consolidating all of Chicago's transportation lines into one company. In 1896, Yerkes's transportation network amassed an astronomical profit of $89 million.

If Yerkes could do it, why not the servants of the people? Hopkins, Sullivan, and their band of corrupt aldermen devised their scheme: First, Hopkins and Sullivan set up dummy gas and electricity companies; second, the aldermen in their pockets persuaded the council to extend a long-term franchise to their dummy corporation. Ogden Gas—named to conjure up a vision of local hero Bill Ogden—was a corporation in name only. It could supply no gas.

The major gas company in Chicago at that time, Peoples Gas Light & Coke Co., naturally did not want competition. Its own franchise was short-term. Logic and discretion dictated that Peoples Gas should buy the long-term lease of Ogden Gas, and so it did. Hopkins and Sullivan received over $7 million for their piece of paper.[1]

While Coughlin and Kenna were not thrilled about the emergence of Hopkins and Sullivan as rivals, they tended to tolerate the new machine. Besides, they were raking in oceans of kickback money from the gambling dens and brothels of the Levee, particularly the new, prestigious Everleigh Sisters' House, which was, by far, Chicago's most elegant brothel.

At some point, the afterglow of Chicago's Fair was bound to fade. When it did, Chicago, too, fell into the country's financial depression. Some work was available on the Sanitary and Ship Canal, still being excavated, but workers all over town were beginning to suffer. Out in Pullman Town, it was becoming ever more difficult to survive. Production of Pullman cars was down, so George Pullman cut salaries, but allowed no reduction in rent or food prices at his company store. Desperate workers called a strike at Pullman on May 11, 1894. No violence broke out during the seven-week strike, and when it became evident that negotiations were not productive, the workers voted to return to work. To their shock, however, they had been "locked out."[2] The strike was a stalemate.

In the 1890s, the railroads ruled America, and as they grew, so did the industry's unions. There was a separate union for every job category—from engineer and fireman to switchman and conductor. Along with unions came union leaders. Eugene V. Debs had been a high official of the Brotherhood of Locomotive Firemen and editor of a labor publication viewed by many as socialist, perhaps even anarchistic. Debs had recently attempted to organize all the unions into a large one, his, which he called the American Railway Union. He had not been successful in Chicago. Not one union at Pullman belonged to the ARU, nor did the workers want any part of Debs himself. He was unfazed. Extremely ambitious, he needed a cause that would demonstrate the strength of his union. During a labor convention at the time of the Pullman strike, Debs persuaded his members to support the striking workers. Then Debs advised Pullman management that if they didn't settle the strike by June 26, 1894, his union of 100,000 railroad workers would boycott all trains pulling Pullman cars. Management ignored Debs. Immediately, every railroad union from Chicago to California unhitched Pullman's cars, effectively halting the nation's railway service. Ultimately, two-thirds of all trains were idled.

Violence broke out. Workers began to stop the few operating trains by setting fires or causing switches to malfunction. Over the objections of Mayor Hopkins and Governor John Altgeld, President Grover Cleveland on July 3 ordered federal troops into Pullman Town to quell the strike. The workers turned back the troops. When the state militia joined the battle, the troops again failed to subdue the workers. Rioting erupted in other cities. It took three weeks and eleven thousand troops to end the boycott.

The Pullman strike left a bloody mark in history, claiming twenty-six lives and leaving close to seventy critically hurt and hundreds more injured. Though unsuccessful in their specific aims, labor leaders quickly recognized that the size of a union made an impact on management and that future labor negotiations could actually improve the workers' lot. In that regard, the Pullman strike was very effective. Certainly it put Eugene Debs on the national map—nor did it hurt that he was indicted and ultimately sentenced to six months in jail in Woodstock, Illinois.[3]

For the most part, Americans did not support the Pullman strike. But the packing house workers at the Chicago stockyards did, and they joined with the railroad workers in a sympathy strike to show solidarity with the labor movement. Times were truly rough between labor and management in Chicago in the mid-1890s. Managers spared nothing in an attempt to defeat labor and to break strikes; in their methods lay the seeds of racial conflict existent in Chicago today, for the companies imported black strikebreakers from Alabama. As these imported workers crossed the picket lines, a riot seemed imminent. Many blacks already worked at the yards, and they didn't like these newcomers any better than the white employees did. The chanting of "nigger scab" went up and down the picket line. The anger of the workers was not limited to the workplace but was carried home and spread to the surrounding neighborhoods. Wives and children threw rocks at any black they saw, with that virulent chant "nigger scabs."

The packing house owners could not have cared less. For the price of train tickets, Armour, Wilson, and Cudahy could hire as many blacks as they chose and pay them low-end wages. But Chicagoans not involved in the stockyards viewed the situation as explosive and blamed the packers. Stung, the packers announced that the hiring of black strikebreakers would cease. Even so, the white workers soon became demoralized. Realizing that the Southern blacks would hold on to their jobs, they capitulated and returned to work after nine days. But not before burning a black dummy in effigy.

Later in the same year, the University of Chicago, attempting to break a construction strike, imported eighty black strikebreakers from Tuskegee Institute. Every other trade walked off the construction site. If it was too early to call it a pattern or even a trend, it was nevertheless clear that the white workers in the city would not work with black workers. It was equally clear that the unions were beginning to chip away at managerial strength.

In the wake of their defeat, the packing house workers gathered around a new leader, Michael Donnelly. The new union, called the American Meat Cutters and Butcher Workmen (AMCBW), had grown rapidly and in 1902 was chartered with twenty-one locals, totaling four thousand members. It hadn't been easy to achieve this solidarity, for many of the meat cutters were from newer immigrant groups. The same old suspicions and fears of each other were rife. But Donnelly knew that the union's most sensitive issue was the way management played the unskilled worker against the old-timers, training new workers to replace the experienced, increasing profits by paying the unskilled a lower wage. He concentrated on this pocketbook issue, persuading skilled workers to join with him in recruiting the unskilled into the union at a higher beginning wage level. The skilled workers agreed—this was the only way both to take away management's weapon and to protect their own jobs. For the unskilled workers, here was a godsend. With pay otherwise hovering between 15 cents and 18 cents an hour, they jumped at the chance to join a union that would fight to give them 20 cents an hour.

When Donnelly met with management to press for the higher pay for unskilled workers, he got a flat refusal. In fact, they announced a pay cut across the board, whereupon Donnelly led the workers out. His timing was poor, however, for unemployment was high. Thousands of Chicagoans were desperate for work. As the 23,000 strikers walked off the job, would the packers attempt to hire unemployed Chicagoans, or would the unemployed Chicagoans cross the picket line? No one will ever know, for the packers, anticipating (and having provoked) the strike, had already recruited thousands of black strikebreakers. Trains rolled in from the worst slums in the South.

As the black strikers crossed the lines, the chant again went up—"nigger scabs." Pleading to maintain peace, Donnelly barely kept his men in check. But as the days went by, frustration, anger, hatred boiled over. The target of the hate was no longer the packers, but all blacks, any black. A black man in no way involved with the strike and his young son happened to walk by the picketers. Five hundred strikers seized and beat them brutally, leaving them for dead. It was if a powder keg had exploded, releasing pent-up fury into the air. Next a black strikebreaker was seized. Enraged strikers cut his eyes out with knives, screaming, "All niggers will get this." They indiscriminately hurled stones at blacks, day after day, until, exhausted, they realized they couldn't win. The company strategy of importing black strikebreakers had worked. In the end, the strikers won nothing. Gloom settled over the back of the yards neighborhoods as dispirited fathers and husbands trudged home to face their families. Scars from any serious strike take years to fade. In this one, the actions of the packers watered and nurtured the seeds of racism in the blue-collar neighborhoods surrounding the stockyards.[4]

For the moment, though, Chicagoans proved resilient again. These destructive strikes had stunned the city, but as soon as they ended, Chicago turned its attention to a more amusing saga.

Residents of the Gold Coast viewed the new expanded lakefront property produced by landfill from the diggings of the Sanitary and Ship Canal as an asset to their own property values. They expected elegant buildings to rise on that land and anticipated no snags—certainly not the obstacle of Captain George S. Wellington Streeter.

On July 10, 1886, Captain Streeter, former entertainer, forester, seaman, copper miner, rogue, and Civil War veteran, ran his second-hand boat, the *Reutan*, aground on a sandbar east of the Gold Coast, about five hundred yards from the beach. Unable to refloat the *Reutan*, Streeter and his wife, Maria, decided to live aboard it. Chicago was in the midst of another building boom, and shortly, Streeter worked out a deal with an excavation contractor to dump landfill around his stranded boat. Soon he had a walkway to the beach and a rocky breakwater protecting his houseboat. The property wasn't huge, but it was rather comfortable, perhaps several acres. Soon, itinerant workers attracted to Streeter's little island came seeking to build shanties on his land. Streeter rented them small parcels of land for a dollar a year.

As Streeter's little waterbound shanty town and its band of itinerant workers grew, the sight rankled the Gold Coast homeowners, who determined to do something about it. Meanwhile, the ever-inventive Streeter had repaired and refloated the *Reutan*—renamed it the *Maria*—for the World's Fair. He used it by day as a popular excursion boat and by night as home, moored to his island.

The question of the island's ownership nagged at everyone. A study of the federal map of Chicago and the state of Illinois convinced Streeter that his man-made island was no part of Chicago. He wrote the government to that effect, advising Washington that as a Civil War veteran he was exercising his homestead rights. When N. K. Fairbank, the Gold Coaster and real estate tycoon, was apprised of Streeter's claim, he stormed out to the island and ordered the captain to vacate forthwith. Streeter replied by brandishing a shotgun and firing a blast of birdshot into the air. When Fairbank sought legal help through his lawyers, Chicago's most prestigious, he received cold comfort; they warned him that any action would tie him up in court for a long time.

Fairbank, now blind with rage, hired thugs to throw Streeter off, but the Streeters, aptly named, were street-smart. They recognized that they were up against a wealthy adversary and in for a long and dirty fight. They quickly replaced the *Maria* with a high-sided scow and turned it into a two-flat home, with living quarters on the second floor and a supply of guns, rocks, and ammunition stashed on the first floor. Once the scow's ladder was pulled up to the second floor, no one could safely board the boat. Moreover, the Streeters had an admirable vantage point from the second-floor window. Visitors could not ambush them. No matter how many thugs, detectives, or policemen Fairbank hired to evict the couple, they remained safety ensconced on their boat.

Indeed, Streeter was on to a good thing. He had little trouble raising the money for lawyers—the migrants' lease money took care of that. When asked why he rented to "undesirables," Streeter roared, "This is a frontier town, and it has got to go through its red-blooded youth. A church and WCTU branch never growed a town big yet. Yuh got to start with entertainment." Streeter had those big shots so frustrated that he was entertaining all of Chicago. When he finally received a reply from Washington admitting that the federal government had no jurisdiction over his affairs out in the lake, Streeter immediately set up a local government, shocking the gentry of the near north side.[5] Their plans for their valuable 126 acres of Gold Coast land might have to be scrapped—land that would one day house Northwestern University, Water Tower Place, Olympia Center and Neiman Marcus, John Hancock, and the Allerton. Streeter and Fairbank, as the latter's attorneys had predicted, would battle it out in the courts for the rest of the 1890s.

Meanwhile, depression or no depression, the Levee District in Chicago's 1st Ward was flourishing. The annual 1st Ward ball sponsored by the notorious Democratic leaders of the ward, Coughlin and Kenna, attracted larger and larger crowds of pimps, prostitutes, gangsters, gamblers, and thugs, who crowded the Coliseum on South Wabash to dance, drink, and gamble the night away. Coughlin and Kenna enjoyed immense power and were on familiar terms with the new mayor, Carter Harrison, Jr., as with his father before him. But after fifteen years of bossing the Levee, they were about to be challenged.

In 1900, Coughlin and Kenna recruited Jim Colosimo, a street cleaner in the Department of Streets and Sanitation, as their new precinct captain and bagman. A bagman, not normally a high-powered sort of fellow, merely collects tribute from the crooked element in the public and ferries that money to the crooked politicians. Colosimo was no foot soldier. He quickly learned the folkways of the Levee and decided that prostitution was too profitable an enterprise to pass by.

In no time, he had six streetwalkers working for him and was known as Big Jim or Big Man of the Levee. He began to expand his horizons.

Meanwhile, the rest of Chicago—including the police and the mayor—paid little attention to the crime and corruption so rampant in the Levee. Instead, Chicagoans were busily moving out of the center city into surrounding suburbs, turning them into lovely neighborhoods of churches, schools, parks, and steam-heated homes. Their major concern was transportation. Yerkes's transit lines were unreliable, shoddy, and dirty, but his payoffs to corrupt aldermen put commuting Chicagoans at his mercy—and would keep them there for some time.

More promising to Chicagoans was the projected opening of the Sanitary and Ship Canal, but St. Louis was opposed, fearing that Chicago's garbage and waste would wash out of Lake Michigan, down the Mississippi, and directly into the St. Louis water system. Rumor had it that St. Louis would seek an injunction to prevent the opening of the canal. Illinois and upper Missouri residents in the Sanitary District decided to take precipitate action to head off any such suit. The date of the opening of the canal was to be January 20. In the early hours of the morning of January 16, however, a commissioner who will be forever anonymous phoned Governor John R. Tanner requesting permission to open the controlling locks at Lockport and let the river waters flow. The governor agreed. As most Chicagoans slept, the locks were opened without ceremony. None the wiser, St. Louis residents filed a suit that very morning, but it was too late.[6] Lake Michigan water was by that time flowing right past their city.

In my family history, the turn of the century was important in another way. Margaret Jane Crane and John Nolan, my maternal grandparents, were married in Holy Name Cathedral. Margaret Mary and Michael Burke, my paternal grandparents, married that same year. The Nolans took up residence in Lincoln Park at 2050 Bissell. The Burkes moved into 1620 North Rockwell Street in the community called Humboldt Park.

In 1910, Charles Comiskey opened the park that bore his name at 35th and Shields. Comiskey, a native Chicagoan and former star of the St. Louis Browns baseball team, had spent $1 million to give the city "the best stadium in the country." Naming his team the White Sox, Comiskey recruited the best players available, not hesitating to steal the stars of the local White Stockings team, a National League club. The White Stockings grandfather Burke had admired in his teens were soon stuck with the inexperienced players on their farm team. Accustomed to the glory days of Al Spalding's White Stockings, sportswriters all over the city began to belittle the White Stockings team as nothing but a collection of cubs.[7] The moniker caught on, and from 1901, Chicago rooted for either the White Sox or the Cubs. Since Comiskey Park, located next to Bridgeport, was on the south side of the city, the White Sox became identified as the south side's team, and the Cubs, playing after 1914 at Wrigley Field in Lakeview on the north side, attracted fans from that side of town.

In the new century, Captain Streeter hung on, but things were not going well for him. In the spring of 1902, John Kirk, a hired killer, was found murdered near Streeter's scow. The captain was convicted of the murder and packed off to jail. He had pleaded innocent all along, and his lawyers eventually proved he had been framed. Governor Altgeld, of Haymarket fame, pardoned him, but going home was not a happy affair, for Maria had died during his nine months in prison. Embittered, Streeter and his squatters fought on.

Big Jim Colosimo was in better shape. He married a madam who owned her own house and took over the business. The brothel proved so lucrative that he could soon set up two rather swanky evening spots—the Saratoga Club and the Victoria, named for his wife. Knowing the streets well, Colosimo constructed an elaborate set of underground escape tunnels for his patrons in case of a police raid. There seemed little need, since Kenna and Coughlin paid off the police on the beat in the Levee.

Colosimo was also becoming active on another front. Using his position in Streets and Sanitation, he and sidekick Mike Carozzo organized the city street cleaners into his own union. This scam provided another source of income—skimming dues—and cheap labor—streetworkers snatched girls off the street to be sold into Big Jim's white slavery racket. All the while, Colosimo and his cronies remained on the payroll of the city.

Carter Harrison, Jr., had campaigned in 1901 as a reformer because he knew people were disgusted with Hopkins and Sullivan, but once in office, he allowed Coughlin, Kenna, and Colosimo free rein. Chicagoans were fed up, however, and facing a reelection challenge, Harrison realized he had to make at least a swipe at reform.

He could deal, he felt, with the issue of vice and corruption by telling Coughlin and Kenna that the Levee had to move farther south, away from residential areas. In that way, he could claim that he had "segregated vice" and thereby placate the voters for a while. The strategy worked. And so did Harrison's attack on the Yerkes transportation monopoly. He took on the robber baron's friends on the city council and defeated an ordinance that would have renewed Yerkes's franchise for *one hundred years.* Perhaps emboldened by success, Harrison fought forcefully in Springfield for the right of cities to own their transit systems. That was the end of the line for Yerkes. He left Chicago for London, where he soon died. The process of structuring municipal control of transit lines began. Harrison was reelected mayor in 1903, but his efforts would come back to haunt him—the city didn't have the money to purchase all of the transit lines.

Yet it was still Christmas every day for Coughlin, Kenna, and Colosimo. The "segregated" Levee was now located between 18th and 22nd streets south, centering on Dearborn and State streets. At 2133 South Dearborn the Everleigh Sisters' House was booming, frequented by the most affluent of Chicago residents and foreign dignitaries.

Well removed from these shenanigans, the Burkes were eagerly awaiting their second child. On December 18, 1903, my father, William Patrick, was born, "right in time for Christmas," as my grandfather would say. Two years later, on September 15, 1905, Katharine Nolan, my mother, was born. Shortly after her birth, Marshall Field's name jumped into the headlines once again.

While honeymooning with his most recent wife in New York, Field was notified that his son had accidentally shot himself and had been rushed to Mercy Catholic Hospital—one of the city's first hospitals, built in 1849 on fashionable Prairie Avenue. Leasing a private train, Field sped home. When you are powerful, you *are* news, but Field was not prepared for the swarm of newsmen when he stepped off the train. The barrage of impertinent questions, the mob following him to the hospital, and the loud clamoring for information completely unnerved him. According to Marshall Field III's biographer, he shouted, "Have you no shame?" and began striking reporters with his cane. He refused to make a formal statement, as did the hospital and the police. Rumors were rife—Marshall Field's son had committed suicide; something to do with the Levee; he had been shot in the Everleigh sisters' exquisite brothel. And so on.[8] Whatever the circumstances, he did not recover. Now the spotlight focused more brightly on the Levee, and women's reform groups would make it a target for years to come. But the short-term impact of young Field's death was a rise in the price of "protection." The police, Coughlin, Kenna, and Colosimo grew ever richer. Young Field's widow and children moved to England.

The Levee was giving Chicago a terrible reputation across the country. Carter Harrison, Jr., could not—or would not—go against Kenna, Coughlin or Colosimo, however, for he needed their political clout. He also knew that the Hopkins-Sullivan faction, angered by his defeat of Yerkes, would work against him in the next election. Worse, the city still could not afford to purchase the transit system, which clattered on with individual companies running the lines. They functioned helter-skelter without long-term franchises, and dissatisfied voters were again grumbling about unreliable transportation.

Then as now, Chicago was a Democratic city, and the exalted Democratic machine rolled on and on forever on, seemingly invincible, election after election. Yet, occasionally, in a Democratic primary, the machine has sputtered. Sometimes in primaries, Democratic blocs even refuse to support any Democrat, throwing their weight instead behind Republicans. 1905 was such a year. The Democratic machine, fragmented by various committeemen vying for power, lacked a single strong leader. The most powerful bloc was the one led by Hopkins and Sullivan.

Chicago now had a large Irish Catholic population. Only about 7 percent were immigrants, so most could vote. Archbishop James S. Quigley craftily orchestrated their loyalty. He had directed that the parishes be no farther than one mile radius from each other, thus pastors could know their congregations well. Also, Quigley was building new schools and churches wherever possible.[9] Shrewd politicians like Hopkins and Sullivan recognized the strength of Irish Catholic voters. They made certain that the streets were swept around the churches (and synagogues) and provided every available city service to the clergy. A pastor had only to mention that some worthy parishioner needed a job for Hopkins or Sullivan to come through.

Harrison was not Catholic, although he had been educated at St. Ignatius and had married a Catholic woman. While he was pondering whether or not to run, Hopkins and Sullivan cast about for a suitably pliable Irish Catholic to back. At the same time, by spreading rumors and planting stories in newspapers about Harrison's alleged ties to Kenna, Coughlin, and Colosimo, they drummed up sentiment against the mayor, who was already in public disfavor because of Chicago's failure to purchase the transit lines.

Enter Edward Dunne, a political maverick. A young Irish Catholic judge who belonged to no one, he took it upon himself to speak loud and often in favor of municipal ownership of transportation. Residents, he thundered, had the *right* to expect safe, reliable transportation. Harrison, of course, agreed with Dunne; no one wished to have the city buy and manage the transit lines more than he. But no matter who got elected, no matter what Dunne said, Chicago could not afford it.

Still, Dunne, the challenger, had no political baggage. Harrison had plenty of baggage, and it was heavy. Realizing that the luster of his name had tarnished and that Hopkins and Sullivan would be formidable foes, he decided not to run. Edward Dunne was nominated by the Democratic Party and elected mayor by an enthusiastic public on April 4, 1905.

CHAPTER 6

Modern Chicago

Hopkins and Sullivan took aspirin and went to bed with ice packs the night Mayor Dunne won the election. An outsider, Dunne did not play the games of the ward bosses. Similarly, eight months after my general election, almost three-quarters of a century later, two ward bosses confided in me that when I beat them and the rest of the machine, they were up all night—commiserating with each other on the telephone, consuming more than a pinch of Jack Daniel's, and speculating about their political fate—for I too wasn't one of them and I certainly wasn't one of the boys.

Dunne was pro-labor, but, ironically, he was barely over the threshold of the mayor's office in April of 1905 when the teamsters called a strike. As Tuttle writes in *Race Riot*, this one would be even more crippling than the meat packers' strike the year before. Once again, company after company imported blacks from the South to man the horse-drawn trucks. So enraged were the striking workers that rocks, knives, and guns were wielded openly on the streets of Chicago as trucks were stopped and all but dismantled by the union. Unlike the stockyards strike, this one was citywide and affected every segment of industry—bakeries; coal, produce, and meat suppliers—violently bringing all commerce to a halt. Emotions run high in all strikes, but rarely has racial hatred been so blatant. Families united behind the strikers and against the black workers. Schoolchildren formed strike associations, condoned by their teachers, vowing to stone any black hired by Peabody Coal Company who attempted to deliver coal to the schools. Blacks who had long lived in Chicago's black belt and were not strikebreakers were stoned even so, sometimes beaten to death. A crowd of jeering children outside Peabody Coal Company encircled and taunted two black men going home from work. The black men in this case were armed and began firing into the crowd, killing an eleven-year-old boy. In retaliation, white mobs ravaged the black belt. Black Chicagoans were dragged off streetcars and beaten, windows were shattered and doors smashed. It was no longer safe to be black on any Chicago street.

By May of 1905, blacks had armed themselves and were firing back at the white gangs destroying their neighborhoods. Several white men were killed. The rioting continued until May 22, taking twenty-two lives. Over four hundred were seriously injured. Mayor Dunne had allowed the strike to rage for one hundred days without ever calling in the militia. Eventually, he moved to act as mediator between labor and management, but in the end the labor movement certainly did not profit from this strike.[1]

Dunne was also beleaguered by the issue he'd raised so effectively: mass transit. The same election that had placed him in the mayor's chair had included a referendum on the issue—with mixed results. Voters had divided pretty much evenly between city ownership and city regulation.

Despite the brutal strike and the headache of mass transit, Dunne did accomplish much of what he set out to do. After he made his first cabinet choices, the machine aldermen were quaking in their shoes, and so was the business establishment. His appointment of Jane Addams to the school board enraged Hopkins, who had disliked her from the first moment Addams began to speak out against the terrible living conditions in his fiefdom, the 19th Ward. Clarence Darrow's appointment as assistant corporation counsel signaled that Dunne was not merely a populist, but a true reform populist. Moreover, for the first time, a mayor appointed labor representatives to many boards and commissions. Dunne also gave some of his supporters jobs in City Hall, where they worked side by side with the machine's precinct captains. When these loyal soldiers complained to Kenna, Coughlin, Hopkins, and Sullivan that the new appointees had never so much as rung a doorbell in their lives but got jobs anyway, there was little consolation to offer: "We don't understand him. We delivered our wards for him." This conversation can always be heard in City Hall when an outsider gets hired.

Taking the bit in his teeth, Dunne finally began to campaign for municipal ownership of *all* the utility companies—gas, electric, and transit. Hopkins and Sullivan, clearly on the run, saw their graft payments dwindling away. Nor were they encouraged when the Illinois legislature passed, at Dunne's urging, legislation allowing the city to regulate the gas and utility rates. Chicago, no longer a frontier town, was maturing.

The school board was raising hell, too, over long-term cheap leases on school properties. They demanded that the sweetheart contracts be renegotiated and that the schools receive the profit. The Chicago Board of Education had been given vast amounts of real estate in Chicago's earliest days. Here was a gold mine, but state law does not allow the money from the sale of school lands to be used for its operating budget—that money may be used for capital improvements only. The Board of Education had long evaded the spirit of this law by leasing out some of its lands, for periods as long as one hundred years. The hundred-year leases ignored the fact that property values rise and fall. Much of the school land in the Dunne term had, of course, risen in value; his Board of Education seemed correct to end this practice and to renegotiate the leases. The school board members, largely labor supporters and social reformers, had no love for the Republican *Tribune* and announced that the paper itself owned some of these sweetheart land contracts, and had since 1895. There were several downtown office buildings on school land as well. Dunne, of course, had been opposed by the *Tribune*, but now he drew down the full wrath of the press. From then on, the *Tribune* would hound him diligently, describing Dunne's administration as filled with kooks, freaks, and socialists. Nor did he win in the courts. In the years since his administration, the original cozy long-term leases have always been held valid. (I have personal experience of this, for many of those hundred-year leases, dating back to 1895, were still in effect in 1979 to frustrate me as I dealt with a financially strapped Board of Education. Schools desperately needed capital improvements, but the long-term lease agreements were again ruled valid. One large piece of Board of Education land was leased to the city itself—the land under Midway Airport. To aid the schools' capital budget crunch, my administration purchased the Midway Airport land in 1981 and gave the money to the school board.)

Most significantly for Dunne, his police chief started cracking down on the Levee. Dunne hated political corruption, particularly the kind that ran wild in the 1st Ward. Religiously, morally, and civically, he was a true reformer. He increased the yearly license fee for taverns from $100 to $500 and enforced that law diligently in the Levee, pledging to use the fees to hire dedicated policemen. One of those dedicated policemen went so far in his zeal as to shut down Kenna's saloon. Both of my grandmothers proudly told their daughters that Dunne could get away with this only because the women's temperance groups were solidly behind him. They liked him for his stand on the Levee but also because he had made it clear that in his view, women would soon win the right to vote in Illinois.

Dunne had turned traditional Chicago on its head, alienating many a power bloc along the way. Water rates were increased for major corporations and residential rates lowered. Zoning laws were enforced. Building inspectors strictly adhered to the building codes and even shut down Marshall Field's store for two hours because of faulty fire escapes.[2] The business community, the aldermen, the hoodlums all awaited eagerly the end of his term. Coughlin and Kenna moaned. Why should a tavern continue to pay them for protection when the mayor was off the reservation? The *Tribune* had been ridiculed because of its sweetheart long-term land lease. In a word, they all knew they had no *clout*.

Oddly, the public, which should have been rooting for Dunne, in fact seemed lackadaisical, much more involved in rooting the White Sox to their league pennant in 1906 than in political realities. The Cubs were to win the pennant and the World Series in 1908. Thirty years later, my grandfathers Burke and Nolan could still describe those races, particularly the 1908 Series, in great detail, and spoke wistfully of the popular chant "From Tinker to Evers to Chance," memorializing the legendary double-play infield, all Hall-of-Famers.

The public seemed to take for granted Dunne's many reforms and was tired of waiting for a resolution of the transit issue. There was, in fact, an impasse. The aldermen favored regulation of the transit system; Dunne would countenance nothing less than ownership. Caught in this impasse were Chicagoans—tired of trains that ran late or broke down, delaying arrival at work, for which some would be docked part of a day's pay. After waiting long for a train, riders could find no place to sit. Many blamed pneumonia and flu epidemics on poorly ventilated and overly crowded trains.

Little has changed in modern Chicago—ask my opponent in the 1979 race for mayor, Michael A. Bilandic. The blizzards that plagued Chicago that winter brought about many of the same conditions riders faced in 1905. Trains ran late, if at all, for days at a time. When the Chicago Transit Authority did get a fair portion of its fleet moving again, some charged that too few trains were allocated to the south side of Chicago—in fact, black Chicagoans stood waiting in freezing cold only to see the trains roll right past them, too overcrowded to stop—and a cry went up: "They've cut our service. The trains won't stop for us." More than anything else, Bilandic's handling of the blizzard caused black Chicagoans to vote against him. Having trains bypass the south side stops was a huge political blunder.

A political rule of thumb is that logjams need new faces. The new face of 1906 was that of a young Republican, Fred Busse, who campaigned for regulation instead of municipal ownership to improve the system. Chicagoans were more than satisfied with that option, especially if it benefited them as effectively as regulation of the other utilities had. The idea took hold, and so did Fred Busse, who went on to defeat Dunne in 1907. Thereby, Chicago rule returned to the business community. Busse's pro-business bias, however, and his apparent support for closing taverns on Sundays would be his undoing. In 1911, the Democrats returned Carter Harrison, Jr., to power.

Despite the corruption and political turmoil of this decade, life in Chicago seemed ever more promising to many immigrants. For my grandfather Burke, Chicago was a far better place than it had been on his arrival in the 1880s. Gone at last, for instance, was the notorious 1st Ward ball, Kenna's and Coughlin's annual blowout for their constituents, politicians, members of the press, and whoever cared to mix with prostitutes, gamblers, pimps, and the other underworld habitués of the Levee. To my devoutly religious grandfather's delight, that corrupt frontier image was being replaced by the founding of United Charities and the Church Federation, an association of every religious group in Chicago.

Chicagoans were beginning to sense a common purpose, a feeling of a family-oriented city. But no common purpose could be discerned in the way Chicago looked. The city had grown so fast there'd never been a plan for its development. In 1909, after three years of work, under the supervision of civic leaders such as Charles Wacker and other members of the Merchants' Club, Daniel Burnham, architectural impresario of the World's Fair, submitted his design for the reorganization and development of Chicago. Basic to his plan was a vision for the functional and recreational uses of Chicago's lakefront, for shipping as well as recreation—for instance, on Navy Pier. Comprehensive connecting networks of boulevards and streets, like the Michigan Avenue bridge and Wacker Drive, would ease the flow of traffic downtown and to the neighborhoods; a large lakefront sports complex including the monumental Soldier Field, marinas, and the construction of the northerly island would spawn Meigs Field off the downtown lakefront. All of Chicago's neighborhoods would have large parks for recreation. The city council immediately approved the plan. The Chicago of today is very much the Chicago of Daniel Burnham's imagination.

While life seemed kinder to my grandfather, and to thousands like him, it was growing more difficult for Big Jim Colosimo. Nash writes in *Makers and Breakers of Chicago* that Big Jim had the misfortune of not belonging to the Black Hand, a growing concern; rather, he was merely an Italian gangster "soloing" under the aegis of old-line bosses Kenna and Coughlin. The Black Hand didn't want any more soloing, it wanted to take over, so three Mafia henchmen called on Big Jim and informed him that they wanted a piece of his business. If they weren't cut in, his cafés would be in trouble. Big Jim, unimpressed by their threats, killed two of the three on the spot. He knew that he hadn't seen the last of the Black Hand, so he hired his own protectors. He couldn't hire bodyguards in Chicago, because most local Italians were reluctant to take on the mob. Instead, Big Jim looked to New York, importing hit man Johnny Torrio as head of his bodyguard detail. Big Jim paid the muscle very well—he even gave Johnny Torrio a piece of one of his smaller café,s the Four Deuces, at 2222 South Wabash, in the heart of the Levee. Round One of the crime war went to Big Jim Colosimo.[3]

Nobody, it seemed, could tame Chicago's crime, but Mayor Harrison felt he had to try. On October 24, 1911, Harrison, pressured by reformers and the women's temperance groups—and possibly firmly believing his prediction that women would soon have the vote—ordered the Everleigh Sisters' House on the Levee closed. For Harrison, who never seemed to survive his own reformist moves, that was again the beginning of the end. Kenna and Coughlin joined with freewheeling political bosses Hopkins and Sullivan to bring him down.

Corruption in the Levee was not the city's only excitement. William Randolph Hearst's *American* had started a circulation war with Medill McCormick's *Tribune*. Hearst had Max and Moe Annenberg running his circulation department; their idea of competition was to rough up the boys who worked the *Tribune* newsstands. When Medill

McCormick (grandson of Joseph Medill) hired the enterprising Annenbergs away from the *American*, Hearst countered by buying the services of vicious street gang members. One of them, Frank McErlane, would go on to fame as the first of Capone's henchmen to use a submachine gun. This armed newspaper circulation war revolved around those least able to protect themselves—the newsboys. Both of my parents, seven and nine at the time, closely followed the harrowing experiences of children their own age, especially newsboy Charles Gallantry.

Young Gallantry, tending his newsstand at Chicago and Robey streets, defied the *Tribune*'s circulation brute Bob Holbrook by refusing to take an additional thirty copies of the *Trib*. He told Holbrook he couldn't sell them. Holbrook repeatedly knocked Gallantry to the ground, but to the amazement of a crowd of onlookers the boy got up defiantly time after time. When some bystanders reached out to help the beaten boy, Holbrook's assistants fought them off until Gallantry could no longer get back on his feet. He had lost consciousness.

His ordeal was not unusual. Newsboys would be beaten, even killed, if they didn't meet their ever-rising quotas. The police offered little protection, since the police superintendent, John McWeeney, was very much in league with Hearst, while the state's attorney, Charles Wayman, was in the *Tribune*'s back pocket. Nor would either paper report newsboy deaths, even including a murder on the very premises of the *Tribune*.[4] The *Daily News* never entered the fray, concentrating instead on hiring prominent writers like Ben Hecht and Carl Sandburg and publishing hard news. This horrifying war continued for years, taking its toll on the children of the poor.

Chicagoans' favorite sport, next to baseball, is a mayoral election, and another election was just around the corner. Like most Americans, they took little notice yet of news reports that on June 28, 1914, Archduke Ferdinand of Austria was assassinated by a Serbian nationalist, an act that would trigger World War I. This was the first election in Chicago in which women could vote. As a girl, my mother was particularly pleased that Illinois had granted this privilege, not only because it validated equal rights, but more selfishly because her mother and her Aunt Laura had spent so much time marching in support of the law. She always made me laugh when she said, "The minute I saw Mother put on her best bonnet and look very proper, I knew she was going to march."

The Republicans were running Bill Thompson, a man of boundless energy and a keen sense of how to build constituencies. It had not been an easy campaign for any of the candidates. The Democratic primary, which ended the career of Carter Harrison, Jr., had been so divisive that it was hard for Democratic Party boss Sullivan to pull the Democratic factions together behind the party's endorsed candidate, Robert M. Sweitzer.

As Douglas Bukowski explains in *Big Bill Thompson*, Sweitzer proved to be a poor choice of candidate, even though Sullivan's power had increased through the years. Sweitzer was tapped because of his German heritage; only five cities in the world had larger German populations than Chicago. During the primary, the Harrison faction had played on ethnic and religious prejudice. One Harrison ally accused Sweitzer of being anti-Semitic, specifically of referring to City Hall as a "synagogue" because of the many Jewish employees. Others accused Sweitzer of joining the Ancient Order of Hibernians instead of German associations. Sweitzer countered this last attack by writing a strong pro-German letter, entitled "The Fatherland," to the German community. It included a promise: "You, your relatives and friends can be of great assistance to Germany and Austria next Tuesday by electing Robert M. Sweitzer."

This missive was seized upon by Bill Thompson in the general election and mailed to the Polish community, the second-largest in the world outside Poland. The Poles, envisioning their relatives in Poland being slaughtered by Germans, flocked to vote against Sweitzer—and for Republican Thompson.

Ordinarily, Thompson would get much of the usually Republican German vote, but taking no chances, he attacked the King of England—a figure seemingly remote from Chicago politics. This sally could also help with the Irish vote. Thus he pirouetted on the ethnic tightrope throughout the campaign. Thompson even courted the black vote, for his base was the predominantly black 2nd Ward. For years, he had been a friend of the Reverend Archibald Carey, a powerful black leader. Thompson received the endorsement of the largest black newspaper, the *Defender*. That was fine with the Democrats. In those days they wanted nothing to do with blacks. (Difficult as it may be to recall, the Republican Party was "the party of Lincoln" to blacks and whites alike at least until the middle of the twentieth century.)

Even so, Sullivan's Democratic machine worked hard, registering people to vote, probably making commitments of all kind of payroll jobs in City Hall, and delivering political favors as fast as possible, perhaps motivated by the fact that with Harrison gone and Sweitzer a winner, the pols would finally be able to unload their secretly owned utility stock in their dummy company, Commonwealth Electric Company. They had been holding this secretly owned stock throughout Harrison's terms—in hopes of unloading it to competing utility companies, since Harrison would have vetoed the granting of any long-term franchise to their company. They were hungry to make the kind of killing they'd made with Ogden Gas ten years before.

Despite these fervent machinations, Thompson put together a winning coalition and in 1915 became the thirty-third mayor,[5] in time to welcome Catholic Chicago's new archbishop, George Mundelein, who would be coming from Brooklyn. The Catholic archbishop of any city in the early 1900s was a very important figure. Each parish church was still the center of daily life, social events, and fund-raisers, the essential backbone of the neighborhood. Catholic Chicagoans, proud to be the largest archdiocese in the United States, eagerly awaited the arrival of their new archbishop. Wisely, he would continue the local practice of building parochial schools before elaborate churches, but he made one all-important policy change, decreeing that there would henceforth be only one parish per district,[6] serving all ethnic groups within that district. No longer would Irish, Poles, and Italians worship at separate churches in the same district. The church ruled with an iron hand, and Catholics all over Chicago fell obediently into line. This new archbishop, it seemed, believed in the universality of the Catholic religion.

Mundelein had in fact come to a terribly divided city. Even the unity of the nation was being challenged, a nation composed still of ethnic groups watching their relatives savaged by war in Europe. Pro-peace groups sprang up all over the country. Jane Addams led peace rallies. Mayor Thompson, over the strong objection of Governor Frank Lowden, permitted the Peoples Council of America for Democracy and Terms of Peace, a huge antiwar group, to hold a rally in Chicago. Socialists Victor Berger and Crystal Eastman, barred from all other Midwestern cities, were allowed to speak.

While such rallies made Chicago appear to be the center of pacifism, that was far from the truth. The Poles, the Bohemians, and the Jews in the city were virulent in their antipathy toward the Germans. Eastern European immigrants agitated to rid Chicago of much of its Germanic flavor. The school board was pressured to change the name of the Bismarck Public Grammar School; it became Funston School.

German could no longer be taught in the public schools. Patriotic organizations sprang up, one of which, the American Protective League, collected the names of German aliens, ran background checks on their activities, and reported anything "suspicious" to the federal government. Under attack, the Germans organized. At rallies some shouted their renunciation of their citizenship and their decision to return to Germany to fight for their native land. Charles Wacker, a prominent German, brought some sense to the dialogue when he addressed a large German congregation and reminded them they were Americans first.

Death came closer to hand than war bulletins when on July 24, 1915, the *Eastland*, a summer excursion boat anchored at Clark and South Water streets, took on a full load of passengers and began to list. As the engines started, the boat capsized. Passersby quickly jumped into the water to try to save lives. Police, firemen, doctors, and nurses rushed to the pier. Over 1,500 people were saved, but 812 drowned. Whole families perished. It was the worst such accident in American history. Both of my parents, ten and twelve at the time, were deeply moved by the newspaper photos.

Most of their memories were much happier, however. As a child, I loved to listen to my mother's vivid stories about growing up in Chicago. Her first ten years were spent in an apartment at 2110 North Clifton Street in Lincoln Park, only a block from her Aunt Laura's home at 2200 North Seminary Street. That one block was very important in my mother's childhood. She hadn't known her grandfather John R. Crane at all, because he died the year she was born. Nor did she remember Sarah Crane, the youngest of her mother's family, who had died of a ruptured appendix a year later at the age of twenty-four. "Medicine in those days was in its infancy as compared to now," Mother would explain, shaking her head. "Such a shame, but that's how it was."

From her descriptions, life seemed quite simple back then, but of course it really wasn't. It was, however, well organized. Monday was laundry day—white wash flapping on the clothesline. Tuesday was baking day. Thursday was club day—not bridge, but a game called euchre, played by Laura, Margaret Jane, and two neighbors. My mother dreaded her mother's turn to have the ladies over, because, of course, the house would have to shine. She and her brother Frank were drafted into service. Lace curtains had to hang perfectly straight to the floor. My grandmother would pin them at the base to keep

Grandmother Margaret Jane Crane Nolan, for whom I am named, circa 1903 at home in Lincoln Park. She is holding my uncle Frank.

them just so. The Tiffany lamp on the mahogany table in the bay had to glow. Frank had the task of rolling up the oriental rug and dragging it out of the parlor into the yard to beat it free of all dust and lint. Mother had to water the huge fern atop its pedestal in the corner of the bay.

She also had to plump up the down cushions on the couch, polish the good silver, and shine the best china. It was no hardship, however, to sample Grandmother's finger sandwiches or the chicken salad that would be served on homemade bread. The dessert would be special, too, and if Grandmother baked a cake, well, it had to rise higher than the cake served at the previous club meeting. After all of the preparations, my mother, Frank, and their younger siblings, John and Mary, were not to enter the parlor until the women were leaving, and then only to say goodbye.

Lincoln Park itself was, according to my mother, a social center second only to St. Vincent's Church and school. On Sunday family outings there were boat rides in the Lincoln Park lagoons, baseball, races among the various age groups, and tennis. For my mother, ice skating in the winter in the park with Frank and their cousin, Bill

My mother, Katharine
Nolan Burke, as a child.

Hogan, was torturous fun, because she always stayed until her toes
turned numb. When she could stand it no longer, she'd quickly rush
home to heat them on the stove. When I asked in amazement, "Why
the stove?" she'd reply, "Where else? It and the fireplace were the
only sources of heat in the house at that time. Why, I used to put my
petticoat on a chair near the stove so that when I got up for school it
would be toasty warm. Frank and I loved to read, and my mother
arranged a spot in the kitchen near the stove for our chairs so we
would be warm in winter."

The prime center of Catholic life in Lincoln Park, St. Vincent's
Church, was the pride of the Crane family. They had participated in
its building. It opened its doors in 1897—three years after the Cranes,
Laura, John, and all the rest, moved into the area. With pride, they
told how in the following year enough money was raised to open St.
Vincent's College next door to the church. It incorporated as De Paul
University in 1907. My mother's fairly solid sports background came
from attending the school's football games in the fall and baseball

games in spring and summer. Together, church and college provided a real sense of community.

A Lincoln Park Christmas was different then. The solemn moment was not celebrated at midnight Mass as it is today, but at 5:00-A.M. Mass, the climax to a lovely Christmas Eve that began with the lighting of the Christmas tree at Mother's house. From outside, it glowed through the filmy lace curtains of the bay windows. The candles would not be lit until Christmas Eve, so wary was everyone of fire. My grandmother placed a covered bucket of water nearby just before she lit the candles, which would twinkle merrily throughout a sumptuous dinner featuring oyster stew. Following the dinner, there would be stories of the past, an exchange of gifts, and then the careful dousing of all the candles. After a rest, the whole family walked to 5:00-A.M. Mass at St. Vincent's, Nolans and Hogans and all the neighbors shouting Merry Christmas to each other into the predawn light.

When the United States entered the World War in 1917, my mother suffered doubly, for her mother, Margaret Jane, my namesake, died that year of pneumonia. Mother was only twelve years old, and her life completely changed after that. In those days, as a sign of independence, women often took out their own insurance policies, and my grandmother's policy—held by the Ladies Catholic Benevolent Association—named my mother and her sister, Mary, as beneficiaries. The inheritance enabled my mother and Mary to attend St. Mary's Convent School in Nauvou, Illinois, with enough left over for college.

Once war on Germany was declared, Chicagoans enlisted in droves, filling 10 percent of the quota for Illinois. Among volunteers to the cavalry was Marshall Field III, who came home from England to serve his country. The almost completed Navy Pier, opened a year earlier, quickly became a training center for troops. As fast as the farmers harvested wheat, Chicago processed it and shipped it out to feed America's military. And like most cities, Chicago participated in Liberty Bond drives to raise money for the war effort. Smaller manufacturing companies retooled and began producing war supplies, while the major steel companies produced and shipped sheet steel for guns, ambulances, cars, jeeps, and trucks. A volunteer Training Corps took the place of the National Guard.

On November 11, 1918, Armistice Day, Chicago went wild. Troops waiting to be shipped overseas instead paraded down the streets of the city and were joined by thousands of residents celebrating peace. Church bells pealed, sirens wailed along the river, residents sang, danced, hugged, and kissed all along State Street, Michigan Avenue, and Wabash and Clark streets. Peace brought great hopes for the future. In February 1919, Chicago staged a tumultuous welcoming celebration for the first Illinois regiment to come home—a black unit, the 8th Illinois. Half a million people jammed Michigan Avenue to salute them. Later in the evening, there was a homecoming ceremony at the packed Coliseum. Mayor Thompson was cheered by most of the biracial crowd, though not by the residents of Bridgeport or the Back of the Yards area, who viewed him as far too tolerant of blacks. Still, Thompson's base, the 2nd Ward, carried him once again to victory that very month and elected also the first black alderman in the city's history, Oscar de Priest.

Bridgeport and the Back of the Yards neighborhoods had not forgotten the stockyards strike. Indeed, race relations in Bridgeport were now sporadically violent against the black community. The source of trouble was Ragen's Colts, a Bridgeport gang that for five years systematically raided the black belt, throwing firebombs, breaking windows, taunting and intimidating blacks. They warned blacks to stay out of Bridgeport and promised that any black who dared venture down Bridgeport streets would be beaten or shot. The *Chicago Defender* repeatedly called for an investigation, accusing the Democrats in control of the area of protecting the Colts and fostering their rampages.

Still, most Chicagoans now realized that the war had changed their city and its racial composition forever. The large emigration of blacks attracted by war-related jobs helped cause a serious housing shortage. Housing was particularly scarce on the south side of the city, the locale of most jobs. The steel mills, the port in south Chicago, the stockyards, the freight and railway depots, and heavy manufacturing plants were there. War-related industries had bunched on the north side along the north branch of the river, so many blacks had settled there as well—in Little Hell, formerly home to poor Italians. The west side, which always had a black population, also expanded. But newcomers largely gravitated to the black belt on the south side, and that area began to spread even farther south to Hyde Park and Kenwood. Neighborhood organizations like the Hyde Park Kenwood Association, originally founded to support such projects as neighborhood beautification and civic improvement, transformed overnight into hotbeds of hatred, determined to prevent any further encroachment by blacks. Those who dared moved in were sometimes bombed out. But go south they did, aided by unscrupulous realtors who did not hesitate to start rumors of blacks moving into white south side communities, rumors that caused waves of panic selling.

Since the boom days of Prairie Avenue, the housing due south of the Loop (the elevated railway tracks looping the downtown commercial district) had turned over twice. The early mansions had first been converted into flats for Irish and German families until they moved out in the 1880s and 1890s; then blacks moved in—and stayed. When the older, established Jewish community on the west side fled the radicalism of the Eastern European Jews, Russians, and Bohemians, they went west to Lawndale, or left the west side entirely for Hyde Park or a new community in the far north side lakefront called Rogers Park. The northwest and southwest sides continued to be dominated by Poles, Italians, and eastern Europeans. The north side Irish, Germans, and Scandinavians flowed up the lakefront, toward Evanston and outlying lakeshore communities. Modern Chicago was taking shape.

With the end of the war came a slowdown in the economy. The returning servicemen wanted their old jobs back, and through the "last hired, first fired" rule of the marketplace, unemployment became a matter of grave concern for newcomers. My father, almost sixteen, had a part-time job after school as a delivery boy for Blums, an exclusive women's store on Michigan Avenue. He worried about losing his job, but, luckily for him, the store kept him on. Most blacks were not so fortunate.

Chicago quickly became a divided and nervous city, ready to explode. The summer of 1919 was typically hot and humid. On a Sunday in mid-July, Chicagoans were sunbathing on beaches along the lakefront. On the south side, black Chicagoans frequented the beach that the white south side community allowed them to use, a beach bounded by 26th Street on the north and 29th Street on the south. About midafternoon, five black young men were floating on a raft that inadvertently passed over the dividing line. When they approached 29th Street, the crowds of white sunbathers spotted them and began to shout and hurl stones. The five victims tried to paddle back, but it was too late. A rock struck one child in the head. His four friends could only watch helplessly as he drowned.

Years of hatred erupted in uncontrolled rage on both sides. Both sides picked up rocks or deadlier weapons and attacked. News of the fighting quickly spread throughout the south side, and more people armed themselves in what would become a race riot lasting five days. Blacks and whites in smaller communities on the west and north side in the Little Hell area also joined the fray. The police were not equipped to handle so large a riot, and Mayor Thompson, caught in the middle, was ineffective.

Gangs of whites, led by Ragen's Colts and the Hamburgs, also from the Bridgeport area, raided the black belt, burning and shooting. When the violence spilled over into the downtown area, the manager at Blums made sure my father skirted Little Hell on the way home and stayed there until the riot ended. Only a combination of the state militia's intervention and torrential rain finally put an end to the rioting. Mob action was responsible for the deaths of sixteen blacks and fifteen whites, with five hundred seriously injured.[7] The police admitted to shooting seven blacks to death.

The 1919 race riot shocked most Chicagoans, especially those who lived out on the northwest side and far north and were not exposed to the crippling conditions of poverty and fear that fueled the hatred. Once I was in politics, south siders and southwest siders would often say to me, "Yeah, you north siders drive us crazy. You just don't know what it's like to see them take over your neighborhood and to have to keep moving."

The race riot was not on the minds of Colosimo and Torrio. Torrio saw a golden opportunity on the horizon—Prohibition. He advised Colosimo to make plans to bootleg. When Prohibition went into effect on January 16, 1920, most Chicagoans, who always opposed any form of liquor regulation, were angry, but the law was soon being enforced. Big Jim Colosimo had made so much money in all the other rackets that he didn't want to bother with bootlegging. Torrio felt otherwise. On May 11, Johnny made an appointment to see Big Jim in his office at Colosimo's café, but didn't show. When the boss walked out to the foyer, shots rang out and he crumpled to the floor dead, set up by his trusted bodyguard, who had imported an outsider for the hit. As the chefs at the nightclub ran out of the kitchen, they glimpsed the fleeing killer. Several of them told the police about an identifying mark, a long scar.[8]

CHAPTER 7

The Roaring Twenties

in't She Sweet," "The Sheik of Araby," and "Yes, We Have No Bananas" were the nation's songs at the start of the Roaring Twenties, when, my mother told us she bobbed her hair, wore her skirts above her knees, and danced the Charleston. Women were becoming quite liberated. The Nineteenth Amendment had finally given women the right to vote.

The one song Chicagoans didn't want to hear in 1920 was "Take Me Out to the Ball Game." The town was reeling—not from bathtub gin or the murder of Big Jim Colosimo, but from the shocking newspaper headlines of the previous year. A two-bit gambler named Billy Maharg bragged to the *Philadelphia North American* that he had "fixed" the 1919 World Series by paying off eight White Sox players to throw the series to the Cincinnati Reds. The newspaper bannered the "Black Sox" story, spurring an investigation encouraged by Sox owner Charles Comiskey. On September 29, when a grand jury was impaneled, Chicagoans realized there must be some truth to the rumors.[1] Twenty years later, both my grandfathers were still unspeakably sad about that revelation. At sixteen, my father just felt taken, but my grandfathers actually felt personally betrayed. They and the Sox had grown up together.

Other sports took up the slack for a time. Alonzo Stagg, one of the greatest football coaches in America, was at the University of Chicago. Fans made the trip to the Midway at the university to watch him coach the Maroons college games. The Northwestern Wildcats were also a fairly good football team. And Chicagoans considered Notre Dame's team theirs too, treating South Bend, Indiana, like a suburb. For Catholic Chicago, "the Fighting Irish" team, coached by the great Knute Rockne, may as well have been the next-door neighbor. My parents used to tell me about the intense football rivalry in those days between Catholic Notre Dame and Methodist Northwestern. Religious slurs were often expressed openly on the football field as well as off, provoking fights among spectators in the stands.

Pro football was just developing in our bailiwick. George Halas of the Decatur Staleys and Ralph Hay of the Canton Bull Dogs met to form the first organization of professional football teams—just twelve days before the Black Sox grand jury was selected. Their league, the American Professional Football League, was a forerunner of today's National Football League. George Halas was one of our own, born in Chicago to Bohemian immigrants. In 1920, he was out there in Wrigley Field struggling to survive with his new team, the Chicago Bears.

But the daily media coverage of the Black Sox scandal upstaged the other local teams. Grandfather Burke would grow teary-eyed as he described Joe Jackson's departure from the courthouse after testifying before the grand jury. He somberly quoted the young newspaper vendor who grabbed at Jackson's leg and shouted, "Say it ain't so, Joe, say it ain't so." Jackson had to reply, "I'm afraid it is, kid, I'm afraid it is."

The end of the postwar depression helped buoy the city's spirits. Mayor Thompson, big in stature, overwhelming in the scope of his public works proposals, and raucous in his rhetoric, soon earned the lasting title Big Bill the Builder. Had there been TV in those days, his commanding personality would have dominated the screen, no matter who else was present. In his second term, Big Bill Thompson certainly heeded the advice Burnham offered with the Chicago Plan— "Make no little plans!" He completed Navy Pier, a three-thousand-foot glass, steel, and concrete structure extending from Grand Avenue out into the water. The recreational side of the pier lay at its most eastern point and included a 3,500-seat Concert Hall housed in what was called the Terminal Building. The Shelter Building on the pier included an open pavilion, concession stands, two decks, and a roof garden. A streetcar ran from Grand Avenue and circled the entire pier. Passengers could stop along the route to admire the freighters anchored at the docks or proceed to the entertainment areas. Chicagoans proudly boasted, "Why, we are five hundred feet longer than the piers of Atlantic City." (Navy Pier was the longest pier in the world, until surpassed in 1929 by Southend Pier in Essex, England.) The pier was an overnight sensation. In the summer, children swarmed over the playground and visited the Ferris wheel and merry-go-rounds as they listened to the music coming from the auditorium. Excursion boat rides to Lincoln Park or Jackson Park cost 35 cents a round trip. Right after the war, Thompson held a Pageant of Progress, a kind of minor World's Fair, and drew a million visitors in two weeks. He also recruited six hundred exhibitors. Choral groups sang on barges anchored off the east end of the pier. There were swimming meets and motorboat races and parachute jumps. Each evening of the pageant ended with fireworks.

One pathetic sight during the festival was poor Ma Streeter, who tied up her houseboat on the east end of Navy Pier and sold hot dogs. The captain's third wife, she was alone now, for Captain Streeter had died of pneumonia about eight months before. Chicagoans love a fighter, a challenger, an underdog, and Streeter had a dandy forty-eight-car funeral procession led by Big Bill Thompson and Harrison B. Riley, president of the Chicago Guarantee and Trust Company. At the funeral service Riley said: "The captain's ideas about law were somewhat at variance with that of the preponderant legal opinion, but he was a gallant and able antagonist nevertheless. We shall miss him more than might be imagined. He kept two lawyers and one vice president busy for twenty-one years."

Harrison Riley spoke that day as if the battle were over, but Ma Streeter continued her late husband's fight for title to his island. She sold enough hot dogs to pay legal expenses right up until 1925, when the federal courts ruled that since Streeter had never gotten a proper divorce from his first wife, Ma was not his lawful heir and, in fact, had no legal claim at all. That ruling she fought in the higher courts until 1935, when she died penniless. Distant relatives filed suit after that and also lost all claims in court.[2] That area of wealth and prestige is now called Streeterville.

With his own brand of showboating enthusiasms, Mayor Thompson worked with Charles Wacker to build the Michigan Avenue bridge, a magnificent bascule two-tiered bridge that in 1920 would connect Michigan Avenue south of the river with the widened North Michigan Avenue. This bridge over the Chicago River was as close as one could get to the spot once called Fort Dearborn on the south side of the river and DuSable's first home just across it. Because of the bridge, Michigan Avenue became a fashionable location. The Drake Hotel anchored it to the north at the Oak Street Beach, and the city's most prestigious hotel, the Blackstone, anchored it to the south. Between them in the twenties—and standing today—would rise the Stone Container Building and the 333 North Michigan Avenue building, across the street from each other at Wacker Drive and Michigan; to the north, the beautiful Wrigley Building, the Medinah Athletic Club, now the Sheraton-Chicago, the Tribune Tower, the Palmolive Building, the Allerton, Nieman-Marcus, Saks Fifth Avenue, Water Tower Place, and the Westin Hotel. Across from the Drake today stands the One Magnificent Mile building, the Bloomingdales building, and the Fourth Presbyterian Church. To the south of the river along Michigan Avenue, the boulevard fronted the Central Library, the massive Grant Park, the Art Institute, Orchestra Hall, the Auditorium, the Field Museum of Natural History, Shedd Aquarium, Adler Planetarium, and finally Soldier Field.

In that decade of the Roaring Twenties, Thompson kept right on building. In keeping with Burnham's plan, his new project was the construction of Wacker Drive, which meant the end of old South Water Market Street, the produce center right off the south bank of the main stem of the Chicago River at Michigan Avenue. This project was greeted ambivalently, because South Water Market Street served as a sentimental reminder of early Chicago. But Burnham was right; the two-tiered boulevard would relieve truck congestion in the downtown area, confining it to the lower boulevard, and provide at the same time a beautiful upper boulevard along the river to Wolf Point, where it would turn south along its south branch. Beneath the entire downtown area, a tunnel system beginning at Wacker Drive and Michigan Avenue provided an underground street system for trucks, cars, and storage.

My mother came home from the sheltered convent boarding school in 1923—to Jazz Age Chicago. Happy to be home and delighted by all the changes, like everyone else, she was mesmerized by silent films and the radio. Jazz was a huge fad, and young middle-class whites—one in twelve Chicagoans now owned a car—traveled to the south side to catch the popular musicians. Because union rules forbade black musicians from performing north of 22nd Street, Benny Goodman, Gene Krupa, and Hoagy Carmichael went to south Chicago to play with black jazz greats to sell-out crowds. At least in

music, there was some integration. The two most popular jazz cabarets were the Sunset Café at 35th and Calumet and the Lincoln Gardens, where the beat of "Tiger Rag" kept feet tapping.

During the era of silent films, Chicago was a moviemaking capital.
One-fifth of the silent films produced in America were produced at the
Essanay Studios, an outfit that expanded from a one-room studio at
501 North Wells Street to its final location at Western and Irving Park
roads. It became the largest film studio in the country. Wallace Berry,
Charlie Chaplin, and Gloria Swanson worked there. But Essanay management made a big mistake—they turned down Mary Pickford.

After silent movies came the next craze, radio, and Chicago was
ready to cash in, thanks to the electrical genius of Samuel Insull. This
Englishman had come to Chicago about the time of the World's Fair in
1893 to take over the Chicago Edison Company after having worked
as Thomas A. Edison's personal secretary in New York for twelve
years. Titles meant very little in those days. Insull had simply performed any task the famous inventor required and gained a wide range
of experience. Soon he pioneered large-scale steam turbine generators
capable of producing such great quantities of electrical energy they
could supply electricity to all of the residential areas of Chicago as
well as to the hungry skyscrapers downtown. A smart promoter and a
shrewd salesman, Insull sold electricity for electrical lighting and
other power uses over a six-thousand-square-mile territory by the end
of World War I.

In 1898, Insull changed the company name to Commonwealth
Edison, but not for promotional or public relations reasons. Committeeman Sullivan was at it again. Just as he and his tight little band in
the city council had floated the Ogden Gas Company, so they now
had a phony electric company—Commonwealth Electric—and, courtesy of the city council, a fifty-year franchise. Insull was expected to
come crawling to buy the franchise, but he did no such thing. Sullivan
and his crowd might have a piece of paper, but Insull had exclusive
contractual agreements to buy any and all electrical equipment with
every manufacturer in the country. The Sullivan clique could purchase nothing having to do with the generation and delivery of electricity. Even so, Insull needed the fifty-year monopoly, so he bought
out Commonwealth for $50,000, a far cry from the $7 million paid for
Ogden Gas, and changed his company name.

With the city's increasing prosperity, electric lights were everywhere along the commercial strips and the downtown area; gaslight

became a relic in the mid-twenties. Because of electric power, rapid transit was now rapid indeed. Commonwealth Edison stores blossomed all over the place, pushing vacuum cleaners, toasters, and washing machines.[3]

In 1922, Big Bill Thompson chose to sit out the election, fearing he would lose. Scandals had rocked both of his terms. In the first term, Police Chief Charles Healy had been indicted for conducting a gambling business on a private phone installed in his City Hall office. Clarence Darrow got him off, but public suspicion lingered. In the second term, right before Thompson would have otherwise declared his candidacy, his most trusted political adviser and friend was indicted for conspiracy to defraud the schools. He, too, would win acquittal, thanks to Darrow's legal genius, but not before the election. These scandals and the voters' assumption that Johnny Torrio's blatant crimes could not flourish without the mayor's acquiescence scarred Thompson. He did not run, but, being Thompson, he didn't stray far.

The jubilant Democratic Party bosses knew victory was theirs if they only chose the right candidate. Roger Sullivan had died and left the reins of the party organization to his protégé George Brennan. Out of the mayor's office for eight years, Democrats were hungry for power. Their candidate, William Dever, a superior court judge, had impeccable credentials. Something of a reformer and very progressive, he had been picked by Brennan to contrast with Thompson's taint of corruption.

The major campaign issue was Prohibition. My mother, like many Chicagoans, was appalled that organized crime thrived on Prohibition. She felt the spread of crime far outweighed any value enforced temperance might have. At any rate, Dever very quickly glossed over Prohibition with the brief statement "I am opposed to Prohibition, but I will stop the crime and corruption, lawlessness and vice."[4] (Dever was first and foremost a jurist. He opposed Prohibition, but he believed in the rule of Law. If a law was wrong, it should be amended; as long as it was on the books, he would uphold it.) He then cleverly changed gears by raising an old issue—municipal ownership of the transit systems. Because of the strength of the ethnic wards belonging to the Democratic organization, Dever won.

Few had listened closely enough during his campaign. The mayor's new police chief, Morgan Collins, immediately cracked down on the cabarets, the black-and-tans, the speakeasies. He even marched into homes if he suspected anyone of making bathtub gin or green beer. This was unsettling to many. When the city's top cop arrested the mother of two small children after finding liquor in her house, that really raised eyebrows. One Democratic leader spoke out against the raids, but Dever pressed on. The *Tribune* editorialized, "When a law does not have the support of the conscience of a people, but when it is regarded by them as tyrannical and unjust, it cannot be enforced."[5] Dever continued to enforce the law with vigor.

Police Chief Collins had even turned down—with fanfare—a $100,000 bribe. Johnny Torrio's power was slipping as the raids undermined his rackets. He moved his operation into Cicero, but the gangs under him began to wonder why they needed him at all and struck out on their own. They soon challenged each other, bombing and killing in turf wars. When even Torrio had his life threatened, he fled to New York in 1925. Where was his number-one scarfaced henchman, hit man, and enforcer—Al Capone?

Doing well. Torrio had given Capone the Four Deuces Saloon at 2222 South Wabash and a quarter of the profits, allegedly $13 million from beer receipts, gambling, and prostitution. Chicagoans were traumatized by the constant gang murders, fearful that they were no longer safe in their own homes. Actually, crime was not getting worse—it was destroying itself. As Scarface moved to take over the streets, Big Bill Thompson moved, too. Knowing Dever could not be reelected after this chaos, he prepared to run again and shrewdly cut a secret deal with Capone—campaign contributions in exchange for protection.

By 1926, Capone was consolidating his complete control of organized crime and Cardinal Mundelein was planning for the upcoming Eucharistic Congress, the first worldwide Catholic celebration of the Eucharist ever held in the United States. Well over 880,000 Catholics lived in Chicago, recognized by Rome as the largest archdiocese in the nation, and Pope Pius XI had high regard for the leadership ability of Mundelein, the church's youngest archbishop. Invitations had been extended to every bishop and archbishop in the world. The archdiocese booked Navy Pier, Soldier Field, and the Coliseum for meetings and seminars. Mundelein asked for the assistance of the police and national guard for traffic control. He left nothing to chance. Once hotels were booked, churches and homes were organized to house the pilgrims and visitors. Hundreds of visiting priests were assigned to parishes so they could say daily Mass. These assignments followed ethnic lines—priests from Italy were assigned to churches of predominantly Italian congregations, etc.

On June 18, 1926, Chicago and the church were ready to receive the hundreds of thousands of guests. Pope Pius XI sent John Cardinal Bonzano as his representative. Today we take it for granted that the Pope travels the world. But sixty years ago the Pope didn't leave Rome. Instead, he sent an apostolic representative to major ecclesiastical gatherings, Bonzano leading a delegation of twelve cardinals, three hundred bishops, and fifty-seven archbishops to to New York aboard the S.S. *Aquitania.* There the delegation was greeted by Mayor Jimmy Walker and 300,000 New Yorkers, who cheered the religious party all the way from the dock to St. Patrick's Cathedral. The delegation left New York for Chicago on a special Pullman Company train refurbished and painted a shiny cardinal red. All night long, radios carried news of the "red special" as it made its way toward Chicago, waved along by cheering crowds. It pulled into Chicago at 9:45 A.M. on June 18. The motorcade to Holy Name Cathedral was greeted by church bells, whistles, car horns, and hundreds of thousands of excited Chicagoans.

In an unusual move, Cardinal Mundelein invited the leaders of all faiths to participate in this historic event, with an official welcome at the Coliseum. The cardinal had promised the Pope that one million people would receive communion on opening day, and they did.

The Congress opened with the formal Mass at Holy Name Cathedral. Each country represented wore its native dress, as brilliant colors of the robes gleamed in the sunlight that streamed through the cathedral windows. At the sight of the participants in their native dress, the crowds for blocks around the cathedral realized what the cardinal meant by religious unity. At Soldier Field, an altar had been constructed on a forty-foot-high stage, so that the ceremony could be seen by all. On a day dedicated to children, 62,000 of them, after practicing for months in their parish schools, sang in unison the "Mass of the Angels." There was a Women's Day and a Men's Day. At a memorable men's evening Mass, just as the benediction began under a full moon, 230,000 men were asked to light and hold up their candles and salute the purpose of the Congress, the Eucharist. The candles were lit, the chorus of male voices singing "Tantum Ergo" filled the lakefront sky, the trumpets saluted, and Chicago's part in the Congress was ended. John Clayton, a *Tribune* reporter, exclaimed with tears in his eyes, "That was the God damnedest, most beautiful thing I have ever seen."[6]

Grandpa Burke was there, along with my father and both his brothers; my uncle Ed was now a seminarian. My grandfather never forgot that experience. For him, as for many other immigrants, the church had sustained his faith through hard times in Chicago. Now, at Soldier Field, my grandfather was given a special seat because of his sons' decision to serve the church.

Unexpectedly, the formal closing of the Congress was a disaster. Cardinal Mundelein wanted to give the religious and the pilgrims a taste of American suburbia by going to the major archdiocesan seminary in Mundelein, a Chicago suburb in a picture-perfect pastoral setting. More than 300,000 accepted the cardinal's invitation, at least 270,000 arriving by special suburban trains. Over 35,000 cars jammed the grounds around the seminary. Moreover, the sky darkened as the procession of religious made their way to the portico of the simple Georgian chapel for outdoor Mass. Suddenly, the heavens opened. The small lakes on the seminary grounds overflowed and the rain soaked everyone attending Mass. There was absolutely no place for the huge throng to take shelter.

Mayor Dever attended all the sessions, but the magic didn't rub off. He had enforced an unpopular law. Never mind that he also completed the Wacker Drive project, straightened the south branch of the Chicago River (thus consolidating the railroad terminal), and built Chicago's first air terminal, Midway Airport. Even Clarence Darrow, at a banquet for Anton Cermak, a powerful ethnic Democratic leader and former Dever supporter, lifted his glass for a revealing toast: "I can't get a drink without going to bootleggers, and I frequently want a drink. I like Tony Cermak 'cause he's wet and 'cause he doesn't make excuses." Inevitably, Thompson defeated Dever.

When I was mayor, the magic of a similar landmark religious event failed to rub off on me, too. As I hosted the visit of His Holiness Pope John Paul II, the Byrne-Daley feud got underway in earnest. Before the Holy Father arrived, the American Civil Liberties Union filed suit to ensure that no taxpayer money would be spent on his visit, thus preserving to the letter the separation of church and state. They won in federal court. Almost simultaneously, Chicago's John Cardinal Cody called me to say that the Pope did not want to be greeted by an official delegation. Viewing himself "the people's Pope," he preferred to meet only with those who genuinely wanted to meet him on their own. I joked, "Well, Your Eminence, between the Church and the ACLU, there really isn't much for me to do." He didn't miss a beat. "There are two things," he replied. "The streets and curbs around the Palmer House, where the papal party will stay, need a little repair. And, come to think of it, the curbs around my house on State Parkway could use a little fixing up, as that is where the Pope will stay."

About a week before the visit, Cardinal Cody called again. "Jane, we'd like you and the city council to be on hand at O'Hare Airport when the Pope arrives." I asked him if he liked his new curbs. He laughed and diplomatically noted, "The whole city looks great."

The day of the Pope's arrival, I could feel the excitement in the air on my way to work. But when I reached City Hall, there were a lot of hangdog expressions in the secretarial pool. My chief of staff arrived to explain that they were being deluged with nasty phone calls protesting my abusive treatment of Mrs. Daley, the late mayor's wife. Daley's daughter, Pat Daley Thompson, had even called one of the City Hall old-timers, who started out in Mayor Martin Kennelly's administration, to ask her how she could work for a person as vicious and petty as Jane Byrne. I was flabbergasted. Then my sister called, telling me that a call-in radio show was jammed with calls accusing me of snubbing the late mayor's widow. Quickly, I turned on the radio. I couldn't at first believe my ears, but I had been around City Hall long enough to recognize an organized campaign. I picked up the phone, called Cardinal Cody, and explained my predicament. Could he issue a press release explaining that no one outside the chancery office had issued invitations and that City Hall had not compiled any guest list? He agreed, then added, "Jane, I wouldn't worry about this. You should know that not only was Mrs. Daley invited, but also I sent a member of the chancery staff to her home with a complete schedule of events for her to choose from." I was hurt and stunned that she or anyone near her would fabricate such a terrible rumor. The loyal Bridgeport phone brigade of the south side was alive and well. As Peter Finley Dunne had written about Bridgeport, "Politics ain't bean-bag."

As Mayor Thompson looked the other way in the 1920s, Al Capone, though exiled to Cicero, planned a complete takeover of organized crime—by which he meant an Italian takeover—and his five-hundred-man gang proceeded to eliminate competing mobster Dion O'Bannion and his mob enforcers, Earl Hymie Weiss and the O'Donnel brothers. Thompson won reelection in 1927. He campaigned hard on the matter of reopening the ten thousand businesses closed by Dever, hardly a subtle message. Independent Republicans Julius

Jay, and myself, with His Holiness Pope John Paul II on the Pope's visit to Chicago in 1979.

Rosenwald, Sewell Avery, Jane Addams, and Edward Ryerson all backed Dever, but Thompson's campaign sailed on Capone's money and the mayor's firm support in the 2nd Ward. When the Democratic Party chairman started a rumor that Thompson would turn the government over to blacks, the indomitable politician roared back that he would give blacks their fair share. Democrats began singing "Bye, Bye, Blackbird" in ethnic neighborhoods to play on racial fears. When the Thompson victory tally rolled in, the Republicans naturally chanted, "Bye, Bye, Dever."[7] Capone had contributed more than financial support to the exercise of the ballot box. He sent well over five hundred goons to various precincts, where they broke the limbs of stubborn adversaries. In precincts where Dever was expected to do well, hand grenades were lobbed into the polling places. It's fair to say that Capone did more than anyone else to help Thompson regain the mayor's office. According to my parents, the general public didn't like the mob violence going on—but stood aside, considering it a matter between the politicians and their cronies.

During Thompson's tenure, Capone would be able—without fear of city intervention—to complete his takeover of organized crime. The gangland bloodbaths ceased, and Chicagoans happily turned their attention to more wholesome entertainment. The Trianon, deemed the "most beautiful ballroom in the world," was going strong. There Chicagoans danced to the sounds of Dick Jurgens, the Dorsey brothers, Guy Lombardo, Eddy (Dancing Shoes) Howard, Lawrence Welk, Art Kassel (and his Kassels in the Air), and Wayne King. Rudolph Valentino performed Latin dances to the music of an Argentine orchestra. An equally grand ballroom, the Aragon, was about to open on the north side. Chicagoans could also listen to music at home, for the bands were broadcast live by WGN radio, sending its signal from the top of the Drake Hotel. The public was packing Wrigley Field to watch George Halas's Bears and the awesome swiftness of the "galloping ghost," Red Grange. The Cubs, headed for the pennant, were drawing crowds. Notre Dame games attracted an exodus of Catholic Chicagoans to South Bend either by car or the Notre Dame Specials that the South Shore–South Bend Railroad provided every weekend to root for Knute Rockne's Irish. Fans then came back to College Inn for dinner after the game. "You missed it," my parents would say confidently. "You'll never have what we had. Ziegfeld, great music, great bands. It was good, clean, innocent fun."

Thompson's gratitude to his gangster ally became self-destructively flagrant. For example, he appointed Daniel A. Serritella, a Republican 1st Ward committeeman and front man for Al Capone, as commissioner of the Department of Weights and Measures. Since that office became the Consumer Affairs Department of today, the mob still was officially my predecessor in my first political job. Thompson's end was coming soon. His slide began in earnest in 1928 when his handpicked candidates for state's attorney and governor were defeated. The vicious campaign—called the Pineapple Primary because so many bombs were thrown—broke Thompson physically and mentally. Not that it troubled Capone. He was too busy figuring out a way to eliminate his last remaining opponent, Bugs Moran. On Valentine's Day, 1929, armed with machine guns, the Capone mob gunned down seven members of the Moran gang. The St. Valentine's Day Massacre was a watershed to Chicagoans; they would tolerate no more violence and terror. They determined to get rid of Thompson in the next election.

Needless to say, my parents never included highlights from the

Capone era in their reminiscences of good, clean fun. They had met at Notre Dame. Practically from first glances, they had eyes only for each other. On August 31, 1929, they were wed at St. Jerome's Church in Rogers Park. During their courtship, they had only one serious argument—about stocks. For their new home, my mother wanted a baby grand piano. My father was a natural pianist, leading songsters at parties, and she loved seeing him in his element and joining the fun herself. But he wanted to continue buying stocks, which were then going up and up and up. An investment for their future, he argued. My mother was adamant; they bought the piano—and a good thing too, because six weeks later the stock market crashed.

A decade that began with a baseball scandal ended with the Cubs' pennant in 1929. Proudly, Chicagoans sang, "Take Me Out to the Ball Game," but they would soon be singing "Buddy, Can You Spare a Dime?"

CHAPTER 8

Buddy, Can You Spare a Dime?

When I was about six or seven years old, my mother allowed me to rummage through her hope chest, where I found her wedding gown and long train. It was a velvet dress, in my eyes unsuitable for a summer wedding. But my mother, always fashion-conscious, explained that she was not the type to be married in a summer gown on the eve of September. Besides, she quickly added, the last two weeks in August you can count on cool nights. It is as if nature is preparing for the entrance of a dry, brisk autumn. Autumn in Chicago is one of my favorite times of the year, and I could picture the season of my parents' marriage. People would still be flocking to the lakefront, soaking up the sunlight as long as they could. Soon the lake would turn a greenish gray, the sailboats and the sun worshipers would disappear, and the icy blasts of winter would descend on the city.

In that autumn of 1929, Chicagoans were looking skyward not only to observe the annual migration of birds to warmer climates but also to catch a glimpse of the new Boeing 80 transcontinental airplane streaking across the sky. The plane provided passenger service between New York and California—a two-day trip. Within a year, Chicagoans could fly directly to Salt Lake City and San Francisco from Midway Airport. Cranes and Burkes alike loved to take an afternoon trip to Midway to watch the mail planes take off and land.

Before the end of the year, Marshall Field was putting the finishing touches on the Merchandise Mart, the world's largest building, standing where Chief Billy Sauganash ruled over his tribe in the nineteenth century. The Mart, a great family attraction for Chicagoans, faced the two-tiered Wacker Drive across the Chicago River at its bend—Wolf Point. Around the bend and down the south branch, Insull was building his corporate headquarters. By this time he was supplying one-eighth of the nation's gas and electric power.

Chicagoans in fact felt very secure in the fall of 1929. They were preoccupied with "talking pictures" and Sunday drives in their Buicks, Fords, Chryslers, Hudsons, and Studebakers. They tuned in to favorite radio shows—to Bing Crosby crooning "Anything Goes," to Rudy Vallee melting hearts with "Tell Me That You Love Me," and to *The Sam and Henry Show*, an instant comedy hit that would soon be nationally acclaimed as *The Amos and Andy Show*. People were also reading the novels of two startling new talents, F. Scott Fitzgerald and Ernest Hemingway. Warnings from the Federal Reserve Board concerning the stock market—the Federal Reserve Board increased the bank rate from 5 to 6 percent—did not seem urgent. On September 3, 1929, as Chicagoans watched Buckingham Fountain in Grant Park close down for the summer, the stock market zoomed to an unprecedented high. Everyone relaxed.

The year before, Democratic politics changed when Anton Cermak outsmarted the entrenched Irish politicians whose constituents had earlier had an important advantage over other ethnic groups—they spoke the English language. A Bohemian immigrant and president of the Cook County Board, Cermak became party chairman, by virtue of the demands from Chicago's burgeoning Bohemian and Polish populations. (Of Chicago's three million residents, 17.8 percent were Bohemian and 13.7 percent Polish.) He forged his victory by surrounding himself with ethnic committeemen, ensuring that various ethnic groups shared in the party's power.

But Cermak also recognized that a new breed of Irish politician was waiting to be tapped, a white-collar group more business-oriented than the old-timers he defeated. For the most part, members of this new wave worked in insurance, banking, and real estate rather than in construction or haulage, and they were intent on winning the money that could be made through local government in these professions. Cermak appealed to these "young bucks." Two of them in particular, Pat Nash and Joe McDonough, would become powerful politicians, preferring to join Cermak rather than wait in line behind the older Irish political leaders.

So it is in politics. I well remember a 1970s Cook County Democratic rally at a packed Medinah Temple. I had a good spot on the stage to observe the machinations of Chicago's politicians, sitting among them as a member of the Democratic National Committee and chairman of the Resolutions Committee of the Democratic National Party. I noticed Mayor Daley motion to Alderman Tom Keane, his powerful finance chairman and floor leader in the city council. Keane had been around a long time, since the early 1930s, as alderman and ward committeeman. The mayor told Keane he wanted to acknowledge the older man's birthday and was going to ask the audience to sing "Happy Birthday." Keane said sternly, "No, don't do it." By the look on his face, he meant it. Daley made the announcement anyway, then asked Keane to say a few words to the crowd—which the alderman did, thanking the crowd, then glancing sharply at those on stage with him before turning back to the assemblage. "The young bucks up here with me didn't mean a word of the song," he snapped. "They would be just as happy if old Keane here never had another birthday." I was holding my breath for fear of what he would say next, as the television cameras kept rolling. But he only smiled an acid smile and added, "How do I know how they feel? I was a young buck once myself."

And so it was in 1929—Nash and McDonough joined Cermak in order to beat out the "old bucks." But there were limits to Cermak's largess. The new and undisputed leader of the party shared some of his power with every ethnic group but two—blacks and Italians. The black 2nd Ward had remained loyal to Thompson. Italians were out on two counts. First, because of Capone's alliance with Thompson, the heavily Italian 1st Ward was Republican. In addition, all Italians were unfortunately lumped together in the public mind with the Black Hand's activities. Cermak pulled all the rest of Democratic Chicago together, though, and proved a strong leader, taking the position that the party was more important than individual personalities. With so many ethnic groups voting together, the Democratic bandwagon could not be stopped, carrying countless elections. Of course, winning meant that all would share in the spoils of victory. Broadly ethnic Chicago was organized politically for the first time. Thus the invincible Democratic machine was built. The old Irish guard muttered, but they were hopelessly outnumbered. When I entered politics in 1960 working for the John F. Kennedy campaign, there was a popular saying around town that if the machine slated Donald Duck for the Senate, Donald Duck would soon be Senator Duck. From the days of Cermak's organization, that saying pretty much rang true.

On October 24, 1929, the Roaring Twenties came to an abrupt halt. Something had gone wrong on Wall Street. Stocks were plummeting in value and no one knew why. Players in the stock market had bought their stock on margin—only 10 percent down. With stock prices dropping so fast, brokers were calling their customers to post considerably more money to cover their margins. A wave of panic selling ensued, because many could not meet their margin calls. The ticker tape was running behind, as brokers were flooded with frantic telephone calls to sell. When the market rallied somewhat that afternoon, Chicagoans breathed a sigh of relief, but some families had already been wiped out. My father, who was working for Inland Steel, was bewildered. While several of his friends and neighbors lost everything that day, the steel industry was operating at 95 percent capacity, a production rate almost unheard of except during wartime. Inland Steel itself was enjoying some of its best business quarters since 1918. My father had always believed in the slogan "As steel goes, so goes the nation." It shook him to the core that his steel barometer was so far off the mark. By October 28, orders to sell far outdistanced buys, and the stock market collapsed. Dreams of the future and 16,338,000 shares of stock lay worthless on the floors of the stock exchange.

Inland Steel's handling of its employees during the Depression impressed my parents. In spite of losses in 1932, Inland tried to keep its work force intact by means of staggered work weeks and shortened hours. The company contributed to group insurance programs and established a fellowship club, employees contributing voluntarily 3 percent of their salaries, an amount matched dollar for dollar by management, to help those who were not making ends meet. Four thousand Inland employees joined. My father said that the fellowship club and Inland's massive contribution of free coal to its employees created a feeling of strong camaraderie. Employees at Sears Roebuck were buoyed by Julius Rosenwald's announcement that the company would cover the first round of margin calls for all personnel. Samuel Insull followed suit for his employees at Commonwealth Edison. That New Year's Eve my parents entertained what they always referred to as "our crowd." As my mother recalled, "As that young crowd, most of them recently married, gathered around the piano to sing 'Auld Lang Syne' and face the next decade, no one could have slightly imagined how much worse the Depression was going to get."

Amid that terrible Depression, my older brother Billy was born. My mother always said, "We were lucky at the time Billy came. Your father's salary at Inland had not been cut yet." The Chicago Billy was born into was a city of long lines of men, women, and children standing in front of soup kitchens. Stale bread sold at discount, 10 cents a loaf. Company after company closed its doors. Banks went under. Well-dressed men sold apples on State Street. A shantytown of wood-and-tar-paper shacks sprang up at Randolph Street and the lake; it was nicknamed Hooverville after the President blamed for the Depression. The shacks were a stark contrast to the magnificent Board of Trade Building just opening on LaSalle Street. Over 600,000 Chicagoans were unemployed. But, my mother often reminded me, everything seemed bizarre at the time.

In 1930, Cermak's multiethnic machine carried every one of its state and county candidates to victory, not by selling any single candidate, but by selling the ticket. "Sell the straight Democratic ticket" was the chairman's marching order. His forty thousand precinct workers were the salesmen. City and county workers kept tally sheets on their individual precincts. On election night, the votes they turned in had to be submitted for signature to the ward committeeman listed on the sheet. Copies of the sheets were filed at the Democratic headquarters. Poor election tally sheets meant the precinct worker was not producing. If he failed to produce, he could lose his job. In his newspaper, the *Chicago Public Service Leader*, Cermak publicized the individual results of every ward organization. There was no hiding place in Democratic Chicago politics, not for a ward boss, not for a precinct captain.

Nor did Cermak tolerate old-line politicians who for their own political power sabotaged the election of colleagues, pretending to support them while swinging their wards behind Republicans. Cermak demanded party loyalty. Loyalty, loyalty, loyalty was preached to the Poles, the Irish, the Germans, the Jews. And this sermonizing worked.

One of Cermak's first acts as mayor was to cut property taxes, providing immediate benefit for the Depression-weary taxpayer trying to hang on. Thousands had been evicted from their homes for their failure to keep up with rent or mortgage payments. He streamlined the bureaucracy, cutting deadwood and merging departments to create greater productivity. After paring the Civil Service Commission to manageable size, he turned over the reins of the party to his loyal "young bucks." Cermak concentrated his energies on two projects—construction of a downtown subway with federal funds and keeping the second World's Fair on schedule. Both would provide desperately needed jobs. Things weren't in fact getting better in Chicago, but they seemed better. (Nothing could dampen the joy in my father's side of the family over the ordination of my uncle Edward. To an immigrant Irish family, the ordination of a son to the priesthood was the fulfillment of a long dream.)

Cermak had one more project up his sleeve—the Democratic National Convention would be held in Chicago in June 1932. I was not born until the following year, but even so my memory of the man nominated that year would be strong. I believed Roosevelt. In the early forties he would seem like a kind grandfather who would keep the war away from Chicago. The 1932 convention was one of the closest and most exciting in American history. After five days, the Democrats still had no candidate. The Al Smith supporters, led by Cermak, held off the determined forces of FDR until California switched, putting the future President over the top. In those days, it was customary for the nominee to wait at home for a formal delegation to call and advise him of his victory, but FDR was an innovator. My mother recalled, "Chicago went wild when Roosevelt broke with tradition and came to Chicago to thank the state delegation personally." Here was another straw of hope—this gratitude, and the promise of a New Deal.

Roosevelt's campaign song, "Happy Days Are Here Again," offered no solace to our family friend—and Insull's right-hand man—Johnny O'Keefe. Everyone needed a scapegoat for the Depression, and Roosevelt was pointing his finger at Samuel Insull. Thousands of people had been wiped out when stock in his utilities empire collapsed. The Democratic candidate threatened to prosecute Insull and anyone else who had failed to protect the public investment in now worthless stock. It made a good campaign issue, but Johnny knew Insull to be a man of integrity who took pride in bringing electricity to the city he loved, lighting the boulevards, powering the rapid transit systems and household utilities.

He shunned New York's financial institutions after his painful experience when the House of Morgan called in loans on his former boss, Thomas Edison, virtually putting him out of business. As his empire grew, he relied on Chicago and London banks. Johnny O'Keefe often talked to my parents about Insull's philanthropic nature. He had guaranteed the margin calls of all his employees at the beginning of the Depression and also set up fund-raising events for the unemployed that pulled in as much as $10 million on several occasions.

When the end came for Insull, he had long considered his work completed in Chicago. He had been in Chicago fifty years and was ready to turn over the reins of Commonwealth Edison and his other companies to his son. Remembering the hostile takeover of Thomas Edison's company, Insull had reorganized in 1928, placing most of his companies in two larger entities, Insull Utility Investments (IUI) and Corporation Security Company of Chicago (CORP). Both holding companies sat at the top of the Insull pyramid, controlling $500 million in assets through other holding companies. Still, there were threats. Cyrus Eaton, a Cleveland Financier, had been quietly buying stock in Insull's companies prior to the crash—and by the time of the crash, asked to be bought out. Insull, again fearing a takeover attempt, finally agreed, with assurance of financing from the Continental Bank of Chicago, to pay Eaton $56 million to buy back the stock. Continental, however, could not complete its part of the agreement. Coming up short by $20 million, it asked New York bankers for assistance. Insull was required to post his resources from IUI and CORP to guarantee the loans, putting him in an extremely precarious situation. If the value of the stock fell sharply enough in the markets, the holding companies' assets could be eaten up just covering the loan. That was exactly what happened. The Depression raged on. The market price of the stocks fell and the banks called the loan. Insull's empire went into receivership. The stock was worthless and Insull was out.

Cermak, meanwhile, was besieged with problems. Fifty-one of Chicago's 228 banks had already folded. Evictions mounted. Determined to get his greatest public works project, the subway, under construction, Cermak worked diligently for Roosevelt, who beat Herbert Hoover for the presidency on November 8, 1932. Cermak made sure Chicago went big for FDR and, immediately after the election, requested time with the President-elect. The White House worked out an appointment for the two while Roosevelt was in Miami for a speech. On finishing his speech, FDR motioned for Cermak to join him in his car, to talk during the motorcade through Miami. A shot was fired. The bullet intended for Roosevelt struck Anton Cermak instead. While the crowd and police quickly subdued a man named Joe Zangara, the would-be assassin, Roosevelt cradled Cermak in his arms as they were sped to Miami's Jackson Memorial Hospital. Cermak's condition was serious. Chicagoans were told the mayor had little chance to survive.

News of Cermak's critical condition had no sooner chattered over the wireless than Chicago's ward committeemen began to meet secretly in small groups around City Hall, jockeying for power. Periodically, various committeemen scurried to their favorite reporters, floating trial balloons concerning prospective mayoral candidates. Some committeemen used journalists to plant rumors about Cermak's condition—as if they had a pipeline to his doctor in Miami. Precinct captains, City Hall employees, fanned out around the building to assure the media that their particular ward boss had the necessary votes to take charge and to spread negative rumors about rival ward bosses.

This maneuvering around Cermak's hospital bed was little different from politics forty-three years later when Mayor Richard J. Daley suffered his stroke early in May 1975. I was about to be named cochairman of the Democratic Party in Chicago and at Daley's insistence had been assuming some of the duties, though I wasn't technically elected to the post till seven months later. Consequently I was able to observe the backstairs plotting. The Daley family's decision to order an immediate blackout on his condition only fueled the rumors that he was severely incapacitated. This created such a vacuum that by the time the doctors gave out any information, the infighting was in full swing. Even a medical bulletin announcing that Daley was scheduled for surgery in ten days to remove the blockage in the artery leading to the brain, and was expected to recover fully, barely slowed the jockeying committeemen.

Three days before a Democratic fund-raising dinner on May 22, Billy Daley, the mayor's son, called and said his father would like to speak with me. I was relieved to learn that the mayor could in fact speak. But what I heard was more a stammering whisper than a voice: "Madam Chairman, I'm fighting my doctors like hell to be at the dinner, but if I don't make it, you are cochairman, you will preside for me. Get a pencil. I'll tell you what I want you to announce."

I was stunned. The dinner was a huge event. Every city, county, state, and congressional delegate plus six thousand guests would attend; $1.5 million would be raised. Clearly, Mayor Daley knew little or nothing about the extent of political maneuvering in his absence; some observers had predicted a coup before the dinner. I had some doubts, also, about my effectiveness as a stand-in, for Daley had been shoving me and other women down Democratic committeemen's throats for the past two years.

After Daley hung up, I sat for a while staring at the phone. How could I prove that this conversation had taken place? My presiding over the dinner and announcing the reelection plans he dictated to me could only be perceived as a raw grab for power. Not wise. I decided to hold a press conference instead. Daley's plans were sound both politically and governmentally. They called for a more open Democratic Party executive structure, including two powerful new deputy chairman positions. The first chair, to be filled by a senior citizen, would represent Chicagoans sixty years of age and older. "We should provide free legal service to seniors in every ward headquarters," Daley had said. "Those attorneys could assist the elderly in obtaining proper social security awards, help them with their taxes and pension claims." The other deputy chairman, for young adults, was to recruit young people not yet connected to the machine. He had added, "Sometimes I think we get too set in our ways. The young can bring new ideas to the party." Daley also wanted to broaden the ward superintendent's job description to include women. "Hell," he said, "the woman is in the ward much more of the time than the men. She'll know what's going on in the alleys, the school playgrounds." That position was controversial. I don't think a woman had been ward superintendent in Chicago since Jane Addams. Anyway, I hoped my announcement of Daley's plans would show the public and the committeemen that he was of sound mind, fit enough to remain as party chairman, and was indeed functioning as mayor.

The press conference was strident. I saw to that, and purposely sent shock waves rolling through City Hall. Not only did I enumerate Daley's programs, I also called the power seekers a handful of "greedy little men" and urged them to have the decency to postpone their coup until after the operation, when it might become clear whether or not Daley would regain his health. Fortunately, Mayor Daley did recover.

Forty-three years earlier, Cermak had not. As he lay dying in Miami, he was visited by a young Irish Democrat from Bridgeport, Ed Kelly. Kelly, a member of the South Parks Commission, was close to Colonel McCormick of the *Chicago Tribune* McCormicks. His surprising flight to Miami signaled a shift, a softening of the antipathy many Irish Democrats felt toward Cermak. "Pushcart Tony" they had called him, resentful that he'd outsmarted them when he grabbed the Democratic leadership. Kelly remained with Cermak for nineteen days, until the mayor's death on March 6, and accompanied the casket back to Chicago. Being seen as caring and solicitous benefited

Kelly politically. Cermak's death not only left the city without a mayor, it also left a void in party leadership.

As the funeral train rolled back toward Chicago, Pat Nash, the Democratic leader most trusted by Cermak, swung into action. He summoned party leaders—all were from the south and west side—to choose an interim mayor. When ethnic bickering broke out, Nash permitted it for a while, but he had the matter locked up, and recommended Ed Kelly, who became the next mayor and the first of the forty-six-year reign of Bridgeport mayors.

The committeemen of 1933, referred to collectively in session as the Central Committee, were jealous and suspicious of each other— just as they are now. But in those days, they had one thing in common—respect for and a belief in Pat Nash, who had spent a lot of time stroking them. He had little to offer, he realized, to the disgruntled Irish leaders from the far south and west sides who accused him of "caving in" to Colonel McCormick, Kelly's backer. To them, Kelly was an outsider, not a member of the Central Committee; he ran no ward and had never even served on the city council. He had not earned the mayor's chair. Nevertheless, Nash was able to push Kelly into office because of the loyalty of the multiethnic coalition—and because of the necessary payoffs. Jacob Arvey, Jewish alderman of the west side's 24th Ward, was elevated to the influential post of city council finance chairman. In a further demonstration of gratitude to the Jewish community, Arvey's former law partner, Barnet Hodes, was named corporation counsel for the city. Respect was paid to the Polish community by retaining Menc Stephan Szymczak, a Cermak appointee, as city comptroller, Kelly also changed the name of Crawford Avenue to Pulaski Avenue, over strong objections from many communities and businessmen located on that avenue. Two more Cermak confidants, Paddy Bauler of the 43rd Ward and Charley Weber, of German descent, of the 45th Ward, were also promoted. With these appointments, Nash cemented a Kelly consensus.

A less civilized succession took place when Mayor Daley died. Well before the funeral, members of his cabinet, the city council, boards, and commissions were summoned to view the body at Nativity Church at 653 West 37th Street, where Daley lay in state. Afterward, coffee was served in the church basement. I went down there expecting a somber gathering and found instead a herd of political animals tearing at the flesh of the mayor's office. Aside from the priest greeting guests at the door, this was certainly not a wake. Men were buttonholing one another right and left. Barely cold, the body lay not twenty feet above, as the climbers jostled and shouted, "Don't worry about him. I already have his vote," or "Well, are you with me or not?" Secret meetings were arranged, and cliques coalesced. I thought it was Chicago politics at its rawest and worst. The king is dead, long live the king—but who will that be?

The new "king" of 1933 demanded total loyalty to the party, just as Cermak had. He and Nash copied Cermak's agenda—support for the Democratic ticket and absolute control of Chicago. Wanting his name and political affiliation uppermost in Democratic minds, Kelly put into place Chicago's unique political network, a vast army of street and sanitation workers, police, fire personnel, and City Hall employees. The reasoning was simple: since city employees were awarded jobs by letters of recommendation from their ward commit-teemen, they were, all of them, foot soldiers of the machine. A system of reward and credit was therefore designed for government projects. If the city fixed a sidewalk or curb, the precinct captain in that area would be notified of the improvement. He would follow up by sending letters to those of importance in his ward and to those who had benefited, taking credit for the repair, citing his City Hall connections, and thanking Mayor Kelly. Thus the ward's gratitude to the precinct captain and the mayor was assured. Kelly also had the precinct captain keep him current with everything going on in the community, such as crime, gangs, racial problems, slum conditions, or dilapidated housing stock. In effect, the mayor had an intelligence system in each and every community.

I was reminded of Kelly in the spring of 1980, when I traveled to Israel for a U.S. Conference of Mayors. There, thousands of years of civilization seemed as yesterday. I walked the stations of the cross on the Via Dolorosa, visiting the Church of the Holy Sepulchre, built on the supposed site of the Lord's entombment. I made the climb to Masada, where Jews leaped to their death rather than be captured by Roman legions, and I traded war stories with Jerusalem's Mayor Teddy Kollek. As the mayor and I took a short walk around the modern city of Jerusalem, I remarked that the people we passed all showed an obvious affection for him. He replied, "Oh yes, well, we are so much smaller than your city. I even have my phone number in the book, and if people want to call me, they call me. You know what you ought to do? Do what I do. I've got a guy on every block. Well, maybe you can't do that, you are too big. Anyway, I have this guy on every block. I can find out about anything going on. I just pick up the phone when I want to know something and say, 'Hey, Joe, what's going on on the block?' Yeah, that's how I keep my fingers on everything. You are too big in Chicago to do that." I stopped in my tracks and started to laugh, back on earth after my tour through ancient history. Jerusalem may seem like a city in a time warp, but urban politics is urban politics anywhere.

Kelly and Nash and the Democratic coalition were solidly in control in 1933 Chicago, but two important chairs still sat empty at their table—one for Italians, one for blacks. The predominantly Italian 1st Ward holds within its boundaries all of downtown, with its financial district on LaSalle Street, its shopping center on State Street, the governmental district on North LaSalle, and some of the city's finest institutions, such as the Art Institute, the Central Library, the Auditorium, and Meigs Field. It also contains Chinatown and a large Italian commercial and residential area. Politically speaking, the 1st Ward is synonymous with the word "mob."

In 1933, Bathhouse John Coughlin was the alderman of the 1st Ward—as he had been since 1892, the heyday of the Levee. Insiders still say that 1st Ward politicians are the best dancers in Chicago, for they can dance on both sides of the street at the same time and never lose a beat. After the demise of the 1st Ward ball, Bathhouse John accommodated to the changing times. He still got his cut of gambling and prostitution money, for the south end of downtown still flourished as the red-light district and gambling clubs thrived under his protection. At the same time, he was alderman for the rest of the powerful, respectable downtown district. He quickly made himself available to the new Kelly-Nash machine. With Capone in prison since 1931, the mob was being run by loyal henchmen who knew that their gambling empire would collapse without protection such as they had enjoyed under Republican Big Bill Thompson. They arranged for their Republican-owned committeeman, Serritella, to meet with Bathhouse John, then Serritella met with Pat Nash. An understanding was reached. The city would go easy on Capone's heirs. Serritella would get a cut from the take in prostitution and gambling, plus the promise that he would never face opposition in the 1st Ward. On the other hand, Nash could count on the Italians in his multiethnic bloc.

With the Italians at their table, the Kelly-Nash team turned toward the black community. Cermak's attitude had been primitive—blacks should be brought into line on their knees. He had fired many of Thompson's Republican black employees and shut down gambling in the black wards. Kelly and Nash reversed that policy, signaling the police to look the other way regarding vice and gambling. Chicago's policy game network (an illegal betting game similar to today's legal lottery) was clearing $30 million a year, making it one of the black community's most lucrative enterprises. Once the black policy kings found that their business had been revived, they climbed quite eagerly aboard the Kelly-Nash bandwagon. Their legions of policy writers made excellent assistant precinct captains of the Democratic Party. But the Kelly-Nash machine went farther, rehiring blacks and placing them in responsible positions. Kelly made the highly visible appointment of Robert S. Abbott, editor of the *Chicago Defender*, to the World's Fair Committee.

Once the machine had successfully co-opted the opposition, it wanted money, big money, to enhance its power. Protection money poured into party headquarters, though Kelly did not personally touch it. Gambling was the province of the committeemen in each ward, who also chose the district police captain. The police captain collected the money from prostitution, bookmaking, policy, etc., for the ward boss. Considerable sums were involved, as much as $12 million to $20 million annually. Chicagoans could place a bet anywhere, from newspaper city rooms to the dining rooms of prestigious private clubs. Half the take went downtown to party headquarters in the Morrison Hotel. Kelly and Nash had their coalition. They also had the support of the business community, which followed Colonel McCormick's lead.

Dever, Thompson, and Cermak had been conscientious about laying the groundwork for the 1933 World's Fair, but Kelly was lucky enough to preside over it. My mother would say, "Chicago looked so shabby and demoralized, and yet just as the first Fair forty years earlier brought hope to unemployed immigrants, so this Fair, the Century of Progress Exposition, brought a glimmer of hope." Four decades earlier, eleven-year-old Franklin Delano Roosevelt had come to the Chicago Fair aboard his parents' private Pullman car. Now, too bogged down in Depression problems to leave the White House, he would press a button from Washington and the Fair lights would blaze on.

This fair would be modern, even futuristic, as would its architecture. Again, the planners emphasized space, water, and color. Man-made islands sprang up along the lakefront from the Adler Planetarium to 37th Street. The pavilions erected on eighty-two acres of land

My father, William
Patrick Burke, in 1980.
Courtesy Dave
Schuessler.

were surrounded by water. One of the islands built for the fair, Northerly Island, is today the home of Meigs Airport. Visitors marveled at the electric refrigerator, shatterproof glass, and a newfangled invention called television. They saw the first aluminum train, the Burlington Zephyr. There were shows and carnival games and Sally Rand, the fan dancer. The police arrested Rand several times a week for indecent exposure, a notoriety that only added to her box office. On opening day, only ten thousand people attended the Fair, but by midsummer, it was drawing a hundred thousand a day. And Chicago hosted twelve hundred conventions, a by-product of the Fair. Of course, the Fair needed a more extravagant showpiece than the Eiffel Tower or the Ferris wheel. A skyride should do it. Joseph Sander writes in the *Chicago Tribune Magazine* that two towers, each 628 feet tall, spaced 2,000 feet apart and nicknamed Amos and Andy, were joined by wire. Rocket cars suspended from the high wire sped six thousand people an hour from tower to tower. In all, the Fair put $200 million into Chicago's pocket. On closing day in 1934, the crowd swelled to 374,000.[1]

The Fair provided not only hope, but also jobs. For my parents' generation, those who came of age in the Roaring Twenties, five agonizing years were now over. By 1934 my father had suffered two pay cuts. His salary was 60 percent of what it had been and there were more mouths to feed. Now things began to look up.

Mayor Kelly had cut the ribbon on opening day in late May to inaugurate the Fair. My mother could not attend because three days earlier, on May 24, I was born. My parents had no way of knowing that the election of Ed Kelly had started a tradition of Bridgeport mayors—or that their infant daughter would be the one to break it.

CHAPTER 9

The Dark Shadow of War

resident Roosevelt kept his word. He put Americans back to
work, and he did not forget his campaign promise regarding
Samuel Insull. Insull hadn't waited around, but had fled to Paris
before he could be brought to trial. Once he realized the federal
government was determined to prosecute, Insull went on to Greece,
which had no extradition treaty with the United States.

I recall asking my parents why Johnny O'Keefe was such a
staunch Republican when everyone else in their crowd was a Democrat. In one voice they answered, "Sam Insull." Insull and those close
to him were upset that he was being treated like a criminal. Several
times, Insull declared he would gladly stand trial if he thought he
would get a fair hearing, but he judged the case against him to be
political. Add politics to the angry, Depression-weary populace of the
time, and Insull's assessment about judicial fairness may have been
accurate. Insull admitted making mistakes, but not egregious mistakes; he did not wish to serve as scapegoat for the Depression. Even
in Greece, however, Insull had no peace. Borrowing money from several friends, he chartered a small cruise ship, hoping to remain safe at
sea, but in Istanbul he was seized by the Turkish government and
handed over to United States authorities.

Facing trial in both state and federal courts, Insull was returned to
Chicago and thrown into Cook County jail with murderers and rap-
ists. From October 1934 to March 1935, Sam Insull's trial dragged on.

He finally took the stand in his own defense, denying any attempt to defraud stockholders. His actions were intended only to maintain tight control of his empire, he said. He also testified that John O'Keefe, our family friend, was a straight arrow and had never been involved in any questionable business schemes. Chicagoans appreciated Insull's philanthropy and his personal kindness to his employees in the early days of the Depression. At any rate, the jury believed him.

After his acquittal, Insull returned to Paris. On July 13, 1938, broken and bankrupt, the former millionaire suffered a fatal heart attack in the Paris subway. He had 85 cents in his pocket. John O'-Keefe and many another would never forgive FDR or the Democrats for the destruction of Sam Insull. Bright and extremely capable, Johnny landed on his feet, getting a job with Colonel Frank Knox, editor and publisher of the *Chicago Daily News* and later Secretary of the Navy.

Mayor Kelly was riding high as he faced his first real election in 1935. Of course, the Democratic leaders took the position that Roosevelt poured federal funds and jobs into Chicago because of the machine's political clout. Early in his first administration, FDR tried to distance himself from the machine, but eventually he, like other Presidents to follow, recognized that in Chicago you don't get much done without City Hall.

The legend of the machine has taken on a life of its own. In reality, it was not really invincible, but Kelly did roll up a smashing victory in 1935. He was endorsed by the newspapers, pushed by the business community, and peddled by the precinct captains. As his newfound black supporter the *Defender* explained: "If you leave it to the west, north and far south side to elect the mayor, then don't be surprised when those things you are likely to want are left to them. Politics is a business; there is no sentiment involved; support is given for support."[1]

Other events of the mid-thirties stood out more dramatically in my childhood, especially the gathering storm in Europe. At the age of eight in the early 1940s I asked my parents how the war in Europe had begun. They answered with a family story about my uncle Ed, who had been sent to Rome by Cardinal Mundelein in 1932 for postgraduate study. Ed was still there in 1935, when Adolf Hitler sent German troops marching through Austria and Czechoslovakia. Ed's presence in Europe worried the Burkes, because they always suspected that

Hitler's move would lead to World War II. It was a happy Burke family that journeyed to New York that fall of 1935 to welcome home Uncle Ed, who had returned aboard the famous steamship *Normandie.* With his doctorate in canon law tucked safely under his arm, Ed was assigned to the Chicago chancery office (the executive office of the church) and took up residence at Holy Name Cathedral Rectory.

My earliest radio memories are the voices of FDR, fiery John L. Lewis, and Adolf Hitler haranguing his throngs. Of course, I followed the radio serials *(The Shadow, The Green Hornet, Jack Armstrong,* and *The Lone Ranger),* but when I heard important political leaders, I couldn't help but listen intently. I particularly liked the booming, self-assured voice of John L. Lewis, who, my father told me, led the United Mine Workers in their fight with the owners of the mines for a worker's right to join a union and for better safety in the coal mines. He went on to explain a tactic bizarre to me—the sit-down strike. It struck me as hilarious that people would actually descend all the way to the bottom of a mine only to sit down. My father was not amused. "Strikes are no laughing matter," he snapped.

The sit-down strikes spread to the steel mills and in May 1937 led to violence at Republic Steel on Chicago's south side. When workers there sat down in protest, company owners called in police to evict them. In the name of law and order, Mayor Kelly put down these strikes as quickly as they erupted, but he could no longer deny that unions were an organized force to be reckoned with. The working man might vote Democratic, but he had no formal agreement yet with labor leaders. When workers called a strike on Republic Steel for May 27, the city's corporation counsel issued a legal opinion that the strikers were entitled to hold peaceful demonstrations. Even so, minor skirmishes broke out between police and picketers. The families of the strikers, about two thousand strong, gathered on Memorial Day 1937 to protest the police actions. The picketers were armed with rocks, the police with guns. Violent fighting erupted. When the police fired, the crowd turned to flee, and some panicked. Several wounded protesters fell to the ground, and others fell on top of them. Anyone who couldn't escape was clubbed. As abruptly as it had begun, the violence known as the Memorial Day Massacre ended, leaving ten dead and thirty seriously wounded from gunshots. Sixty protesters were hospitalized by police beatings, and three policemen were injured when struck with rocks and clubs.

The *Tribune* had praised police work during the strike, and now the mayor echoed that praise. As in the days of Haymarket, the police had again been manipulated by big business, and again many Chicagoans felt that police brutality was not justified. Forty-five hundred public-spirited citizens organized themselves community by community and met at the Civic Opera House to demand an investigation. A citizens' commission was established. Arthur Goldberg, then a prominent labor lawyer, wrote the report of its investigation, which found the police guilty of instigating violence and charged the city administration with a cover-up.

Mayor Kelly knew that if the working class turned against him, he would be finished. He moved quickly on two fronts. He set up meetings to forage a relationship with the leaders of the Congress of Industrial Organizations (CIO). Next he intervened in a stockyards strike, negotiating a settlement the strikers could live with. Eventually, a trade-off agreement was hammered out with CIO officials. Police would not intervene in future strikes if labor endorsed Kelly in 1939. And so labor entered the densely packed Democratic fold. In four years, the Kelly/Nash machine had co-opted all—blacks, the mob, the business community, and now the labor movement. Those components (with the exception of a predictably solid black vote) still make up what is left of Chicago's Democratic machine.

Kelly and his machine rolled on, trading on the goodies of federal relief programs and construction jobs. An ardent Roosevelt supporter, Kelly secured the Democratic Convention for Chicago in 1940. To many mayors, the President admitted his uncertainty about running again, but he didn't want to turn his back on his country while war raged in Europe. This may well have been Roosevelt's way of testing the water, evaluating his political support among the party's bosses. Politically, it is not unusual for an incumbent to have his close supporters orchestrate a spontaneous draft. Kelly wanted Roosevelt. Kelly was a big-city boss, and big-city bosses controlled the convention and chose the party's candidate. It followed then that Kelly would pack the galleries and issue floor credentials to his precinct captains.

The political coup of Roosevelt and Kelly occurred on the second day of the convention—a coup that would have been the envy of Joseph Medill and Anton Cermak. Wanting further confirmation of his chances, Roosevelt sent a letter to the convention to be read by Democratic Chairman Altan Barkley of Kentucky: "The President has never had, and has not today, any desire or purpose to continue in the office of President, to be a candidate for that office, or to be nominated by the Convention for that office. He wishes to make it clear that all the delegates to this convention are free to vote for any candidate."[2]

Kelly was already familiar with the contents of the letter. As the audience sat stunned, a voice, seemingly omnipresent, boomed throughout the hall: "We want Roosevelt. America needs Roosevelt." The surprised galleries picked up the cue, joined in the chanting, and began to march around the floor. Kelly made sure that no one noticed who had started the stampede. In fact, it was no one inside the hall, but Superintendent of Sewers Thomas Garry, stationed down in the basement with a microphone hooked up to the hall's public address system. Sight unseen, he led the stampede for FDR, and the spontaneous draft soon followed. The bond between the Roosevelt administration and the Kelly/Nash machine was now even stronger.

In these childhood years, I was making a trade-off or two myself. For the sake of my beloved riding lessons I agreed to endure ballet and swimming instructions. We had moved to Sauganash from a Rogers Park community called North Town (I was in third grade at the time), and our new school, Queen of All Saints, arranged riding lessons at the Kirby Riding Academy near Northbrook for any students who were interested. They gave me some of my greatest thrills as a child. But the Burke children were lucky enough to find excitement in the classroom as well. We all fell under the spell of my mother, who truly loved books. When she was sent to boarding school after Grandmother's death, one of the sisters sensed her loneliness and led her to the library, saying, "You will find many good friends in those pages." Indeed, she had, and Mother wanted us to learn this valuable lesson. She would serve us after-school refreshments around three-fifteen. When I was seven, Billy ten, and Edward five (and freshly awakened from his afternoon nap), we'd sit around the kitchen table, munching on graham crackers and jelly or homemade peanut butter cookies and fruit juice, listening to my mother read poetry and short stories. On one occasion, she announced that we were going to the movies the following Saturday to see The Wizard of Oz. We had, of course, heard the music from the film on the radio. My mother was proud that Mother Goose (1897) and The Wizard of Oz (1900) had been written in Chicago by Frank L. Baum. And she often read us "Little Boy Blue," the famously poignant poem by Eugene Field, a writer for the Daily News.

She was not alone in her respect and love for writing. The Chicago of that time was at the height of a golden age of literature and journalism, attracting the curious and the ambitious from all over the Midwest. Humorist George Ade rode in fresh from Kentland, Indiana, to join the *Chicago Daily News.* Theodore Dreiser arrived from Warsaw, Indiana; Sherwood Anderson from Clyde, Ohio; Vachel Lindsay from Springfield, Illinois. Ben Hecht came to the *Daily News* from Racine, Wisconsin; Ring Lardner to the *Tribune* from Niles, Michigan; Carl Sandburg to the *Daily News* from Galesburg, Illinois. All wrote fresh, realistic evaluations of the city and became known as the Chicago school of journalism.

On Sundays, we always went to my paternal grandparents' home for dinner. My father's clerical brothers, Ed and Joe, came as well.

The Burkes were a completely different kind of Irish from the Cranes, very religious, going to Mass every morning. Coming from these different backgrounds, my mother and father viewed many things differently, which made for a perfect balance in the way they raised us. For my father's parents, religion had truly been the center of life. He would never just say good night to us; it was always "Good night, God bless you." When his relatives said goodbye, it was "Goodbye, God bless you." There were many other right-from-Ireland expressions. It was typical of the old country, as well, that my father, as the eldest son, was the favorite child. Handsomely "dark Irish" with piercing blue eyes, he could do no wrong. Of course, he was very bright, did well in school, and always helped his family as much as he could. He turned his intelligence to business and was successful, but he never learned to be overbearing or abrasive in competition. He would not knowingly hurt a soul, and he never wanted to hear a catty word from us children. If one of us made a cruel remark about someone else, he would get a stern expression and say, "If you can't say something nice, keep it to yourself." It's not that he stifled us. He encouraged us in school, in sports, in every contest. He wanted the best for his children.

When I was growing up, I was fascinated by my grandparents' house, which was filled with statues of the Virgin, Sacred Heart pictures, and other signs of devout, trusting faith. I loved the Sunday dinners when my clerical uncles brought their friends and told stories about the different peoples living in Chicago.

Uncle Ed was already vice-chancellor of the archdiocese, a power unto himself in those days, near the peak of the church hierarchy in town. It would become his great disappointment in life that he did not make bishop. When he reached his late forties, new stars had appeared. When Cardinal Meyer was appointed, it was also a case of a new broom sweeping clean, I suppose. He asked Ed which parish he'd like to be assigned to. My uncle was, as always, straightforward: "I'm not asking to be assigned to any parish. I've served Holy Name since I came back from Rome. If you're ordering me to leave here and take a parish, I will, because I took the vow of obedience, but it will not be voluntary on my part. I want you to know that." The cardinal hesitated a few days, then called him back in. "There are two good openings," he said. "One in Winnetka, one on the northwest side. Which do you want?" Again, Ed would not choose. "I'll obey," he said, "but you'll have to send me." He was duly sent to St. Bartholomew's on the northwest side. He really declined after that. He never really enjoyed parish work, although he did like being back with the people. It was too late to change; power had been the all-important thing. As the second most powerful cleric in the diocese, he had done a lot of good, made important decisions, and instituted changes, such as establishing the first bilingual teaching centers in Chicago.

Uncle Joe, even in the eyes of the family, played a lesser role, acting as pastor at St. Joseph's. He was something like Father O'Malley in *Going My Way*, a happy-go-lucky priest who was a great golfer and a fine singer. In different ways, both brothers left their mark.

As far back as 1908, the Black Hand had been met with resistance by the White Hand, an Italian organization aided by Protestant churches established in the early German settlements and still functioning when the Italians moved into those neighborhoods. The White Hand opened settlement houses. Missionaries from Olivet Baptist Church at 1441 North Cleveland and from Moody Bible Institute worked the streets and gave children alternatives to the Black Hand. It was not at all unusual when I was in school in the thirties and forties to see the pastor or the clerics on the basketball courts playing ball with their teenage parishioners. Some of this influence remains today, but not enough to cement a neighborhood together in the old way. It seems that the public expects government or the police to take the place of family and religion.

Perhaps government really has become the last hope for community. In the spring of 1979, just after I had been sworn in as mayor, I noticed an increase in gang crimes in the Puerto Rican community. I called a meeting with the acting superintendent of police, Sam Nolan, who was a friend as well, and Thomas Hughes, a police commander in charge of gang crimes. Hughes seemed to feel that I could not possibly understand the nature of gang violence. There was nothing he could do to stop the crime wave, he informed me, because the gangs were retaliating against each other; the crime pattern was cyclical. If that was the case, it seemed clear to me that it was our job to break the cycle.

I asked, "Do you know who will shoot the next gang member?"

"Yes. He and his gang are holed up in a basement on Evergreen Street." He gave me the address.

"And do you know who will be shot?" He did.

I couldn't believe there was nothing we could do to stop this killing. I suggested to Hughes that he pick up the intended victim and arrange to have him visit relatives in Puerto Rico.

Hughes snapped, "There is such a thing as his constitutional rights."

I turned to Nolan and suggested that through the Police Department's community relations officer we find the name of the child's priest or minister and have him get the parents' consent to send their son to Puerto Rico for a while.

Hughes interrupted, "You don't understand. These people don't care about their kids."

I responded, "Commander, are you telling me that the parents would prefer to claim the body of their son off a slab in the morgue rather than to send him safely out of town?"

Sam interjected, "We will try to get it done, Mayor—today, if possible."

Later that afternoon, he phoned: "Mayor, the package is on an Eastern flight."

"Did the parents approve?" I asked.

"Most gratefully, Mayor."

I said, "Sam, there have to be major changes in the cavalier way these gang shootings are viewed, beginning with the transfer of that Commander."

"Well, you may get a beef on that, Mayor. Commander Hughes is from Bridgeport, and, as I understand it, he's a close friend of the Daleys."

I said, "Sam, transfer him out and put in the most sensitive but toughest policeman you have."

Thirty years earlier, the gangs would have been handled by churches and families.

In 1939, Kelly won reelection two to one. I was six and not much interested in Kelly's reelection—for my sister, Carol, had just been born. Had I been older, I still would not have cared much, for the two wards I grew up in, the 50th and the 39th, were against the machine. Sauganash adults only infrequently discussed the Democrats and then only to dismiss the machine as corrupt.

On September 3, 1939, my father called from his office: "Turn on the radio. I can hear newsboys yelling in the street!" The radio reporter confirmed my father's fear—Britain and France had declared war on Germany. At dinner that evening, the radio was the focus of our attention as reporters covered the first fighting of the war, predicting that it was only a matter of time until America joined her European allies. Our parents reassured us nervous children that we were safe, Europe was far away. The newsreel at the Saturday matinee, however, brought the war close to hand, as we saw pictures of bombed-out homes, schools, and hospitals, and orphans our age or younger roaming the streets. The national mood was still antiwar, but the government was preparing to fight.

In May 1941, New York's Mayor Fiorello La Guardia, who was director of the U.S. Office of Civil Defense (OCD), announced that Chicago had been designated a Special Defense Unit and named Kelly chairman. The Special Defense authorization came here because of Chicago's heavy industrial base. The steel mills, the railroad center, the many manufacturing companies, the shipping center on southeast Chicago's Lake Calumet Harbor—all were vital to the war effort. The Army declared Chicago a critical area and gave it a priority rating for OCD protective equipment. The city soon had air raid sirens, sandbags for the air raid shelters in the subway systems, federal allocations for special security watchmen.

Even though we were not yet at war with Germany, all the preparations going at full speed certainly made me think we soon would be. Kelly had already established the Chicago Commission on Civil Defense the previous December, so he was well ahead of mayors in the rest of the nation, having lined up 100,000 civilian volunteers, established servicemen's centers, and sponsored aluminum collection drives. Recycled aluminum could be used for military parts. The recycling of paper involved us and all the other kids in school paper drives, making us feel we were aiding the war effort. Once recycled, the paper could be reused for boxes and wrapping papers for war products. Consumer production was at a minimum. My mother missed nylon stockings and wore a rayon type, as did all women during the war. Yet I never heard anyone in Chicago complain. We knew the nylon would be used for parachutes. To me, with the vivid newsreel notions of an imaginative child, that would mean safety for a paratrooper invading Germany in the dark of night.

On Sunday, December 7, 1941, my brothers and I were playing in front of the house when Mother summoned us inside. She was not a good actress, and as she told us that the Japanese had bombed Pearl Harbor, she began to cry. Like many other Americans, I had never heard of Pearl Harbor. When I asked about it, Billy said, "That's close to California. They could be here tomorrow!" Billy was always excitable. My mother explained that the Japanese had not declared war against us, even though they had bombed the American naval ships in Pearl Harbor while the crews were still in their bunks, and most of the sailors had gone down with their ships. I felt my legs tremble. While I had expected we would go to war in Europe when the time was right, I didn't expect our sailors to be bombed without warning, while they slept. I was frightened and sad.

Suddenly I thought of my father, who had gone to a Bears game. Would he get home safely? Almost immediately, he entered the house. The attack on Pearl Harbor had been announced at the football game. For the rest of the day and half of the next, we huddled around the radio waiting for news. On December 8, we heard Roosevelt address a joint session of Congress: "Yesterday, December 7, 1941, a date that will live in infamy, the United States was suddenly and deliberately attacked by the naval and armed forces of the Empire of Japan. Over two thousand sailors died aboard the sunken ships. With the unbounding determination of our people, we will gain the inevitable triumph, so help us God."[3] I gazed around the room at my mother and brothers, Roosevelt's stentorian voice ringing in my ears. I didn't understand everything he said, but because of the strength of his voice, I was no longer afraid. In fact, I became angry that the Japanese had dared to attack us.

As my parents listened to Roosevelt's speech, my mother worried that her younger brothers would have to serve, and perhaps my father, too. Her fears were realized when both her brothers, John and Frank, enlisted. Frank went Navy and was off to the Pacific campaign. John went into the Army and on to the European campaign. Uncle Frank was a signal officer on the aircraft carrier *Yorktown.* I was too young to recall now if it was the first or second *Yorktown.* The first *Yorktown* sank after doing glorious and victorious battle for Midway Island on June 4, 1942. He had served on either the *Hornet* or the *Enterprise* intermittently, and I believe after the second *Yorktown* was commissioned, he was reassigned. Whatever the case, during a sea battle off the Marshall Islands in the Pacific, a crippled returning plane went out of control as it reached the deck of the carrier. The plane missed the landing hook and spun around on the deck, and its propeller severed my uncle's arm at the shoulder. Uncle John, much luckier, would come home unscathed.

During the war, my father, who was in charge of sheet steel allocation, often had to travel to the mills on the south side. When he worked on Saturday, Mother urged him to take the three oldest, Billy, Edward, and me, with him. She always said as we trooped out the door, "Make sure you teach them the city." The trip to the mills took about two and a half hours, and Dad did indeed teach us the city as we traveled along on our war-weary tires. The first thing he mentioned as we approached Lake Shore Drive at Foster was that North Lake Shore Drive and the Lake Shore Drive bridge had been built with WPA funds during the Depression as Roosevelt's contribution to giving people desperately needed jobs. At Lincoln Park and Fullerton Avenue, he'd point out that state funds had helped to finish the park during the Depression. I thought it was beautiful with its lagoons and wonderful zoo.

He told us how neighborhoods on the north side were changing. Many people were coming to Chicago in search of wartime jobs, so housing was at a premium. Landlords seized that opportunity to convert spacious rental apartments into smaller apartments and even rooming houses in Lincoln Park, Uptown, and Edgewater on the north side. When we drove past Potter Palmer's mansion, he recalled the development of State Street and how as a teenager he had delivered packages to the impressive mansions there. If we took Michigan Avenue out to the mills, we'd pass the smart shops, look over at Holy Name Cathedral on Chicago Avenue, and take in Cabrini Green, a housing project built with federal funds during the Depression and bursting at the seams with job seekers. Our father pointed out Navy Pier and Northwestern University's downtown campus, both being used as training centers for the Army and the Navy. As we passed the old Water Tower, I'd think of my forebears the Cranes, who had walked these streets at the time of the great fire.

We would continue south on Michigan Avenue, passing the *Tribune* building. My father told us that the *Tribune* building stood next to the site of DuSable's home. Past the Michigan Avenue bridge to Wacker Drive, my father would turn right so he could show us Heald Square, named in honor of General Heald, the general who was leading the troops and families of the first Fort Dearborn to Indiana when they were ambushed by the Potawatomi raiding party. The square itself was dedicated to the victims of the Fort Dearborn massacre.

Usually we stopped for lunch in Chinatown, Greektown, or Little Italy; none was far from the Loop. Since meat was rationed, we loved going out for lunch and savored the Greek-style lamb chops or the wonderful meatballs and spaghetti. My mother was pleased, too, for our lunches away from home saved her red meat points to use at the butcher's later in the week. After lunch, we'd go back to Michigan Avenue and past the Art Institute, the Central Library, and the Auditorium Theater, which had been turned over to the USO. Then we would turn east at Congress and back to South Shore Drive, past the Planetarium, the Field Museum, and the new Administration Building of the Park District (also built with WPA funds), past beautiful parks along winding roads and miles of lovely beaches, including Rainbow Beach Park (built with WPA funds), and the city's new south side water filtration plants.

Once past the University of Chicago, we could see the flames from the steel mills shooting high into the sky. All of the mills—U.S. Steel, Wisconsin Steel, and Inland Steel—were working at full capacity for the war effort. At Inland, my father would hurry off to his meetings, and we'd take a tour of the plant, including the roaring blast furnaces, and watch the sheet steel rolling off the lines. This steel was mostly used to make tanks, planes, and ships, but some was allotted to Pratt & Whitney on the southwest side for airplane engines.

In the southeast community where Inland Steel was located, hordes of working-class newcomers, particularly Mexicans, lived among harbors, railroad yards, and railroad repair yards. The port was lined with barges for loading Chicago's merchandise. Passenger trains were being converted to troop trains. Germans, Swedes, Croatians, Mexicans, blacks, and Irish were all working together. I saw that Carl Sandburg's words about us were true—"Hog butcher for the world," "toolmaker," "stacker of wheat," "player with railroads," and the nation's "freight handler." "Stormy, husky brawling city of the big shoulders."[4] His poem, which we often read in school, came vividly alive to me. We were the nation's breadbasket, butcher to the world from our stockyards on the southwest side, tool and die maker from the many small factories and mills around the city. And all working for peace. I was thrilled for the people of my hometown.

As we headed north toward home, we would again pass the University of Chicago. Unknown to most residents, Enrico Fermi and others were working there, exploring the nature of atomic energy. On December 2, 1942, these scientists produced the first nuclear reaction, secretly inaugurating the terror and promise of the atomic age.

On April 12, 1945, President Roosevelt died, just as it seemed that the war was coming to an end. I was terribly shaken, for Roosevelt had been President of the United States all of my life. I trusted his every word. When Vice President Harry Truman took over the office, I felt sorry for him, because he lacked the bearing and eloquence of FDR. Suddenly, history seemed to accelerate. At the end of April, Adolf Hitler committed suicide, and eight days later, Germany surrendered. Just over three months later, the first atomic bomb fell on Nagasaki. Shortly thereafter, Japan surrendered. For the first time in most of my life there would be peace throughout the world.

CHAPTER 10

Postwar Prosperity

hicago really took off after the war. Shortages quickly became a thing of the past. Nylons, antibiotics, and plastics of all kinds proliferated. We moved gratefully into a drip-dry world. Sauganash had remained sparsely populated during the war, surrounded by wooded acres and prairie, a home for wild roses, marigolds, and daisies as well as abundant wildlife, including the wild pheasant our springer spaniel, Duchess, chased through the tall prairie grass. Overnight, in the late forties, all that vanished. In its place were neat single-family housing, green sod, and evergreens.

Even so, postwar Chicago faced a tremendous housing shortage, not least the Burke family. On November 24, 1945, arrived the baby of the household, Mary Jill, making us a family of eight. As we drove off to Thanksgiving Day Mass my father announced that we must find a larger house. We had lived for five years at 6242 North Keeler Avenue, in two stories and three bedrooms. My father mentioned a call from a close friend in Winnetka. Two houses there were about to go on the market.

Most of Chicago's northern suburbs were only fifteen minutes by car from our house, but to Billy and Edward and me, Winnetka might as well have been Pittsburgh. We formed a battle plan, enlisting Mother: each of us would find a specific disabling flaw no matter what Father took us to see in Winnetka. Billy might trip on a stair; I could complain about a board moving under the carpet, or the lack of cross-ventilation, or cracks in the basement floor. I am certain that by the time we finished looking at suburban homes, my father felt he had shown us nothing but tenements. We were firm in our resolve—we'd not leave Chicago, not ever!

Fortunately, a larger home became available in Sauganash; my parents grabbed it at once. But we were the exception. Chicago's population had remained fairly static since 1940, growing only 6.6 percent in ten years. Now it exploded. By 1950, the metropolitan population stood at 5,560,000, including 3,621,000 of those within the city limits. From the end of the war on, the mayor faced a major combination of problems—a shrinking tax base, thousands of returning veterans, a tide of Southern immigrants, and little decent housing.

In addition, a steady stream of middle-class families left the city, and industry decamped as well. The lure of the suburbs was inevitable—ample and cheap land, enough for free employee parking. Shopping centers sprang up, attracting such long-lived downtown monopolies as Marshall Field's, Carson's, and Saks. The city could hardly compete with suburbs that didn't have to shoulder the costs of a big and aging city; small police and fire departments were sufficient for suburban communities. Sanitation demands were tolerable, and school systems moderately sized.

The mayor and the city council responded to Chicago's housing needs by authorizing new public housing under the Chicago Housing Authority (CHA). WPA housing in Chicago had always been a good thing, run without political interference under the strong leadership of a black woman, Elizabeth Woods. Continuing her practices as head of the CHA, she was not a favorite of the pols.

Most CHA housing was built in all-white neighborhoods. But since at least 20 percent of the returning servicemen and most of the newly arrived Southerners were black, Commissioner Woods decided that 20 percent of the available housing would go to blacks. Herein lay the seeds of fierce conflict. Where would the 20 percent be? The big blowup occurred over a targeted project near Midway Airport called Midway Homes. Residents of that area protested against this incursion of blacks into their community, some going so far as to seize the units assigned to black families. The ever political Kelly cautioned Elizabeth Woods to be more moderate in integrating communities and to limit the influx of blacks to 6 percent in keeping with the city's overall percentage of black population. But for the residents who lived near Midway Homes, even the proposed 6 percent was too much. When the first black family tried to move in, hundreds of community residents barred the way. Kelly sent four hundred police to protect them, and did so again for twenty more black families who followed.[1]

The mayor's continuing protection of blacks at Midway Homes did not ease the intimidation and harassment. He had in fact been blindsided by the housing issue. In 1943, secure in a huge victory, he had declared Chicago an "open city racially." After that, Congressman Bill Dawson, the powerful black boss of five black wards, handled all of Kelly's race relations. Now racial hatred was out of the closet. The city's battle to build scattered-site public housing in white neighborhoods began at Midway Homes, but it didn't end there. It has been waged by means of court-ordered construction in the face of community hostility for forty-five years.

When Mary Jill was born, my father drove all five of us older children down to Mercy Hospital on historic old Prairie Avenue. My mother came to the hospital window to wave to us and to hold up the new baby for us to admire. We were very excited about seeing both of them, but were terribly shocked at the ugliness of the neighborhood, filled with crumbling frame houses and sagging front porches, and the stench of rotting garbage. We had driven by Prairie Avenue and the pretty neighborhood park nearby many times, but actually to be in the community was another matter. Rusting abandoned cars and trucks littered the empty fields, and poorly clad young children played in the snow. A friend of the family had sent my mother Arthur Meeker's book *Prairie Avenue* to read during her hospital stay. As soon as my father brought it home, I devoured it. Meeker had grown up on Prairie Avenue during its grandest days—a far cry from what I was seeing. He portrayed Christmases there and the parties thrown by Marshall Field I and the rest of Chicago's elite.

As Father drove us home, we bombarded him with questions. "Well, part of this is due to poverty," he said, "and part of it is due to the war." He reminded us about Daniel Burnham's 1909 Plan for Chicago. The city had stuck to the plan under the hand of the Chicago Plan Commission. "But nobody foresaw the Depression, and no one could predict World Wars I and II, which delayed construction," he added. "I am sure that now the war is over, they will demolish all of this poor housing and replace it with new and better."

My father was prescient. Mercy Hospital had been a main fixture of Prairie Avenue during its golden days. The hospital's executives now had to make a major decision—remain in the blighted community or abandon their past for the greener pastures of the suburbs. I hoped they wouldn't leave, and fortunately the powers kept Mercy where it was. With Mercy Hospital, other south side institutions, such as Michael Reese Hospital and the Illinois Institute of Technology, along with the major businesses in the area, banded together to form the South Side Planning Board. In a public/private-sector partnership, financed partially by the New York Life Insurance Company, they created the hundred-acre Lake Meadows. Racially mixed mid-income high rises went up; Michael Reese expanded, as did IIT, all with the help of Mies van der Rohe, the great architect of the 1940s.

William Le Baron Jenney, inventor of the modern skyscraper, had replaced heavy masonry and concrete structure to build upward with wrought-iron and steel beams. Mies van de Rohe went even further, incorporating glass between steel beams. Soaring towers of glass with panoramic floor-to-ceiling views of the city stood in place of the slums. He was soon copied in most of Chicago's new high-rise residences. The creation of Lake Meadows gave the rest of the south side the necessary spurt, and for years buildings were demolished and land cleared from Lake Meadows to its almost identical twin, Prairie Shores, to the property around the University of Chicago, including Hyde Park, and Kenwood.

Slum clearance was the order of the day on the south side. Officially labeled urban renewal, this type of rehabilitation was dubbed "negro removal" by Chicago's blacks. I, like everyone else in the white middle class, I suppose, had thought that clearing away slums and substandard housing was desirable. I was in my teens, and naive. Though it seemed to me that the poor children I had seen around Mercy Hospital were getting an opportunity to move out of the old frame wooden housing and into clean and warm towers of glass, that wasn't the case. The new high rises were built only for middle-class blacks and whites. Faculty at IIT, say, or hospital staff from Michael Reese lived in these new buildings. Nor was this relocation well reported by the press. In fact, the slum clearance was praised. No one consulted the poor who were being removed. Few considered the effects on a child suddenly torn from neighborhood and friends, on a family uprooted. Profit was the motive, and it was wrong.

Slum clearance occurred on the near north side as well, west of the Gold Coast. In the North LaSalle Street redevelopment the centerpiece was the Carl Sandburg housing complex for middle- and upper-income tenants. Townhouses and high rises galloped up block after block of near north side land. Here, though, it was the private sector at work, financing the construction of the complex while the local government (using federal funds) bulldozed the buildings, cleared the land, sold it at competitive rates, and assumed the responsibility for relocating displaced residents—and again, no one noticed the devastation of the lives of those ripped from their community.

Integration did not touch us on the north side, where most neighborhoods remained stable. We did, of course, read about the upheaval of urban renewal and the housing shortage, but never evaluated the human equation. Chicago's school problems would hit closer to home.

During the Depression, Kelly had made massive cuts in the school budget; he had fired fourteen hundred qualified teachers, eliminated some of the curriculum, and cut vital programs. But, ever the wily politico, he had appointed several political influentials to teaching jobs; wanting to placate labor, he had also retained over five hundred politically appointed janitors. In reaction, Robert Maynard Hutchins, president of the University of Chicago, had lashed out, "The precipitous actions taken by the Board of Education in the summer of 1933 were based either on a complete misunderstanding of the purpose of public education, a selfish determination that its purpose shall not be fulfilled, or an ignorant belief that a system that has been wrecked can still function. The economic and social condition of Chicago will be worse for twenty-five years because of what the Board of Education has done."[2]

Even so, the schools had limped along through the end of the Depression and during the war, when thousands of blacks immigrated to Chicago in search of war-related jobs. Not only did whites resist integration in housing on the south and southwest sides, they fought it in the schools as well. Blacks, primarily limited to the south side's black belt, showed little interest in migrating to the north or northwest. In 1945, there were student strikes in the all-white schools on the south and southwest when blacks attempted to enroll. Kelly courageously stated that blacks could enroll in any school they wished—and once again he backed up his policy with a police escort. Not many blacks dared venture into white classrooms, though, and terrible overcrowding blighted the primarily black areas.

As a seventh-grader reading about these overcrowded schools, I wondered how students could learn. We were somewhat overcrowded in our private school as well, because no building materials were available during the war, but it was nothing like the segregated black schools. The press downplayed the strikes of the white students, but the hatred developing among kids my age was clear to me, and disturbing. My parents were understandably concerned. Mother said her mother always told her the "greatest sin is unkindness" and we should imagine how we would feel if we were being discriminated against because of skin color. My father was optimistic. "Once the war ends," he said, "the Board of Education will build more schools, and the children will get a good education."

But when the war was over, the National Educational Association investigated Chicago's schools and issued a gloomy report not limited to Depression and war-related situations. NEA charges struck at the heart of Kelly's abuse of the school system and censured the compliant Kelly-appointed school board. James B. McCahey, president of the school board, was a Kelly satrap, routinely appointing politically sponsored teachers to temporary positions. Once these unqualified teachers were hired, they stayed, becoming an extension of Kelly's machine. Like the precinct captains, they kicked in political contributions to the mayor's fund-raisers and cheered on cue at political gatherings. Some major Chicago textbook companies stopped supplying books to the schools because once they were awarded any contract, the mob came by for a cut of the profits. The NEA had also discovered that the school board passed over low bids for school supplies in favor of a supplier with political clout, who in turn made payoffs to committeemen and school personnel. From teachers to principals to contracts, the machine ran the schools.

As my father had predicted, it all came to a head in 1946. Citing the NEA's charges, the North Central Association threatened to withdraw accreditation of Chicago's public high schools unless the superintendent and the school board resigned and an independent board chose the future chairman and members of the new school board. Kelly, feeling the wrath of angry parents, obliged, but his exploitation of the education system would haunt many mayors to follow. I get angry, even now, when I think about the masses of uneducated children "pushed" through a system that finally collapsed in the fall of 1979, when I had been mayor for six months.

On a more positive note, Kelly built the State Street subway and finally settled the transit problem plaguing many administrations by forming the Metropolitan Transit System. He also announced plans for the Congress, the Dan Ryan, and the Kennedy expressways, but he wouldn't be around to break ground. Ward Committeeman Jacob

Arvey, favorite son of the Jewish bloc, returned home a war hero in 1946. The Democratic Central Committee, tired of Kelly and his boss rule, ousted him as party chairman and gave Arvey the job. He wouldn't be dangerous to their mayoral ambitions, because Jewish flight to the suburbs had left him without a powerful constituency.

In 1947, as I was about to graduate from elementary school, Chicagoans selected a new mayor, Martin H. Kennelly. Local politics had little appeal to me then, but national politics was a different matter. In 1948, Harry Truman would run for election. Most of my friends didn't like Truman. I did. He made me laugh when he threatened to punch a reporter in the nose for criticizing his daughter Margaret's singing voice. I enjoyed his piano playing and wisecracks, but mostly I enjoyed his spunk and admired the strength he unexpectedly revealed when he had to step into Roosevelt's shoes. In contrast to sophisticated Tom Dewey, the Republican nominee, Truman seemed appealingly down-to-earth. As the campaign moved along, political pundits predicted he was through. I didn't think so.

So it was a great shock to me one evening at the dinner table when my father announced his support for Dewey. "Dewey!" I shouted. "You can't be for Dewey!" I was only fifteen, and my father appeared taken aback by my intensity. I almost burst into tears as I scolded him for being a turncoat. I reminded him of the Depression and of all the projects a Democratic President had bestowed on Chicago—the bridges, Lake Shore Drive, housing, the eight-hour work day, the reopening of the banks, jobs for Chicagoans, the minimum wage bill.

My mother chimed in, "Don't waste your breath. Your father has gone 'big business.' He forgets what it was like for those before him, and the benefits that will help us in our old age." My mother never forgot how hard the Cranes had worked to make something of themselves. And she had seen her family sink to near poverty under the weight of medical bills generated by her mother's long illness. During the Depression, my mother put away money from her household allowance just as her mother had done. She had also taken out an insurance policy to guarantee my college education. She would take no chances.

My father had never before shown any sign of male chauvinism to me, but that evening, I thought he seemed condescending about our support of Truman. I got furious. "You'll see. Truman will win!"

Our dinners were not peaceful again until the election. I was persistent. I told my father, pointing to Dewey's self-assured smile, "The

American people won't buy this." A week before the election, when Mrs. Dewey admitted she had already picked out the curtains for the White House kitchen, I shouted, "What gall!" On election night while we waited anxiously for the returns, my father serenely played his favorite songs on the piano. Very much enjoying his apparent advantage in the political battle in our house, he struck up "The Missouri Waltz," chuckling, "That's where your candidate will be tomorrow morning, and with that, I say good night."

I stayed up for the returns. Finally, when it was undeniably clear that Truman had won, I took the stairs three at a time and snapped on the light in his bedroom. "Get up! Get up! There's an emergency downstairs!"

Half asleep, he lumbered down the steps behind me. By the time he made it to the living room, I was already at the keys, playing "The Missouri Waltz." He didn't get it. My mother was laughing as he turned to her and asked, "What's the emergency? Why did she get me out of bed?"

My mother said, "The people spoke, Bill. Truman was reelected."

In my victorious excitement, I was now playing "God Bless America." My father was stunned.

The Burkes were a large family, and on Sundays we still gathered for dinner at Grandmother Burke's home. Uncles Joe and Ed were always there. Joe had been assigned to St. Margaret of Scotland's Church on Chicago's south side, and Uncle Ed had risen to chancellor of the archdiocese under Samuel Cardinal Stritch. My grandparents' place was the only home my uncles had outside of their parish rectories. Both grandparents encouraged the two priests to bring their friends home with them on Sundays—and they did. It was exciting to listen to the various priests talk about their parishes and the special customs of each unique neighborhood, and fun to read in the papers about their progress up the ecclesiastical ladder.

A lot of the priests who came to our family dinners were becoming pastors and bishops. The Reverend Raymond Hillinger, the pastor of Angel Guardian Orphanage, became Bishop Hillinger, but he remained like a beloved uncle to us when we'd sit around in his quarters and talk over hot chocolate. So, too, with Bishop Cletus O'Donnell and Archbishop O'Brien. The cardinal's residence was a different matter, however; we had not grown up with him. When Uncle Ed took us for visits there, I would be half frozen with awe. Cardinal Stritch knew it and tried very hard to put me at ease. He had the gift of kindness. I never realized, however, that any of this was special—the seat of Chicago Catholicism was just part of Uncle Ed's territory as chancellor.

Over the years, as I listened to Uncle Ed's tales of diocesan politics, I came to see that church bureaucracy was not so different from City Hall in its ethnic groupings—Italian priests to Italian parishes, Polish priests to Polish parishes, right on up the line to bishops. Nor was the church hierarchy free of power struggles. The chancellor and vicar-general of the archdiocese were powerful, for both had the cardinal's ear. When Ed was chancellor, Monsignor George Casey was vicar-general; they had formed their own cliques and avidly competed against each other. Cardinal Stritch was very wise in the matter. He took the best advice that each had to offer. For the competitors, there was often much more at stake in their battles than merely choosing monsignors. The contracts for the construction of all the schools and churches as well as the insurance policies on all church property were awarded by the executive board, which thereby could attract sizable contributions. Nor was it unusual at Christmas for a wealthy contractor to make a personal gift to a priest or a religious: "Please, Father, say one hundred high masses for all the deceased members of my family." Such tokens of esteem were more than acceptable in the church. After all, priestly salaries were not lavish.

Thirty years later, during my time as mayor, John Patrick Cody was the Chicago archbishop. Pope John XXIII had called Vatican II into session in the early sixties "to open the windows, and air new policies." Some changes were fairly superficial. Catholics might now eat meat on Fridays, and altars were turned so that the priest faced the people as he said Mass. It was not trivial, I thought, that Mass would no longer be said in Latin, but in the native tongue—and I didn't like it. I had enjoyed being able to attend Mass in foreign countries and always understand the words because of the universality of Latin. Also, nuns were no longer required to wear religious habits and began wearing lay clothes. Sunday after Sunday I would leave church astounded, and occasionally dismayed, as the old customs were ripped away.

For a while there were two churches—old and new. Cody was definitely "Old Church." It was not uncommon to read about the conflicts between the young priests and laity over his refusal to share power, and many viewed him as autocratic and domineering. I didn't share this sentiment. To me, the title "cardinal" also meant "Prince of the Church." The glittering robes and the cardinal's ring were marks of royalty. That was ending, and the cardinal didn't accept it well. Even the financial records of the church listed the cardinal as "Corporation." He totally and singly controlled church finances, answering to no one. Even today, if one is injured on church property, say, and files a lawsuit, the action is against the Cardinal as a Corporation Sole.

In March 1981, a friend called me in City Hall to say that the *Chicago Sun Times*, then under the editorship of James Hoge, meant to publish a series exploring the personal and bureaucratic life of Cardinal Cody. Included would be such matters as his award of a church insurance contract to the son of a female friend in St. Louis, the cost of the cardinal's early home, a slew of his personal expenditures, and even the costs of redecorating his official residence. The series would urge a federal investigation into the cardinal's handling of church money. Hoge, according to my friend, had said, "We've really got him—he can't survive this."

At this point, the cardinal was quite ill and suffered attacks of senility. The exposé would do no one any good, and I doubted that the federal government had jurisdiction. Besides, the revelations were not shattering. Relatively little money was involved. My friend suggested, "Why don't you call Hoge? Remind him he'd breaking the story a few days before St. Patrick's Day, and with the cardinal leading the parade, one million Catholics would be furious at the *Sun Times*." I did call Hoge, mentioned the parade, and added, "Surely you know church funds are separate, and even if the rules of the game have changed, what is the good of destroying a dying old man?" Hoge was interested in only one thing—how I had learned about the story. I asked him again if he knew the cardinal was dying, but he didn't answer. Then I gritted my teeth and called a high-ranking priest from Holy Name and asked him over to my office. I despised having to inform the priest about the potential scandal. I didn't want to be "in the know" about any of it, but I thought the church should be forewarned—hence, forearmed.

My term as mayor had been preceded by an era of attacks against the Establishment—business, government, institutions, professions. And now the church. I had a good idea the newspaper account would be filled with innuendos, half-truths, and a few verifiable facts. It would be destructive and demoralizing. The priest sat across the desk and heard me out. "Well," he said, "some inquiries were made a while ago, but they amounted to nothing." I repeated what I had been told about the specific allegations in the series and told him about Hoge's alleged threat. Marshall Field v was the publisher of the *Sun Times*, and Cardinal Cody had presided at his wedding. The priest asked if he should call Marshall. I thought so. No other choices seemed viable. I do not know whether or not the priest ever talked to the publisher, but the *Sun Times* series did not run until several months later.

At that point, the U.S. attorney, Dan Webb, had no choice but to investigate. The government's response was key to the series, as it lent credibility to the accusations and, of course, sold more newspapers. The cardinal quickly became a subject of ridicule, and people began dropping buttons into the collection box instead of money. The church hired top-rate lawyers, and the investigation proceeded. The aging cardinal, hospitalized twice during the investigation, could hardly walk during this ordeal.

Several months later, on vacation in Palm Springs, I turned on the news and heard speculation that Cardinal Cody would soon be indicted. I was so outraged I decided to call Ed Meese, then U.S. Attorney General. As mayor, I had had many conversations with Meese about governmental matters when he was President Reagan's Chief of Staff. Improper or not, I phoned him, explaining that I was not asking a political favor or trying to tamper with any proceedings of the Justice Department. As a private citizen, I was incensed. What had happened to the respected rules of the federal investigation and the secrecy of the grand jury proceedings? As both a Catholic and a mayor, I abhorred the harm caused by the leaked stories.

Meese replied that no U.S. attorney relished leaked stories about indicting a cardinal. I was sure Dan Webb, the U.S. attorney in Chicago, wasn't leaking the stories, but somewhere in his office an investigator was currying favor with the press. The conversation ended with my urging that the secrecy of the grand jury be honored.

The *Sun Times* received the National Headlines Award for its series April 1; Cardinal Cody died on April 25. As I stood near graveside during his funeral, I realized how greatly times had changed. How different from the days when no one would have dared savage so cruelly a dying cardinal. Little came of all the hoopla, anyhow. The grand jury returned no indictments. The case was closed on May 26.

In 1951, though, when I was a college freshman at St. Mary of the Woods in Terre Haute, Indiana, I would not have believed that an archbishop would be tainted by local politics, which I didn't follow very closely. National politics interested me much more than Chicago's. During the summer between my freshman and sophomore years, the city hosted the Democratic National Convention at the newly refurbished International Amphitheatre in the old stockyards area. Our neighbor Andy Frain owned an ushering service that handled security, and the Frains invited us to share their choice convention box, situated only fifty feet from the stage. My Republican-leaning father was not eager to go, but I was, despite being stitched up from a recent appendectomy. As the divisive 1952 convention drew to a close, President Truman appeared in an attempt to unify the party and rally us around Adlai Stevenson, former Illinois governor and now the presidential nominee. When Truman started across the stage, I jumped unthinkingly to my feet, punched my fist in the air, and shouted, "Give 'em hell, Harry!" Had this raucous voice been inside me always? Truman looked up, smiled, and waved. I had startled everyone around us, including my very proper father. I felt a yank on my skirt (a yank familiar to me over the years) as my mother said, "Sit down, you'll split your stitches."

That fall I transferred to Barat College of the Sacred Heart College for my sophomore year, because I missed my family and the big city. Barat was in Lake Forest, only half an hour from home. My major was premed, and I fully expected to become a doctor. The following year, though, I met Bill Byrne, a six-foot-two, blue-eyed, blond Notre Dame junior majoring in the Great Books Program in preparation for law school. We dated almost steadily from our first meeting. By senior year, I was soft on medical school and sweet on Bill. We planned to marry. In the early fifties, American boys were almost certain to be drafted. Most at Notre Dame, including Bill, had joined the ROTC or the NROTC so they could finish their schooling and graduate as officers. All faced three years of service after graduation. If I entered medical school in Chicago, I might not be able to finish—for marriage to a serviceman usually meant a nomadic life.

Bill and I graduated from college in 1955 and were married on New Year's Eve, 1956, in a very Catholic wedding involving two bishops, scores of monsignors, and the cathedral chorus. Uncle Ed officiated. Many of our friends were officers in the Navy and the wedding was military, crossed swords and all. Our first home was in Pensacola, Florida, where Bill was in basic flight training school to become a Marine pilot. From there we went to Kingsville, Texas, for Bill's jet training.

In Kingsville the reality of Bill's line of work sank in. Jet flying

My first husband, Bill Byrne, in Sorin Hall at the University of Notre Dame, 1953.

was in its infancy and quite dangerous. One day in 1957, Bill had just left home after having lunch—in fact, his car had barely pulled away—when I heard a terrible bang and then a noise that was surely an explosion, followed by the wail of sirens, many sirens. I ran outside, but, oddly, none of my neighbors joined me. Then it hit home. I was new here, but everyone else on this base knew what a jet crash sounded like. I sat down on a crate—we were still unpacking—and thought to myself, Someone on this base is going to get a phone call that will change her life. Not I, for Bill had just left, but waves of nausea kept rushing through me. I soon learned to control my fear, but every time I heard a jet crash, I grew sick at heart, praying that my phone wouldn't ring.

When I was mayor, the bleak prospect of having to make that kind of call lurked just beneath the surface every day. The duty I most hated was sitting with the kin of a slain police officer or a fallen firefighter. I knew too well what lay in store for them. First the radio news bulletin, then waiting for the call or for someone from the district to come to your door with the terrible news, to comfort the families as they demanded to know how, where, and the most difficult question of all—why. Then, as friends in the Police or Fire Department showed up, I noticed the sense of solidarity and strength the friends in uniform imparted to the bereaved. I'd watch their faces as they struggled with the shock of their loss. Usually I arrived at the hospital before the family did. Wives and children would rush in, hoping that the worst wouldn't be true. I could feel their grief. Often, particularly in the case of a policeman, the death was brutal. Numbed, families were usually beyond any comfort I could give. Soon they'd realize that nothing remained to hold them at the hospital, and they would go home.

A mayor has great power, but she or he cannot safeguard those who safeguard the city. In 1981, Chicago lost three young police officers, victims of brutal murders within five days of each other. Sitting with the three families had drained me, and the deaths were, of course, very demoralizing to the eleven thousand police officers and their families. I knew that the New York Police Department's Emerald Society had a bagpipe band, so we arranged through Mayor Koch's office and the Chicago Police Department's Emerald Society, at no taxpayer expense, to bring in the New York bagpipers. We also contracted for a fine group of Chicago artists, Franz Benteler and His Royal Strings, to play during the funeral Masses. Between the softness of the violins and the strength of the bagpipes, a quiet dignity and pride for the fallen officers and their families filled the church. For all future police and civic events, we established our own bagpipe band in the Chicago Police Department's Emerald Society. It was my personal way of saying thank you to the finest police department in America.

After nearly three years of marriage, I had lost a baby and given birth to a baby girl, Katharine Crane Byrne, named after my mother and grandmother Crane. Bill and I had been transferred many times—from Pensacola to Kingsville to Miami, finally landing in Cherry Point, North Carolina, in 1958. Bill had been in the Marines for four years and was scheduled for release in June 1959. We longed to settle down. My mother fell ill in May, and I flew up to Chicago with infant Kathy to be with her until she recovered from surgery. Bill had to log his cross-country flight time for the month and decided to join me in Chicago the last weekend in May. We would hunt for a house, and Bill would look over law schools. Mother had been home only two days, but she had outdone herself, baking a cake and cooking Bill's favorite dinner. The weather was turbulent on the day of his flight.

Bill, first row, first left, with his training squadron in Pensacola, Florida, 1956.

Bill phoned to say he would not fly until early the next morning if he didn't get weather clearance within the hour. A heavy fog lay over Chicago that night, and I went to sleep early in my old room, anticipating the trip to the airport.

Very early, around five, the phone rang in my parents' bedroom down the hall and awakened me. I remember saying to myself, "I knew he would get into Glenview early but not this early." I looked out, and it was a beautiful, sunny day, a wonderful contrast with the rain and fog we'd had the day before. I grabbed my robe and started down the long hall corridor to talk to Bill. Then I saw my father coming out of his bedroom. He just looked at me and went on past, tears welling in his eyes.

"Oh, Dolly, Dolly, I'm so sorry," he said, using the nickname he had invented for me when I was a baby.

Uneasy, I went into the room and saw Mother sitting up in bed, staring straight ahead. I just walked over to the phone, thinking I should pick it up. It was beginning to dawn on me that something was terribly wrong. I saw that the phone was back in its cradle. My mother was beginning to cry.

"Oh my God, my God," she said. "I would easily have traded places this past week with Bill."

I was not going to accept this. I grabbed the phone anyway, but there was no one there. I sat down on the edge of their bed, looking at my parents, and I felt a wave of great anger because I still did not know what had happened to my life.

"Where is he?" I screamed to my father. "Is he hurt?"

My father shook his head. He could only mouth the words, "He's dead. It happened at twelve-thirteen last night, right outside Glenview."

I was numb. I turned to Mother and said, "Please, Mom, don't be crying. I'm going to need your help. This is going to be hard to get through."

I went out into the hallway. I felt like crying, but my mind was racing, trying to digest a thousand things. Had it been painful? Had he known? Where was he lying? It was unbearably sad that my Bill had died alone. I went to my bedroom and knelt down by the window to pray. It was such a beautiful day . . . if only he had waited. After I had prayed for the repose of his soul and asked God for strength to endure this loss, I turned, still on my knees, to look at Kathy in her crib.

She had loved him in her few months of life. They had played great games together. She couldn't say "Dada," but she'd managed a version of his name that tickled him: "Bull." Her hands were open and relaxed in sleep. Well, I thought, you went to bed with a father and will wake up with your life changed. Those were the days of male identity to everything. At school, she'd be expected to have a father. She'd be whispered about with pity.

I put my head on the slats of the crib and held on for dear life. In the back of my mind came this thought: If you don't give her an identity of which she can be proud, she will have none.

I knew what I had to do. I had to be both mother and father and achieve a name for her. Of course, nothing so logical was clear at the time; the thoughts came and went, started and stopped. The phone rang. A Navy officer wanted to express his sympathy. I leaned down and kissed my sleeping Kathy. This is not going to touch her, I thought. No matter what, this grief will not touch her. I will make sure of that.

Bill was buried with honor, as only the military can muster. I sleepwalked through it, supported by the Marine Corps squadron and of course my own family.

I was twenty-five and a widow. I had never really known any deep hurt—until then.

CHAPTER 11

The King Maker

When I left Chicago in 1956 to live at various Marine bases across the country, I was amazed to find that the city's image was rather tarnished. Typically, people showered me with cracks about Al Capone, political bosses, and racism. The people I met through the service seemed to know more about the mob and the machine than I did. I was routinely defensive, responding that I'd never met a gangster in my life and knew little about Daley, who'd become mayor only months before I left home.

Clearly, Richard J. Daley, though a newcomer on the national political scene, was already famous, if not notorious.

His had been a particularly vicious campaign, from the primary through the general election. When Daley, chairman of the Democratic Party for only a year, decided to challenge the incumbent mayor, Kennelly, many Democrats along the northern lakefront and northwest side were skeptical of this son of Bridgeport. They didn't want a return to Ed Kelly's style of bossism. There was also concern that allowing Daley to be both county chairman and mayoral candidate concentrated too much power in one man, one area, and one breed of politician. Daley tried to ease the suspicion by pledging that if elected he would resign as county chairman, a promise he would never honor. He defeated Kennelly in the primary.

In the general election, Daley was blistered by Robert Merriam, the Republican candidate, who repeated the charges of bossism and foresaw a "wide-open city." Merriam linked the entire seamy history of the machine to Daley, charging that prostitution would again thrive and gambling flourish. Daley repeated his pledge to resign as chairman if elected mayor and began trotting out pictures of himself and his large family, declaring that as a family man he could never wink at vice and crime. Stories began to appear in the media portraying Daley as a daily communicant—not a bad thing in a Catholic city where the church was still a law unto itself, as powerful as any local administration. The machine catered to it and all other religious institutions. If, for example, there was a blizzard, the church property, parking lots, and streets received the same swift and efficient snow removal services as hospitals, police stations, and fire stations. It wouldn't be politically expedient to alienate hundreds of worshipers arriving for church services only to find themselves stuck on snow-clogged streets or unable to park. The police and fire captains made periodic courtesy calls to pastors, rabbis, and preachers. Major policy decisions at City Hall, such as exemption from water taxes, benefited churches and charitable institutions. Church zoning approvals and construction inspections were rushed through official channels. Daley had all these favors in the bank.

The Democratic nominee also spattered dirt. Playing upon white fears of black encroachment on the south and southwest sides, the family man frequently reminded residents that Merriam was a divorced "left-winger" married to "a part Negro."[1] It was a nasty campaign.

I came home for good in 1959. Because I wanted Kathy to have a father figure in her life, we moved back in with my parents in Sauganash. Friends of mine resented the credit Mayor Daley was taking for the Loop's ongoing downtown building boom. It would have happened, they'd say, no matter who turned the first spadeful of dirt at ground-breaking. And they were right, for the whole country was booming in the early and middle fifties.

Shortly after returning home, I had occasion to visit a dentist at the University of Illinois Dental School on the near west side. I was shocked to see seven high-rise CHA housing structures there, a complex stretching for ten blocks. The near west side had always been a melting pot—principally Italian, but with stable settlements of Mexicans and blacks. Many a time during college Bill and I had gone with college friends to Little Italy for pasta. No more. The Congress and Eisenhower expressways had cut through parts of the west side. Hospitals had gobbled up even more land through expansion.

My father couldn't understand my surprise. "It's going on all over the south side—urban renewal keeps taking away the old housing." Cabrini Green had also expanded by two thousand units the year before, most of it high-rise, just like the new high rises that replaced the slum housing we'd seen at Mercy Hospital years before. My friends my age treated Daley's massive public housing and urban renewal with scorn, feeling he didn't care what neighborhoods he destroyed, because he was just looking for kickbacks from contractors, road builders, and architects. I wasn't putting too much stock in their opinions about Daley—most of them had moved to the northern suburbs. It seemed easy enough to criticize from afar. They had turned their backs on Chicago and were now comfortable Republicans anyway.

There wasn't much coverage on TV or in the newspaper of what life was like in public housing, and we didn't hear the views of the tenants. I think the general feeling in Chicago was something like "Well, they are better off than they were in the old, dilapidated housing." It took years to learn the truth. The majority of tenants had come up from the rural South; living packed together eighteen stories up in the sky was unnatural and even frightening. Children raised in crowded apartments had no room to breathe, study, or let off steam. No longer could they run out the back door into a grassy yard to play—they had to take elevators (much too small and too few for the number of users) to get outside.

There had long been talk of turning Navy Pier into a port for passenger steamship lines; now, instead, a new Port of Chicago stood ready to receive cargo ships from all over the world on the southeast side. Midway Airport, long too small to handle area traffic, had yielded to the newer O'Hare International Airport, already the busiest airport in the world. Modernization had taken its toll on the meat-packing industry. Cudahy had closed the doors in its Back of the Yards operation before I left; but by 1959, Armour had closed as well. It had become cheaper for packing plants to go to the cattle—that is, to smaller pig and cattle towns—and ship packaged meat directly across the nation. The railroads were still going strong, but only because of "piggyback" shipping, a method Chicago pioneered. No longer Carl Sandburg's hog butcher to the world, we still produced one-quarter of the nation's steel and iron, and over a quarter of its radio and TV sets. But a new word now described Chicago—"metropolitan." Many of these newer industries had located in the suburbs.

To celebrate the opening of the St. Lawrence Seaway, which

linked the Great Lakes to the Atlantic Ocean via Canada, Chicago planned a state dinner for Queen Elizabeth in June of 1959. The British monarch's visit posed ironies. Most of Chicago's Irish took pride that a Back of the Yards son of Bridgeport could greet her as an equal, but others considered any fraternization with the British as near betrayal. The *Britannia* dropped anchor off Monroe Harbor, and amid a twenty-one-gun salute, sirens, and water showers from fireboats, the Queen stepped into Chicago. Mayor Daley came of age politically with her visit, which went off without a hitch and wiped away his image as a run-of-the-mill ward boss.

While Daley catered to big business, reducing tax assessments by 8 percent during his first term, he also increased police and fire protection and instituted a street-lighting program in the neighborhoods. Pleased and feeling a greater sense of security, voters responded overwhelmingly in Daley's 1959 reelection bid. When I asked my Republican friends how such a supposedly incompetent mayor could carry forty-nine of fifty wards in his 1959 reelection campaign, they blamed vote fraud in the machine wards. And, they'd go on, since anti-Daley voters realized they couldn't beat the corrupt machine, they simply didn't bother to vote. Indeed, voter turnout *was* down at least 9 percent since Daley's first election in 1955.[2] But that's how it always was for Daley—people either liked him for his solid nuts-and-bolts government or loathed him as a corrupt machine boss.

At any rate, the machine had never been stronger. Daley, mayor and chairman, held the jobs of over forty thousand city workers in the palm of his hand. He and such clout-heavy committeemen as Thomas Keane, finance chairman of the city council, John D'Arco, boss of the 1st Ward under Daley, Parky Cullerton, assessor and northwest side committeeman, and Congressman Bill Dawson, committeeman and boss of the south side, decided the fate of all the political offices and jobs in their realm. They chose all candidates for sheriff, assessor, county clerk, state's attorney, the Metropolitan Sanitary District, and the judiciary—all the way up to the slate of candidates for the justices of the supreme court of Illinois. The Democratic labor unions were docile, and most of big business, as during the Kelly and Cermak regimes, worked for the straight Daley ticket.

Benjamin Adamowski, who had opposed Daley in 1955, was the only fly in the ointment. A prominent leader of Chicago's Poles, he could have been eased in as a powerful committeeman under Daley. But he bolted the party in 1956, ran for state's attorney on the Republican ticket—and won. Here was a perfect example of the cohesiveness of Chicago ethnic groupings. The Democratic Poles deserted the party to vote for one of their own—even though it was the office that machine Democrats most hate to lose control of. The state's attorney of Cook County can investigate (or not) just about anything, and an ambitious incumbent in the post can use the media and the office's power to rise politically.

Naturally, the machine bosses never forgave Adamowski. He had been one of them—a ward boss, a member of the state legislature, a city council member. Not only had he bolted the family, he had beaten the Daley machine at ground zero in a Cook County race.

Adamowski battled royally with Mayor Daley during his three years as state's attorney and well into the 1959 mayoral election. Many in Chicago believed Daley wanted Adamowski defeated for reelection more than he wanted John Kennedy to win the presidency. A rival as state's attorney can be a loose cannon. (I know this well, for Daley's son, Richard, once he became state's attorney, readily attracted headlines for investigations of my administration. In politics, the procedure is referred to as "dirtying someone up." Daley convened at least five grand jury investigations of my administration in his first two-year period as state's attorney—before announcing his own candidacy for mayor in 1983. No one in my administration was ever convicted, but that sort of news never catches up with the headlines.)

While all this was going on, I knew little about such power politics, for I had hopped aboard the John F. Kennedy bandwagon. In the spring of 1960, I was moved by Kennedy's radio speech sensitively acknowledging the grief of families who, in one "peacetime" service activity or another, had lost husbands and sons in the Cold War. They were indeed soldiers and heroes, he said. I agreed. I had always known my Bill was a hero. Then Kennedy challenged us to aspire toward a better world, to follow him across a "new frontier." I felt inspired to take that walk. My sister Carol headed the Young Democrats at Barat College. This was not a particularly significant position, because most Barat students were Republican. In fact, Carol's Young Democrats numbered only ten, but she was an avid Jack Kennedy supporter and through a close friend met Jack's sister, Eunice Shriver. Her husband, Sarge Shriver, *was* significant—president of the Kennedy-owned Merchandise Mart and president of the school board. Shriver also served on many business boards, including some my father had been named to.

Carol spent her pre-convention Saturdays down at the Merchandise Mart working on the fledgling Kennedy campaign. There was excitement in our household when Kennedy won the nomination. My father, though not particularly enamored of Kennedy at first, was practically steamrollered into supporting him by my mother, and our dinner-table conversations became quite heated. Finally, my mother asked him how he could forget the prejudice and hatred Al Smith had endured in his run for presidency. Perhaps her thinking was colored a bit by the stories she had heard from Great-Aunt Laura about the Know-Nothing movement and the ridicule the Irish Catholic immigrants had withstood. Whatever the case, her punchline was "Bill, you can have all the money in the world, and play your golf with your business friends at the best country clubs—but until this resentment of Irish Catholics is gone forever, you'll be a second-class citizen, and so will all our children and grandchildren. Do what you want!"

My father finally came around, volunteering for the Illinois Businessmen for Kennedy Committee, and Carol was appointed assistant executive director of the Kennedy headquarters in Chicago, a paid staff position. The Kennedys had been canny. They wanted to sustain the momentum following the convention, and with help of the Merchandise Mart's staff, they opened the new headquarters the very day after the nomination at 333 North Michigan Avenue, a building that stood where old Fort Dearborn had guarded Chicago in the eighteenth century. Machine democrats did not work at Kennedy's headquarters. In fact, his office was set up specifically to lure independents and others who would have nothing to do with the Daley crowd.

The Merchandise Mart served as a clearinghouse for six Midwestern states and all of their local Kennedy headquarters. Shriver was loosely in charge of the Kennedy effort in the Midwest, and Bobby Kennedy ran the entire national campaign, along with Larry O'Brien and Kenny O'Donnell. They functioned out of Washington but were responsible for all local offices. As the Kennedy effort moved into full swing, word reached Chicago staffers that Mayor Daley was not pleased to find a Kennedy headquarters in *his* city. And word reached John Kennedy in Washington that there was to be *one* Democratic organization in Chicago, not two. The campaign would be directed by the mayor, not a bunch of independent swells. Seeking to prevent a rift, Bobby Kennedy and O'Donnell flew to Chicago to explain to the mayor the strategic importance of a separate Kennedy headquarters in Chicago. Daley let them cool their heels for five days before agreeing to see them.

Rumors mounted at headquarters that the office would probably be closed, and that Bobby Kennedy, not known for patience, was calling Daley everything under the sun. According to O'Donnell, however, the meeting was cordial, but the mayor stood firm: no headquarters but Democratic headquarters, no campaign chairman but Daley. Bobby was intolerant of bosses and fumed in private. O'Donnell shared his bias, but realized Jack couldn't win in Illinois without Daley. The matter was resolved only when Joseph P. Kennedy, patriarch of the clan, appeared on the scene and convinced Daley that it would be a terrible public relations blunder to close the headquarters. Kennedy would look like a tool of the bosses. Also, there was a headquarters in every other major city; it could look as if Chicago were being slighted. Daley compromised. The headquarters would remain on Michigan Avenue and he would control *all* campaign events. In short, nothing could be planned in Chicago without his permission.

Carol was still a college student, despite her ground-floor position in the Kennedy campaign. She begged my parents for permission to take off fall semester and continue to work through the entire campaign—but to no avail. My parents insisted she stay in step and graduate with her class. Carol turned to me to take her place. I was immediately tempted, but I had never before left Kathy for long periods during the day. (There weren't as many working mothers in 1960 as there are today, but I imagine the feeling is still the same, one of guilt and anxiety at the thought of not being available if your child needs you.) It was a hard decision. But my mother, eager for me to rejoin the outside world, insisted that a woman who had raised six children could certainly take care of Kathy while I was off at work.

And so I entered politics in mid-August of 1960. I had a fervent desire to see Kennedy win, and an even deeper belief that he would. I was inexperienced but dedicated, and I soon learned that most of us campaign workers were in the same boat. Shortly after I started, headquarters buzzed with the news that JFK was coming to Chicago. Kennedy, Daley, and Congressman William Dawson, who always attracted huge black crowds, would tour several new housing projects on the south side, then the nominee would drop in on his headquarters. The visit was scheduled for Saturday, so I brought two-year-old Kathy with me.

As Kennedy went through the line at campaign headquarters shaking hands, he stopped and looked down at my daughter. She was wearing a pair of Junior Navy wings that Bill had pinned to her diaper when she was born. Jack commented on the wings. To avoid an awkward situation for Kathy, my mother quickly explained that her father had gone to heaven. Kennedy stroked Kathy's head and said, "Isn't that nice for you, Kathy, to have a daddy in heaven?"

There followed a "photo opportunity"; the committee chairmen sat on a couch flanking Kennedy. He signaled me to bring Kathy over, and when he sat her upon his lap, the flashbulbs popped. That photo appeared in all the Chicago papers, with accompanying stories about how Kennedy hated the cliché of politicians kissing babies, but had broken that tradition in Chicago. On Monday morning, there was a glossy of the photo on my desk with a note attached from the communications director of the Kennedy campaign: "Kennedy usually doesn't go for this stuff, but he held the *Caroline* [his plane] an extra half hour to get the picture and Kennedy authorized it to be released to the press." Friends in the service sent me copies from the *Stars and Stripes*. Even the *Bridgeport News* ran the shot. Many staffers felt that Kennedy too rarely showed emotion, so this was good politics. How clever to be photographed with the child of a dead Marine officer! But I had seen the compassionate look in his eyes when he understood that Kathy's father was dead.

Daley's antagonism toward our headquarters and overseer Sarge Shriver did not abate. A dispute arose, for instance, over our plan to establish a speakers bureau. Most campaigns have such a group of civic and political leaders ready to stump various constituencies for the candidate. Daley was decidedly against the idea, however, and hit the ceiling when he learned that Sarge had appointed Stephen A. Mitchell, former national chairman of the Democratic Party and an ardent Stevenson supporter, to head it. Earlier in the year, Mitchell, who was definitely from the liberal reform wing of the party, had run for governor in the Democratic primary against Daley's candidate, Otto Kerner, a former judge who happened to be Cermak's son-in-law. Mitchell's campaign had been aimed squarely at machine politics, and Kerner had trounced him.

Matt Danaher, Daley's chief of patronage, called headquarters about the Mitchell appointment: "Daley is absolutely livid. He is blue with rage. You people are committing suicide. Tell Sarge to drop that name."

Now Sarge turned blue with rage. His honor was at stake, and he would not go back on his word. He roared that he was sick of Daley's tirades.

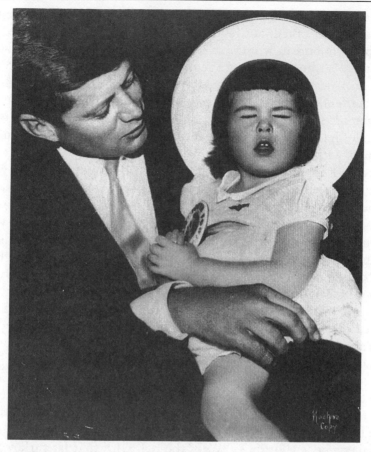

An inspiring moment in my young adult life, when candidate John F. Kennedy was photographed with my daughter Kathy following the jet crash that took the life of my husband and Kathy's father, Marine officer William Patrick Byrne. There began my walk across Kennedy's New Frontier.

The furor boiled for three days. Finally, Danaher called again: "Daley says to put Mitchell's name in the wastebasket today or there will be no further cooperation between Democratic Party headquarters and Kennedy headquarters."

Danaher was also talking to O'Donnell, who informed Bobby, who in turn flew to Chicago to mediate the dispute. Once again the nominee's brother had to cool his heels for several days waiting for Daley to see him. Finally, Bobby and Daley worked out a solution—on the mayor's terms—that succeeded in avoiding public embarrassment. Mitchell wasn't fired, but Kennedy headquarters simply decided that the speakers bureau would have to be canceled because of a lack of resources. Without a bureau, there could, of course, be no chairman.

It was with some amusement that I watched Kennedy's out-of-town staffers, all prominent men in their own right, plea for time with Daley in order to pay a courtesy call. But Daley would never see them. Principles had been established: the boss speaks only to the candidate and rules with an iron fist.

Joseph Kennedy was an exception. Still, although he always got in to see Daley the very day of his arrival, the senior Kennedy stayed behind the scenes, for polling indicated that a sizable slice of the electorate was put off by him. It was never public knowledge when Joseph Kennedy came to town or met with Daley. That kind of information would give too much credence to talk of JFK's debt to back-room political deals and a certain party boss. I liked Joe Kennedy. He never talked politics, only family. He seemed bemused that Jack, who had never expressed any interest in politics until Joe Jr. died, had entered politics at all. "Jack was such a shy kid," his father would say, "always reading books."

A few weeks before the election, Jack Kennedy himself flew in for a rally. His advance men arrived a week before to work out the logistics—the motorcade, press coverage, strategy for organizing a crowd. This team's leader, a politician from Massachusetts, called Daley's office to coordinate. Of course, his phone call was not returned. After three days, he was furious: "Well, the hell with that fat turkey Irishman. I was sent here to do a job, and I'm going to do it." He made plans for Kennedy to land at O'Hare Military Air Base, printed fliers announcing the time of the Senator's arrival, organized volunteers to distribute the fliers, and hired sound trucks to get the message out into the neighborhoods.

As soon as the fliers hit the streets, one landed on Daley's desk in the party chairman's headquarters at the Sherman Hotel. One of the mayor's political secretaries, Mary Mullen, promptly called us: "The mayor doesn't want Kennedy to land at O'Hare, he wants to welcome him at Meigs Airport on the lakefront in downtown Chicago." We explained that thousands of fliers were in circulation; sound trucks were out on the streets. There was *no* way to change airports. She persisted: "Cancel your event at O'Hare. The Senator will land at Meigs." Civil war threatened. Again, Danaher called O'Donnell to complain about the upstarts at Kennedy headquarters.

I don't think anyone at headquarters really cared where Kennedy's plane landed. It just seemed so ridiculous to be overruled once the public had been informed. O'Donnell explained the situation to Senator Kennedy, who ducked, saying, "Let the pilot decide." The pilot chose O'Hare, citing generally poor weather conditions and fog along the late in late fall.

That was the last straw for Daley. He acted as if his municipal airport were being attacked and his civic pride challenged. He called our office himself: "I don't care what the pilot says, the best engineers in the world built Meigs Airport. It is a perfectly safe airstrip and Kennedy will land at Meigs."

At headquarters, we distributed the VIP credentials that listed O'Hare, and the machine geared up for its welcome at Meigs. I happened to work late on Friday evening before the Sunday event. Answering the phone, I was surprised to hear Joseph Kennedy's voice. He wanted to know whether the airport contretemps had been resolved. I said no. He needed to hear no more. As I left headquarters, I had no idea where the Senator would actually land. On Saturday, I received a telegram from Mayor Daley inviting me to welcome Senator Kennedy at Meigs. I was instructed to bring my telegram with me. This was puzzling. Neither Mayor Daley nor his staff knew me. They must have got my name through our headquarters.

Sunday afternoon my mother, Kathy, and I drove down to Meigs. Using my telegram as a passport through police control points, we were led to a VIP room at Meigs, a very crowded and smoky room filled with machine politicians who, to judge from their comments, were there only because they had been summoned by "Buddha." Buddha, I learned, was of course the insiders' epithet for Daley. I understood that Kennedy couldn't risk alienating Daley, but I was disappointed that he'd apparently caved in. Suddenly, loudspeakers blared, "The Senator's aircraft is about to touch down. Won't you join the Senator and Mayor Daley on the reviewing stand." We filed out and up onto the temporary reviewing stand. Before us was Daley's crowd, some 25,000 people carrying Kennedy signs and waiting for the plane to land. Instead, three helicopters appeared over Grant Park. As they swooped lower, I spotted Kennedy and Mayor Daley waving from one of the choppers.

Kennedy hadn't disappointed the crowd at O'Hare after all. He had landed there and then landed again at Meigs, via helicopter. Politics is certainly the art of compromise. That was the last coherent thought I had at the rally.

Almost on cue the crowd roared its approval of Kennedy. The signs were bobbing up and down the way precinct captains have been trained to make them do for years. Such stomping and cheering I had never heard. It was a staged demonstration running away with itself. The police barriers were knocked over, and the crowd started pushing toward the reviewing stand, which began to shake. The police tried in vain to hold back the crowd. One officer grabbed me: "You, with the kid, get in that squad car over there. She's liable to get trampled." My mother, Kathy, and I readily followed orders. The Senator and the mayor climbed into an open car, and the motorcade began to move through the crowd, which by now was out of control, pushing down fences and even turning over a squad car in their wake.

In two weeks, the presidential campaign would end. Kennedy had scheduled Chicago only once more, for a Daley-sponsored torchlight parade from downtown out to Chicago Stadium. Daley's campaign strategy was for the Senator's momentum to peak during the last two weeks of the campaign and not before. The Mayor wanted big wins for his candidates—Kennedy and Dan Ward, a super-clean law school dean handpicked by Daley for state's attorney. We heard that ward captains were being directed to trade votes if they had to, sacrifice lesser candidates if they couldn't sell the whole ticket, but to bring in Kennedy and Ward at any cost.

A few days before the torchlight parade, Mrs. Edison Dick, a prominent member of the Women's Board of Directors at Kennedy headquarters, came into the office and handed me a check for a thousand dollars from her friend Mrs. Marshall Field. I thanked her, but Mrs. Dick seemed less than friendly. She said she had been talking to Adlai Stevenson, her very close friend, who was in California working hard for Kennedy, and he had told her how disappointed he was not to be invited to the torchlight parade. "After all," she added, "he *is* the former Democratic governor of Illinois and was the standard-bearer for the party twice."

I had a feeling this might be a replay of the Stephen Mitchell issue. It was quickly explained that the parade was sponsored by Mayor Daley and the Democratic organization; in fact, Kennedy staffers weren't even certain of an invitation themselves. Still, a call would be made to Democratic headquarters on her behalf; perhaps Stevenson's name had been omitted in error. Mrs. Dick said she would check back later.

The inquiry was made. A Daley aide responded, "This whole matter has been thoroughly discussed with Bill Blair, Stevenson's administrative assistant, and we have been assured that Stevenson thoroughly understands. Those liberal WASPs are all the same. The only reason they are working for Kennedy, halfheartedly at best, is so Stevenson will get some party post after the election."

Not long afterward, Mrs. Dick returned in high dudgeon. When the above situation was explained, she huffed, "Oh, pooh, what does he know?" and stamped her foot. "I just hung up with Stevenson, and it isn't true. He wants to come." As she spoke, her face flushed. She was holding a piece of paper in her hand and started waving it around: "This paper has Stevenson's private number in California. I demand that Senator Kennedy call him and personally invite him to the parade. You might advise Senator Kennedy while you are at it that neither I nor my friends have ever been known as Catholic pushers, you know."

I was shocked. Had I heard her correctly? That neither she nor her friends would normally work for Catholic candidates? As Mrs. Dick bristled, the paper with Stevenson's number fell from her hand, which was literally trembling with anger, and wafted to the floor.

Thoughts of the old Know-Nothing Movement raced through my mind, of Joseph Medill and his editorials about the drunken Irish crowding the jails, of the ruthless drive to relocate the immigrants from Chicago after the Great Chicago Fire, of the smug way Lake Forest residents bragged about settling in Lake Forest in order to escape the shanty Irish. Who, I asked myself, do those people think they are? The Catholic immigrants helped build this city and this country. The Irish hadn't stolen land from the Indians. They hadn't conspired to steal lakefront property. They hadn't boxcared thousands of unsuspecting black men to Chicago to break strikes.

So irate was I now that I didn't notice Mrs. Dick's precious piece of paper on my foot. She glanced down at it. The proper thing, of course, was for me to pick up the paper and graciously return it to Mrs. Dick. She was much older than I. I had been trained to step aside and let any older person precede me. It was so easy for me in my sitting position to reach down and pick the paper off my foot and hand it to her. It was the gracious and proper thing to do, all right. I could hear my mother saying, "This is your chance to show her what is right; ignore her ignorant religious slur." Mrs. Dick knew that I knew what was expected. She looked at me, and then at the paper sitting on my foot. I caught her gaze, and turned away from her. She could retrieve her paper only by bending down and taking it off my very Irish Catholic foot. As she did.

Soon thereafter, Daley triumphed again. The torchlight parade—sans Adlai Stevenson—was so well regulated that the last float had not left the starting position before Kennedy's plane was airborne again. One hundred and fifty thousand people marched to the stadium. The vaulted streets shook as bands, ward organizations, and labor unions marched behind the candidates, who were accompanied by a police caravan.

In contrast, election day was quiet, so quiet that when Shriver called from Hyannis throughout the day, there was absolutely nothing to report.

It had never occurred to me that Kennedy could lose, but as the evening dragged on and the food wilted, I grew concerned. Some of the states considered Kennedy shoo-ins went to Nixon. Shriver called yet again quite late in the evening. There was great concern about the continuing silence from downstate Illinois. There have always been as many vote-fraud stories about downstate Illinois as about Cook County. As the evening wore on, television commentators had more and more to say about the strangely sparse vote returns all over the state. Shriver called again—Kennedy had talked to Daley, who advised him to go to bed and get some sleep. "Daley said he knows what votes are out downstate," Shriver continued, "and he knows what votes are out in Chicago, and that Kennedy will carry Illinois."

Even if it took all night, Daley would hold back results from the huge black belt of Chicago's public housing. Behind this lay a sophisticated, well-informed fear. So concerned was Daley about downstate Republican vote-stealing that he'd ordered Congressman Dawson not to release his vote tallies. Without Chicago's numbers, how would downstate know how many votes to steal?

As the last votes from downstate were tallied, Daley finally released his results, and Illinois went over the top for Kennedy. Jack Kennedy was the President-elect of the United States. Richard J. Daley was a President-maker.

CHAPTER 12

The Challenge to the Machine

P olitics is addictive, and by the end of 1960, as we closed down Kennedy's headquarters, I was hooked. All of the Kennedy staffers were making decisions about the future. The Shrivers were off to the Peace Corps. John R. Reilly, Bobby Kennedy's Midwest advance man, was going into the Attorney General's Office. Deeda Gerlack, a Shriver neighbor who had scheduled teas and appearances by the Kennedy women, was about to marry Bill Blair, who would be appointed ambassador to Denmark. Margaret Zuehlke, the executive director, turned down a Washington job offer, as did I, in the administrative office of the Peace Corps, for she was marrying a local attorney, John Robson. I couldn't uproot Kathy from the security of my parents' home.

Those of us who didn't opt for Washington got a letter of introduction to Mayor Daley. I never used mine. The motorcades were behind me, like the teas and the crowds and the cheering. Unknowingly, the Kennedys had pulled me out of my mourning and through the hardest year of my life.

I had a child to raise; reluctantly, I considered leaving politics for teaching. A teacher's day was shorter. I would have a schedule roughly like Kathy's. I enrolled at both the University of Illinois and Northeastern College to take courses in education. A double-track schedule would halve the time to obtain a teacher's certificate. Within that year, I completed the required sixteen hours, passed the

179

exam, and began to teach fourth grade at the Field School in Rogers Park.

I wished for only one memento of the glory days—the President's signature on that picture of him holding Kathy. Midway through his administration. I sent my request through Evelyn Lincoln, his personal secretary. The autographed picture came quickly, along with an invitation for Kathy and me to sit with the President for half of the Army/Air Force football game at Soldier Field on November 1, 1963.

Once again, it was Daley's show, and he packed Soldier Field with over 66,000 people to cheer on the teams and Kennedy. Since my parents had tickets too, Kathy and I rode to the game with them. At the stadium, my father asked a policeman where I was to go. I showed my invitation to the officer, who told us to follow him, assuming that all four of us had been invited. We were led onto the field and up a temporary stairway to a huge box, actually a reviewing stand. The front was draped with a flag bearing the seal of the President of the United States. My parents were very uncomfortable. Laughing, I shoved them ahead of me into the box. When the Secret Service approached us, I said brightly, "We are the Byrne party." My father, a shy man, squirmed and whispered, "You won't be satisfied until you have your mother and me arrested and thrown out of the park." I noticed that the chairs were marked by name. I told my parents to sit in the seats marked Jane and Kathy Byrne. My daughter and I went into the back row of unmarked seats. My father sat uneasily next to the superintendent of West Point, who kept referring to him as Mr. Byrne. Dad was admirably stoic.

Soon after we were seated, an announcement was made over the public address system that President Kennedy had canceled his appearance because of a bad cold. As we milled around, dismayed, I ran across old friends in the President's party. John Reilly, at the time President Kennedy's nominee to become a commissioner of the Federal Trade Commission, urged me again, "Janie, come on out to Washington. Kennedy is creating a golden age for America." I longed to be a part of that dream, but for now, it was enough to have Kathy sitting in the President's box amid the military brass. Perhaps after the next election, Washington would be possible; Kathy would be old enough then.

There was to be no golden age, however. Only three weeks later, John Kennedy was shot in Dallas, and the nation turned on itself in fear, anger, and grief. My response was somewhat selfish. For me, he had symbolized a hope that if I pulled out of my own grief, I could have a useful life. In a sense, Kennedy's golden age would have given more meaning to Bill's death.

The tumultuous sixties crashed down upon us. I could see it in my younger sisters, both students at Barat College. Donna, a junior, and Mary Jill, a freshman, had a different agenda from that of my generation. Civil rights, women's liberation, suspicious challenges to government policies—these had been all but nonexistent in the decade after World War II. My friends and I had been content to be in college, to enjoy the academic challenge and the social life. To this day, I feel that if Kennedy had not been murdered, he would have orchestrated a more temperate pace for social change, eliminating much of the agony of the sixties—the distrust, the killing, the bombing, the pervasive sense of disillusionment among the young.

It was on the very cusp of 1960s changes that I took Mayor Daley's advice, recalled in my opening pages, and met with Alderman Shapiro. I asked to become a volunteer in the political work of the 39th Ward and to be allowed to join the ward organization. I started attending meetings and became friendly with a few of the old hands.

An annual political event in Illinois is Democrat Day, held at the State Fair in Springfield. It attracts a healthy number of representatives of the wards and townships across the state. It's really a sort of political bazaar, a place to rev up the troops and compete for jobs and slots on various tickets. I went down in 1964, and on the train back to Chicago, two precinct captains asked me, "Why are you here with us? What are you doing at all the ward meetings? You don't have a job or anything."

That was easy. "I like Democratic politics."

They thought that a stitch. "But aren't you going about it backward? We try to work our way up to where you are, and you're sort of working your way back down." (They meant from Kennedy headquarters to grunt work at the ward level.)

I chuckled inwardly, "Whaddaya know? I'm being *seen*."

When Daley's schedule permitted, I made my mandated visits to his inner sanctum. During one, several months after the fair, he asked if I would ring doorbells for the next local election. I agreed, but had to point out, "So far as I know, no one has ever rang doorbells in Sauganash." And I wasn't looking forward to it, either.

He asked, "Do you know what to do?" I didn't. He said, "It's real simple."

Okay, here was the mayor of Chicago, maker of Presidents, on ringing doorbells: "You just ring the bell. Take all your candidate literature with you. When the Missus answers the door, you just say, 'Hi, Mrs. Brown. I'm your neighbor from down the street. I'm working for the Democratic Party's candidate. I wonder if I could tell you something about the candidate?' That's all there is to it."

On my first day, I gathered up my literature, announced to my family that I was off to ring doorbells, and walked down the street praying that no one would be home.

It isn't easy for me to knock on someone's door uninvited and disrupt his or her day. Sauganash is a friendly community, but people there mind their own business when it comes to a neighbor's politics. As I turned up the walk at the O'Connor house, I realized that I knew "the missus," but I didn't know her at all well. I felt horribly out of place. As soon as the door opened, I repeated Daley's little speech, word for word.

To my astonishment, Mrs. O'Connor said, "How nice of you to want to tell me about your candidate. I've just taken an apple pie out of the oven. Why don't you come in and have a piece while we talk?"

Well, I thought triumphantly, this isn't so bad. As she turned to enter her house, I flashed a V for victory to the four faces peeking from my parents' bedroom window—my mother, Kathy, Donna, and Mary.

As the day wore on, I encountered a few nos and heard "I like you, Jane, but I could never vote for the machine" a few times. But overall, I was encouraged. In fact, I figured I had turned the precinct around. On election day, hospitality and apple pie to the side, I found I had swung only a possible seven votes.

Apparently having seen enough, Mayor Daley sponsored me in my first government job. Lyndon Johnson's War on Poverty had been declared, and the agency overseeing it locally required a staff. My career there began in the late summer of 1964. Downtown staff—social workers, educators, and urban planners—worked on programs affecting the quality of life in neighborhoods, such tasks as cleanups, athletic and senior citizens programs, and assistance with sanitation, nutrition, baby care, and health care. Professional politicians were conspicuously absent. And the central office attempted to reflect the ethnicity of those living in poverty: 80 percent black, 15 percent white, and 5 percent Hispanic. This was some place for a thirty-year-old "lace-curtain Irish" girl from the north side! Perhaps Daley wanted this neophyte to see another side of life.

Chicago's antipoverty program was administered differently from those elsewhere in the nation. Instead of federal funding going directly to social service organizations, the money went to City Hall, which funneled it to the Chicago Committee on Urban Opportunity. This agency was treated as another branch of city government—that is, its chairman was Mayor Richard J. Daley. He wanted control of the federal funds for two specific reasons. There'd be political benefit because the agency dispensed thousands of jobs, and there'd be personal aggrandizement, because Daley's name would appear on each and every check.

The day he sent me to the agency, he said, "Watch yourself. There are some real thugs over there, and the rest of them won't be happy until they take this," pointing to the mayor's chair. As a newcomer, I was observing training sessions of community representatives, defined as the "hard-core" poor. Once trained, they were supposed to go back into their communities and advise residents about opportunities offered by the agency, explain government services available, and ultimately recruit other unemployed people as community representatives. In most cases, this activity was their first job ever.

At the end of the sessions, counselors invited the new employees, most of them women, for coffee and cake at a focus-group session. When a counselor asked what problems the representatives foresaw in making the program work, the answers were usually shocking. The intensity of disrespect for local government and the program in general, as well as their training, came through loud and clear. I had never before been in the same room with anyone who lived in abject poverty in the black ghetto. In one meeting, a woman suddenly started shouting, "This whole thing is a pile of crap! You expect me to go into the community and tell people about all the help the city is trying to bring them. They'll laugh in my face. What do I tell them about the slum landlords and the lousy buildings we live in where we pay double the money that you whites pay for decent housing? They see us coming, and we can't live where we want to. What about violations of the building code going to court, and they get continued and continued while the damned crocked politician pockets the fix money?"

Others started shouting, "Those Health Board inspectors are on the take, too! Have you-all seen the filth in our stores? Bugs and rotten food—they bring down here after it spoils in your neighborhood, but they sell it to us at a mark-up. And what are you going to do about the lousy taverns destroying our young men? Do the cops shut them down for selling to minors? This whole neighborhood is owned by the syndicate and crooked politicians. That old fat King Daley sits downtown getting his cut of the money from the payoffs to let them destroy us. Tell him to take his big foot off our necks and keep his lousy job! I got too much self-respect!''

As several people stormed out past cheering neighbors, I sat back, stunned by these accusations, though I wasn't sure I believed them. I most assuredly did not believe that Mayor Daley belonged to the syndicate. Also, the Chicago Committee on Urban Opportunity, including the downtown office where I worked, was 80 percent black. I had never heard that kind of talk downtown. I shunted it aside, but I could not forget the blowup.

Black colleagues in my office were not outwardly militant. They went along with the program but kept a jaundiced eye out for the expected Chicago political shenanigans. Partly their suspicion stemmed from the agency's domination by Daley. Unlike my coworkers, I did not feel that Daley sought control specifically to keep blacks in check. He kept everyone in check.

Only once did Washington seek to bypass the machine. Many ministers, priests, and social workers on the south side were working on leaders of a Woodlawn gang to go straight. Sarge Shriver bought the concept of funding the gang in the antipoverty program. Hardly anybody else did. Most of Chicago hated the very notion of a ''street gang'' and abhorred the thought of tax dollars going to criminals. I teetered on the fence. Despair reigned in other communities like Woodlawn. Yes, the young needed leaders, but on the other hand, this particular gang was deeply involved in extortion, drugs, and murder. I found it hard to believe that money alone could make a dent in the real causes of poverty—lack of education, absence of job opportunities, and broken, despairing homes. It also occurred to me that Daley might be politically afraid of the gangs. Perhaps he associated them with Ragen's Colts and the Hamburgs. Like many in Bridgeport, Daley had made his way up the Chicago political ladder by virtue of gang membership; he had belonged to the Hamburgs, a much milder group than Ragen's Colts. Gangs provided muscle as well as money. Was there really much to choose between belonging to Ragen's Colts in the 1920s and 1930s and the Black Stone Rangers in a ghetto of the sixties?

When Daley heard about Shriver's renegade funding, he beelined to Lyndon Johnson, and the poverty agency had to organize a summit meeting, a lunch attended by the mayor and Shriver. Daley was aswim with anger at Sarge. Most inner-city blacks I knew wanted Shriver to win and bypass yet more funding past City Hall. I strolled over to the luncheon with a former alderman, Morris Hirsch. He'd been demoted by the machine and now worked as a planner in the antipoverty agency. I asked him the question of the day: "What do you think—which one will back down?" He looked pointedly at me and said wryly, "Once there was a king, who had ten thousand men. He marched them up a very high hill and marched them down again." Smiling, he went on, "We are all like those soldiers. Daley is marching us up the hill. We'll sit at a stacked luncheon, with payrollers— either city workers, or approved agencies receiving funds from us. Nothing will happen—nothing will change."

True. Over lunch the mayor tediously spelled out his conviction that the program should be managed by elected officials answering to voters at the ballot box, not by self-proclaimed leaders answering to no one. Mayor Daley had the thing locked up. A little show of unity, a genuflection from Sarge, and that was the end of direct funding.

My black friends at the agency thought that Congressman Dawson had been politically declawed by Daley. Since 1945, he had run all the south side black wards, handpicking aldermen and generally behaving like a boss. Around 1957, however, Daley had begun to burrow in, undermining Dawson's power and transforming the black aldermen into what the press called the "silent six." Working in the antipoverty program, I got to know them: Claude Holman of the 4th Ward, Ben Lewis of the 24th Ward, Kenny Campbell of the 20th Ward, Bill Harvey of the 2nd Ward, Ralph Metcalfe of the 3rd Ward, and Bob Miller of the 6th Ward. They were cooperative and actually seemed rather firm about their requests, sometimes demands, for jobs and improvements in their wards. Silent they were, however, on council matters and policy decisions. Of course, with the exception of Leon Depres, the independent alderman from Hyde Park, white aldermen were silent as well. Alderman Thomas E. Keane, finance chairman and boss of the council, second in power only to Mayor Daley, ruled with an iron fist, cagily meting out perks and plum assignments. To be an alderman was to vote as he directed and to speak out only with permission.

I soon learned a lot about the civil rights alphabet soup of the sixties—SNCC (Student Nonviolent Coordinating Committee),

CORE (Congress of Racial Equality), and CCCO (Coordinating Council of Community Organization). All job applications were forwarded to City Hall for clearance by the patronage office. I began to notice a pattern: no applicant linked to SNCC, CORE, or CCCO ever got hired. To Daley, these acronyms meant protester, agitator. Not so the NAACP applicants, however, who also spoke out often on civil rights. Why were they routinely hired? Because of the machine. It was known that Congressman Dawson had directed six hundred precinct captains to buy memberships in the NAACP, paying the entry fee himself.[1] In fact, my black coworkers were convinced that the machine controlled the Chicago offices of the NAACP and the Urban League.

One issue could always unite Chicago community action groups—education. Minority neighborhood schools were so overcrowded that classes met in three shifts a day. New schools took a long time to build, so the superintendent and the school board rushed in portable trailers to ease the overcrowding—an unpleasant stopgap measure. Meanwhile, more money seemed available for schools in the better neighborhoods than in the minority communities. Demonstrations about school conditions became virtually a daily occurrence, led by Al Raby, head of CCCO and a man of determination. He was not going to disappear. On the other hand, Mayor Daley had a fierce pride in his city and his works, including the school system. In 1963, he had been mayor for eight years and was pounding away at the image of Chicago as "the City That Works."

Most Chicagoans were unaware of the depth of this school crisis, primarily confined as it was to the black community. Even the phrase "black ghetto" became an issue. Daley denied that any such thing existed in Chicago. Activists jumped on that statement as proof of his insensitivity. Numerous groups in formerly dispirited black communities joined with Raby in protest. The school trailers were nicknamed "Willis-Wagons" in derision of School Superintendent Benjamin Willis. Almost every day, Raby and his followers marched from Buckingham Fountain in Grant Park down Michigan Avenue to Madison Street en route to City Hall to protest, bound and determined to prove to the mayor that they had the kind of strength a politician counts—growing numbers. In one march alone, twenty thousand protesters surrounded City Hall. Once, marchers sat down at the corner of State and Madison and tied up traffic throughout the lunch hour and into the afternoon. Even black gangs like the Black P. Stone Rangers (as the Black Stone Rangers now called themselves) and the Disciples came together on the south and west sides to join in the demonstrations downtown, chanting "black power" and "Willis must go." Every evening, television carried footage of the day's protest into the homes of shocked middle-class white residents. For the first time, conditions in the black communities were receiving attention in the city's major news media. Comedian and social activist Dick Gregory joined Raby on the protest line, lending credibility and garnering yet more coverage. The machine could neither prevent this civil disobedience nor stop it. Ben Willis resigned.

Working in the antipoverty program gave me a close look at this anger spilling into the street. It was frightening. Bombs exploded downtown, Molotov cocktails were hurled into the fringe white neighborhoods. When the chant became "Daley must go," he finally acted. For one thing, he pressed the antipoverty agency to ease tension in the poorer neighborhoods. The machine always thinks if you give someone a job they'll get in line—the credo that "every man has his price." Half of the programs weren't even fully written, but no matter. Whole clumps of people went on the payroll. The dissenters were not quieted. In fact, many a new employee on Daley's payroll marched along with Raby during the lunch hour. Within our agency, employees grew suspicious of each other. The city seemed ready to burst into racial strife. On June 12, 1964, a police officer attempting to arrest a Hispanic protester faced a drawn gun. The policeman shot the protester in the leg, and a riot ensued. For two nights, squad cars were set afire, as were the stores along Division Street. Finally, the police, aided by religious leaders and social workers, were able to bring the riot under control.

Angry people of all colors and backgrounds are capable of mob violence, as I would learn during my first mayoral campaign in the late summer of 1978. At a press conference, I charged that ghost voters were listed on the City Election Board's voting rolls, and I cited Rosie's Grill, a coffee shop in Bridgeport, as the center of payoffs for jobs handed out in that ward. That evening, while I was speaking in a black community, I was surprised to see a camera crew pull in. Previously, the media had paid little attention to my campaign, since it was assumed that no one, especially a woman, could beat the machine's incumbent candidate, Mayor Michael A. Bilandic of Bridgeport. After my speech, a woman reporter from ABC-TV asked if I'd go with her crew to Bridgeport and repeat my charges standing in front of Rosie's Grill.

Of course I would. She offered to take me along in the sound truck, but I wanted to drive and agreed to meet her in Bridgeport for the television spot, which would air live on the ten-o'clock news. Sound trucks and television equipment always draw a crowd. When I arrived, children had gathered around as the crews assembled the tripod lights. Residents sitting out on their front porches—the Bridgeport grapevine—seemed friendly enough. One couple offered me a glass of iced tea as I waited to be interviewed. The producer decided to line up the children in a semicircle behind the reporter and me.

A few seconds before going live, I spotted a group of about ten men and women with baseball bats walking toward us down the middle of the street. I figured a baseball game had just ended in a nearby park. The instant the bright lights popped on, the group divided, strode to the ends of the semicircle, and tapped the children's ankles with the bats. To get away, children began pushing and shoving one another. The reporter gamely tried to continue the interview, but a bat knocked over one of the tripods. The lights crashed to the ground. The shoving and jostling intensified. Unable to broadcast, the reporter quickly wrapped up, "As you can see, we are trying to come live to you from Bridgeport with former commissioner Jane Byrne."

The interview was over. As the crowd dispersed and the crew retreated to its truck, I walked across the street to my car, thinking, I hope all of Chicago saw that. Then, as I reached the driver's side, I heard just behind me the sharp bang of a bat against the back fender. I jumped inside, locked the doors, and found myself surrounded by threatening men and women. When I turned the ignition, two men jumped on the hood and spat on the windshield. A man perched on the roof leaned over and banged on the glass, while others bashed at the doors with their bats.

I looked back. No sign of the television crew. I glanced toward the porches for possible friendly support. Everyone had disappeared. I edged the car forward. I didn't dare accelerate for fear that one of the mob on the car would fall off and be injured, in which case I could face charges of hit-and-run. The police assigned to Bridgeport were usually local residents; they'd defend this mob. I crept for several blocks, gripping the wheel. The last of the crowd began to jump off only when I swung my car onto 35th Street and headed toward the Dan Ryan Expressway. Clearly, the remnants of Ragen's Colts and the Hamburgs of Bridgeport were still around.

Back in 1965, Daley, an astute politician, well knew the consequences of polarization, for he and Chicago were living through a deep and widening polarization from 1963 through 1966. The south-west side white community was no less disenchanted with him than the black community that had helped him move into City Hall. He lashed out, throwing down the gauntlet to Chicago's blacks: "There will be law and order on the streets of Chicago!" Here was a no-win situation for Daley. More acts of civil disobedience would surely follow. White voters interpreted Daley's stance as a signal that he would not allow blacks to take over the city, but, finally, he was powerless.

Al Raby's following grew, greatly assisted by the arrival of Dr. Martin Luther King, Jr., for a July 24, 1965, march, thirty thousand strong, on City Hall. Daley refused to meet with King and Raby; the school crises did not ease. Early in 1966, Dr. King announced that he and Raby were establishing a Chicago Freedom Movement, and in January, he and Coretta moved into a west side apartment.

Once Dr. King took up residence in Chicago, the city fell under an intense spotlight; all the television networks sent reporters to Chicago. Daley's ego was on the line. He had to win. He announced a massive slum clearance program. Dr. King countered with the announcement that his Chicago subsidiary—Operation Breadbasket—would immediately stage more boycotts. Daley's town was suddenly up for grabs. Labor, big business, most black ministers (especially those receiving federal dollars from the antipoverty program), the black committeemen, their precinct captains—all were being challenged by Martin Luther King, Jr.

In the 1960s, polling was not as common as it is today. Certainly the black committeemen weren't polling. Surrounded by their own yes-men, they felt secure, as did their precinct captains, who went out to calm their constituents, promising great rewards if they stayed in line. None of these hacks wanted King coming into their wards and pointing to slum conditions they had accepted. The very life of the machine was at risk. What was to prevent King from starting his own vote-getting organization? King marched and boycotted; black gang activity increased; tensions between blacks and whites on the southwest side in areas like Bogan and Marquette Park reached a fever pitch. When Dr. King and the black activists announced additional boycotts, white anger seethed and the unrest again spilled over into the Puerto Rican community.

Dr. King called for an organized demonstration on July 10—Freedom Sunday. On that day, forty thousand protesters converged on City Hall as the civil rights leader posted a list of social, political, and economic demands on the front door. The demands were ignored. When sporadic riots erupted in many sections of Chicago, Dr. King planned two marches into all-white neighborhoods to produce "creative tension." One was slated for Bogan, the other for Marquette Park. The targets were real estate firms, because of their discriminatory practices. These two protests produced the worst racial violence Chicago had yet witnessed. White gangs set cars on fire and pelted the marchers with rocks. I know that the police did their best to contain the rioting, but they became themselves a target of hatred for protecting the marchers. At one point, a rock struck Dr. King in the head, almost knocking him to the ground. Mayor Daley was in serious trouble. His political base was that southwest side, where his neighbors were furious with him for allowing dissension to disrupt their neighborhood.

In truth, the protests were becoming self-defeating. Dr. King, who believed in nonviolence, found he could not control the more militant blacks. A cooling-off period was in order. On August 26, Daley, backed by a group of religious, political, labor, and business leaders, held a summit meeting with Dr. King and his supporters under the umbrella of the Chicago Conference on Race and Religion. Not much of consequence was accomplished. More swimming pools would be built in black areas, and sprinklers would be attached to fire hydrants to provide some relief from the summer heat. Both sides publicly pledged improved communication and cooperation. King had his symbolic victory and retired. After the dust cleared, however, there was no doubt that the Daley machine and its conservative allies, including the black aldermen, had won the battle of the long, hot summer of 1966. Daley flew to Washington to meet with LBJ to discuss a $2 billion federal program guaranteed to clean up the slums in this country. Earl Bush, Daley's speechwriter, saw to it that the meeting was well covered in the press.

Change was in the air, however. Although the challenge from the "Movement" people had been beaten back, the black machine was no longer monolithic. Several of its leaders were delighted that King had spoken out against Daley. A black woman, Dorothy Tillman, an advance person from the Southern Christian Leadership Conference, remained in Chicago to carry on King's work, as did Helen Latimore. And a young preacher, Jesse Jackson, was appointed by Dr. King to the permanent leadership of Operation Breadbasket. Machine precinct captains and ward committeemen scoffed openly that "after taking care of King, those three"—Tillman, Latimore and Jackson—"won't be any more nuisance than a fly." My instincts said otherwise.

In part, I think Daley got bad advice. I told him every time I visited his office about the brooding, angry nucleus of dissent in the black community. But others, chiefly Dr. Deton J. Brooks, the executive director of the agency administering the antipoverty program, apparently painted a rosier picture. Daley would always counter, in a tone of disbelief, "Why doesn't Dr. Brooks mention that to me?" I probably should have said, "Like so many others around you, he is afraid to tell you the truth," but I didn't. To most, the racial tension seemed to subside. Chicago settled back into its old routines, but soon "We Shall Overcome" rang throughout America and the Vietnam War heated up. 1968 was on the horizon.

CHAPTER 13

The City That Wasn't Working

I n late 1966, I got a phone call from Neil Hartigan, an administrative assistant to the mayor. "I know you worked at Kennedy headquarters," he said. "A small group of us would like to set up a similar campaign for the mayor's next race. I wonder if you'd like to help out?"

Neil was machine through and through—his father had been the committeeman of the 49th Ward—but he was hoping to reach the uncommitted and young Democratic voters who abhorred the machine. I thought it smart of him to try, but I could see the pitfalls he was going to create for himself. Just as Chairman Daley told candidate Kennedy, there was no need for a second Democratic organization; the committeemen wouldn't want any secondary headquarters opening in their wards, Neil Hartigan or no. Of course, Neil knew how to capitalize on his position superbly. When his secretary made his calls, she always said "the mayor's office" was on the phone, and when you rushed to answer, there was only Neil.

Probably, then, it would take the committeemen a while to determine whether Daley was telling him to do all that he was doing in their wards or he was soloing. The second pitfall I foresaw was that all of the other young Turks mentioned frequently as future mayoral contenders at that time—Dan Shannon, former Notre Dame football star and now a Park District commissioner; Congressman Danny Rostenkowski; Jim McDonough, commissioner of streets and sanitation—would be alert for signs that Neil was engaging in a power play. I looked forward to watching all of this.

The name of Neil's new political organization was Chicago-67. We all worked hard organizing coffee and tea parties in the homes of supporters citywide. Various members of the Daley family attended these teas to talk about their father, the man, accompanied by a cabinet member to speak about the mayor's governmental accomplishments. We organized events for the young professionals who worked downtown, fashion shows with a Chicago flavor in the lobbies of large Loop buildings. The mayor would appear on the ramp as the highlight of each show; meanwhile, tons of literature regarding his programs and plans for the future were disseminated. Need I explain that Neil would be at every event to introduce him?

I had now worked in the antipoverty program for Mayor Daley for three years. He was focusing hard on expanding the downtown area, and he knew how to initiate the growth of his city. Arrogant, tough, humorous, too boisterous at times—and defensive—Daley was like Chicago itself. I liked him and thought he was doing a good job. I accepted Hartigan's invitation to work on his new political committee for the mayor's reelection campaign.

The committee turned out to be a great success, attracting new energy and vitality to the mayoral race. Neil was definitely a comer, and his was a fresh approach, a far cry from the stale "I can get you a new garbage can" pep talk from the precinct captains. But he was beginning to pay a price, for jealousy in politics is savage. His Chicago-67 events were subject to loud speculation: "He's doing this for himself"; "He's using the mayor and the mayor's office to build his own power base"; "Daley doesn't need Chicago-67, he'll win in a walk anyway." No speculation about a successor was ever encouraged by Daley or his family, even though he had already been in office for twelve years and the subject was written about often. In this case, though, the mayor feared neither Neil nor his ambitions, figuring that the other young Turks would eat him up. Actually, the young Turks never had their feast, because Hartigan went on to become the Illinois attorney general. (In 1990, he would come within sixty thousand votes of the governor's mansion.) But in Chicago politics the most important role is mayor. It is *the* role. Machine politicians don't care who Illinois sends even to the U.S. Senate; in fact, that seat is considered a kick upstairs and out.

In February 1968, Chuck and Mary Daly, friends of mine who

came to Chicago following Kennedy's death (Chuck had been a White House adviser),[1] invited me to their home for a small fund-raiser to defray the cost of Pierre Salinger's unsuccessful Senate race in California. I debated about going. The Kennedyites were encouraging Bobby to enter the presidential race. Mayor Daley, on the other hand, was already making plans for the Democratic National Convention to be held in Chicago in August, and he was openly committed to Lyndon Johnson. Daley's maxim was the same as Cermak's: *nobody* is for *anybody* politically until the chairman tells *everybody* whom to support. Also, I had certainly not forgotten how Daley grilled me at our first meeting for supporting John Kennedy. Of course, the Daly's had invited a Kennedy group. Finally, I rationalized that since I was indeed in the Kennedy camp myself, I might as well go.

During the party, I asked Salinger if he planned to attend the convention. I was taken aback by his response: "No. If I want to give blood, I'll donate it to the Red Cross." Vietnam protesters had organized sporadic incidents in Chicago during 1967, but without the violence characteristic of occurrences in California and Washington and at many campuses. I asked him if he was serious. He didn't hesitate. "Yes, I think you are going to have every kind of protester imaginable in your city. It will be a mess." I could not agree with him.

In early March, the mayor's secretary, Leona Warnecke, phoned to ask me to appear at his office right after lunch. Only five blocks separated One North Wacker Drive, home of the antipoverty offices, from City Hall, but psychologically it was a world away. As I waited in the mayor's outer office, I tried to change my mind-set. What was he up to now? I hoped it wasn't the Kennedys again. It wasn't.

As I entered his inner sanctum, Daley got right to it. There was an opening in the Department of Weights and Measures. I began taking notes, thinking he wanted me to find someone from the antipoverty program for the position. "It pays about eighteen thousand a year and carries with it the title of commissioner." I continued to write, grateful he didn't mention Chuck Daly's party. "Are you opposed to accepting it?"

I looked up in disbelief. "You want *me* to take it?"

He said, "I believe, if I am correct, you will be the first woman commissioner serving in any major cabinet in any major city in the United States. Your office will be here in City Hall. Tell no one that I am going to submit your name to the city council tomorrow."

Once again he was being pure Daley—having to add some element of intrigue. But he wasn't finished yet.

"No one got this cabinet position for you." Jabbing a pointed finger at me, he went on, "There is a big difference if I personally appoint someone—instead of taking the recommendation of a committeeman, businessman, or member of the clergy. That other person isn't mine, but when I appoint personally, that person is handpicked by me—and *is* mine. You owe your loyalty directly to me; you answer only to me. If anyone claims they helped you get it—and they will—I want you to know the truth." Indicating the chair directly to the right side of his desk, he added, "That is your chair. If you have any trouble in the job, get in here." He pointed again to the chair to reinforce this statement. And he again growled, "You answer only to me!"

I was getting in over my head. I knew nothing about the department. Daley obviously enjoyed his role as power broker and delighted in surprising me. No wonder they call him Buddha, I thought. He always looked the same—conservative blue suit, white shirt—but his behavior was very changeable—beneficent as he passed out the title of commissioner, playful as he sprang his surprise by asking, "Are you opposed?" He was somber as he explained the meaning of a personal appointee, obviously proud that he had such power, and he enjoyed letting me know that he even selected the chair in which decisions would be made.

It was a funny thing about that chair—I took his original statement as a figure of speech—but he meant it literally. In the nine years of my commissioner that followed, he'd always say, at every one of the many group meetings I attended, "Janie—sit there." What significance there was to that chair I don't know. He prided himself on stories in the papers that no one really knew him, and it was much too soon in my young political career for me even to try to understand what was significant and what was show biz.

My thoughts were jumbled as I walked back to my office. I had certainly never expected a cabinet post, and there was the difference in our ideas about presidential candidates. What if Daley continued to support LBJ? Loyalty was demanded, and loyalty is what I wanted to give, but I didn't want to choose between Daley and Bobby Kennedy. On the way back to my office I decided to stop off at St. Peter's Church in the Loop to consider Daley's offer. I feared the responsibility, but I came out of St. Peter's convinced I should give it a try. Following the mayor's orders, I told no one at work, but I did tell my parents and Kathy, who were overjoyed.

I spent some time checking up on Weights and Measures. The name had been officially changed earlier to Consumer Sales Weights and Measures. (Later, I would have the name changed to Department of Consumer Affairs.) I also learned that, contrary to the mayor's information, the department was located at 320 North Clark, not in City Hall. He was like that—name changes and locations were of no significance.

Neither of us could have anticipated the tremors that my appointment activated. Initially, the press had a grand old time stereotyping me as a petite blonde in the male bastion of Daley's council. Not that I'd said one word to any reporter, but soon I was doing nothing but. Camera crews ambushed me all over the place. Suddenly I was fielding a slew of questions, and was glad I had done some research. The notoriety created by the appointment did not quickly vanish, though in the long run Daley was praised both for recognizing that the age of consumerism was upon us and for appointing a woman.

Mayor Daley was a complex man. He wielded incredible power, yet saw fit to ask me if I looked down on the Democratic organization. He had a constant need, in fact, to defend the machine. He took speech lessons to improve his diction. I came to believe that Daley was a shy man with something of an inferiority complex. He was in every way the boss, and at times a tyrant, but he could also be magnanimous. Anyone down on his luck would get help—if Daley went to the wake of a friend, he'd stop in every parlor at the funeral home and express his condolences. Yet he knew he had to be tough or lose control of the monstrous machine; otherwise it would cast him aside, as it had Dunne, Kelly and Kennelly. Slate-making, which was tantamount to winning, occurred every four years. The machine could ruthlessly dump the mayor—and slate whomever it wanted.

Statewide slate-making had occurred the last week in February, just before my appointment was announced. At a slating session, a potential candidate must appear before party leaders to present credentials. Most such performances are *pro forma*, but not all, for Illinois party leaders can reject a candidate summarily, denying a voice to the candidate's constituency. Adlai Stevenson III had appeared before the slate-makers asking to be endorsed for the governor's office. He had been speaking out against Johnson's policies in Vietnam at every opportunity and was candid enough to admit that he would not support the President and his views on Vietnam. In other words, he rejected the machine concept of "taking the ticket from the top to the bottom." Stevenson was a top vote-getter for the party, but the bosses nonetheless denied him any spot on the ticket. Outraged, he threatened to form a third party.[2]

Minnesota's Senator Eugene McCarthy was running hard in the New Hampshire presidential primary. These rumbles figured in the congratulatory phone calls I received from Kenny O'Donnell, John Reilly, and Chuck Daly, who all asked if Mayor Daley ever spoke about Bobby Kennedy. "Bobby doesn't want to split the party. McCarthy is stealing Bobby's base. Daley would be so helpful. Bobby wants any type of encouragement from Daley, even if it has to be covert," they said. I had no inside information for them. Daley was not confiding in me.

Just before the New Hampshire primary in March, Daley summoned me again. As I approached City Hall, I assured myself that he probably wanted to drill me on confirmation-hearing behavior. Once again, I would be surprised.

"How are things going?" he asked.

I said things were fine but I hadn't expected so much publicity. Daley seemed to have nothing more of importance to say. It was one of those awkward moments when we uneasily made small talk. I wondered if he had forgotten why he asked me there, or if he had changed his mind about expressing something. I had been in and out of his office hundreds of times throughout almost four years in the antipoverty program—this had never happened before.

Before this tête-à-tête could go further, there came a tap on a side door that led to a small room right off the mayor's office. Daley's guards stayed there. One of them stepped into the office to say there was a private phone call in the next room.

Excusing himself, the mayor took the call, leaving the door wide open. I could not possibly miss Daley's loud greeting: "Hello, Mr. President! How are you, Mr. President?" It dawned on me that Daley wasn't talking to the president of Marshall Field's but to the President of the United States, and he was practically shouting. "Don't worry about young Adlai, Mr. President! He's not going to form any third party, Mr. President! I had the lad in here just yesterday. I explained to him, Mr. President, that you don't desert the party in bad times; you take the ticket from the top to the bottom, Mr. President. He understands, Mr. President. Why, I even told him how we all supported his father twice for the presidency even though we knew he was a loser. We weren't quitters. We worked like hell for him. We didn't turn our backs on him. I told him, Mr. President, that just because the head of the ticket is in political trouble and could lose he shouldn't turn his back, just as we hadn't turned our backs on his father." The mayor roared on, "This is going to be a bad year for

Democrats, Mr. President. I told him that. He understands."

I was incredulous. The last and most powerful big-city boss in America had just told the President of the country that he would lose the election. What was Daley doing? Publicly, he supported Johnson. In fact, he liked Johnson, who had poured tens of millions of federal dollars into Chicago. But political reality was in the saddle.

After hanging up, Daley came back into the office, sat down, faced me, and said quietly, "That's all, then." I was dismissed, never knowing why I had come or why he left the door open. Much folklore surrounded Mayor Daley, and many surmised that he *always* tested his cabinet for loyalty. Was he testing me, using me? To this day I do not know.

At the time, I decided he was using me. That evening, I phoned Chuck Daly. Mary said he was in New York with Kenny O'Donnell and gave me Kenny's phone number. I hesitated before dialing. With my blood pressure gone sky-high, I made the call: "You asked me if Daley has cracked even a little. You asked about any sign regarding his feelings about the national mood. Perhaps this is nothing—I don't know. You will have to draw your own conclusions." Then I repeated what I had overheard. He thanked me and said he regarded Daley's conversation as good news. I added: "I can only tell you what I heard and how I would feel if I were Lyndon Johnson, and Mayor Daley told me the ticket was in trouble because I headed it."

Kenny responded, "I'll be joining the Senator later tonight. We'll let him draw his own conclusions."

On March 12, Johnson barely squeaked by the New Hampshire primary. McCarthy, with virtually no money and a bandwagon of college kids for campaigners and strategists, almost defeated an incumbent President. It was clear now that the split in the Democratic Party was deeper than a few college protesters. Bobby's move had to come soon, or McCarthy would gain unbeatable momentum as *the* challenger to Johnson.

Four days later, Kennedy declared his candidacy, and the following day he marched in New York's St. Patrick's Day Parade.[3] As I viewed the television coverage, I recalled John's book, *Profiles in Courage*. To my mind, Bobby was now being extremely courageous, undoubtedly risking his political future and perhaps his physical safety.

Several days later, I was confirmed by the full city council, with one dissenting vote from Alderman Leon Depres, who was said to be targeting Daley, not me. If so, Depres chose to fire a very cheap shot. "Daley works in strange and mysterious ways," he said. "One day we'll find out what skeleton in Daley's closet is this woman. She is probably being hired, certainly not for her qualifications, but to look good in publicity pictures with the mayor. Why doesn't he hire a photographer's model instead?"

I was mortified by this attack and had mixed emotions about how to respond. On the one hand, I felt like asking the mayor to withdraw my name, but on the other, I had a tremendous urge to slap the alderman. As soon as the meeting ended, I rushed to the phone to get solace from the one person who always knew what to say, my mother. "Just do the job you were chosen to do and prove to the alderman how wrong he is." That attack would not be the last, and that advice would always prove to be the best response.

On March 31, a warm spring day in Chicago, Lyndon Johnson scheduled a televised speech from the Oval Office. Like much of the nation, my family gathered in front of the television set to listen to the President explain and defend America's policies in Vietnam. At the conclusion of his prepared statement, as he removed his glasses, I suddenly, intuitively, knew what he would say. I turned to my parents. "Here it comes. He's going to tell us he is not a candidate," I said. My father told me not to be silly.

Then Johnson intoned, "I shall not seek and I will not accept the nomination of my party for another term as your President. But, let men everywhere know that a strong and vigilant America stands ready to seek an honorable peace and stands ready tonight to defend an honored cause, whatever the price, whatever the burden and whatever the sacrifice that duty may require. Thank you for listening. Good night, and God bless all of you."[4]

My father was stunned. He asked, "How did you know?"

I said, "Because I heard Mayor Daley tell Johnson he would lose."

The country had been in continual turmoil over the war, but with Johnson out of the picture, perhaps events would become less chaotic. As for me, now I could be both a Daley and a Kennedy loyalist, for surely the mayor would declare his support for Bobby. What a month, I thought—I became commissioner, LBJ decided not to run for reelection, and Bobby Kennedy announced for the presidency. All of this in three and a half weeks! There certainly are surprises in politics, and they come in no certain order. It was all emotionally gripping to me. I liked it.

As I happily plunged into my work as commissioner, I began to pick up on some ancient Chicago political realities, among them the meaning of the term "payroller." After a week on the job, I had yet to meet any field staff—the fifty inspectors of supermarkets, gas stations, and so forth who monitored all phases of commerce and supposedly protected consumers by assuring compliance with the Consumer Protection Ordinance. I asked Deputy Commissioner Raymond Fahey, who had served as interim commissioner until my appointment, where the staff was. He kept assuring me they'd be along, they'd be along. Indeed, on April 1, he ushered thirty of them into my office. They seemed uncomfortable as he explained that on the 1st and 15th days of the month the staff would appear in my office to drop off their time and worksheets and pick up their assignments for the next two weeks.

I was flabbergasted. The 1st and 15th were paydays, of course, and that was seemingly the staff's primary connection to my office. I laughed shortly and said, "Not anymore. You'll come in every day for your assignments." There was much grumbling the next few days as the old routine gave way to the new.

The tragic news of April 4 blared over the television set as my family and I ate dinner. Martin Luther King had been shot. Several minutes later, another news bulletin announced his death. The reaction around the table was a mixture of shock and dismay and dread. Another U.S. leader shot. Another sickening, tragic murder. We watched the televised account of events, though nobody wanted to face the reality of this death. His supporters at the Lorraine Hotel in Memphis looked lost and frightened. Suddenly I had an awful premonition that this killing would trigger a terrible reaction. There would be violence in Chicago.

The next day, a Friday, my intuition was confirmed. Grief turned to violence across the country, and Chicago geared up for another riot. All morning long, reports trickled in of trouble mounting on the west side of the city and sporadic looting on the south side. I could feel tension in the air as I crossed the river from the north side, using the Clark Street bridge, heading for City Hall and the emergency city council memorial session Daley had called for that afternoon. An army of helmeted police on motorbikes and in squad cars and vans was turning onto LaSalle Street. Inside City Hall, police roamed the building and stationed themselves along the corridor to the council chambers.

The last eulogy spoken, the last hymn sung, the ceremony drew to a close. I heard the shuffling of feet in the hallway outside the chamber doors. Then the door opened, and in swept a horde of police with the Reverend Jesse Jackson in their midst. The mayor signaled Jackson to join him on the platform. Here was a scene to contrast with the riot photographs of 1966. Daley and Jackson posed beside each other. The mayor wanted this photograph circulated throughout the black community as quickly as possible.

But it was more than cynical politics. Even though he deeply disliked Jackson, Daley created this opportunity in order to plead for community peace. He did not want his city torn apart yet again. And Jackson understood. He gave a militant speech on behalf of black aims but added that Dr. King had preached the doctrine of nonviolence. In that spirit, Jackson asked for an end to all violence in Chicago.

Mutterings and negative comments in the back halls of council chambers came from black and white aldermen alike. "Why did Daley do that?" someone said. "He gave that guy credibility. Why did he give him a place of honor on the podium in front of all the cameras?" It seemed to me that Daley had had no other choice.

Starting down LaSalle Street back to my office, I was startled to see large crowds rushing toward the train stations. As I continued my walk north along LaSalle to the bridge and across the river, I heard sirens. The city became eerily silent as people rushed out of the Loop. Looking west, I saw coal-black clouds rising hundreds of feet into the spring air. It appeared that the whole west side was on fire. I felt nauseated. When I reached my office, I was handed a note, a directive from the Mayor to send all personnel home. By the time I reached the Kennedy expressway, heading for Sauganash, the sky over the west side was orange with shooting flames and ever blacker with smoke. According to radio reports, the National Guard had been called in. The city council memorial session and Jesse Jackson's appeal had failed.

The burning continued throughout that April night and the next morning. Finally, the mayor requested that President Johnson send in troops. By Sunday, all was quiet on the ravaged west side. The loss from arson and theft—the insured part, at least—amounted to about $15 million. Well over eighty police officers had been injured. Nine civilians died, and forty-six were injured by guns.[5]

The media are ever so good at covering tragedy. A shocked Chicago could view the myriad details of looting and burning every day on television. The public was in an uproar. Those who witnessed the burning firsthand had seen fire engines and firefighters showered with rocks, broken glass, and sometimes bullets as they attempted to quell the fires. They saw teenagers smashing store windows and fleeing vandalized stores with television sets and furniture. Everybody was angry—white Chicagoans at the rioting, black Chicagoans at the years of deplorable living conditions and derisory schooling.

Mayor Daley detested this portrait of his city. The city that worked was clearly not working. Under tremendous pressure to control the profoundly outraged reaction to Dr. King's murder, the frustrated and furious Daley made a terrible mistake. Besieged at his next press conference by a barrage of questions as to whether the violence could have been prevented and whether police had acted effectively, he lost control. Daley stated that he had directed Superintendent of Police Jim Conlisk to "shoot to kill" during the initial phases of the riot. Conlisk denied this. Headlines about the "shoot to kill" order bannered the afternoon edition of the *Chicago Daily News.*

The television news at five and ten led with the explosive press conference. It was a bad time for Daley. Too late, Daley explained that he meant arsonists to be the only targets of police guns. The public wasn't buying it. Daley had been unlucky. Earl Bush, his sensibly liberal and quite savvy press secretary, had been on vacation in early April and hadn't made it back to Chicago to take up his role as Daley's alter ego.[6] Bush would never have let such an edgy Daley call a press conference. But the damage was done. In misplaced anger, the mayor fired Bush, but he was too valuable to do without and was reinstated within the week. (I was pleased that Bush was reinstated, because he was one of the smartest advisers the mayor had.) Thereafter Daley was known as the shoot-to-kill mayor.

While Daley coped with the crisis, I found myself sought out as an expert on consumer problems. A theory was making the rounds that poor people looted stores because they were tired of price-gouging and inferior merchandise. *Time* magazine phoned wanting to know how many west side stores had been prosecuted for marketing inferior merchandise and for price-gouging. I asked Fahey for that information, only to find the cupboard bare. He was in an awkward position, having been passed over in favor of a woman twenty years his junior. As acting commissioner, he had set up a system of office hearings.

When city merchants violated a consumer law, they received a warning letter advising them to appear in the commissioner's office. After these hearings, nine times out of ten, Fahey had given only a verbal slap on the wrist for the infraction. According to his files, the same merchants were hauled into his office time and again for the same violations. Was the department not required by law to prosecute the violators in court? I asked. He admitted it was. I asked him to order all inspectors to appear in my office the next day, to discontinue the office hearing citations, and to give every inspector an arrest book, with numbered pages. I wanted a copy of all citations.

Fahey was not happy. "You'll be sorry if you do away with those hearings. Just wait until someone gives a ticket to a store with clout and the ward committeeman calls you and tells you he'll have your job in the morning if you don't fix it."

I said simply, "Mr. Fahey, have the inspectors in tomorrow."

He wasn't through, though. "When you get that call, what will you do?"

I replied, "I'll tell the committeeman to go to court, because that is where the case will be heard."

In the next two weeks, I inspected the west side myself, assisted by a supervisor and a research assistant. I was determined to find out if grocery and other retail stores were as unconscionable as rumor had it. We inspected and wrote arrest notices in several of the larger chain stores. But what we needed was more black inspectors familiar with the black community and its stores, inspectors the local residents would trust. The area itself was ravaged for block after block on Madison Street. Vacant spaces stared at us from empty hulks, or brick rubble lay piled where buildings had once stood. It was unsettling to be out and about there, for the mood of the people was sullen. Whatever my department did at that point was dismissed, surely with cause, as too little, and too late. We were not wanted, and we knew it.

Meanwhile, a national political question hung in the air: was the mayor supporting Bobby Kennedy? In fact, Kennedy was trying to phone Daley, but Chuck Daly told me that Buddha wasn't taking his calls. June 4, the night of the California primary, I joined my family in front of the television set to watch the returns. From the Ambassador Hotel in L.A., Bobby gave his victory statement, flashed his V for victory signal, and declared, "Now on to Chicago!" I was thrilled. "On to Chicago!"

Seconds later, I was aghast to witness the murder of yet another

Kennedy. After he was shot, I tried frantically to think whom I could call to find out whether Bobby had survived. But everyone I knew was in California with him or en route to other states to push the campaign forward.

Throughout the night and into the next day, we waited until the announcement came—"Senator Kennedy has died."

No more of this, I thought to myself. I seriously contemplated leaving politics. My mother advised me to put off the decision for a while.

About a month later, Patricia Daley called. "Jane, my father said you don't seem happy. It's Bobby, isn't it?" I admitted I was heartbroken and tired of politics. She said, "Well, you knew, didn't you, that my father was for him? Surely you knew, didn't you? He loved him. My father felt that if he had come out earlier for Kennedy, what happened would have happened that much sooner. My father felt there were people who wanted to kill Bobby, and if he gave him credibility, they'd get him. You know that, don't you? You must have known that."

I didn't understand the drift of what she was saying, and I wasn't sure I believed her. Had Mayor Daley suspected a plot? If he had declared for Bobby sooner, would Bobby have been in jeopardy? Patricia's remarks sparked even more questions in my mind. I felt like crying.

Instead, I said, "I wanted to believe that your father supported Kennedy. Thank you for telling me."

There was a long pause. Then she said, "My dad wonders if you will help out with the Democratic National Convention."

CHAPTER 14

It Can't Happen Here

n 1968, most Chicagoans were bone-weary of demonstrations, threats of riot, arson, and looting. Yet more was on the way, to judge from the press, which was touting the Democratic National Convention as a cinch to make Chicago a focal point of violence. Like so many others, I had lost my enthusiasm for playing host to the delegates, alternates, VIPs, dignitaries, celebrities, and world media stars who would come here. After Bobby, the other candidates seemed flat. Just the thought of the bands and balloons gave me a headache. What would be or could be the answer for the war protesters—and who could bring together the divided Democrats, now including regulars, liberals, and dissidents? Why did Mayor Daley even want it here?

While Chicago had been hit hard on the west side during the riots that followed Dr. King's murder four months earlier, we hadn't been the only city to erupt. Lyndon Johnson's presidential commission and a local committee appointed by Mayor Daley were established immediately, charged to investigate the root causes of ghetto riots. Federal Judge Otto Kerner headed up the presidential commission, Federal Judge Richard B. Austin ran the local one. The local commission wasn't a bad place to start in politics. One of its members, young corporate attorney Dan Walker, an independent Democrat, would become governor of Illinois in 1972.

According to the Kerner Report, the riots flowed from poverty and pent-up frustrations after decades of black segregation in housing, public and private, where the poor were preyed upon by unscrupulous merchants and landlords and violent youth. The report charged that rent for inferior housing was high and ghetto food prices higher. It was not uncommon for merchants to peddle stale bakery goods, wilted produce, and spoiled meats in those communities. The merchants and landlords had always finessed this practice, claiming that higher insurance rates in the poor neighborhoods forced higher prices.

Much of this ghetto gouging directly affected me, since the Department of Consumer Affairs was expected to monitor Chicago's retail and wholesale practices. The day the Kerner Report was released, I had an appointment to see the mayor. I didn't expect to find him in a very good mood. Nor was my agenda designed to improve it—the Kerner Report had come down hard not only on cheating in the minority communities but also on our need for federal grant money for hiring inspectors from within those communities.

Daley reacted predictably to the "Presidential Commission Report"—he disagreed. He felt that the riot expressed despair over Dr. King's death and nothing more. He was stung by the disorders, for after thirteen years as mayor, he so identified with Chicago that the matter was a personal affront. He was boss. It couldn't happen here. When Daley rejected Kerner's suggestion that merchants were cheating the poor, I told him that the charges were true. I had inspected the ghetto neighborhoods and found food prices were sometimes 10 to 15 percent higher than elsewhere. His head snapped back, and he stared at me, incredulous.

In fact, I felt that just about anything would have helped at that time—tax incentives, the Community Development Program, anything. I felt that Bobby Kennedy would have come up with imaginative, effective programs, but at least the Johnson White House was trying to address the most galling of problems in minority neighborhoods.

Twelve years later, the dramatic difference as the nation swung rightward was driven home when several of us mayors were invited to a meeting in Reagan's White House. The subject was "Enterprise Zones," a hot concept in the early 1980s. Don Regan, Secretary of the Treasury, opened the meeting: "As we begin and before you ask, there will be no 'tax incentives' to this program. I repeat—no tax incentives." That being established, I saw little purpose in pursuing this pet new concept; private industry would not cooperate in inner-city development for nothing.

Reagan's meeting ran the gamut, though, as one of my colleagues suggested the following: "Mr. President, this may sound foolish to you, but as I travel across the country, I see vast areas of empty lands. I just wonder if those couldn't be declared 'Enterprise Zones'? I don't think any of us would mind sharing our top-heavy load of poor minorities. It's just that some of our cities seem to get all of them. I mean, couldn't we devise some cataloguing system of lands and offer them to the minorities and ship them out there?" Cataloguing people!

To my great surprise, the President replied, "No, my good man, I do not think it's silly. It might be a very good idea." The subject dropped, but I did not recover quickly. The last time anyone catalogued people and shipped them by boxcar was to the gulags in the "Evil Empire" of Soviet Russia. The press forever lurked in the circular drive outside the White House ready to pounce on a good interviewee. On that day, this particular mayor bit her lip and headed straight for the waiting car. If that story leaked out, it wouldn't leak from me.

As the 1968 convention drew near, I could not imagine who among the Democrats could unite the diverse groups congregating in Chicago. It was thought that Vice President Hubert Humphrey would continue Johnson's policies down the line. Eugene McCarthy was considered too liberal by most Americans, and his tremendous early popularity in California and New York had waned. Kennedy had won both of those primaries. McCarthy still had a following of antiwar protesters, but they were not delegates to the convention. In his book *Boss*, Mike Royko described the preconvention climate: "The *Tribune*-owned American went on an almost daily binge of eye-popping headlines and stories about the plans to disrupt the convention, taking every threat literally and seriously. The *Tribune* itself sniffed around for the great communist conspiracy it suspected of backing the protesters. It has one reporter who does nothing but ferret out supposed left-wing involvement in the membership of any organization the *Tribune* dislikes."[1]

From a distance, it seems nearly impossible to credit an article by William F. Buckley, Jr., which reported that the radicals were going to contaminate Chicago's water supply with LSD.[2] But many citizens and most of Chicago's police believed what they read. Local television threw fuel on the emotional fire. Each evening brought images of Yippies practicing their martial maneuvers and karate exercises in Grant Park. Leaders of the National Mobilization Committee to End the War in Vietnam were interviewed daily. Their posturing, provocative statements and foul language—"Fuck LBJ," "Fuck the pigs,"

"Fuck Daley"—insulted most Chicagoans. The police were always referred to as pigs. Constant burning of the American flag angered me. Demonstration leaders were predicting that their numbers would swell to 100,000. Organizers of the protests sought permits to hold a march to the convention hall and to sleep in the park. After they called Mayor Daley "a paranoid suffering through a bad menopause," their chances of obtaining those permits were slim to none.

Adding spice to this mix was a strike called by the International Brotherhood of Electrical Workers (IBEW) earlier in the month, making it nearly impossible for the media to set up a proper convention communications system.

Daley was not intimidated. The convention would be held in Chicago. He'd show the world a peaceful, orderly gathering.

As a rule of thumb, Daley held the media in low regard. Cabinet officers were directed never to take the calls of the press or answer their questions—unless all was first cleared by Earl Bush. It was a rule I didn't follow. I knew I was running a good department and I didn't fear the media's questions. This antipathy toward outsiders was not new. The clannishness of the Bridgeport Irish politicians was fed by a feeling that everyone was against them and looked down on them. Knowing that the networks abhorred his controlled city, Daley reasoned, why accommodate them? He had a thousand weapons. A reasonable network request to park mobile TV vans at hotel entrances so as to cover the arrival of star-quality politicians was denied. Any other American city administration would have granted permission. The press was required to pass through metal detectors at the International Amphitheatre, a chilling reminder of the fragility of the First Amendment. Daley's most glaring move was assembling 25,000 troops in Chicago to keep the peace. On the other hand, to many Chicagoans, myself included, the thought of 100,000 people threatening anarchy seemed equally chilling.

The press played the machine's absolute intolerance of the media big, and Daley finally relented on some permits, though not until the media big shots, the vice presidents of the three major networks, sought an audience with him (a turn of events he probably desired in the first place). They'd come at last to him, the boss—just as I had seen the powerful have to do from the Kennedy campaign of 1960 on.

Since Robert Kennedy's death, I had lost interest in the convention. I was more or less on the sidelines, doing the minimum. I worked a bit on the hospitality committee and helped assemble a nice welcoming package of toiletries along with a "things to do while in Chicago" brochure.

In my own family, a striking generation gap appeared. My parents thought the Yippies a bunch of spoiled and scruffy malcontents, but my two younger sisters were shocked when the protesters were denied permits to sleep in the parks. Donna, a college girl herself, felt the city should welcome them, install portable toilets, and let them be. "They are just kids trying to get Daley's goat, no danger to anyone. Why doesn't he see that? Now he looks bad. What harm can they do in the parks?" Chicago's long-standing ban on sleeping in the parks cut no ice with her.

At any rate, Daley invoked that ordinance, and at 11:00 P.M. on Sunday, August 25—convention eve—the police moved into Lincoln Park, where some of the demonstrators planned to sleep, to send the Yippies packing. There was, of course, no place for these youngsters to go. Every hotel was booked full of delegates, dignitaries, and political groupies. Police supervisors I talked with after I became mayor claimed not to know who issued that order to sweep out the park, but it was a messily indiscriminate police action, snaring Yippies, bystanders, and newsmen alike. After the first sweep on Sunday and the negative publicity—several newsmen had been beaten—I figured an order would be issued calling off the police. No way. The parks were swept again Monday night, triggering another melee. Silence from the mayor's office was read by the police as approval.

In the convention hall itself, security police were omnipresent. Everyone had to show a security badge and pass through the metal detectors. I went out to the hall Monday and Tuesday, but gave my pass to my brother Billy and his wife for Wednesday night. Security was so tight that they, like many delegates, felt they were being treated like potential assassins. Conventions are normally happy affairs. This one turned dreary and oppressive. To make matters worse, emotions were running high throughout the hall. McCarthy's delegates, as well as the holdover Kennedy delegates, pushed for a strong statement in the platform in favor of the ending the war. Meanwhile, Mayor Daley was still trying to prove that no one could take over his town. For days he had huddled in his office with the striking IBEW leadership and management. Thus closeted, he wasn't getting a full picture of the mood on the street. He eked out a compromise of sorts with the electricians that brought more telephone service to the Amphitheatre, though not as much as delegations felt they needed.

I watched the fateful Wednesday evening of the convention on television. There were rumors that LBJ was flying to Chicago to bid farewell to the delegates. Perhaps that explained Daley's actions—putting the U.S. Army on standby, positioning the National Guard at Soldier Field. Maybe, I thought, he's afraid that someone plans to kill the President. The Reverend Ralph Abernathy of the Southern Christian Leadership Conference presented another dilemma; he planned to lead a procession of poor people out to the Amphitheatre by mule wagon. Any hint of another black uprising after the west side riots terrified the mayor.

That was outside the convention hall. Inside was no better. I watched a security guard jump NBC's John Chancellor, throwing him and his equipment to the floor. Next a TV commentator announced that Mike Wallace had been taken into custody and that other newsmen were being attacked in the hall. The television screen zoomed in on a stolid Richard Daley, surrounded by his ward bosses and other members of the Illinois delegation, toughing it out. The hall itself was emotionally charged as a battle raged over the party platform. Most members of the platform committee wanted to skirt the Vietnam issue, but the McCarthy/Kennedy contingent filed a minority report repudiating American involvement in the war and demanding that we bring home our troops. Party professionals like Daley reasoned that since Humphrey would inevitably gain the Democratic nomination and was a member of Johnson's team, the party couldn't condemn the actions of the past and still hope to sell a candidate who was an integral part of that past. Mayor Daley told me he had asked Ted Kennedy to make a run either for the top spot or the vice presidency, but the Massachusetts Senator, still mourning Bobby's death, refused. Ted told Daley that his wife, Joan, was adamant about his not campaigning; she refused to be the last Kennedy wife to take the long walk to Arlington. Had Kennedy agreed, or even come to Chicago, I believe he could have persuaded the mayor to be more moderate about control of protesters and the heavy security in the hall.

As the political battle raged in the hall, my television screen was suddenly filled with demonstrators in Grant Park breaking through the police lines. They had vowed to march to the Amphitheatre, and now the major battle of the convention raged. Several times the crowd was ordered to disperse and return to the park. At the same time, the police began pushing the crowd back. The pressure on the perimeter of the crowd propelled those in front of the line into the officers' faces.

The constant chanting and taunting took its toll on exhausted, fearful police, who exploded at Balbo and Michigan. Caught in the melee of radical organizers who wanted to provoke the police were thousands of innocent, sincere kids seeking an end to the Vietnam War. Like the long-ago strikes at Pullman and Haymarket, the situation blew out of control. On the ground floor of the Hilton Hotel, the windows of a bar called the Haymarket Lounge were smashed by rocks, provoking the police to sweep the park from all three sides. Nightsticks cracked heads, and rocks flew back in retaliation. Stink bombs fouled the air. The kids trying to escape could run only north up Michigan Avenue or directly into the Hilton lobby. Either way, they were clubbed, as were the media. No one was in command. Television cameras trained on the faces of those running or being dragged by police. The carnage seemed endless.

Most delegates at the Amphitheater viewed the battle on their TV monitors, but the mayor was not watching. Suddenly, a delegate from Wisconsin asked that the convention be adjourned to another city, where it could convene far away from Daley's storm troopers in blue. Abraham Ribicoff, governor of Connecticut, stood on the platform and shook his finger at Daley, accusing him of being responsible for the "Gestapo tactics of your police." The mayor and the entire Illinois delegation stood and shouted at Ribicoff. Daley cupped his mouth and shouted words that were forever denied and debated— supposedly, "Fuck you, Jew."[3] Here was a Daley I had never seen. After his outburst, he sat down quickly and drew his finger across his neck, signaling *cut*—shut off the mike. Whoever was in charge of the mike shut it off—briefly.

Tears sprang to my eyes. Everything had gone wrong. In the middle of the fight at Balbo and Michigan, Abernathy's mule train wandered down Michigan Avenue, right into the melee. I sighed with deep relief that nothing happened to him to trigger more trouble. I needn't have worried; the black community, wary of the police, the National Guard, and the U.S. Army, had stayed home.

I believed that Richard Daley was mortally wounded that night. The protesters would heal. So would the reporters who got roughed up. No one died. But Daley will not heal, I thought. This man who had striven to rise from Bridgeport politician to respected national urban leader was cut down in a twenty-minute riot. As Daley stalked out of the hall, amid horrible booing, I sensed that he realized how far he had fallen. I shut off the television.

Battle lines were clearly drawn now. Daley's supporters rose to defend him, but they were outnumbered. Every major network ridiculed him for the tight security, for losing control of his police. Even so, he would not hide. On the last evening of the convention, his people from Bridgeport packed the galleries, waving placards proclaiming, "We love you, Mayor Daley." This, too, became the subject of media mockery.

Kenny O'Donnell and his wife, Helen, were in Chicago for the convention. Surprisingly, so was Pierre Salinger, who played an active and provocative role in Grant Park, condemning the handling of the convention over loudspeakers. As the tumultuous week drew to a close, Kenny invited me to lunch. I just didn't want to see him. When he asked me to recommend a nice restaurant, I said, "Every restaurant in Chicago is nice." He asked if he detected sarcasm. I said, "Yes, you do. Where were you all? Where was your input? You Kennedy people just stood around wringing your hands and looking shocked. What could have gotten into Salinger? He was out there in the park acting dismayed at what he saw when he had predicted it to me six months earlier at Chuck Daly's. At least, Chuck Daly called me last Sunday to suggest that I advise Mayor Daley to ease his restrictions on the press or the press would blast him. None of you showed any leadership or any loyalty."

When I came up for breath, Kenny said, "I guess you don't care to go to lunch." I admitted I didn't. He said, "I've been trying to locate Matt Danaher"—Daley's patronage chief—"but I can't find him. I wanted to give him two messages for Daley." Kenny asked me to relay them. The first was "In a poll of delegates on the floor of the convention, eight out of ten delegates side with Daley." The second was "When I stopped for a drink at the Pick Congress last night after the session, two of the most prominent Democrats on the national scene said they were going to get Daley."

"Who are those Democrats?" I asked.

Kenny replied, "That wouldn't be cricket."

After the convention, Chicago remained hot and muggy, as well as exhausted and bitterly divided. We all looked forward to the long Labor Day weekend. Running continually through my mind were the tumultuous events surrounding the convention and O'Donnell's two messages. Completing my backlog of work over the long weekend, I called the mayor's office to make an appointment for the following week. To my surprise, Daley was in his office. I figured he had surely taken some time off after the convention fiasco. But no, why didn't I come over now? Downtown Chicago was deserted, only five days after the National Guard and the U.S. Army had rolled down Michigan Avenue.

The mayor usually called me Janie, but when he turned official, he always boomed, "Commissioner." This was a "Commissioner" day. He looked as hard and angry as he had at our first meeting almost five years earlier. He had assumed an air of bravado, but the frustration and hurt were clearly evident.

"I hope you found out what kind of people the Kennedy people are," he said. "There wasn't a man among them. They have no guts."

I replied, "Mr. Mayor, I can't explain the actions of some of the Kennedy men"—like Frank Mankiewicz, who publicly insulted Daley from the podium of the convention hall—"but O'Donnell's the leader of the Kennedy clan, and he seemed sincerely concerned. What should he have done? His candidate, his leader, who might have prevented all this, was gone. I don't like being in the middle of this all the time, but you won't take their calls half the time, and the other half of the time, I spin my wheels wondering if you even want me to deliver their messages."

"What are the messages?" The first one was easy to repeat, but with a very dry throat, I barely got out the second. I was unprepared for the mayor's response. The veins on the sides of his temples pulsed, and his hand dropped hard against his desk.

Without looking at me, he asked, "They'll get me? Is it to be physical?"

I felt deflated. "Surely, Mr. Mayor, O'Donnell didn't mean that. Surely he would have reached you himself if that were the case. Send Danaher to Boston. Have him get the names of those two top Democrats." Then I made what to him must have been a most stupid and naive remark: "Mr. Mayor, how could it be physical? They are Democrats."

Daley was philosophical. "Well, one can't totally protect oneself. We've certainly seen that in the last few years. But if it is to be political, well, hell, there have been a lot of people trying to get me for a long time."

On my way back to my office, I crossed over the Clark Street bridge of my ancestors and looked down at the dirty water along the stem of the Chicago River. So much of Chicago's history had taken place along that river and still did. Only five nights before, police had been ordered to man the bridges along Wacker Drive in order to keep demonstrators in Lincoln Park from crossing to join forces with the demonstrators in Grant Park. Rumors had swept City Hall that Alderman Keane had driven from bridge tender to bridge tender ordering them to raise the bridges to cut off traffic. How similar to the Lager Beer Riots. I thought of earlier days, of Indian tribes living peacefully along the river's banks and of how they fished and hunted in unpolluted waters. The free and open way of life of the earliest settlers and trappers along the river was gone. The flutes and the banjos that had played in the Sauganash Hotel along the Chicago River—they, too, were gone.

The battle of the bridges that had raised a cathedral to unite the north and south sides of Chicago had served its purpose only to a limited degree. "Convention capital of the world," we called ourselves. I thought of the earlier Chicagoans who hosted a convention that nominated Abe Lincoln right across that river in the Wigwam Hall, a nomination hailed by sirens of a happier kind. As I entered my building on the north bank of the river and gazed out on the burned buildings of the west side and at the water, flowing westward, I remembered my ancestors, who settled not far from my office. I thought of the waves of immigrants who packed its banks from south branch to north, the Germans, Scandinavians, and Irish. I thought of the old buffalo trail down to the river that became a thoroughfare for waves of immigrant Poles to the northwest side. I thought of the ugly flames and the demoralized spirit of the west siders. What a contrast to the spirit of earlier Chicagoans who had rebuilt after the fire.

Perhaps the west side could rebuild again. I took one last look across the river at the empty hulking skyscrapers and the empty streets and thought, 'You've been through worse than this, Chicago. You'll be fine.'

Within the month, Mayor Daley increased his security guards and installed a push-button door outside his office.

Most Chicagoans knew that serious mistakes were made during the convention, but were ready to move on, rather than dwell on the fiasco. That was not the case with Mayor Daley. U.S. Attorney Thomas Foran announced a federal investigation of the convention riot, and the Federal Commission on the Causes of Violence, the same commission impaneled to investigate the riots after the assassination of Martin Luther King, also announced an investigation. This time Democrat Dan Walker headed up the commission in Chicago.

Meanwhile, the Department of Consumer Affairs, once Serrittella's corrupt domain, was in for a revitalization. I had little time to look backward. My place was out on the streets, checking stores, working with my inspectors.

One Saturday morning that fall, Mayor Daley called asking me to stop in to see him later in the day. When I got downtown, he appeared quite chipper as he passed along the complaint of a few businessmen that my inspectors were harassing the National, a grocery chain. I assured him that the National deserved more than it was getting, since several of its stores were blatantly cheating the poor. Their meats almost always contained upwards of an ounce less than claimed on the label. Fresh price tags were frequently glued over expired package labels. A crate of eggs calling for a dozen might contain only ten or eleven or include several cracked eggs. Such cheating was worth thousands over time to the store manager. The National continued to cheat customers; we continued to write arrest notices. The National must have thought we were playing some sort of game and an appeal to Daley would crimp enforcement of the law. He made no such suggestion.

At length, the manager of National's meat operations came to see me—not for the first time—to say he wanted to cooperate. I mentioned that we *had* been cooperative; we'd set up training classes for their butchers. He smiled. "Oh, Commissioner, that's not what I meant. We wanted to cooperate enough with you to put a pretty little mink around your pretty little self."

I stared at him in disbelief, then showed him to the door, warning him to clean up his act or he'd be before the state's attorney for an attempted bribe.

The following Saturday morning, the mayor called me in again about the same matter. My anger was apparent. He said, "Don't take my telling you this as my way of stopping anything you are doing in regard to cheating. I never meet with anyone without informing the commissioner. Did you offer to cooperate?"

I said, "Mr. Mayor, they wanted to cooperate with me by putting a pretty little mink around my pretty little self. I don't know if that comes with the job or not, but as for me, forget it."

The mayor turned red. "You did the right thing. I didn't know. I don't take, either."

I took this opportunity to ask Daley's opinion about the November presidential election, only ten days away. He was angry with Hubert Humphrey for innuendos that the Democratic campaign was in trouble because of the convention upheaval. The machine was supporting the nominee, but with little enthusiasm, concentrating most of its effort on the state's attorney's race on behalf of Edward Hanrahan. Daley wanted no more Adamowskis to plague him with investigations, no more headlines. The machine worked so hard for Hanrahan in 1968 that he received 200,000 more Chicago votes than Hubert Humphrey. There was another significant development in that election. The black community, a constituency the machine counted on, stayed home to the tune of more than 100,000 votes. Daley lost the top of the ticket to Nixon, the governor's office, and the attorney general's office. In the short time since the convention, Daley's stock had dropped precipitously.

Worse, Dan Walker released a stinging report on November 30, labeling police action during the convention nothing less than a police riot. Walker's report pleased liberals in the Democratic Party, and he became their hero. Thus, we entered a new period of Democratic attacks against the machine, an anti-Daley movement so strong that it would carry Walker into the governor's office in 1972.

Much of the rapport Daley enjoyed with big business downtown was dissipating, too. After the machine's poor showing in the November elections, the business community grew more outspoken. I got a good dose myself when I represented the mayor at the Better Business Bureau's annual dinner. When the master of ceremonies mentioned Daley, loud booing arose across the ballroom. It was startling to hear his name ridiculed in public. Many committeemen began to distance themselves from him. The public disaffection took its toll. Whether related to this disapproval or not, the mayor became ill toward the end of the year. Flu, the public was told.

During Daley's absence, I learned even more about payrollers. An article in a supermarket trade paper described the inspectors in my department as "vultures out of control swooping in on supermarkets with no rationale or justification sometimes two or three times a day" and concluded, "Something smells rotten in Consumer Affairs."

I called the publisher to demand proof of the allegations, and he gave me the names of seven store managers or owners who would talk with me. Fearful of retaliation, although at first I couldn't figure out why, they requested that their remarks be treated confidentially.

Only four of the seven appeared for a meeting at my office. I asked why the other three hadn't shown up, since the meeting was confidential. One explained, "Commissioner, we are taking a chance. We are just as frightened as they are." But why? I asked. "City Hall," came the reply.

I hadn't a clue what they meant—I *was* City Hall in a way—and my temper began to rise.

"You are certain there won't be a flood of city inspectors coming after us?" they asked. "No building inspectors, no fire inspectors, none of that?" I affirmed the confidentiality. One of them offered, "A short time after you came here, the word went out that you were strict, and we would have to pay a higher price for protection. We were to join a club called the 'I had lunch at the Bismarck,' then we would no longer be bothered." The Bismarck Hotel, directly across the street from City Hall, was a hangout for politicians.

Flabbergasted, I asked, "You pay to cheat? How much?"

Previous to my stint, they had paid $50 a week; now the price had doubled, and these merchants couldn't afford the Bismarck Lunch Club membership anymore. That was the only reason they came forward to level with me. I reassured them yet again there would be no retaliation. On the other hand, I scolded them for being little better than the inspectors.

I alerted the city's Department of Investigations, and the carnage began. Within a few weeks, more than a third of my department had to be fired. The investigation caused much internal dissension. Inspectors began to distrust one another. Tires were destroyed with ice picks and threats flew around the department. Not that we got rid of all the bad apples. The crooked inspectors who remained decided to undermine my position with the powerful committeemen. Having been around far longer than I, they knew which law firms were well connected and which grocers had retained them. These inspectors began writing frivolous arrest notices for those stores. For example, certain grocers and the manufacturers of vanilla wafers were charged with fake labeling. There is no vanilla in the vanilla wafer; it's made with a product called vanillin. Incredibly, the inspectors cited stores selling oyster crackers, as well as the manufacturer, because they contain no oysters. Walgreen Drug Stores was cited for not having *all* of its "advertised articles on sale."

This was not random birdshot. The corporate attorney for Walgreen, the maker of vanilla wafers, and the manufacturer of oyster crackers was the powerful finance chairman of the city council, Alderman Thomas Keane. When he phoned to make an appointment with me on behalf of Walgreen, I had no idea that the inspectors were using these tactics to get me. They had actually aimed two shots with this maneuvering. First, an angry Keane might well go straight to Daley. Second, if I didn't file the arrest notices in the courts, they could say I had done a political favor.

Keane came in with his clients separately. To my surprise, he delivered a lecture to the Walgreen representatives, advising them that a new day had dawned in America and in Chicago—"the age of consumerism." His clients pledged to post signs at each cash register notifying consumers that if demand for an advertised sale item exceeded supply, a coupon would be honored when the item was back in stock. I knew the courts would throw out the vanilla wafer and oyster cracker cases (the labeling was approved by the feds), but I let all cases, even the frivolous ones, go forward; none resulted in a prosecution. In the end, everybody came to realize, I think, that the department would be run honestly. Many of my inspectors were on the receiving end of threats, and I had several intimidating phone calls in the middle of the night. I mentioned the calls to Richard Elrod, the city's prosecuting attorney. He could not do much about them, of course, but he could act on news that inspectors in the west side were being warned to stay away from a supermarket called the Red Rooster. Before the end of the year, Elrod had sixteen convictions against the store.

Concerning the riots, there was no caving in on the part of U.S. Attorney Thomas Foran. His federal investigation of the riot during the convention climaxed in February 1969, when indictments were brought against eight protest leaders: Abbie Hoffman, Jerry Rubin, Tom Hayden, Rennie Davis, David Dellinger, Lee Weiner, John Froines, and Bobby Seale. Foran intended to try them under the antiriot section of the 1968 Civil Rights Act, charging them with conspiracy in crossing state lines to provoke a riot. Now there will be a prolonged and sensational trial, I thought, which will overshadow the fact that Chicago is putting the convention behind it.

The month before, Mayor Daley had returned to office, apparently recovered after a long on-and-off absence. Some weeks later, from my place on the reviewing stand during the St. Patrick's Day Parade, I noticed that the commissioner of health, Morgan O'Connell, repeatedly urged the sixty-seven-year-old Daley to put on his heavy coat. As the parade ended, O'Connell offered me a ride back to my office. We were barely in the car when he blurted out, "Dick has got to take it easy. If the medical world knew what really happened to him, they would have been flying big-name specialists in here from all over the country. I am of the belief that when one artery starts blocking up at his age, it will shortly be joined by all the others. I have him on high-blood-pressure medicines now, and I check him every morning in the office. If he rests and takes his medicine, he'll be okay. He'll be as good as if he'd had arterial surgery. Dick's really a very lucky man, lucky to have pulled through it, and he's pretty much his old self, but he's got to be careful." I sat back in the car, disheartened by the doctor's diagnosis and dismayed that he had been so candid. Some details remained murky. Had Daley suffered a mild stroke or a mild coronary? Flu, however, was still the culprit in the official version.

Early that summer, the mayor strode into a cabinet meeting, obviously agitated, waving a newspaper and saying, "Where are the women? Where are they?" The only woman in the room, I apprehensively awaited his next words. Pointing to newspaper photos of two gang leaders, he asked, "Why don't they show the mothers of these victims on page one? Why don't they show the innocent dead child being returned to a mother's arms?" Daley's subject, I saw now, was the killing of two innocent teenagers caught in the crossfire of rival gangs. But he wasn't so much upset about the specific incident as unhappy in general at the press for riding herd on him with one screaming headline after another.

In truth, Daley had a big police problem. One of the wildest trials in American history—against the Chicago 8—was in full flower. Daley wanted none of it, so he distanced himself from the police issue as well as he could. His press aides planted stories to the effect that while Daley backed the police (of course), he disapproved of what they'd done in Grant Park. I found myself somewhat amused at this cabinet meeting. Jim Conlisk, an excellent superintendent of police, very bright, super-clean, and incorruptible, had been all but stripped of power in front of the whole city. Subsequently, Daley had been harshly judged by his own Commission on Violence. Now gang wars blazed in the streets. Daley was like a worm on a hook. He needed the police and yet had no confidence in them. Conlisk sat there red-faced as Daley stormed that the gangs had to be stopped.

Then Daley said it again—"Where are the women?" Suddenly, in his softest and most humble voice, he said, "I guess I'm old-fashioned, but I still believe that the hand that rocks the cradle rules the world. You can't tell me, no matter how modern we've become, that that has really changed. If we read of anything about civilizations, we find that they were great because they had strong women. We have to activate and organize our women. We have to get women who are in the home, in the neighborhoods, to stand up and say enough is enough." A voice inside of me asked, "Where are we going with this?" Daley was charged up. "The police can't do it alone. They need the help of those in the community. They need the help of women, mothers. They need the whole community to back them."

The meeting was interrupted by his secretary warning that his appointments were backing up. He closed the meeting. "I want all of you to think about these issues. Janie, come into my office." I waited as he ran through his appointments, then I went in. He asked, "What do you think? Can we organize the women? You're good at organizing. Do you think I'm right? We need women. Why don't you think about it? You have access to women's groups. You're always out in the neighborhoods. See what you can do."

Back at my office, I talked to some of my black women inspectors about his suggestions. They told me the success of such a program depended on tremendous support from the mayor's office personally as well as from individual police commanders. Sheer terror ruled the streets of their community. "We could try," one of them said, quickly adding, "Commissioner, I send my own children to a private school in the suburbs to get them away from the gangs, but even they have to pay their dues to have safe passage to the bus. It's terrible out there. Any mother that stands up to the gangs could face retaliation, maybe even the murder of one of her own children."

Mayor Daley was hell-bent to take on the gangs, elevating this issue to a top priority of his administration. He called a summit meeting of the top police, State's Attorney Hanrahan, the chief court judges, business leaders, and several cabinet officials. Taking his cue from the Mayor, Hanrahan declared all-out war on gangs, creating a special antigang unit. This unit targeted groups such as the Black Panthers. FBI Director J. Edgar Hoover did his bit for confusion by labeling the Black Panthers the most dangerous of threats to the internal security of the United States.[4]

On December 4, my clock radio woke me with the news that Hanrahan and fourteen police officers armed with search warrants for a cache of weapons had raided the apartment of Fred Hampton, the controversial local head of the Black Panthers. Hampton and his associate Mark Clark were killed in their beds. Hampton was viewed by many in the black community as their leader and spokesman. This raid would spark dramatic political changes in the civil rights movement in Chicago.

CHAPTER 15

The Tumultuous Seventies

Mercifully, the sixties drew to an end. After Christmas 1969, my family (Mom, Dad, and Donna, who still lived at home) and Kathy and I flew to Bal Harbor for a vacation. I particularly looked forward to this traditional pause, for it gave me a chance to be with Kathy, and an opportunity to take stock of the past year and plan for the next.

In the ten years since my husband had died, my daughter had all but grown up. My loving parents, brothers, and sisters had taken us in and made our home secure. That New Year's Eve, standing on the promenade deck of the Sea View Hotel and gazing at the stars over the ocean, I said a prayer for the New Year. The year would need it, for it seemed that 1970 would begin where 1969 had left off.

The Chicago 8 trial was still grabbing headlines. This was a true loggerhead situation for Daley; he wanted the defendants convicted of conspiracy, while they were determined to prove that the trial was a mockery of justice. For the benefit of the media, they created daily guerrilla theater. Their behavior, their costumes, their painted faces—red streaks across their noses, green cheeks—all looked pretty stupid to me. There were constant press reports of disruptive actions and shouted obscenities. Federal judge Julius Hoffman warned that if this continued, the eight would stand trial bound and gagged. That same day, Bobby Seale called the judge a pig. Hoffman kept his word. From then on, Seale sat in the courtroom chained and gagged. Once again, Chicago was in the spotlight as new protests began—this time regarding the conduct of the trial. The gag in no way stopped Bobby Seale from making noise. The judge now declared him in contempt of court and sentenced him to a jail term.

Down on my level, I continued to be harassed by threats and buffeted by evidence of corruption in Consumer Affairs. A memo I wrote recommending closure of the Red Rooster still languished in the mayor's office. I didn't know just why. Initially, I hadn't pestered Daley with details of enforcement because of his preoccupations, first with the west side riots and later with the convention fallout. Then he had fallen ill.

Throughout this period, my department cracked down on cheating supermarkets as never before. The effect was positively Newtonian—for every action, there is an opposite reaction—and this reaction put our inspectors in jeopardy. Many of Chicago's merchants were, if not happy with the old system, at least comfortable with it. For decades they had bought protection in subtle ways—carrying insurance with the company of the ward committeeman's choice, buying a fistful of tickets to his fund-raiser, or taking healthy ads in his souvenir book.

Thus was drawn the indistinct line between protection and the right to steal. Merchants who were wired to committeemen had a standard line—"The committeeman is a friend of mine"—and if that didn't stop a diligent inspector, a phone call would be made to the committeeman. It was not unusual for inspectors caught in such a dilemma to ask me what they should do. I knew if we bent the law once we would have to bend it for everyone. I always said the same thing: "If the store is cheating, write the citation." This was quite difficult for the inspectors, because frequently an inspector will owe his job to a committeeman's sponsorship. Commissioners came and went, but the ward committeeman would always be there. It had been only a matter of time before the boil festered and broke. I'd had the wit to protect myself early on; I'd memoed every significant action and sent a copy to Daley. He knew, or could have known, about the lunches at the Bismarck, and about a $5,000 cash bribe offered to a supervisor in my office to stop the Red Rooster letter of revocation from reaching Daley's office.

Out of the blue, in April, I was called to the mayor's office three times in one day. Each time it was to tell of a committeeman's visit, a visit to complain about me. "Janie, what are you doing over there to get everyone so upset? Five different committeemen have been in today. There has to be something behind this." I was accused, he said of being anti-machine and too tough on everybody, merchants and inspectors alike.

Had he read my memoranda? No, he said; what memoranda?

Well, the mayor got an earful after that, especially about the Red Rooster, which seemed to have real clout—five committeemen no less to plead for it. By the time I finished, my throat was dry.

"Why didn't you come in and tell me these things?" Daley asked.

"It all seemed to peak when you fell ill, Mr. Mayor."

Emotionally, I wasn't happy to be in this position, but I also knew I couldn't change. As the first female commissioner I couldn't show fear of the committeemen's power. Daley would have to choose— follow through on the revocation and back me, or side with them. His own stock both within and without the machine was low; it was a perfect time for the committeemen to strike.

But there was another course. I said, "Because of the negative press you are receiving over the convention, some committeemen have grown restless and distanced themselves from you. I don't believe they should be allowed to use me to shove you to gain or keep their support."

"What does that mean?" he asked.

"I'll resign," I said, and I left his office fully intending to do so.

I was barely back in my office, however, when Johnny Daley, the mayor's nineteen-year-old son, called for some Bureau of Labor statistics regarding the cost of living, facts he needed for a college paper. He made an appointment to see me the next day, a Friday. In truth I really didn't want to quit—I hated the thought of losing to those committeemen—but I also knew I was pushing Daley to back me at a time when he didn't need the heat.

A family man in politics involves the whole brood. Just as Daley had had his daughter call me about Bobby Kennedy, so his son's call had been a plant. He was too proud a man to let me know what he was going to do—he was stalling—and he probably didn't know the course he would take himself. One thing I knew for certain—unless something good happened by the close of business the following day, I'd have my answer and I'd leave.

Friday morning, when my secretary brought in my mail, there was a hand-delivered invitation to the gala Democratic fund-raising dinner. The card enclosed from the mayor invited me to join him on the dais as an honored guest. The dinner would seat seven thousand and on the dais would be presidential candidates, labor leaders, big businessmen, and only the most important politicians. My inspectors would never have to choose again between the threats of a committeeman and the directives of the commissioner. That place on the dais said, "She has clout," "She is backed." I was thrilled. The Red Rooster would crow no more.

Shortly after, Daley called in the hearing officer and the revocation hearing began. Through this period, Daley's support of me never wavered. Despite his mounting political troubles, he treated me without fail as a valued colleague. Later that day, his son called. He wouldn't be needing the statistics after all. Counting on Mayor Daley, I planned new consumer legislation. Morale in the department skyrocketed.

Even as I rejoiced, I sadly remembered Dick Elrod, who had helped me build a case against the Red Rooster. In the fall of 1969, the Weatherman faction of Students for a Democratic Society staged a "Days of Rage" campaign in downtown Chicago. Assigned to street duty to provide legal counsel to police, Elrod was caught in a window-smashing spree. He tried to tackle a chain-swinging Weatherman and struck his head against cement. He was permanently paralyzed.

To my mind, nothing recent had so deeply divided Chicago as the slaying of Hampton and Clark. The city was still in an uproar over the shootings. Not a few in the black community considered the deaths of Malcolm X and Fred Hampton as a systematic murder of their leaders. The Black Panthers claimed that without provocation, the police had fired close to one hundred bullets into Hampton's apartment, willfully murdering him as he slept. City Hall was a caldron of rumor. Police officers cited FBI reports that the Panthers were well armed with a cache of machine guns and rifles stored in the apartment. So, the story went, the police staging the raid did not know what to expect. The police insisted there was no conspiracy to kill Hampton and Clark. Officers reported making their way in the predawn hours down dark corridors, hearing shouts within the apartment and then a shot fired at the police. Thinking the Panthers intended to open fire, they responded.

Oddly, the state's attorney's office did not seal off the apartment, and for weeks, Panthers conducted tours of the apartment to prove their case. The media discovered that the holes in the doorway of the apartment—described as bullet holes in a photograph released by

Hanrahan—were actually nail heads. Journalists and reporters did an immediate about-face, and an outraged black community and most black aldermen screamed for an investigation. Black members of the Illinois house and senate joined them, the most notable of these politicians being Harold Washington. In response to this tumult, Representatives Shirley Chisholm and Adam Clayton Powell of New York and Charles Diggs and John Conyers, Democrats from Michigan, held a congressional hearing in Chicago five days before Christmas and demanded that a federal grand jury look into the case.[1] Clearly, Hanrahan could not explain away the police raid.

Mayor Daley the politician put his personal feelings toward Stevenson behind him and slated a solid ticket for the 1970 off-year election. Adlai Stevenson III, often considered the liberals' future candidate for mayor, headed the ticket as the Senate candidate, thus eliminating any mayoral future. Dick Elrod, though paralyzed, was slated for sheriff. Daley worked hard to win this election, for his popularity was still sagging. Stevenson was expected to attract the liberal Democratic voter, Elrod to carry both the Jewish and law-and-order blocs. On May 15, a federal grand jury indicted Hanrahan, but the federal indictment could only press federal charges, such as civil rights violations. The more serious charge of murder must be tried in state court. The federal indictments made a Cook County grand jury investigation politically necessary, so Daley quickly called for a "special prosecutor" and appointed a prestigious attorney, Barnabus J. Sears. Perhaps, Daley hoped, the investigation plus his other gestures to the black community—a city college named for Malcolm X, a street for Martin Luther King—would encourage them to vote the machine slate.

Back in August 1970, a new alderman, Michael Bilandic, of the 11th Ward, the home of Bridgeport mayors, came to see me about phosphates, a substance that had been implicated in long-term water pollution. As chairman of the Environmental Control Committee of the city council, Bilandic was sponsoring an ordinance to remove phosphates from laundry detergents. He wanted me to testify before his committee on behalf of the measure, but the issue seemed more environmental than consumer-related, so I said the ordinance should be handled by Environmental Control Commissioner Wallace Poston. Then I promptly forgot about the issue.

That afternoon, a very animated Mayor Daley summoned me. Inflation was getting worse, and he was worried. "People vote pocketbook," he said. "They don't tend to take the violence and protests into the voting booth when money and their family's welfare are at stake." He asked me to "put together the facts on what basic hamburger was selling for two years ago at this time. Survey the whole marketplace—the price of a three-bedroom apartment or home, shoes for kids, milk per quart, you get what I mean? Start now. They have that price-per-pound law. It should be easy. Don't tell anyone why you are doing it."

As the elections drew near, Earl Bush unfolded Daley's plan. "The boss said he wants to take out ads in *TV Guide* showing the huge jump in prices since Nixon and the Republicans took office. He believes in brainwash, brainwash, brainwash. He wants voters to see Republican prices versus Democratic prices every time they turn the page of *TV Guide*. He's giving me a small budget for radio spots sending out the same message."

About two weeks later, as I drove down the Kennedy expressway, there it was on the radio—"Everything costs more under Republicans." Soon, housewives in supermarkets seemed to take up the refrain.

Daley's strategy worked. The riots, the Democratic Convention, the "days of rage," the shooting deaths of Black Panthers, Hanrahan's indictments, all evanesced in the voting booth, and the Democratic Party smashed the Republicans at the polls that November.

The victory seemed to buoy the Democratic organization, quelling whispers that "the old man ain't got it anymore." I was glad for Daley. The past two years had been tough for him, and he was sick. Following the election, the press got off his back and once again proclaimed him kingmaker. They hinted that the landslide victory of 1970 meant another run for mayor. I was doubtful; surely his family would dissuade him. In December 1970, however, he announced his candidacy.

About mid-February of 1971, I feared that the campaign was running too smoothly. There had to be a hitch, and before too long, there was. Bilandic's phosphates law had passed, calling for a gradual phase-in of nonphosphate detergents. As I entered my office one morning, every light on my phone was blinking. My secretary explained that all of Chicago's television stations wanted to accompany the inspectors on their rounds to enforce the new law. I had been afraid of this—that the public would think the new law had been sponsored by the Department of Consumer Affairs. I asked my secretary to refer calls to

Environmental Control, but they kept streaming in. At length, she came into my office: "Commissioner, you'd better take these calls. Every chain store is phoning, saying the inspectors are removing *all* the laundry soap from the shelves. They're mad."

It was even worse than that; grocers were being arrested by Environmental Control employees for noncompliance. I called Commissioner Poston to ask what he was doing. A capable fellow, he was more accustomed to working with corporation executives than with the public. His department was indeed busily and indiscriminately confiscating detergent and arresting owners. "We are on top of it," he said. "After all, Bilandic is the mayor's alderman."

This would not do. It had to be based upon some misunderstanding. I asked my supervisor to obtain samples of the detergents and get them tested for phosphates by an independent company. Next, we all met with the mayor—Commissioner Poston, Earl Bush, Alderman Bilandic, and I. Daley listened patiently. Poston looked terrified. He was caught with the problem of empty shelves, angry store owners, and shoppers whose laundry was getting dirtier by the day—all of it right before the mayor's upcoming election.

"We are on the side of the angels," Bilandic declared. "We are environmentalists. Who can argue with saving the lake?"

Glancing at me, the mayor asked, "Why do you seem opposed?"

I answered, "Mr. Mayor, this city has claimed greatness for reversing the flow of the Chicago River for as long as I can remember. We bragged that we had pure lake water because our sewage doesn't flow into the lake. Now we are stripping shelves all over the city to save our lake? I don't think there are any phosphates in the lake."

Bilandic switched gears. We needed to get rid of phosphates to help our downstate neighbors. At length, we reached a bureaucratic decision: we would invite the merchants and representatives of the major detergent manufacturers to meet with the mayor to discuss the problem.

Science actually resolved the issue. According to independent testing, phosphates could not be found in any of the detergents. The problem was the labeling on the boxes. The Department of Environmental Control had made the arrests without testing the product, which, as I saw, was phosphate-free. Rather than flouting the new law, Procter & Gamble, Lever Brothers, and Colgate were simply, as was allowed, using up their old inventory of boxes.

I sent a note to the mayor. Perhaps retailers should post signs to the effect that there were no phosphates in the detergents. At the meeting with the merchants and manufacturers' representatives, Daley rose as only Daley could to thank them for complying with the law. Still seething, the retailers asked for assurance in writing that they would no longer be harassed. Mayor Daley thought his word was sufficient. They responded, "It's not because of you, Mr. Mayor. We have gangs coming in demanding protection money. We have Jesse Jackson with his boycotts. We need no more extortion on phony issues. We also need well-informed inspectors."

The mayor relented, directing Earl Bush to issue a press release explaining the situation and revealing the result of the independent testing. There it ended, a tempest in a bureaucratic and political teapot, but real enough while it lasted and a pretty good example of how screwed up a careless government can be.

For the 1971 election, I again worked citywide with members of the Daley family, setting up coffees in hospitality suites for residents in high-rise buildings. We could reach as many voters as are usually found in a whole block of single-family houses with just one tea or coffee. At these rallies, the Daleys shared personal anecdotes about their father, and I discussed his contributions to the city. The last Sunday of the campaign, I held a tea at my parents' home. My whole family worked on the invitations. Over a thousand people waited in line—it trailed through a heated tent in the yard—to shake Daley's hand. The conspiracy trial of the Chicago 8 (Seale had returned to Judge Hoffman's court as a separate defendant) was over. The jury cleared some of the defendants of conspiracy to incite a riot, but convicted five of them. Daley reasoned that half a loaf was better than no loaf at all and moved quickly to put it all behind him.

He performed a new balancing act perfectly. To his own southwest side base, he positioned himself as Mr. Law and Order, having stopped the black marches into their community. He gave the liberals Adlai III, and by championing my consumer ordinances and most of Bilandic's environmental ordinances, he painted himself as a liberal who sought an environmentally safer world and advocated consumer issues.

Young and liberal Republican Richard Friedman, Daley's opponent, did his best. He tried to make an issue of the violence of the past four years, but without any substantial Republican backing—most businessmen supported Daley—he might as well have gone on a vacation. Friedman thought he had a sure issue early in the campaign when Federal Judge Richard B. Austin ordered the Chicago Housing Authority to build public housing in all areas of the city. Anger spewed out of the southwest side. Even the north side was alarmed for the first time, fearful of the crime they associated with public housing. The uproar in the neighborhoods spread to the aldermen, who vowed such housing wouldn't be allowed in their all-white wards.

Daley sidestepped the issue neatly, announcing a program called New Towns in Town, planning whole new communities on old industrial sites and old railway yards. It was a program I suggested to him, but I can't take the credit. John R. Reilly, an FTC Commissioner who had worked alongside me in the John Kennedy campaign, gave me the idea. The program appeased white voters and didn't alienate the blacks. After the election, however, Daley directed the chairman of the Chicago Housing Authority to challenge Judge Austin's decision in a higher federal court, where it developed a life of its own—the case was still in the courts when I became mayor in 1979.

Daley ran a strong campaign, rolling out the reliable machine vote. He had to win big, and he did, carrying 70 percent of the total. Some of us, however, observed that 1971 saw the lowest voter turnout in mayoral elections in forty years, and it worried us. Still, Daley's reelection augured well for the new year. If his health held up, working in his cabinet would continue to be rewarding.

Then came the Hanrahan affair. The grand jury was in session all this time and was bringing its work to a conclusion, but at an April city council session, the doors of the chamber were suddenly flung open, and there stood State's Attorney Ed Hanrahan. Nobody in the council room knew it, but Hanrahan had been indicted by Special Prosecutor Barnabas Sears and he was mad as hell. The cameras rolled, and that evening Chicagoans learned not only that Hanrahan was indicted, but also that the superintendent of police was named an unindicted co-conspirator.

Nothing is quite that simple, however, in Chicago politics. In a show of true neighborliness, Chief Judge Joseph Powers, a Bridgeporter who had once been a lawyer in Daley's firm, refused to accept the envelope containing the indictment. Therefore, they couldn't be announced, for the law requires the chief judge's reading. This charade persisted through one legal maneuver after another—who wanted a hand in indicting a machine state's attorney?—until the indictment finally made its way to the state supreme court. Judge Powers then had no choice but to arraign Hanrahan.

Meanwhile, to those of us who worked closely with the mayor, something was amiss in City Hall. Oh, the government was working—Corporation Counsel Richard Curry informed me that my legislative package of sixteen new laws would be ready by budget time in August—but President Nixon's new U.S. attorney for the Northern District, Jim Thompson, was pushing an investigation of political corruption in Cook County. I heard Earl Bush reassure a terrified coworker: "The mayor didn't mean it. He's not himself. He has a lot on his mind." In late June or early July, I was scheduled to see Daley. As I waited in the anteroom, one of his former law partners, Judge George Schaller, breezed in to see him. This was probably not good timing for me, I suspected.

As Schaller left and I entered, Daley clearly was beside himself, practically snorting steam. In the seven years I had worked for him, I had never seen him so upset. Shortly after his April victory, newspaper articles mentioned that a federal grand jury was looking into alleged political payoffs between racetrack officials and politicians. I did not connect the mayor's horrible mood with that scandal, which hit closer to home than I would have dreamed. According to the press, targets of the investigation were Federal Judge Otto Kerner (the former governor of Illinois and author of the Kerner Report), one of his assistants, and several local politicians. The mayor and others in local politics truly believed that Nixon was using Attorney General John Mitchell to destroy the Democratic machine and that the young and ambitious Jim Thompson was more than willing to play the hatchet man.[2]

Daley angrily insisted that he knew nothing of any racetrack stock deals. Throughout the summer and into the fall, though, those receiving stock found their names in the media, their identities apparently leaked by someone in the U.S. attorney's office. Once again, it was raining Daley headlines in Chicago. Schaller's former law partner, Judge William Lynch, had held stock for Democratic politicians and made a lot of money on his own holdings when he sold his stock at full market value.[3] So had the president of the Cook County board, George Dunne,[4] and Congressman Dan Rostenkowski.[5] Every day, newspaper headlines blared out additional details, linking the scandal to the mayor because of his past association with Schaller and Lynch. As county chairman, Daley had put Schaller on the bench, and through his clout with President Lyndon Johnson, had attained a federal judgeship for Lynch. It was hard to believe that the mayor knew nothing of the racetrack scandal; yet he repeatedly assured me that he was completely in the dark. If I hadn't seen Daley's reaction to Schaller's visit with my own eyes, I would not have believed him.

As all the headlines were breaking and federal grand juries were poking around members of the city council, the government continued smoothly. Daley's questions at my budget hearing were sharp. When I discussed the sixteen consumer protection laws, all ready to go, he advised me not to release them all at once. "Release them one or two at a time. You get more mileage that way. The voter can't absorb sixteen laws at one time. String it out."

And that is what we did. Each law sponsored by the mayor came before the city council, making headlines: the grading of meat, posting octane amounts on gas pumps, the toy safety law, banning lead in interior paints, price marking on packages. (It isn't enough to have a scanner at the checkout counter. Scanners make mistakes.)

In addition to consumer laws and the budget, the mayor faced some difficult political decisions, for slate-making was on the agenda. To my dismay, the Democrats reslated Hanrahan, then on trial. I felt the pillars of City Hall tremble. Many members of my staff spoke of resigning. They were ashamed to work in City Hall. I naively thought the Democrats had made a terrible mistake, but Daley and the Democratic leadership didn't think ethics, they thought numbers. In a county-wide election, blacks are a minority even now and were probably not even 10 percent at that time. Hanrahan was a law-and-order man—the fighting state's attorney had been, after all, raiding an apartment in order to get guns off the street. J. Edgar Hoover's opinion of the Black Panthers carried weight. Stir in, I'm sorry to say, the racism shot through Chicago and in particular around Daley's base, and it is easy to see why Hanrahan was reslated. I didn't know much of that then.

The black community was outraged; that was evident by the angry faces in City Hall. I brought up the matter with Earl Bush, who responded, "But what if Hanrahan is acquitted?" That bothered me, too—was I prejudging a man? This, I thought, I'm going to watch carefully. The black committeemen were gloomy; they doubted they could win reelection with Hanrahan on the slate.

Then came another twist. Thirteen days later, the Central Committee (as the committeemen in session are called) unslated Hanrahan, replacing him with Judge Raymond Berg. Hanrahan ran anyway, as an independent Democrat, and, incredibly, defeated the Democratic machine-backed Berg in the county primary. Actually, the machine did a double-cross and secretly worked for Hanrahan. Along the way, running a law-and-order campaign that appealed to white neighborhoods, Hanrahan became a symbol, the one man who would control Chicago's gangs. The black community vowed to defeat him in the general election. Jesse Jackson established classes under the aegis of Operation Push, instructing black voters how to split a ticket. Daniel Walker (of the Walker Report) had also beaten the machine candidate for governor in the primary. The independents, fed up with machine corruption, rallied around him. Politics amid scandal was the order of the day.

The Democratic Convention was coming up that summer of 1972 in Miami, and the party customarily elected convention delegates during the February primary. For the machine it was business as usual; the usual labor and business leaders were pushed through at the state party convention. The National Democratic Party, however, still smarting from the 1968 convention, had drafted new regulations requiring that each delegation include women and minorities. Delegates could also be elected later than the February primary, according to the national party's new rules, at Democratic Party caucuses in the various congressional districts.

Jesse Jackson and an independent alderman, William Singer, seized this opportunity. They ran their own delegate slate, elected them in caucuses throughout the city, then challenged the regular Democratic slate before the National Credentials Committee—and won, because the machine had stubbornly not nominated enough women nor a mixture of minorities. Machine delegates figured they'd take the fight to the convention and argue that they'd been duly elected in a primary by all the people, not in a caucus in somebody's living room. On national television, though, the Daley Democrats lost the convention-floor fight. A sign of the times—Mayor Daley had not attended the convention, remaining instead at his summer home in Grand Beach, Michigan. As the vote against his delegation was taken in Miami, I realized I was seeing Daley's power slip away. In the past twelve years I had watched him go from being John Kennedy's kingmaker to being an all but hollow figurehead. Perhaps Kenny O'Donnell's warning that powerful politicians were gunning for Daley had come true.

It is customary following a national convention for new members to be elected to the Democratic National Committee. Daley had, despite his Miami defeat, come out publicly for the McGovern ticket, and the nominee, eager to be conciliatory, had offered to select a compromise slate of new members. That's where I came in. One Saturday in late August, as my daughter and I returned home from shopping, my mother ran out to the car: "The mayor has been trying to reach you." She leaned over and kissed me. "Congratulations. You are the new Democratic committeewoman from Illinois. He wanted to tell you himself but couldn't wait any longer. He left this number."

I was dumbfounded. In truth, I did not know what Daley had gotten me into this time.

Of course, McGovern's campaign was a disaster. I soon had to go to Washington for the election of a second vice presidential candidate. Tom Eagleton had bowed out because of disclosures about some earlier psychiatric troubles. Even when I was invited to sit on the stage at the DNC meeting, I identified with Chicago and felt ambivalent. I had entered politics because of John Kennedy, stayed because of Mayor Daley and Bobby Kennedy. While I recognized the shortcomings of the machine and of Daley's role as big-city boss, he had never compromised my role as a commissioner. As national committeewoman, however, I neither believed in my candidate nor thought he could win. Times had changed, and so had I. Now Daley was in trouble, and so were the Democrats. The fifty-nine regular convention delegates bickered, furious over the Miami outcome and somehow blaming Daley. The national ticket was weak; few would work diligently for it. Back home, investigations and indictments were rife. The independent and anti-machine voters were rallying around Dan Walker's run for the governor's chair. Hanrahan had been acquitted, after all, but the damage had been done. Most Chicago blacks wrote off the verdict as just another rigging of a trial by a machine judge.

And so it went. On election day, Nixon carried Illinois big. McGovern carried only one state—Massachusetts. Walker went in as governor, and Bernard Carey defeated Ed Hanrahan's rogue candidacy. Black voters expressed their displeasure by crossing over by thousands to the Republicans.

The new state's attorney and the U.S. attorney were now sniffing around City Hall, poking into the affairs of Chicago's Democratic officials, who now had no friend in the governor's mansion. Rumors abounded in 1973 that the feds hoped to hook the big fish, Daley himself, but as far as I was concerned, they wouldn't succeed. In my hearing, he constantly lectured his cabinet, "Don't take. Don't try to profit from working in government."

Yet early in February, Chicagoans awakened to startling head-lines. The mayor had ordered that better than $500,000 a year in commissions be transferred to the agency at which his son John worked.[6] The insurance covered City Hall, O'Hare, Daley Center, and Chicago Park District facilities. Once again, there were the famil-iar snickers and hallway huddles. To make matters worse, Mayor Daley responded irritably to the press: "If a father can't help his son, they can put some mistletoe on my derrière." That statement shocked me; I hoped he hadn't said it. Johnny was the nicest of Daley's sons, in my view, and there were so many avenues in the private sector where he could have done well, with or without his father's help. The whole episode made no sense. The newspapers and TV kept it alive—it was the first time in his twenty-year career that Daley's enemies could pinpoint personal gain through the use of his office. Rather than back down, he fired Dave Stahl, his chief adminis-trative officer, who had carried out the mayor's decision.

I waited a few days before seeing the mayor. Surprisingly, he was not defensive: "I did not do what Stahl told *Chicago Today* I did. Johnny told me at breakfast one day that he and the Flanagans, the actual owners of his firm, thought they had found a way to save the city money. They told me the city had been cheated all these years. I got so mad. Those other guys"—politically connected firms—"had used the city badly." The mayor grew teary-eyed. "Here were some young, clean-cut kids who were going to save the city money. What I said to Stahl was, *if* what Johnny's group is saying is true, and *if* they can save the city money, give it to them." Daley peered intently at me. "It is important that you know that."

It wasn't important that I know that—I worked for the man. I looked at his watery eyes. If I had answered I would have said, "Mr. Mayor, those tears are not for the city; those tears are because you've been suckered and you know it well." This was a matter for Daley and sons—a family matter I could not have and should not have become involved in.

Several days later, Governor Walker's people did their thing. Headlines shouted that Johnny's company was not even technically certified to accept the award of the city's insurance business.[7] State's Attorney Carey then announced a grand jury investigation to deter-mine whether any state laws had been violated. Events were spiraling out of control.

The largest shock wave struck in July when Earl Bush resigned. For months, rumors had flown he would follow Stahl out because he had recommended that Daley apologize for the insurance award. But there was another reason—Earl Bush was under investigation for secret ownership of an exclusive advertising contract at O'Hare. I shook my head. I hoped that was not true.

Late that summer, a City Hall reporter, Jay McMullen, invited me to lunch. He was doing a story involving my department, and I was pleased to get away from the constant muckraking at City Hall. Mayor Daley hated the press, so I doubted he would care for Jay's taking me to lunch. Thirteen years older than I, Jay had covered City Hall since Martin Kennelly's administration and knew the City Hall ropes far better than I. He had won the John Jacob Scher Award for investigative reporting for a series exposing city giveaways to developers of valuable streets and alleys in Gold Coast and downtown areas. The series didn't win him any popularity awards in City Hall. He had also received a special category award from the Chicago Newspaper Guild for "combining the amusing with the significant in the coverage of City Hall."

I found him to be exactly like the guild award's description. He could combine the amusing and significant aspects of everything! He was not a Chicagoan by birth—he hailed from Pekin, Illinois. He had worked as assistant city editor of the *Peoria Journal* until he was hired by the *Chicago Daily News* in 1947. It would be the first of many luncheons. It was a start-and-stop relationship. We practically sparred about government, the people in it, Chicago itself, and, of course, all the pols. There was always so much going on for both of us. I, as the new member of the Democratic National Committee, found myself off to Washington more times than I thought necessary, but was also busy staying ahead in consumer protection while keeping the department *straight* throughout all the flaming corruption headlines. Jay was equally busy covering it all. I can't even recall exactly when Jay and I started to date. There was something very exciting about him. I realized our casual luncheons had blossomed into love.

Meanwhile, there was no getting away from the fact that City Hall was fairly paralyzed by scandal. Otto Kerner had been convicted of bribery, conspiracy, mail fraud, and income tax evasion. Alderman Paul T. Wigoda was indicted for income tax evasion over a substantial bribe.[8] Matthew J. Danaher (once Daley's patronage chief and his closest political adviser), clerk of the circuit court, was indicted on conspiracy and income tax evasion.[9] (He died before he could stand trial.) Alderman Thomas Keane, the powerful finance chairman of the city council, was indicted on seventeen counts of mail fraud.[10] Earl

Bush was indicted and later convicted.[11] (The conviction was over-turned in 1989.) I became depressed over the mire in City Hall. Had Daley let all this happen?

On January 17, 1974, my mother fell ill. I called the doctor, who diagnosed a coronary over the phone and advised us to rush her to the hospital in an ambulance. My father had all but collapsed in shock. The doctors were encouraging, judging it to be a small event that did little damage, but I was skeptical. A day later, she suffered a second and fatal heart attack.

Mother had been my pillar of strength, my fighter through a man's world right from the rope swing on, the parent who consoled me through the dark days following my husband's death. She was a hu-morous, strong woman, way ahead of her time, a listener who would allow you to talk your way through your problems. She had also been a second mother to Kathy. As each of us made our way into the intensive care unit, many thoughts of my life shared with her rushed through me. Couldn't I pull her back for just a while—just even one more laugh together? It was too late; she was drifting away. As I sat by her bedside, I took her hand and prayed she would be welcomed to eternal peace by her mother, whom she loved so dearly, and by all the Cranes who had gone before her—please God. I took a two-week leave of absence from my job. The mayor was kind. So was Jay. But the void in my life was painfully large.

At length, I returned to work and more scandals. In early March, headlines bruited that the state real estate exams taken by John and Bill Daley had been fixed.[12] Next came the revelation that Michael Daley had been retained by AVM Corporation in 1972, after which that corporation had been awarded a $9.2 million contract for voting machines for Cook County.[13] Shortly thereafter, Michael was trans-ferred to AVM's school cabinet division. The company then won a $747,000 contract for school cabinets.[14] Then came the rumors that the IRS was investigating Daley himself. In early May came more screeching headlines that Michael and Richie's law firm had nego-tiated a highly favorable lease for one of the car rental companies at O'Hare.

During a lunch hour in May, I drove to Presbyterian St. Luke's Hospital to visit one of my deputies scheduled for heart surgery. A surprising collection of television equipment and reporters clogged the hospital entrance. As I walked in, a reporter shouted, "Do you know the condition of the mayor?"

I couldn't imagine what he was talking about. Asking one of the hospital security staff, I was told, "Mayor Daley's in the emergency room. He's in bad shape."

The seventy-two-year-old mayor had finally suffered a very public stroke. My mind shot back to Health Commissioner O'Connell's diagnosis on St. Patrick's Day three years earlier. Now, I understood; the king had slipped so gradually off his throne that only a few had noticed, and those few had begun to feather their nests, secure in their knowledge that Daley was in no shape to call them to task.

CHAPTER 16

Daley's Last Hurrah

After the Miami debacle, Daley had begun to assign me various tasks he didn't care to get involved in. One of them, hard on the heels of Daley's reelection in 1975, was a sure enemy-maker. The lakefront had become increasingly independent in its voting patterns: Democratic aldermen were being defeated regularly; residents were crossing over in droves or not voting. Daley wanted me to set up a counter-independent organization from the 49th Ward (Rogers Park) to the 42nd Ward Gold Coast.

My eyebrows rose almost to my hairline. "Mr. Mayor, you'd better think a little harder about that."

He replied, "I already have, and if these machine committeemen and aldermen can't meet the wishes of the people, we'll defeat them with our own new breed."

Plainly put, I was being asked to set up an organization to defeat Daley's own party members. "Whatever people you get," he instructed, "they have never met with me. They have to act as true independents and attack the machine. I'll provide the money to establish offices, buy equipment and whatever else they need, but it can't be traced to me. That would blow everything."

Daley also wanted me to organize Democratic clubs in the Republican suburbs. One top-notch lawyer I recruited reflected the insecurity of the suburban groups: "I'll go along with this if you are certain that's what Daley wants. But I surely hope that while I'm out there ranting and raving and attacking the machine, someone finds a way to inform the machine's judges who have my cases that this is just a little game we are playing and that I'm really a loyal Democrat."

When the North Shore suburban office opened in Kenilworth, Daley and I drove up for the festivities. He apparently felt it was time to show his hand. He reasoned that he was chairman of all of Cook County, and if these new independents invited him he would go. I felt strange. In 1960, during John Kennedy's campaign, the machine wanted nothing to do with Democrats it couldn't control. Everyone connected with Kennedy was branded independent, dilettante, or liberal. Now I rode in the mayor's limo into the liberal Democratic lion's den. In 1960, Daley had branded me a "northsider, one of them." Now the suburbanites branded me as "machine."

Now, as Mayor Daley lay in the hospital fighting for his life, I was getting bashed by suburban committeemen for interfering in party business, and, no doubt, for talking the mayor into this suburban foray. I was learning that collecting enemies comes easily in politics.

Another week dragged by. No one—neither family nor hospital—would confirm the stroke. The family, angered by critical press coverage of Daley's sons during the past year, ordered a news blackout, a blackout that was never lifted.[1] Inevitably, wild rumors flew: Daley was deranged; he was totally incapacitated. The doctors at Presbyterian St. Luke's recommended surgery on the blocked left carotid artery to prevent another, more crippling stroke, and in mid-May, it was done, successfully. According to Len O'Connor in his book *Requiem*, "Daley's surgeons decided among themselves, Dr. Eric Oldberg concurring, that nothing was to be gained by informing Daley that his right carotid had been discovered to be totally blocked and quite beyond surgical repair. Indeed Daley went to his grave not knowing that for an extended period of time, he had been functioning on the blood supply of one carotid not two."[2] The public was never informed.

Strokes were too much of my life in 1974, for my father suffered one in September and had an operation similar to Daley's. In the space of six months, my boss and my parents had been struck down. Daley took the summer to recuperate. When he returned, he replaced Earl Bush with Frank Sullivan and his long-time appointments secretary with Tom Donovan, his Bridgeport neighbor and patronage chief. Bush's attorney startled many with testimony which in general stated that Bush still wrote the mayor's speeches, adding, "The mayor's sons aren't supposed to know about it. Bush had to pick up his assignments early in the morning or late at night at the mayor's home."

From the time Daley's sons had passed the bar, Bush said, he had been shut out. The boys wanted to be their father's sole advisers.[3]

As I considered Earl's testimony, it occurred to me that several other talented younger men had also been pushed aside. Neil Hartigan was the lieutenant governor, a meaningless job. Dan Shannon, a Park District commissioner, was ultimately stripped of his post for supposed disloyalty. Bill Clark, the former attorney general, often mentioned as a mayoral contender, was not reslated. John P. Coghlan, criminal attorney and campaign worker, had alerted the mayor when the U.S. attorney's office subpoenaed files from the accounting firm of Peter Shannon. Shannon's firm did all of the mayor's accounting work. According to Frank Sullivan in his book *Legend*, Daley retained Coghlan, who gave him a copy of the parts of the federal subpoena pertinent to Daley. When Daley met with Coghlan to discuss the subpoena, Michael Daley was present. Coghlan was fired, according to Sullivan, because he asked Michael to leave the room—a request Coghlan made to protect his privileged relationship if ever questioned by federal attorneys about the meeting. It made no difference that Coghlan's request was correct and prudent; he was fired.[4] Here was danger, but I made up my mind to stay at my job. I worked for the mayor—not his sons.

After Daley's stroke, I felt sure that he would not run again in 1975. I was incredulous when he told me he would.

"You don't seem pleased," he said.

"Well, Mr. Mayor, if your doctors don't want you to run . . ."

He interrupted, "I asked them if they could give me any assurance of a longer life if I didn't run. They couldn't. My family has okayed it. Let's face it. I'm an old man. How many years do I have left, anyway? No, I'm going to die right here in this chair with my boots on. And you are going to have to help me. At the next Central Committee meeting, I'm going to announce your appointment as co-chairperson of the Democratic Party of Chicago and Cook County."

My heart raced. Here was Daley's last hurrah. He had spoken earlier of my becoming co-chairperson, but I'd put him off. I had too many titles already: commissioner of consumer affairs, member of the Democratic National Committee, chairman of the Resolutions Committee of the National Party, commissioner of the Illinois State Commission of the Status of Women. Five committees were too many. Nor would I be easily accepted in the job. I felt as if I were walking on eggshells.

At the next meeting of the Cook County Central Committee,

Daley announced me as co-chair. He also named a co-committee-woman in every ward. And then he forced a roll call, assuring an affirmative vote. When Daley wanted something, he did not pussyfoot. As might be expected, several on the committee were out of sorts, muttering that he had gone soft in the head or was trying to "rev up" the women's vote for his election.

I was barely back in my office that December of 1974 when Daley summoned me. "I told you so," he said. "It wasn't so bad, right?"

I replied, "Mr. Mayor, I hope you make it past St. Patrick's Day. Every year, as we all march happily together, I keep feeling the darts in my back. I think this year, I'll march at the back of the line."

Daley was cool. "They'll get used to it. I'll tell you how I plan to make them accept you as an equal. Someone is always dying. There will come a Monday when I have to go to a funeral. I'll set the committee meeting for that morning. As I leave for the funeral, I'll say, 'Janie, your co-chairperson, will preside in my place.'" Right down to last rites, Mayor Daley could be political.

And so it happened. During a slate-making session for circuit court judgeships, Daley rose and left the room to attend a funeral. The ruse was not a complete success. I was officially in charge, but, as the candidates filed in, some committeemen simply ignored the proceedings and played gin rummy. I could not gain their attention. When Daley returned to the meeting, he chewed them out for their lack of respect.

I expected Daley's 1975 campaign to be a piece of cake. Following the stroke, a sympathy vote was sure to rise for him. Alderman Singer, who had challenged Daley's delegation in Miami and won, was the opposition. Singer had money and hired New York media consultant David Garth, who enjoyed a reputation in political circles for shrewd campaigns, notably Ed Koch's. Garth's work on Singer's behalf marked the first time a Chicago candidate had brought in an outsider to run a campaign. Daley had other opponents—State Senator Richard Newhouse, a black, and Ed Hanrahan, who jumped into the race amid talk of efforts to split the old machine coalition.

Immediately, Daley's campaign sputtered. I couldn't put my finger on it at first, but gradually, it became evident that the mayor's sons were cutting him off from trusted associates, a fact I learned as co-chair. I would later read in Len O'Connor's *Requiem* that even Mary Mullen, who had served as his personal secretary for over thirty-five years, was eased out, and that informal observers were saying,

"You see, as the Daley kids get older, they kept taking over more and more, advising their dad more—especially Michael the lawyer. . . ."[5] They screened his appointments. Personally, I was uncomfortable around the children. Daley had rammed me down their throats, and I knew they resented that. After I became co-chairperson, Michael, by far the brightest of the boys, had grown stronger at party headquarters and was now the lawyer for the Democratic Party.

At the mayor's political office in the La Salle Hotel, two signs hung over the door in the corridor—one read "Democratic Party of Cook County," the other "Democratic Women of Chicago and Cook County." The mayor had told me to chose the office I wanted, but only one had been available on the floor—quite small, but large enough to make a statement. The hotel agreed to redecorate, after Michael insisted that painting and recarpeting be done at the hotel's expense. Though his father was insisting that the office look first-class so that the committeewomen would feel equal, Michael was slow to okay the cost of a modest desk, étagére, bookcase, and lamp; it took months for the poor furniture dealer to be paid. Though small, the office was quite lovely, contrasting sharply with the wood of the chairman's office. His was dark because the drapes were always drawn as a security measure. The chairs were dark and massive as well. On the walls hung the pictures of past Democratic Presidents. I never was comfortable in there; it looked depressing, and everybody always whispered.

Not long after the opening of my new office headquarters, the mayor called me in. His sons were in the room. Michael would represent the party in legal matters, the mayor said. "That means when he tells you to do something, Janie, nod yes, but privately to yourself say no." I smiled weakly. "I want to start this thing off right about the women and your role as co-chair. I'm going to make it clear to the secretaries outside there first." He called in two of the political secretaries. "Janie is co-chair. You are to treat her as my equal, just as if I was here. This is for real. If she wants you to do something, you do it." He turned to Michael. "Have you got that, too, Michael?"

Michael's face turned purple. Neither Johnny nor Billy seemed particularly happy, either. I'd have welcomed a closet to crawl into.

One day, while I was meeting with the mayor about some political plans and strategies, Billy casually strolled in—"Hi, Dad . . . hi, Jane"—and went through the office to the conference room. When the door closed behind his son, Daley jerked his head backward toward the closed door a couple of times, still talking. Not sure what he meant, I shrugged. Our conversation continued, but he jerked his head even more vigorously and began tugging his right earlobe between his fingers while pointing his thumb toward the door.

I couldn't keep from laughing, now that I had caught on. We were dealing with the most basic nuts-and-bolts campaign matters. Didn't the Daley family know what everyone else in the inner circle knew in the last couple of years—that the mayor was no longer making decisions of much substance? Less humorous was the image of this aging man losing his grip on power, while some of the people closest to him were circling around, milking the last drops of his dwindling power.

If politics was Chicago's sport of kings, development was not far behind. A change in residential living had begun slowly in 1964. Charles Swibel, the chairman of Chicago Public Housing, along with architect Bertram Goldberg, had pioneered the development of Marina City. Twin-towered, corncob-shaped high rises were built at Dearborn Street on the north bank of the river. One sixty-story tower was entirely commercial, the other residential. Not since the Great Chicago Fire when Chicagoans fled the central city had it been thought that any significant number might want to live there. Marina City proved that they did. As a result, exclusive high rises were popping up close to the Loop. North Michigan Avenue had changed, too. Its elegant couture shops, such as Stanley Korshak, Blums, and Powells, were joined by Saks Fifth Avenue and Bonwit Teller. Two new high rises went up, the ninety-five-story John Hancock building and Water Tower Place, which combined retail shops, the Ritz Carlton Hotel, and condominiums.

As in any big and aging American city, neighborhoods in Chicago seem constantly to revive themselves. Such was the case with Lincoln Park. From its lovely days at the turn of the century, it had followed the pattern of Chicago's earliest neighborhoods, a period of grandeur, then decline, quickly becoming the home for the city's latest arrivals. A wonderful thing was happening to Lincoln Park in the 1970s. Many of Chicago's young couples were reclaiming the old graystones, renovating them, and returning the neighborhood to its former loveliness. These young couples were independent politically and demanded city services as their just due, not as a political favor. The major problem looming ahead for them was education. They planned to educate their children in public schools, and they meant for those schools to be good.

That's where Alderman William Singer came in. Taking his cue from his own independent constituents, he railed against the school system, striking a solid chord with every parent of a child in the public schools. No better target could have been found. The school system was turning out students with reading and math scores among the lowest in the nation. The dropout rate was very high in minority neighborhoods. Singer articulated programs for bettering the schools, including an independent, elected school board and a vocational training program to reverse the dropout trend.

The kind of candidate who could get under an incumbent's skin, Singer blamed Daley for dismal public education in a mud-slinging campaign. Pollution, too, became an issue, for he linked Daley to polluters through alleged cronyism and sweetheart deals. The same charges were levied about the school board. Disquiet ran through various neighborhoods over unethical financial disclosures involving Daley's sons. The accusations sent Daley reeling, but the mayor was in no shape to counterattack.

Instead, his campaign focused on his accomplishments while in office. During the twenty years he had served the city, he had been responsible for tremendous accomplishments along Chicago's lakefront and downtown, while maintaining the highest bond rating a city can hold. He kept the schools open when schools were struck all over the country, as he kept buses and trains operating while other cities had to curtail transportation services. He negotiated labor disputes for the Chicago Symphony and contributed city funds to their international tours. As for the revolution of the 1960s, he did as well as the last of the big city bosses could. Even so, none of the three major newspapers endorsed him. The *Tribune* was especially critical, reminding one of their treatment of Ed Kelly at the end of his political career.

On election day in February, Daley invited Kathy, now in her midteens, and me up to his suite for dinner. "We'll watch the returns together," he said. I suppose the election was never really in doubt. Daley would win, even though some earlier polls had given the nod to Singer. Small tables were scattered around the room. My daughter and I sat at the table with the mayor and Mrs. Daley, along with the Reverend Gilbert Graham, a close religious confidant of the mayor's, and the younger Daleys sat at scattered nearby tables. We dined on filet mignon, baked stuffed potatoes, and tossed salad. I barely touched my food. If I'd had my druthers, I would have eaten nothing until election night was over. Conversation was awkward. Finally, the mayor said, "Let's see what the people have had to say." Someone put on the TV, and we watched the returns come in.

Undoubtedly, a lot of people would have enjoyed being in my spot sharing Mayor Daley's victory for an unprecedented sixth term as mayor. And perhaps I was merely tired—I had worked very hard in this reelection campaign. But there was something else. I knew he had invited Kathy and me there as a token of appreciation for the work I had done. But the more he tried to include me that night, the more the family wished me gone.

Many ward committeemen, smelling blood in the water, had already been busy building coalitions. But they were denied one last time. Daley got his mandate, carrying 75 percent of the total in every ward in the city, although only 60 percent of the registered voters turned out, the lowest voter turnout in the city's history.

We all went down to the victory platform together. This was a first. Nonfamily had never appeared on an election-night stage with the Daleys, aside from clergy. The main ballroom of the Bismarck was jammed with cheering party workers. As Daley delivered his victory speech, I gazed out at the crowd. Many an unfriendly face returned my gaze. In fact, I was reasonably uncomfortable all evening.

A while later, I was asked to arrange a meeting between Daley and Barbara Burns, an Assistant Secretary of Health, Education and Welfare. Although a Republican, Burns respected Daley and wanted to bring her literacy program to his attention. As we sat talking, she said, "It's easy to see why Jane gets so much done with you behind her." (Our department had been singled out by Ralph Nader for excellent performance, though he said he was surprised that so much could be accomplished in Chicago.)

The mayor angrily cut her off: "Stop right there. Janie and I have had to go through all that dirty talk about us. Haven't we, Janie? The little whispering campaigns, those small, dirty minds—it's going to stop. We've taken it, but it's going to stop!"

My pulse must have hit three hundred beats a second. I was aghast. I'd heard the rumor that the old man was soft on Byrne, but no one had mentioned it to my face. And now Daley was, unwittingly, passing it along to a stranger. The meeting continued, but I didn't hear another word. I was numb, waiting for the end.

When I mentioned Daley's outburst to my secretary, she said, "Commissioner, that rumor is still making the rounds, and it's coming from Bridgeport."

I said, "My God, the mayor is a sick old man. Even if he weren't sick, he's too decent a man for any of that." In addition, the news that Jay and I were close to announcing our engagement had appeared in social columns, and not least, those who knew me would certainly not give credence to such slander. Was I considered so influential I had to be shot down?

In November, as I prepared for my budget hearing, Tom Donovan invited me to the mayor's office to meet with him, Daley, and the corporation counsel, Bill Quinlan. I had no sooner sat down than the mayor dropped his bombshell. "Janie, the records of the Vehicle Commission and those of the commissioner have been subpoenaed." He handed me the subpoena. "We are transferring that department into yours in the new budget. Take it over this afternoon. Secure everything and have an audit done to protect yourself."

Daley was always one to take precautions. "Secure everything" meant "Do not allow any public documents to leave the files." Once the former commissioner left, the files were my responsibility. If the Justice Department looked for a certain file and it turned up missing, I could be accused of deliberately losing it in order to obstruct justice. For the same reason, Daley preferred that outside auditors inventory all records and documents. "Be careful," he said. "It's a tricky crew."

Thinking back to the corruption that had prevailed in Consumer Affairs when I first went there, I said, "Mr. Mayor, this is where I came in—another dirty department."

Daley stared at me ruefully and nodded, "Just do it, please, Janie."

My department did its best to dig in quickly. One of our first aims was a tough safety-testing program for cabs, but in government, reform often comes slowly. Profitable habits, even when unethical, are hard to break. Two divisions of the same company, Yellow and Checker, controlled the taxi business in Chicago by holding over 80 percent of the medallions. Daley did not want them to continue selling or leasing their medallions even though the smaller independent cab companies were allowed to do so. The street value of the medallions was $25,000 each. I didn't think that we were on very good constitutional ground—trying to prevent one group of cab operators

from selling their medallions but allowing others. I discussed it with
Bill Quinlan, then the corporation counsel, who agreed.

Daley responded, "I don't deserve to sit in this chair if I allow one
cab company that controls eighty percent of all the cabs on the streets
to walk out on this city and dispose of city licenses at twenty-five
thousand dollars apiece." The amount of profit on city property was
staggering, for Checker had 1,500 licenses, Yellow 2,166, and the
independents only 934. Daley went on, "How can we regulate three
thousand, six hundred and sixty-six independent cabbies? How can
we protect the public? No; they are not going to get away with it. It
wasn't part of the agreement."

"What agreement?" I asked.

Daley said he had fought them over their monopoly in 1959 all the
way to the state supreme court. In a suit settled out of court, he
insisted, old man Markin (original owner of Checker Taxi Company)
had agreed that the licenses would never be sold or leased. "He agreed
right here in this office." Daley thumped the table.

I asked what he wanted me to do with the 270-odd licenses my
department had confiscated from Yellow Cab for holding them in a
drawer and providing no vehicle for them. He said, "We should hold a
lottery and let cab drivers win them at the actual city rate of the
medallion." That seemed fair. Daley added, "Yellow will never get
them back."

In late spring of 1976, Alderman Edward Vrdolyak of the 10th
Ward called on me. Vrdolyak was a smart, energetic lawyer, someone
the mayor recommended keeping in front of you at all times. David
Markin, chairman of Checker Motors Corporation, which manufactured most of Chicago's cabs, wanted the alderman to act as the mid-
dleman in all disputes between the taxi company and my department.
Then in late spring, the mayor, unknown to me, decided to handle
the medallion matter himself—and in a most surprising manner.

I was going ahead with plans for the lottery when I was called me
into Daley's office. I was shocked by his appearance. Always meticu-
lous, he was disheveled today. His shirt collar was open, his tie loose.
He seemed short of breath, and out of him came a gurgling and clicking sound from deep in his throat. I figured he was experiencing side
affects of his medication. What he said was even more alarming. Contrary to his advice to me, he had struck a deal with Checker Cab and
wanted the medallions returned to Checker. I was amazed, but I
didn't pursue the matter, because Daley didn't seem focused enough

to grasp my questions. His condition saddened me; no less did the low morale in the taxi division when I told them about his decision.

I took Kathy with me to the 1976 Democratic National Convention in New York. On the night of Jimmy Carter's acceptance speech, we learned that the mayor had been told that Carter would stop to shake his hand on the way to the podium. As we aimed our cameras, the nominee skipped the mayor and headed straight for the podium. Daley had been the victim of another power play. It was clear that the 1968 convention was still costing him and he would never again be treated as a political leader by the national party. This slight alienated the Illinois delegation, who barely turned out for the top of the ticket.

Carter became president, but election night was also a disaster for Illinois Democrats, for we lost both the governorship and the state's attorney office. Daley left the following morning for Florida and a long vacation. Routine budget hearings took place in his absence amid a barrage of pernicious rumors. According to one, Daley had slated his own candidate for governor, the popular Michael Howlett, in the primary in order to defeat Walker, who had been traced as the leak of the story that Billy and Johnny Daley's state insurance exams had been fixed. Then, the rumor went he had thrown Howlett to the wolves in the general election after making a deal with Thompson to give covert support if Thompson agreed to drop a federal investigation of Daley and his sons. There are always rumors of deals and tradeoffs in politics. But this deal was totally fabricated. According to the *Tribune*— wish being father to the thought—Daley was through; he had lost the ticket. Photos of various committeemen touted as possible successors appeared in newspapers. Chicago's political arena had turned into a cesspool.

Daley returned from vacation nicely tanned and seeming fairly fit. On December 16, I advised him about an upcoming city council hearing on the regulation of taxicab leases, and we briefly discussed a Christmas party for committeemen and their wives. At four that afternoon, he summoned me to headquarters. He was in a foul mood. It was clear he had read the press coverage that took place during his absence. "I'll put on no party for the likes of them. Let them kick me out. I'm sick of them, anyway. I didn't kick Arvey out, either. I've always taken the blame for kicking Arvey out as chairman. Well, it was Joe Gill who got him—not me."

Daley was rambling, about things that had no connection to me, recalling the distant battles of his long political life. As he rolled on, I could almost see him slipping into the past. He began to pack his attaché case. With a dry sob and tears in his eyes, he looked up at me and said, "To tell you the truth about it, they could have had this chair a long time ago if there was one decent man among them!"

The following Monday, the mayor and Mrs. Daley arrived at the Medill Room of the Bismarck Hotel for the annual cabinet Christmas breakfast. I dreaded it. In fact, I now dreaded most occasions that centered on the once powerful mayor. We all rose as the Daleys entered and proceeded to the head table. The mayor looked gray; his powerful face sagged. The cabinet would pretend they hadn't noticed his slippage and all would make merry by the book for Christmas. Our combined gift to the Daleys was two round-trip tickets to Ireland. As I looked around the room at all the officials seated at the U-shaped table, an odd thought struck me: I was one of the youngest there, but I had been in city work longer than most of the group. For some, it was their very first Christmas cabinet breakfast. And many, it seemed to me, were simply going through the motions of running the city—with no idea of what it had been like in Daley's pre-stroke days.

My taxi hearing went smoothly that afternoon. As I walked toward City Hall to report, a dispatcher from Fire Alarm (the telecommunications office of the Fire Department) caught me by the arm and told me the mayor had been rushed to the hospital. "We dispatched the ambulance," he said grimly, "but based on the equipment they are calling for, he might already be gone."

Feeling numb, I sat down in Daley's outer office as Tom Donovan and Michael Bilandic walked in. By coincidence, they had just come from a luncheon meeting at which they had discussed procedure if and when the mayor died. Without going inside, they slowly closed the door to Daley's inner office, then left for the hospital.

It was over. For sixteen years, I had watched Richard J. Daley, fought with him, fought for him, valued his support. He had been my teacher. I glanced again at the closed door. I could only think, may Richard Daley now rest in peace.

CHAPTER 17

The New Mayor of Chicago

After the initial television blitz—Daley's collapse and death, footage of the family following the hearse escorted by the flashing lights of the fire and police cars on the trip back to Bridgeport—succession became the next topic of media saturation. This was puzzling, because it was understood—and was tradition—that in a mayor's absence because of illness or death, the president pro tem of the city council serves in his stead until the council selects an acting mayor from within its own ranks. The popular election follows.

Wilson Frost, a black alderman from the south side, was president pro tem, but Jay, Kathy, and I watched the news in disbelief as Frost, surrounded by aides, went up to Daley's fifth-floor office only to find the doors locked and the office under police guard. Frost had been publicly humiliated. What was the point of this exercise? The machine may have been set against Wilson, but he would have occupied the post for a week at best. For the sake of unity and fairness, why not adhere to traditional order? Of course, the lockout sent shock waves rolling through the black community, and black leaders' vow to fight the lockout threatened an already uneasy peace in the neighborhoods. What would Daley's "Toddlin' Town" become now that he was gone?

As the city officially began its period of mourning, I called Tom Donovan, who was, along with Alderman Michael Bilandic and Richie Daley, actually running the show. "Why has Frost not been allowed to preside?" I asked.

"Are you kidding?" Tom responded. "If he ever got in there, we'd never get him out." The words of a true son of Bridgeport. Tensions ran high throughout the week, with demonstrations at City Hall and one black organization after another threatening retaliation. The machine just rolled on.

Most meetings regarding the mayor's successor were covert, but, as is usually the case in City Hall, everything was leaked. Obviously, Bridgeport was still in control. Young Richie Daley was the new Democratic committeeman of the 11th Ward. The Daley machine was still "the machine." For at least twenty-two years when Mayor Daley said "Jump" the other committeemen asked, "How high?" As patronage chief, Tom Donovan held thousands of jobs in his hand and had seen a lot of action since Daley's stroke. Most aldermen/committeemen just sat around like Pavlov's dogs waiting for his signal, and Tom took his signal in turn from his new committeeman, Richie. As for Wilson Frost, he was machine, too; he was used to taking orders. Though militant members of the black community pleaded with him to place his name in nomination and fight for the election in the city council, he steadfastly demurred.

When all of the trade-offs were in place, the city council finally convened and elected Alderman Michael A. Bilandic of Bridgeport as acting mayor. Bilandic could not also serve as chairman of the Democratic Party, however, as Daley had, for he was not a committeeman. The committeemen were vying with one another for that post all over City Hall. The contest eventually narrowed to one between Ed Kelly, superintendent of parks, and George Dunne, president of the Cook County Board. At one point, it looked as if Kelly had the votes to win. (The strength of the vote for committeeman is a weighted vote established by voter turnout in the previous election.) Bridgeport residents, who enjoyed over 40 percent of the jobs in City Hall, had enough precinct captains to deliver the highest vote. It was finally agreed that Dunne, in his late sixties, would be a lesser threat to Bilandic or Richie Daley. After all, Kelly, as 47th Ward committeeman, delivered the second-highest vote of all the wards, and, as parks superintendent, he had quite a few jobs to dispense himself. Dunne was therefore elected chairman. During the behind-the-scenes maneuvering and the buttonholing of committeemen, I asked Donovan about Dunne. "If he has his way, he will be the next mayor. That will be no good for any of us." I wasn't so sure myself that I wanted to be part of "us."

When Dunne won, it seemed obvious that he had a right to choose his own co-chairwoman. I sent him a congratulatory note saying that I would be happy to support his selection. I received my reply in a most unusual manner. Two days later, as I drove to work, a reporter on the car radio announced, "We now have the first post-Daley casualty in the reorganization of the Democratic Party. Jane Byrne was just unceremoniously dumped as co-chair. The new chairman also stated that he was disbanding the Democratic Women's Group in its entirety." Dunne obviously cared little for women politicians.

Twelve years later, in 1988, this blatant chauvinism was showcased by the media when NBC's Channel 5 aired a report on sex for jobs in county government. Two female employees of the Cook County Forest Preserve disclosed that they had been forced to have sex with Dunne, still chairman of the Democratic Party and president of the County Board. That exposé launched rockets in Chicago politics. The women appeared on TV for three nights running giving chapter and verse on what they had to do sexually to get hired and promoted. The machine rallied behind the ancient Dunne. The regulars around the Democratic Party watering holes thought it was a riot. "I wonder what kind of vitamins George takes?" they liked to joke. Dunne denied the charges. When the two women were suspended by his county supervisor, one of them attempted suicide. Nothing ever came of the NBC disclosures. I found it terribly sexist and felt deeply sorry for the two women.

Bridgeporters Tom Donovan and Ed Bedore, the budget director, still included me in City Hall decisions. Bilandic had promised the council he would serve only until the mandated election in 1977, one year hence, and not run for reelection himself. But he seemed to have settled in, and Bedore and Donovan were clearly planning for his campaign.

Michael Daley had served as counsel to the Democratic Party of Cook County under his father's chairmanship, normally not such an action-filled spot, but Michael was beginning to have his troubles there. George Dunne had right away asked to see the party's books, only to be told that the cupboard was bare. "No Money Left," headlines blared. Here was a swamp. The public seemed apathetic. It was politics as usual to them. But politicians were incredulous. There were no political contribution reporting laws in Chicago until 1975. No one could know how much had been raised for twenty years. On average, however, every mayor's war chest *since* 1975 had averaged $1.5 million to $2 million a year after a mayor's fund-raiser. The late mayor never had to spend much money on his reelection campaigns; his solid machine would deliver the victory. Nor did he hire political consultants, and he bought little TV advertising. A conservative total of $10 million to $20 million in missing funds was bandied about. To this day, nobody knows whether there really ever was much money, and I doubt that anyone ever will. Michael was replaced as the party's attorney.

All through this 1977 period, Michael Daley was calling me. At first I thought that he was perhaps lonely—there had to be an emotional letdown. He had had so much power, been right in the thick of things, and his and Richie's law firm had so many city contracts. His calls were not specific—just general questions about things going on at City Hall. After several calls I began to suspect that Michael, Richie, Billy, and John were slowly being shut out of the mayor's office. I wasn't surprised; they had stuck it to many people in their careers.

Meanwhile, it seemed to me that City Hall was dead, had no driving force. Bilandic delegated most of his work to Donovan. He enjoyed cutting ribbons and sitting in the big office, but he did not seem to enjoy the long hours entailed in being a real mayor. Also, Bilandic was a creature of the city council. His buddies were aldermen; he had little in common with the cabinet types who dealt with the nuts and bolts of city government. I felt the administration slipping into mediocrity. Cabinet meetings didn't take place on a regular basis; the once rather close camaraderie between officials slipped. It was as if everyone was waiting for a signal. The formerly shiny bright lobby of City Hall seemed dingy and dark. It was winter, and the salt and water tracked in on the marble floors was no longer washed away several times a day. The lobby was also truly darker because Bilandic, always the environmentalist, had lowered the lights to conserve energy. I found the whole scene lacking in energy, drive, purpose.

In May, I told Michael I might leave City Hall. I was still not quite sure why he was calling so often. It was uncharacteristic of him. Was he calling others in the pipeline? What kind of information was he seeking? Once, when he was frankly criticizing the Bilandic administration, I said, "Why don't you go to the horse's mouth?"—meaning Donovan. "After all, you people put Bilandic in there. He's your mayor." I did not know that the mayor and Donovan were irritated by the occasional press speculation that Bilandic had been put there only to save the chair for Richie. It would be much later before anyone would learn the truth: Bilandic and Donovan were making their own plans, which did not include taking orders from the Daley boys any longer. It was thought by many that they intended to become the new Bridgeport powers.

I decided I would finish drafting new ordinances regarding taxis, limos, and sightseeing buses, and see them through passage in the council, but that would be it. I would then resign, a decision I shared with Michael. He agreed that the administration was lackluster, but he could find no suitable alternatives in the crowd of younger politicians.

The taxicab regulation ordinance that had been approved in committee the day Mayor Daley died finally came before the full council, and it passed, as I expected. Bilandic was not concerned about that kind of nitty-gritty. He had other things on his mind; principally, his campaign for mayor. The black community vowed to slate a candidate to take on the machine as revenge for the treatment of Wilson Frost. After several attempts to find a willing candidate, they finally drafted State Senator Harold Washington. Former Congressman Roman Pucinski and Hanrahan were also candidates. Given this field, I thought Bilandic would win in a walk. His campaign was low-key, and Chicagoans did not become interested in the race or in him. Perhaps no one could have stirred them so soon after Daley's death. Besides, the election was only to finish out Mayor Daley's term.

On election day, Bilandic carried thirty-eight of fifty wards. Pucinski carried only seven north and northwest side wards. Washington carried five wards, or 10 percent of the vote. As in the previous election, voter turnout was low. A total of the dissenting votes revealed a high percentage of voters opposed to Bilandic and the machine. Nevertheless, Bridgeport was still in power in 1977.

The day after the election, Donovan called to discuss a rumor of a cab strike, but I predicted it wouldn't happen. The union was forever announcing strikes, but when the day arrived, the overwhelming number of drivers went to work, because they needed the money. Moreover, the union leadership was weak and disorganized.

Nevertheless, Tom asked me down to Bilandic's office to discuss the matter. When I got there, Ed Bedore, still the budget director, was waiting. As the three of us entered the mayor's office, Tom said, "We have to make it snappy, because the Bogan people are coming." A group of mothers from the Bogan area were apparently en route to protest a school busing issue. I was puzzled. After the many vitriolic demonstrations that had scarred Chicago, a delegation of mothers and grandmothers hardly seemed threatening. Besides, things had quieted down in the southwest side neighborhoods of Gage Park, Marquette Park, and Bogan, areas targeted by Martin Luther King's open housing marches of the 1960s. Resistance in these areas to any public housing, open housing, or busing of children was nothing new. Yet Bilandic hastily led us out the back door of his office to that of the corporation counsel. From there, we were spirited up an internal staircase to another floor and down an elevator to the Clark Street side of the building. Then we were hustled into the mayor's limousine, which sped us along the Dan Ryan Expressway. This was certainly a novel way to do city business.

As it turned out, we were headed for Midway Airport, where we took over a conference room and waited for David Markin, the Checker Cab president. Bilandic had Tom call Corporation Counsel Bill Quinlan to join us. This was going to be quite a meeting. For starters, since none of us had expected to be at the airport, we had no reports in hand for reference, no records at all.

Donovan had brought along my department's outside audit of the cab companies' records, a document I had given the mayor weeks earlier. The audit indicated that cab company profits had increased dramatically since they switched to leasing, a rise not hard to understand. Prior to leasing, cab drivers had worked on commission, paid a share of the meter total at the end of the day. They were treated as employees, and the company therefore bore the normal expenses of any company—pension plans, health insurance, and general overhead. Leasing made the drivers into independent contractors, relieving Checker of all employee responsibilities. Any meeting about a strike would have to deal with cab company profits, but nobody here was talking about a strike. This conclave, it became clear, was about a rate increase. Stunned, I asked the mayor to read that page of the audit relevant to Checker and Yellow Cab company profits. Bilandic glanced quickly at the figures and then, without reference to them, asked Markin's representative, Jerry Feldman, to get his financial package together and have the companies' attorney approve it. That terminated our meeting.

We returned to the limousine, and again I suggested to Bilandic that he read the audit (which cost the city $11,000). Bilandic didn't think I should say any more about that audit and said that after all we didn't know what standards they had used. Not until then did I realize what I had just sat through. Our ridiculous gyrations to avoid the Bogan delegation had been a setup to a secret meeting about a rate increase. When I reached my office, I was just about in shock, but it was turning to anger. Almost immediately, Harry Golden of the *Chicago Sun-Times* barged in: "What was the meeting about with you, Donovan, Bedore, and the mayor?" Of course, so many city workers at the airport saw our delegation that it would have been impossible to keep it a secret.

I angrily replied, "Don't ask. I don't want to talk about it." When he persisted, I snapped, "A taxicab rate increase, that's what it was about." I'd put him onto a hot story, and I was delighted. Perhaps adverse newspaper headlines would scare the mayor and stop this.

I had now decided definitely to resign. Jerry Feldman called to say that he understood what the mayor meant—"Have your figures look good." He explained how he would do so: "I'll take some of the administrative costs and transfer them from the commission drivers' operation to lease operations."

Now he was implicating me, drawing me into this scheme. I called Ed Bedore to relay Feldman's conversation and told him firmly I didn't like one bit of this. About a week later, I was summoned to the mayor's office to meet with Bilandic, Feldman, the union head, Donovan, and Bedore. The mayor began the meeting by folding: "I think it is established that to provide quality service there will have to be a rate increase." In my view, he had given away any hope of negotiation. Feldman's request for an increase, it seemed, would be allowed.

This ticked me off. "You do know that this is totally outside the law?" I objected.

Feldman coolly replied, "The law should be changed."

Ending with small talk and discussions of the public relations aspects on all of this, we all assembled in the mayor's press conference room to announce that the unions and the major cab companies had settled their differences. There would be no strike. Bilandic was playing a "Daley"—the great negotiator. But in my view, he had settled nothing and had quietly orchestrated an unnecessary rate increase, a fact never mentioned at the press conference. At the end, Bilandic passed out loaves of sourdough bread to the press, a memento of his recent trip to San Francisco for the U.S. Conference of Mayors.

Dough, sour or green, was certainly on my mind. The fare hike seemed clearly illegal to me. City law allowed a 14 percent cab company profit, fares as against expenses. Figures were validated by a sworn statement once yearly. If the fares were not 14 percent above expenses, the city council could raise rates.

Checker and Yellow had muddied all of this formerly clear water. About 70 percent of their cabs were now leased to independent contractors, who of course reported no gross fares because they paid a straight leasing fee to the companies. I'd gone to bat for a law requiring cab companies to lay out their leased cab figures to the Department of Consumer Affairs. The law had been in effect for six months, but Checker and Yellow had consistently refused to send the paperwork. Now no one in the city really knew what their profits were. It also troubled me that my predecessor, James Y. Carter, had been indicated and convicted of bribery for his dealings with the cab companies. I had kept every memo regarding the fare increase. My brother Edward, an attorney, advised me to put all my notes into one omnibus memo. And he approved of my plan to authorize Bansley & Kiener, the Consumer Affairs Department's auditing firm, to compare the figures the cab companies submitted to the council with the figures they had already submitted to my department. In addition, I had turned over the previous audit to the Federal Trade Commission.

Bansley & Kiener found discrepancies, which I reported to Mayor Bilandic on November 7. On the basis of these new figures, he could easily roll back the increase, I reasoned. The Consumer Affairs Department in turn asked Checker to explain why the figures submitted to the department differed from those given the city council. Besieged, the cab companies sought to turn the tables. They began to insult my inspectors. Replies to written requests for information slowed to a trickle. And just as suddenly, we were being investigated by the press. Out of nowhere came one *Chicago Tribune* reporter, Bill Griffin, and then another, towing an investigator from the Better Government Association, a civic-oriented group primarily concerned with acts of misconduct in government. Right or wrong, the BGA has always been called an arm of the Republican Party. The subject, ostensibly, was department policy toward limousine licensing. I was annoyed, to say the least. Consumer Affairs policies were an open book. I agreed with three of my deputy commissioners; this was a fishing expedition at best and harassment at worst.

Griffin returned. He wanted copies of all our proposed ordinances for taxis and limousines. He also wanted to see an exclusive airport contract dealing with bus service from O'Hare to many of the downtown hotels. The bus company in question, Continental Bus Service, is a subsidiary of Checker Motors. Technically, it operated illegally, since no one in the taxi business could by law own another type of city vehicle license. The bus company had gotten around the law for years by operating on an Interstate Commerce permit. Our new set of proposed ordinances would remedy that: Checker would have to divest itself of the bus company, or the city would have to change the law. This news seemed to turn the *Trib* a bit. Bill Griffin wrote a story favorable to my department.

I was still troubled by the rate increase and was doing my best to expose it. In confidence, I gave Griffin a copy of my omnibus memo, which included all the notes on the rate increase and the Midway Airport meeting. He and the *Tribune* could investigate a real issue, if they cared to. None of this limousine Mickey Mouse. Then I decided to call U.S. Attorney Thomas Sullivan, without telling anyone—not even my brother or Jay. The next day, I arrived at the U.S. attorney's office with another copy of the omnibus memo and met with him and a group of his assistants. My message: if it was wrong, I wasn't part of it, and I wanted my records in his hands. The U.S. attorney warned me to keep our meeting secret, lest the investigation be thwarted.

To this day, I don't know where the leak came from, but in a small story the *Chicago Daily News* revealed that there were discrepancies in the taxicab figures. There was clearly a leak somewhere, and I felt the story was pointing to me. Suddenly I seemed to be attacked through questions being fed to the media about discrepancies in the figures.

The media jumped on it. I was so infuriated that when Channel 2 asked me to go live on the evening news, I wasted no time in making it plain that City Hall was not going to pin the blame on me for the council's decision to approve the fare hike. If they wanted a fight, I'd give them one. On Saturday, November 12, I went into my office and photocopied every pertinent document and letter, including every one of the unanswered letters to Checker asking for an explanation of the discrepancies in the two audits. As I was about to leave, Dave Caravello called. He worked for Walter Jacobsen, the top TV anchor in Chicago, and did much of the footwork in tracking down leads for Walter's personal on-air commentary, *Walter's Perspective*. "Commissioner, I have gone over the tape of last evening. I smell a deeper story here. Can I come and see you?" When we met, I handed him a copy of my omnibus memo, mentioning that Bill Griffin also had a copy. Both were off the record, I added. "Griffin is free to investigate, but not through me. I don't think I'm going to be here much longer. When the time comes, you can release it."

A city council meeting was scheduled for the following Monday. I went, as always, but was very uncomfortable. As I sat in the cabinet box, a northwest side alderman, Tom Cullerton, came over to me and said quietly, "Don't let those guys rattle you. If anyone moves to embarrass you, sixteen of us are prepared to walk out. We are all sick of what is going on around here." I felt a wave of relief. I wasn't alone. Nothing was going to change, but at least I wasn't alone.

Later, Walter Jacobsen called: "Our legal people have okayed release of this memo. When can we go with it? You know, don't you, that they'll have to fire you if we go with this. I'm not pushing you into it." Jacobsen feared a leak before his scoop, but leaks are constant. City Hall usually knows hours before a big story actually breaks. The CBS legal department was now in the know. Soon Bilandic would be, too.

I said, "Walter, go with it whenever you like." I really didn't care anymore. My memo had been with the U.S. attorney for almost two weeks.

When I told Jay that I had given a copy to Jacobsen, he almost fell off his chair. "They'll come at you like bobcats," he said.

In need of fresh air, Jay and I walked over to St. Peter's, where I said a prayer in hopes that I had done the right thing.

When my brother called and learned what I'd done, he reacted viscerally. He later told me his hand shook so badly he had a hard time putting the phone in the cradle. "I *think* you are covered," he said. "The only thing, which isn't serious, is that they'll continue to level charges at you that you should have come forward sooner." Swearing him to secrecy, I admitted going to the U.S. attorney to urge him to investigate, and said that he had asked me to keep it to myself. Edward gasped, then said, "Well, you are in for a rough ride of it. But Mother would be proud."

Walter Jacobsen called back to say, "We are going with it tonight. We are also going to promote it on radio as well as TV. You should leave early. The press will hound you."

I had a speaking engagement at St. Mary of the Woods Parish Church, where my sister Jill was a communicant, but as the speech was not on my public schedule, I wouldn't be found that evening. I warned my father he might be besieged by the media. A large turnout at St. Mary of the Woods surprised me, for many top-ranking city officials, as well as Billy Daley, lived in the parish. (I expected them to close ranks around the mayor.) As I finished talking about consumer issues, a note was slipped to me on the podium—NBC had phoned for an interview and wanted to send a film crew. I declined. I didn't want to turn the situation into a three-ring circus. Besides, I thought my memo spoke for itself.

On my street, television lights illuminated the house. The press jammed street and yard, so I drove past, phoning my sister Carol from the car to see how my father was handling the commotion and to have her ask him to unlock the back entrance. As soon as I hung up, Jay called. Reporters were swarming all over him asking where I was, and his editor was shouting at him for a copy of the memo. I drove to his office, gave him a copy, then headed home again.

As I parked in the garage behind the house, a set of lights went on, and I saw a police officer near the garage. He said, "You don't need to go in the back way, Commissioner. I know you and I know your father. I'll escort you in the front way."

I felt myself getting teary. I said, "Officer, City Hall will be angry at you."

He replied, "Don't let them see you cry. There are a lot of people who feel like you do. Put your sunglasses on. I'll be proud to escort you."

Front way it was—right past the hordes of press. Those kind words were about to trigger an avalanche of tears accumulated during at least five months of tension and anxiety. Knowing the machine and its ways of retaliation, I was concerned about that kind police officer. I called Kathy and Jay, reassuring them I was fine, although I was very cold, almost numb. Round One was only beginning, and already I was drained and exhausted. Machine insiders would consider me a traitor.

In the morning, the press turned up again, but not bearing the news I expected: Bilandic's request for my resignation. I decided to go to my office and pack my personal belongings. At City Hall, the inspectors and deputies were working frantically on the records of the taxi companies, hoping to preserve the integrity of the department. The previous evening, Bilandic had appeared on the ten-o'clock news, denying allegations of an illegal fare increase. His denial didn't wash. The press hounded both of us. Aside from the two of us, most city officials refused to comment, except for Edward Vrdolyak, who sniped at me. "I feel sorry for her. It's her age," he said, intimating I was menopausal. Bilandic and I wound up taking lie detector tests, and we both "passed." When Channel 2 polled Chicagoans for their opinion on which of us was telling the truth, I won decisively. It seemed there was nothing else in the headlines but "Taxigate."

On November 21, Michael Daley called: "Don't get yourself too far out on a limb. You know the press loves 'let's you and me fight.' "

I said, "Michael, you knew all about this. I told you about the Midway meeting at the time. That was four months ago. It has gone too far. I can't turn back. We'd better not talk to each other anymore. Not until it's over."

I did not know whether he was consulting with Bilandic and Donovan. The saga dragged on in the media. The phone didn't stop ringing. This was becoming the longest week of my life.

The day after Michael's call, as I pulled in front of City Hall, a radio bulletin informed me that I had been fired. Inside the building, there were mixed reactions. Smiling faces greeted me as I walked through the front door, but in the elevator to the eighth floor, city workers appeared terrified to be in the same space. My brother Edward was waiting in my office. Camera crews were all over the place. As I got to my office, the entire downtown staff of about forty rose to their feet, clapping and cheering, tears streaming down their faces as they saluted our efforts. I can't cry, I thought. When I saw what was going on in my private office, I grew cold with anger, instead. Plainclothes policemen and an assistant corporation counsel oversaw the stripping of my personal effects. They had not asked for this assignment, but I felt humiliated by them nonetheless. Thrown casually into a box were my autographed picture of Mayor Daley and the photo of President Kennedy with Kathy sitting on his lap.

I ordered them to leave. I should be allowed to pack my own things. The counsel, Martin Healy, turned to my brother. "Ed, I don't like this at all. But I'm under orders."

He shot back, "If you don't like what you're doing, why are you doing it?"

I jumped in. "Are you proud of yourself?"

He said, "No, I'm not. But I'm under orders, and you know what that means. They've told me to inventory everything and send your things to you."

I retorted, "Neither you nor anybody else will touch any more of my personal possessions."

Edward grimly interceded, "If you don't get out of here this min-

ute, I'm walking across the street to the courts to get an injunction to
stop this."

With that, Healy called his boss, Bill Quinlan, relayed our conversation, and added, "The TV people are here filming it all." That did
it. He was given the go-ahead to allow me to pack my things in private. Little did he know that I had already removed copies of all files
germane to the rate increase, and of course I had not yet publicly
revealed my meeting with the U.S. attorney.

The entire staff cheered again as we said goodbye. I handed over
my car keys to Deputy Commissioner Terry Hocin. Walking toward
the elevator I noticed that no one hung around in the normally active
hall; there were no small groups chatting and sipping coffee. The
taxpayers were getting a full day's work that day as the cameras
trailed along beside me. A few custodial workers waved goodbye and
blew kisses. "Goodbye, Commissioner, we'll miss you."

I turned. "Oh, don't worry. I'll be back." I hadn't intended any
challenge to the administration; it was simply my way of saying "See
you around." Television news loved it, though, and played the words
as a promise that I planned to return to City Hall. That set off new
fears in Bilandic's coterie.

As I waited for a cab, passing drivers honked and flashed the
thumbs-up sign. Pedestrians yelled, "Give 'em hell, Jane." Frankly,
the notoriety frightened me. I had been scheduled to address an influential lakefront community organization, the North Dearborn Association, the following evening. I assumed that the engagement, to
be held at a very posh Gold Coast club, would be canceled when I lost
my job, but I received a telegram to the contrary. The group had
already sent out press releases announcing the speech, so television
cameras were on hand. Between the time I left home and my arrival,
the club's board members canceled the meeting. As cameras rolled, I
was informed I would not be allowed to speak after all. Then the
program chairman of the neighborhood organization rushed through
the throng, grabbed my hand, and yanked me past the doorman. Since
his organization had paid for the meeting room, he was determined
that I speak. I spoke. I detailed the entire story of the rate increases,
and again people cheered. I drove home on the Kennedy Expressway,
gratified by the horns honking as people smiled and flashed the
thumbs-up sign. These people were urging me to "keep going," but I
had nowhere to go.

Committeemen wondered aloud to the press why I had turned the trivial issue of a fare hike into such a controversy. If Bilandic wanted to interpret the city's law loosely, that was his business, I reasoned. If he was doing a political favor for someone at the expense of the consumer, that, too, was his decision. I wasn't going to pretend that the company figures I had in front of me the first time were not real. Let them play games. I simply couldn't. In fact, they were stupid to take me to Midway that day. But once there I did what I had to do. Most of the Bridgeport crowd dismissed me as a "crazy broad," allowed by Daley "to become the Joan of Arc of consumerism because it made him look good." Others reasoned that Daley had kept me ignorant of the endemic corruption practices of City Hall.

But times were changing. Soon, and surprisingly, I began to get invitations to address Kiwanis, Rotary, and Lions clubs all over the suburbs. People could be kind and idealistic. Knowing City Hall, Bilandic's pals must have been flabbergasted. According to the rules, if you fought City Hall, your name came out of the Rolodex.

Ironically, my first thoughts of running against the machine originated, in a way, with the machine. Periodic press quotes, always attributed to insiders, went something like "Just watch. She's going to run for mayor." The thought had not even entered my mind in November of 1977, but grass-roots support was building on its own. Whenever Jay and I went out to dinner, people came over to our table to ask for my autograph and say, "Go for mayor, Jane." Many in the black community urged me to run. It was at first overwhelming.

On the legal front, finally, both State's Attorney Bernard Carey and U.S. Attorney Thomas Sullivan, responding to continual nagging from the press, announced they were looking into the taxi fare hike. The day before Thanksgiving, I spent seven hours cooperating with two assistant U.S. attorneys. As I sat there, I thought back to a conversation with James Hoge, editor of the *Sun-Times*, who had called me to suggest that I write an article for his newspaper. His first question was "What are you going to do now?" Then he said confidently, "The mayor will not be indicted on anything. I have it on high authority that the U.S. attorney has no appetite to indict."

This information disturbed me. I said, "Well, we'll have to see. We'll just have to wait and see." That's what I was doing with my life those days.

Whenever we children were troubled, my mother would say, "Go for a walk and get some fresh air. Clear out the cobwebs." So I frequently went for long walks. Because I'd been so preoccupied before,

I'd made no preparations for Christmas. I drove out to Old Orchard shopping center to buy red candles for the candelabra and the mantel. While I browsed in Marshall Field's, I heard, "It's her. There she is. It's Jane Byrne." Suddenly I was surrounded by well-wishers. "Go for it, Jane. Give 'em hell, Janie." There was literally no place I could go in the shopping center without attracting kind and friendly attention.

Meanwhile, the machine treated me to annoying reminders of its power. For a time, there was police surveillance. I called them on it, publicly, and it stopped.

After the holidays, TV anchorman Bill Kurtis called to ask for an interview. I declined, explaining that my notes were in the hands of the U.S. attorney and I had nothing to add to the controversy. He said, "Our surveys indicate that our viewers still want to see you and want to know what you are doing." I had been kept going only by my own conviction of being right and by public support. It is amazing how much energy the public generates in a public figure. If they really were interested in me, I might as well let Bill Kurtis come to my home.

After the interview, a group of friends, including Edward, suggested we take our own poll to gauge voter reaction to the idea of my candidacy for mayor. The results were encouraging—not surprisingly, considering how Bilandic had squeaked through the previous April. Put the 10 percent black vote with the dissatisfied white 30 percent, and it wouldn't take that much additional support to win. Also, voter turnout in the last three mayoral elections had been terribly low. If disenchanted voters could be lured back to the polls, a challenger could upset the incumbent.

My interest in running was stifled somewhat by rumors that the *Chicago Daily News* would fold, and so it did. On March 4, Jay and I were both out of work. We decided to deal with reality after St. Patrick's Day. On March 17, we were married at Queen of All Saints Basilica. When we returned from our honeymoon in the Bahamas, Jay had an interview with Morgan Finley, clerk of the circuit court, seeking a spot in his press office, and seemed to have the job. But this was Chicago, where nothing is so simple. The machine would act true to form. The newspapers were sniffing around and a day or so later, Harry Golden, Jay's erstwhile colleague in City Hall, called to ask if he was pursuing a job with Morgan. Jay was noncommittal, but the next day an item appeared in "Kup's Column" in the *Chicago Sun-Times* suggesting that he had hinted he might have the job in hand.

After I read the article, I turned to Jay. "There goes your job."

Sure enough, Morgan called that morning: "The mayor's office is putting a helluva lot of pressure on me, Jay. I can't hire you."

Clearly, there would be scant money for any campaigning. Jay finally landed two part-time jobs, one with a public relations firm in the suburbs and another as part-time reporter with the *Sun-Times*, where he was safely tucked away in the real estate department. I had caused him many a problem in finding work, but he and Kathy continued anyway to urge me to make the race. So I announced, ten long months before the Democratic primary of 1979.

Ours would be a historically low-budget campaign. From her trust fund, Kathy, now in college, covered the cost of the phone deposit and first month's rent on campaign headquarters. In most primary campaigns, the money and the rules favor the incumbent. While it is mandatory to report sizable campaign contributions in every city, Chicago's law requires disclosure of all contribution over $150. The business community knows that the machine checks the contributions lists, a fact of local political life that hampered my effort to raise money. I was, however, flooded with speaking engagements. Veteran political reporters seemed unimpressed by my candidacy; I suppose they reasoned that a woman had never before been mayor and that no one could beat the machine candidate anyway. Hugh Hill, a seasoned television political reporter with ABC, nonetheless asked me, with great drama, "What do you think the former chairman of the Democratic Party of Cook County, Richard J. Daley, would think of you doing this?"

Instantly, I replied, "I think he'd vote for me."

Responses from the living were quite different: "She turned on us," or "She couldn't have done this on her own. Jay's to blame for this."

Nevertheless, my campaign had momentum with the people. I received many invitations to the block clubs and black churches. As a commissioner, I'd had a chauffeur; now, riding about in search of streets I'd never heard of, I saw firsthand what neighborhoods looked like when you got away from the expressways. The west side had not improved substantially after the 1968 riots. Children played in the shadows of burned-out buildings near collapse. In Englewood, 63rd Street was lined with buildings crumbling from old age. Did I have tunnel vision? Had I forgotten the hopeless, angry voices of community representatives at training sessions during my time in the antipoverty program? I judged myself guilty. I had forgotten. I had been so obsessed with consumer issues that I never noticed the plight of the city's neighborhoods. I saw despair in the faces of senior citizens, forgotten and lonely. Many expressed fear of the gangs that roamed their streets, grabbing their purses or their social security checks. Was this the Chicago I loved? Yes, and it was a part of Chicago I wanted to change.

One of my volunteers, Julius Harris, a black senior citizen, worked hard to get me speaking dates in senior public housing and black churches. Most of the time, he met me and escorted me in. One Sunday, however, he couldn't show up because of illness. He had scheduled speakings at three churches within a short distance of one another. I parked my car and walked toward a huge church that seemed a logical destination. When I passed three teenage boys, I asked them the name of the church. One of them answered, "Ain't you Jane Byrne?" I nodded. "That's the church of a payroll minister. They won't let you in there." I understood. He was a "stay-in-line minister" who knew he would get federal community grant funds only if he stayed on the team.

Most businesswomen seemed enthusiastic about my campaign, but strange obstacles arose. A paralegal living on Lake Shore Drive scheduled a coffee for me in her condominium. Two days beforehand, she called to cancel. The president of the condominium association had told her that if I spoke, the county assessor would raise the building's taxes. Similarly, senior citizens in public housing were advised by precinct captains to vote the party line or they would lose their apartments. I tried to reassure these groups that voting was a private act, that nobody knew how an individual voted, but fear of eviction was spreading from one public housing complex to another. In addition, most employees in public housing were politically sponsored. It would have been against the law, of course, for them to bar me from speaking in these buildings, but every so often I'd come around after booking the time only to find most tenants out on a city-sponsored shopping trip or some such event. I was delighted when one senior citizen coordinator, Vera Edwards, addressed the group following my speech: "When the precinct captain comes and threatens you, don't listen. When they come around election week with their chicken and sweet potato pie, you eat their chicken, you eat their sweet potato pie, but you vote for whomever you like." (I had to laugh at the irony. Vera was politically sponsored herself.)

A young Puerto Rican seminarian took me into his community to shopping centers and churches. There we were on Division Street—in the heart of the old Polish community—winning Hispanic votes. Angel Correa, a supervisor for the *Chicago Tribune*'s morning delivery carriers, and his wife worked vigorously on my behalf. He had his workers fold my rather skimpy literature into the newspapers they delivered. He even plunked a Jane Byrne bumper sticker onto Bilandic's limousine.

In all my appearances, I was stressing what I thought to be the real issues facing Chicagoans: collective bargaining rights for all city employees and the creation of new jobs through a strong program of economic development; more magnet schools, which had greater success than the traditional neighborhood schools and drew the most talented children from a wider area of the city; more police and security at public and senior citizen housing; and the appointment of a black superintendent of schools. By way of qualification, I stressed my years of administration in Consumer Affairs. Most important to me, however, I spoke of hope, a new openness in government, and a renewed energy in the neighborhoods.

As Christmas approached, I was campaigning on Division Street, not far from Cabrini Green, a low-income housing project. Two young black women, one carrying a toddler, stopped to shake my hand. I thanked them and, turning to the child, asked, "What is Santa going to bring you for Christmas?"

The mother looked at me with a forlorn expression: "We live in Cabrini Green. Santa doesn't come there." I was terribly moved by her sobering response.

On the last night of the year, I knelt down to say my usual New Year's Eve prayer and to reflect on the past twelve months. The response—or lack of it—from the U.S. attorney was a major disappointment to me. When I last met with him, he said something to the effect that while they admired what I'd done, respected my courage, did not think what had taken place was right, and didn't approve of it, their jurisdiction was limited to one narrow statute and they could not find that the actions violated that one statute. After that speech, I had dejectedly left his office.

Toward midnight, I opened the window to let in some of the beauty of the evening. The city was covered with almost two feet of fresh snow. A blizzard had hit Chicago. Horns blew, and revelers called out, "Happy New Year," echoing up to me in the canyon of high rises.

Near the end of January, about twenty inches of snow fell and the city all but halted. From the airport to mass transit to simply walking down the street, Chicagoans were frustrated and buried in snow. Campaigning became extremely difficult. But by mid-February, polls began to indicate the seemingly miraculous: I could win. On election day, February 27, Chicago was drenched in sunshine, something Chicagoans hadn't seen much of since New Year's Eve. Jay opened the drapes and said, "Look outside, honey, the sun is pouring down on Chicago. It's your day!"

People came out to vote in record numbers. I had worked hard to lure the disaffected to the voting booths. My press secretary, Andy Bajonski, told me that all three major stations were prepared to project me the winner as soon as the polls closed. I was concerned, however, that the machine might steal votes.

In my suite at the Ambassador West Hotel, our election-night headquarters, I turned on the television set to the six-o'clock news: "Jane Byrne has done the impossible." There was great rejoicing in my family. With them, I went downstairs to a ballroom crammed with cheering supporters. Gazing out over a crowd bursting with energy, I repeated Bobby Kennedy's inspirational message: "Each time a man stands up for an ideal, or acts to improve the lot of others, or strikes out against injustice, he sends out a tiny ripple of hope." Hope had beaten the machine. The margin of victory was slim—twenty thousand votes. Almost half the city had voted for Bilandic.

Power is a difficult asset to manage. There was no longer any privacy in the family suite. I arrived at the hotel in a taxicab and would go home with a police escort. As we exited the hotel, I experienced the real magic of winning—so many Chicagoans shouting their good wishes as they stood in line for blocks around the hotel. At home, as horns blew on Michigan Avenue, I gazed out at the lake and thought of the immense effort required so long ago to remove a sandbar that clogged the mouth of the Chicago River, making way for the future. I felt on February 27 of 1979 that we had swept away, for a while at least, decades of intimidation and control.

CHAPTER 18

Great Dreams for Chicago

On Inauguration eve, April 15, I sat in my living room. The panorama of the city stretched out below me. To the east, the lake curved south from Oak Street to its gracious bend, meeting the shores of Indiana. Directly in front of me was Navy Pier, due east of Streeterville, where Chicagoans had picnicked decades ago, danced on the roof garden, and sneaked a bit of liquor during Prohibition. There "Cap" Streeter's wife had maneuvered her old scow up to the pier to sell hot dogs and sandwiches during the second World's Fair in 1933. Bilandic deserved credit for reminding Chicagoans of the fun and camaraderie to be had at Navy Pier when he instituted an annual celebration called Chicago Fest. Bathed in soft lights, directly below me stood the indestructible Water Tower and its Pumping Station. Both structures, made of a creamy stone, shone with character. Within the Water Tower there were still watering troughs for the horses of the carriage trade. I'll bring the horse-drawn carriages back, I thought; they're good for sightseeing and tourism.

Two blocks to the southwest of me stood Holy Name Cathedral, built of the same creamy stone, a trade-off for the Dearborn Street bridge. Bishop Lyne would offer a private Mass in the cathedral chapel an hour before I took my oath as mayor the next evening. How moving that gesture was for me! I envisioned my ancestors making their way to the cathedral to worship. My grandmother had been schooled there. It was a long way from their days of ankle-length skirts and

Irish woolen shawls to tomorrow night's Mass. Who among them would have believed that from second- and third-generation Irish-Americans would come not only a north sider, but the first woman to be mayor of Chicago?

Farther south, the Magnificent Mile ran to the stem of the river. There stood a pinnacle of power, the mighty *Chicago Tribune*, very near DuSable's original residence on the river's edge. A plane skimmed just above the water and touched down at Meigs Airport. And far away to the south, the flames from Hammond and South Chicago's oil and steel refineries shot into the sky. From the den on the west side of our home, I could view the southwest side beyond Midway and the northwest side out to O'Hare. The press labeled those two heavily ethnic areas the "bungalow belt" because of the array of single-family houses. To me, they weren't any kind of belt, but a chain of small towns, each distinct from the others. All of these areas had been annexed.

My reminiscing swung back to the primary victory, which had caught so many off guard. Labor, big business, both the major newspapers—all had endorsed Bilandic, and lost. Many machine loyalists vowed they weren't going to take it lying down. According to several radio reports, some of the committeemen/aldermen had asked the Socialist Party candidate to step down so one of them could take that spot in the general election.

But most of the pols had been coming around to make their peace almost as soon as my 1979 primary election win was official. George Dunne had phoned his congratulations, offering to set up a series of small breakfast meetings with the committeemen. "You won, and we'll have to work together," he said. Frankly, I was in no mood to work with Dunne or any committeemen following that bitter primary fight. They had thrown everything at me that they could. Too many of them were old hat—closed to new ideas—and had not changed their attitudes toward women, even after the humiliating Miami convention. Many of them, but certainly not all, had been around much longer than I. Surely, if they had really cared, Chicago's neighborhoods wouldn't have been in the shape they were in. I wasn't "one of the boys," and I didn't want to be. But Don Rose, my liberal consultant, said, "You were elected by a very narrow coalition. You must reach out to embrace the whole of Chicago. The machine has the power in the council to stymie your programs."

So I agreed to the breakfast meetings. The first one didn't start off too well. My old friend Matt Bieszczat, who had refused to vote for me as co-chair of the Democratic Party even at Mayor Daley's behest, did come into the meeting room, but he wouldn't sit down. "I refuse to break bread with this woman," he growled. "She plans to give the police and firemen labor contracts. She's out to break the machine. She's out to break the organization." With that he marched out, slamming the door.

For a minute, an embarrassed silence hung in the room, then the others began to laugh along with me. Danny Rostenkowski said that maybe we should slow down a minute—maybe things weren't so funny. He said that at a prayer breakfast in the White House yesterday, President Carter had asked him, "Danny, what's going to happen to poor Chicago now?" If the President of the United States was worried about us, things might not be so funny.

They all lowered their eyes and mournfully shook their heads over the dismal prospects for Chicago. Are these people crazy? I asked myself. I worked in City Hall for over fifteen years, yet they are treating me like an invader from outer space. President Carter didn't even know me. Assuming he actually made the remark, his bias probably stemmed from an image of the big, reliably efficient machine: "the city of big shoulders." Big shoulders belonged on men. Similarly, when I met later with the Democratic leaders of the house of representatives and senate in Springfield, they had nothing to hand me but problems. The vote wasn't there for the Equal Rights Amendment. Did I really want to support the reduction of sales tax on food and drugs? Wouldn't that cripple the city's budget?

Richie Daley had phoned to congratulate me a few days after the primary. I knew the call had cost him something to make, for Richie was still ward committeeman of Bridgeport, the home of Chicago mayors for almost half a century. He knew the tenor of the breakfast meetings. "You know, most of the guys, they're scared. Why don't you give them a call and reassure them?" He ticked off a list of thirteen or fourteen names and phone numbers. I had barely hung up when Don Rose reminded me it was time to leave for the first of a long list of campaign stops.

When I returned to campaign headquarters at 5:30 P.M., Richie was on the line again, asking why I hadn't called those guys. I was taken aback. He was nervous, but also demanding. I mentioned my full campaign schedule, then caught myself wondering why I was expected to provide an explanation. Was I being brokered? If Richie had told those alderman I would call, he'd lost face when I hadn't.

Michael Madigan, Democratic Minority Whip in the Illinois house, phoned to tell me he was meeting with his captains to turn them around to support me in the general election, and he said he wanted me to know that nobody spoke for him, not even Richie Daley.

Then came a call from John D'Arco, the committeeman of the 1st Ward, the ward with alleged ties to the crime syndicate. One didn't hear much about the mob in the 1960s and 1970s, because of the coverage of the protests of the sixties and the corruption and scandals of the seventies; it was as if they had disappeared. But D'Arco was reputedly the mob's go-between at City Hall. "What's Daley doing?" D'Arco asked. "He called me down here in Florida to tell me to wait for your call. Who is he to tell me that?" D'Arco added, "I'll deliver my ward. I'll give you no trouble, but I'm not going through anyone any more than I did with the old man."

Alderman John Aiello called next and nervously asked, what he had done and if he was on bad paper—a phrase from the Mayor Daley era; it meant someone was displeasing to him. He said Richie had told him that he had squared things with me. In almost nonstop fashion he explained that he had supported Bilandic because Bilandic was the choice of the party and not because he had anything against me. I asked him why he was calling. Because I hadn't called, he said. I asked him if I had told him I would call. He of course answered no.

I was gulping down a quick dinner in my office when Richie called again to tell me he thought that most of the guys were probably at home now for dinner. He suggested I give them a call. He also said he wanted to see me, but not in my office in the Monadnock Building, because there would be too many reporters hanging around.

My brother Edward's law firm was down the hall from my office, and I agreed to meet Richie there. As for the phone calls to the aldermen, I reminded Richie I wasn't the mayor *yet* and had nothing to discuss with the aldermen that couldn't wait until after the general election.

I wanted to talk to a councilman I could trust, someone who'd advise me on the antics of other council members—and calm them down. Richie, I now realized, had stirred them up, and God knows that creates all kinds of damaging, mischievous rumors as to who's on first, who's in, or who's out with the new administration.

I phoned Vito Marzullo, dean of the city council. He had worked his way up through the ranks and, though nearly eighty years old, was canny and sharp. Vito had nothing to gain by giving me advice, as he couldn't resist pointing out. "Mayor, I need nothing. Anything I say to you is for your own good, the good of the city and the Democratic Party. What you did is similar to an earthquake. Everybody's upset. Everybody's going in different directions; nobody knows where they stand. What you did was okay, but rest it for a while. Don't make any drastic changes right away. Let the dust settle. They are all jockeying for position. Let things simmer down. George Dunne didn't do right by you and the ladies, but don't retaliate. You will be the mayor. What can George do against you? You'll have all the jobs. He's been around for a long time. People are used to him. Don't make any more drastic changes."

Everybody was telling me to go slow, as if Chicago really was experiencing seismic tremors. And I hadn't even been elected yet! Angry and worried, big business had taken to calling me a "populist." Business's point was that when Cleveland elected a "populist" mayor, the city plunged into bankruptcy.

When Richie and I met in my brother's office later in the week, the purpose of his visit quickly became obvious. Richie was then serving as a state senator, but his head was hardly in Springfield. He had dreams of reorganizing the city council from behind the scenes, of choosing the chairs of the various committees himself. These creatures of the machine—drop most of them in a bag, shake them up, and you couldn't tell them apart. All were after the same things—power, money, patronage. I stopped listening to his schemes, but Richie persisted. Soon I gratefully excused myself; I was late for a campaign stop. We agreed to meet again.

Finally, on April 3, the anticlimactic general election took place. There was never much doubt that I would win; Chicago hasn't elected a Republican mayor since Big Bill Thompson. The Republicans had slated investment banker Wallace Johnson, and the Socialist Party candidate was Andrew Pulley. For a city that had slipped election after election in its voter turnout, the trend was reversed that day. Just as the sun had beamed down on the snow-clogged city on February 27, it shone out again. Over 800,000 marched to the polls in an election that most Chicagoans knew was a sure thing. Whatever magic was taking place in Chicago, it was wonderful. My final vote was 671,189 to Johnson's 132,261. My capturing an astonishing 82 percent of the vote was bannered in all the newspapers, with the

Election night, April 4, 1979, when I received 82.11 percent of the vote.
COURTESY ASSOCIATED PRESS.

subheadline that I had beaten Daley's all-time record total. While I carried Bridgeport and every other ward in the city, I knew many Bridgeporters were hurt.

The lobbying heated up. Finally, Ed Vrdolyak, the most powerful alderman in the city council, as well as my nemesis during the Taxigate scandal, surfaced. Charles Swibel, the twenty-year chairman of Public Housing, called early one morning shortly after the general election. Although we had served together in Mayor Daley's cabinet, I didn't know Swibel well. In the past, he had been severely criticized by the liberal wing of the Chicago press. One of the hottest issues in Chicago during the 1960s and 1970s was the building of public housing in white neighborhoods. Such building had been mandated by federal court order, but Swibel, doing Richard Daley's bidding, had challenged that decision in the courts, tying up the issue for years. Meanwhile, public housing had stayed where it was, mostly in black and poor neighborhoods.

Swibel stated he was calling on behalf of Vrdolyak. "Eddie wants peace. He doesn't plan to fight you in the council. He will prove that to you today by passing the condominium ordinance exactly as you drafted it over a year and a half ago."

I suggested to Swibel that I could pass it on the floor of the council without Vrdolyak's help, as Eddie well knew. Swibel asked if I would at least take the alderman's call. I said, "No, I don't trust him. I will never trust him."

Of, course, Swibel insisted that Eddie would never doublecross him—he guaranteed it. Politics is finally the art of compromise, and Swibel had been a trusted ally of the late mayor. I met him halfway. "You tell Vrdolyak that he should go through you whenever he wants to talk to me. I will never talk to him without a third party. I warn you—if his word is broken or yours ever is, you will have no access to the office of mayor." Such was the climate of Chicago politics on inaugural eve, April 15, 1979.

The next evening, my entire extended family—Jay, Kathy, my father, five brothers and sisters, and well over twenty-five nephews and nieces—attended Mass in the Chapel of Holy Name. How I wished my mother could have been there! At the end of Mass, we moved by motorcade south toward City Hall. As we passed over the river from the north side to downtown Chicago, I winked at the Dearborn Street bridge. For the first time in a quarter of a century, the motorcade to a mayoral election came down LaSalle Street from the north. Yet City Hall stood solid nonetheless, its pillars strong enough to bear the shock of my election.

I had asked a childhood friend, Federal Judge John Powers Crowley, to officiate. The oath was solemn and impressive: "I, Jane Byrne, do solemnly swear that I will support the Constitution of the United States and the Constitution of the State of Illinois, that I will faithfully discharge the duties of the office of Mayor of the City of Chicago according to the best of my ability, so help me God." Following the swearing-in, I held an open house in the mayor's office, inviting in all Chicagoans to see it. I wanted those thousands of people who had voted for me without the inducement of patronage to know I truly represented them.

After being away from government almost two years, I couldn't wait to start. The council reorganized itself, with no interference from me, except for two positions. Through Vito Marzullo, I asked that Wilson Frost be allowed to remain finance chairman. I also chose Alderman Richard Mell for the position of president pro tem of the

An awesome moment. I took the oath of office as mayor of Chicago on April 16, 1979. The late federal judge John Powers Crowley, a childhood friend, administered it. COURTESY JACK LENAHAN, *Chicago Sun-Times.*

council. I notified George Dunne that I would not oppose his reelection as county chairman, but he had to win on his own.

I had retained Mayor Daley's two personal bodyguards, whom I'd known for about ten years before my election. Like everyone else who had been close to him, we periodically engaged in the sport of swapping Daley stories. Once they got talking about the time, toward the end of his life, when he took a sudden fancy to bottled water. From time to time, Daley would ask his bodyguards to pick up a case, but he never gave the guys any money. After a while, satisfying the mayor's thirst had become quite costly. "Honest to God," one of them whispered, "I'm even afraid to tell this now, in case his fist comes punching right out of the grave." They started collecting the empty bottles and filling them with our plain old tap water from Lake Michigan. They carefully resealed each one, terrified that Daley would catch on, but the mayor remained well pleased. When guests came over, he always offered them glasses of his fine bottled water, extolling its virtues of purity and clarity, while his bodyguards trembled in their boots. This whole story was told *sotto voce* . . . just in case.

Mrs. Richard J. Daley and sons Michael, William, Richard, and daughter
Ellie arriving at my inauguration in 1979. COURTESY JACK LENAHAN,
Chicago Sun-Times.

The heavy winter snows had melted, leaving a wake of garbage
and debris throughout the city. My first official act was to order a
citywide cleanup. As we began to organize the massive effort, Clark
Burris, the city comptroller, advised: "Mayor, please keep the spending down. I know you want the cleanup, but please keep it down."

"Down to what?" I asked. "Be specific."

He replied gloomily, "Down to nothing." Burris was projecting a
shortfall in the city's budget—a large shortfall. "We'll be lucky to
meet payroll through the end of the year," he said. Specifically, we
might run out of money by November, and we were facing a year-end
deficit.

"How did this happen, Clark?" I asked.

In those chambers we'd all grown used to lowering our voices.
Clark lowered his to a whisper. "Well, federal revenue funds kept

diminishing." And in an even lower voice, as if afraid the late Richard J. Daley might hear and judge him disloyal, he added, "Daley just went on spending as if the funds were pouring in. Mayor, maybe we can work something out with the unions and the state and still have the cleanup."

After Clark left, I sat for a moment, letting this bad news sink in. Not to meet payroll could be interpreted as bankruptcy. The world knew us as "the city that works." If Chicago went bankrupt now, the blame would be pinned on the "dizzy blonde." I could hear the political dinosaurs crowing across the land, "Chicago elected a woman mayor, then went bankrupt." A sadness swept over me. The great dreams I had for Chicago would of necessity be put on hold.

I had longed, first of all, to better the quality of life in many of Chicago's neighborhoods. The older communities were now home to Chicago's most recent arrivals—Mexicans, Puerto Ricans, Cambodians, Laotians, and Koreans, all pursuing the American dream. Having walked the city streets canvassing for votes, I was painfully aware of their substandard housing, crumbling sidewalks, the lack of money even for proper garbage cans. Landlords inherited property, repeating the pattern of the Prairie Avenue crowd, but abandoned it and no longer tried to help the new arrivals. The machine protected the landlord all the way to the machine judges in court. In fact, as long as a newcomer wasn't a citizen—a voter—he or she just didn't count. The machine controlled the Board of Elections and kept it underfunded, preventing a thorough professional canvass. The names of previous tenants long departed from this world remained on the voting rolls.

I next met with officials in the Department of Public Works and the city's architect. The picture they presented of Chicago's infrastructure wasn't much prettier. No bridges had been rehabilitated, many needed to be replaced, and some were on the verge of condemnation. The sewer and water commissioners sang the same tale of woe: no money for new sewers or sewer lines or water lines. "Well," I asked myself, "what the hell does work?"

The chairman of the Chicago Transit Authority, James McDonough, came in to see me. "You are going to have to take a strike at the next round of union negotiations in November. You will have to break the COLA"—the automatic cost of living increase currently built into the drivers' contract. This was the era of the Iranian oil crisis and 20 percent interest rates, and the country was suffering rampant inflation. Each time the cost of living rose, the drivers' salaries followed smartly behind. "I hate to saddle you with this, but there is no other way," he said. He added a discouraging report on the CTA's rolling stock. Many of the trains were so ancient they hadn't survived the winter, and hundreds of buses needed replacement.

These reports were oppressive. I needed to do something positive. When Bilandic inaugurated the ChicagoFest at Navy Pier, it drew enormous crowds. Recalling what I had learned about the neighborhoods of Chicago during my campaign, I thought, Why not transform ChicagoFest into ethnic fests right in each of the neighborhoods? Wouldn't that help restore pride in these communities?

My idea created a furor. The restaurant lobby—a big player in ChicagoFest—was furious; there was no business for it in neighborhood events. Suddenly, I was besieged. Editorials intimated that I was mean and spiteful to ax a festival that had brought happiness to so many people. Kathy, now a senior in college, stormed into the mayor's office protesting my even thinking about changing Chicago-Fest. Polling showed that more suburbanites than Chicagoans attended the Fest, but city residents also supported it. Thanks in large part to Kathy's persuasive ways, the Fest continued, but neighborhood festivals were planned as well. Some of these local gatherings drew as many as 200,000 people into the parks. We had little trouble sponsoring them financially; the seed money came from the hotel/ motel tax fund, which was earmarked for the promotion of tourism in Chicago.

Over everything loomed the fiscal crisis. Jay wryly phoned me one day from the *Sun-Times*. Jay said that Jim Hoge had called him in and said he had heard that I was going to interview a Don Haider for budget director and that the city's finances were none too good. Jay said that Hoge thought Haider was the one for the job. True, I was talking to Haider, a former Chicagoan then working with the Carter Treasury Department, but was it not peculiar for a boss to call in an employee to suggest a choice for a top city position?

On the other hand, everybody was chirping in with advice. Both Burris and Don Haider (who got the job) cautioned me to keep the city's financial condition to ourselves. If Moody's and Standard and Poor's in New York discovered the truth about Chicago's financial condition, they would lower the city's financial ratings. Creditors would be troublesome, too; a bankrupt city would be buried under an avalanche of bills.

I didn't care for their advice. It made me uncomfortable because it was deceptive in a sense. Burris and Haider suggested a "midyear correction" as one way to work out of the hole, but the remedy required laying off two thousand people. As rumors trickled through City Hall, I made up my mind to tell Chicago's taxpayers the truth at my next press conference. No more cover-ups. In answer to the inevitable question, I said, "There will have to be layoffs because the city has a deficit of somewhere around one hundred million dollars." Terrible mistake. I *should* have said, "The city has a current *shortfall* with projections of a deficit if immediate action isn't taken." Burris turned green. Not only had I said the dreaded "D" word, I'd used it in a technically incorrect way. Walking back to my office, I realized the journalists would jump on this; you can't have a deficit before one actually occurs. The newspapers were soon full of stories claiming that I "shot from the lip." In any case, the taxpayers at least knew now that the city rested on a shaky financial foundation.

The spring 1979 session of the state legislature began. Two of my assistants, Bill Griffin and Michael Brady, a former legislator, told me that Governor Jim Thompson's people wanted a meeting to discuss the Crosstown Expressway funds. These federal funds had been allocated thirteen years earlier during Lyndon Johnson's presidency. The outcry from residents of the northwest and southwest sides had been vociferous; they wanted no destruction of their neighborhoods or relocation of their homes, many of which were in the path of the projected expressway. Mayor Daley did not give up on the idea, he just put it aside, characteristically waiting for the opposition to soften.

Now the state wanted to make a deal. Thompson wanted to split the money—close to $2 billion—with Chicago. These funds, Washington decreed, could be spent on infrastructures of any kind, as long as the projects were related to transportation. The money was sorely needed to repair rusted bridges, construct new streets, buy new transit cars and buses, and correct the notorious S curve of the bridges at Lake Shore Drive and the river. Also, there had been a sputtering effort for years to get started on an extension of the north side Rapid Transit all the way to O'Hare and a Rapid Transit connection from the downtown area to Midway Airport. Splitting up the federal funds would give a break to the state, sure, but with our shaky financial condition, Chicago could not possibly come up with its local share required to draw down the entire federal grant. Our share of the split, $1 billion worth of construction, would provide badly needed jobs; moreover, the state had agreed to pick up the city's local share of the funding of all of the projects. This was a very good deal for Chicago. City taxpayers would spend not one penny for these projects. The plan was explained to the legislative leaders of both parties and to Washington, and an agreement was signed. No city agencies existed to handle construction of this magnitude; we had to build a group to handle them. In the next four years, under the supervision of Public Works, hundreds of millions of dollars flowed in for design, architectural, engineering, and construction contracts.

Right away, however, the carping began, as Bridgeport denizens moaned, "Well, she's killed the old man's dream of a Crosstown Expressway." Lost in this grumbling was the fact that no expressway coalition had ever come up with a way to fund the ten-year-old idea. Costs had more than doubled in that period.

The Carter administration, meanwhile, lurked around the fringes, darting in and out with overtures of help that amounted to very little. The liaison to the White House for Chicago's mayor's office was presidential assistant Jack Watson. At length, he phoned to say that Carter would be more responsive to me and my city. I mentioned that I was having a sit-down dinner as a fund-raiser and that so far ten thousand tickets had been sold. It was a tradition to invite the President to Chicago. If Carter was interested, he would be welcome. I also offered to have a breakfast for him at my home, to include community leaders, TV station managers, and newspaper editors. The next call I received was from the President, effusive in his gratitude.

During this period, I made a quick trip to England as part of the U.S. delegation to Earl Mountbatten's funeral. I was scarcely on the ground again at O'Hare when my legislative assistant and liaison to the governor, Mike Brady, gave me the latest political news—Richie Daley, in his capacity as state senator, had recently met with labor representatives and told them he was going for the immediate elimination of the tax on food and drugs. Several months earlier, Governor Thompson and I had publicly sponsored the elimination of the 3-cent tax on food and drugs over a three-year period—a penny off a year. Inflation was killing government budgets. We needed the remaining 2 cents. Richie was way out of line in his demands. He wasn't even the chairman or leader of the senate. This was a grandstand play that had to be stopped. I had to make Richie realize what the total and immediate elimination of the sales tax would do to the city's already strapped financial condition.

When he came in to talk, with both Griffin and Brady present, I pointed out that we *were* eliminating the tax, but the city was desperately short of funds; we had already taken steps to cut spending in the face of the estimated $100 million deficit at the end of the year. The city *could go under.*

He replied, "Somebody made a deal." To this day I don't know what he was talking about. He was surely close enough to Ed Bedore, his Bridgeport neighbor and Bilandic's budget director, to know the city's finances were in bad shape.

As the liaison to the governor, Brady interjected, "No, Richie, no deal was made. The reality is, the city needs the money."

Daley said, "If you didn't make some deal, Madigan"—Democratic Minority Whip—"did."

Brady said, "Richie, I'm trying to give you the reality of the moment. The city is broke. Let me put it to you this way. The city that your father loved and built could easily go under. We need that tax to pull us through this fiscal year and to help with the year-end deficit. Think about it, Richie, your father's city!"

Brady may not have touched a chord with Richie, but he brought a lump to my throat. The three of us sat there in the mayor's office awaiting his reaction. There had been a sullen look on his face when he first came in; now these words enraged him. He glared threateningly at Brady, as if to say, "How dare you mention my father's name?" Then Richie rose, nearly knocking over a chair, and strode from the office.

I slumped back in my chair. I didn't understand this; it was so very clear the city needed that money. For a minute no one said anything. I looked around at the office, trying to put myself in Richie's shoes. His father had ruled here for twenty-two years. Now, nothing even looked the same. Mayor Daley's massive desk had been moved down to the purchasing agent's office. It and the matching chair were too big; they had engulfed me. One spends a lot of time at that desk and it has to fit. Yes, Room 507 was different, but I thought, times change. Everything changes. Why was Richie doing this? "He doesn't care," I finally said.

Richie Daley and I didn't speak again during my four-year term. My sales tax position prevailed in the legislature. Only much later would I realize he had been positioning himself for the opening salvo in his race for mayor.

The unavoidable layoffs began. Close to 40 percent of the city's employees lived in Bridgeport and another 10 percent in Beverly.

Next thing I knew, Bridgeporters organized a two-pronged attack: a public relations campaign and a legal battle. The public relations campaign was simple. So many times had the press reported that Richie must avenge the loss of the mayor's chair that the public expected him to run against me in 1983. He held a press conference forthwith and vowed he would protect his people. Of the many thousands of Bridgeport jobs, only sixty employees had actually been laid off in the first cuts of three hundred. But those sixty filed lawsuits, claiming they were fired for political reasons—for their support of Richie Daley. There was a law against that in Chicago, though of course political support had been the only way to get a job with the city for most of the century. The public relations campaign was effective, mixing new charges with old, stirring animosity against me for scuttling Daley's Crosstown Expressway, failing to invite Mrs. Daley to the Pope's reception, and vindictively firing sixty Bridgeporters.

I didn't endear myself to the firemen, either. During my campaign I had promised to bring collective bargaining and ultimately labor contracts to city government. Other aldermen in addition to Bieszczat were against this plan; Richie, as I knew, was fervently opposed. After my last Bridgeport appearance prior to the April election, the Daley family had invited me over to Richie's house. At one point, he asked me to step into the kitchen. He asked me if I was really going to give the police and firemen a contract. Yes, I said.

He said the rest of the trades weren't for it. Since Richie's law firm represented several unions, I had no reason to doubt him. I replied that I had promised the contracts and I planned to go ahead with them. He said I was making a mistake, as they were my two front lines and I should want to control them.

I knew well what old machine control could mean. If a policeman didn't look the other way when told to—such as not showing up in a court case for a speeding ticket if the speeder had clout—he might find himself walking a beat in some godforsaken spot. It might mean not passing the sergeant's exam. Although one-half of the sergeant's exam was written and could not be tampered with, the oral half could easily be fixed. I had heard enough of such threats during my campaign. Enough—there would be collective bargaining for all city employees.

Consequently, when elected, I immediately directed the corporation council to start drafting a collective bargaining ordinance. As mayor, I didn't have the legal authority to grant a contract, but the council could give me that power by authorizing such a law. So the legislative process began, and while I knew it would take a while, I was pleased to have it on track.

In government there are always two or three or even more programs in a state of bureaucratic development at the same time. After I had been on the job only four or five months, I was juggling a lot of balls—trying to cut enough from the 1979 budget to reduce the projected deficit for the end of the year, working on the budget for 1980, and moving the Crosstown Expressway trade-ins along, first in Springfield, through the legislature, and now into the reality of projects in the Public Works Department.

There was little time for politics, aside from reports that plans for my September fund-raising dinner were coming along well, including the arrangements for Carter's time in Chicago. I was therefore surprised when John D'Arco, the 1st Ward committeeman, came to see me. "I don't like what I'm hearing from some of the Italians in Richie's ward. He's telling them to slow down the ticket buying for your fund-raiser. This is no good. The kid can't go around being a disruptive, spoiled brat. He's got to get behind you for three years. Then, if he wants to take you on, that's his business. There's a family gathering this weekend." The D'Arcos and the Daleys, it turned out, were celebrating the christening of Johnny and Mary Lou Daley's new baby. "I think I'll talk to Richie at the party and remind him what his father said to all of us during the McGovern mess. You remember how McGovern tossed all of us out of the convention in Miami? Yet Daley was a Democrat—and when it came to working for him and delivering for him after he was nominated, Daley delivered. McGovern won Chicago because Daley delivered. You won, too. Richie has to get behind you. What do you think? Want me to talk to the kid?"

Not wanting to be indebted to D'Arco, I told him to use his own judgment.

Apparently, D'Arco did talk to Richie, because shortly afterward two assistants in my office mentioned an 11th Ward political meeting at which Richie had exclaimed that now he knew how I had won the election—with the help of the mob, because I had met with John D'Arco.

This was nuts. Not only was D'Arco close to the Daleys by marriage, he was seventy years of age, a veteran politician. Everybody talked to him. He'd been a behind-the-scenes powerhouse with Thomas Keane when both backed Mayor Daley in the ouster of Kennelly in 1955. Yet the Daley forces began tut-tutting in disbelief over D'Arco's name and offering up phony rosaries for my soul.

Other problems dogged my fund-raiser. Bill Griffin mentioned on several occasions that the Carter people were pushing hard for the dinner to be an endorsement of his administration. He thought they were billing it as such with the national media. That hadn't been the idea. For one thing, the machine had lost much of its clout after the Democratic Convention in Chicago. It could still deliver at the local level, but not nationally. Even the county and state level was a mixed bag. I had told Jack Watson, Carter's assistant, that with the President's numbers in the national polls so very low, I would be helpful if I could. The purpose of the invitation had in fact been to give Carter a platform to address ten thousand Democrats and spell out new initiatives and new directions, not to endorse his past actions. It wasn't good for the country to have a President with such a poor approval rating. This was a break for Carter, not for me—we'd sold the ten thousand tickets long before he was invited.

As a courtesy and in keeping with political protocol, I had invited George Dunne, still chairman of the Democratic Party of Cook County, to join me in escorting the President into McCormick Place Exposition Center, where the guests were seated for dinner. As we waited in the VIP suite for the big shots who preceded us on the dais, George began haranguing Carter about his failed promise to submit all federal job openings to the Democratic Party of Cook County. The President hardly heard Dunne and didn't respond to his thrust. He seemed preoccupied, reserved, subdued. I surmised that he was in this mood because there wasn't going to be a formal endorsement at the dinner.

We were finally signaled to enter. The hall looked beautiful. The three-tiered speakers' table had been transformed into a replica of the *Delta Queen*, the paddle boat President and Mrs. Carter had recently vacationed on. On the dais sat the elected officials of the Democratic Party, business leaders, labor leaders, and, for the first time, interested and concerned community leaders. Carter's very general speech drew a tepid response. My speech was caution itself, but rather than send the President's group away completely empty-handed, I said, "If the convention were held tonight, I know who I would vote for." This conditioned endorsement of the President was a trial balloon—an old trick of Mayor Daley's. A sigh of relief seemed to rise from the dais, but little response came back from the crowd.

There was another undercurrent at the dinner, one I found both troubling and amusing. On the dais sat representatives of the two major factions of the Democratic Party—George Dunne, the old warhorse county chairman, and Don Rose, my television consultant. Rose was considered a radical, anathema to the party regulars, though he had virtuously shaved off his beard for the occasion. The two factions would bounce me back and forth between them for the next four years.

Jay and I spent the night at the Conrad Hilton, for very good reason; the Secret Service was laboriously securing our apartment for the President's morning visit. Between the sniffing of dogs, the installation of his hotline red phone, and the scurrying about of the caterers, there would have been little room for us. We had invited about seventy-five people to greet Carter and hear what he had to say.

Shortly after Jay and I arrived home the next morning, a minor disaster occurred. Marshall Korshak, the former city treasurer, bumped into one of the women carrying a huge hot cocoa server and it all went crashing down on white carpet. Of course, that had to be precisely one minute before the President arrived. What a mess! Worse, I was very disappointed with the spirit of the reception. It turned into nothing more than a photo opportunity session in front of the mantel. This was truly disappointing, for I had expected the President to deliver a strong message about the economy.

Following the breakfast I accompanied Carter by helicopter to the far southern suburbs. In the air, he showed little energy and was very quiet. He made a perfunctory address to the group assembled there, again breaking no new political ground.

As we were about to enter the presidential limousine to return to Chicago, Carter was stopped by the entourage of newsmen and women who accompanied him. I got into the limo; finally, he joined me there. He turned a little toward me and said, "The press just found out that we have been cleared by the Justice Department of any wrongdoing in the peanut farm investigation." (This was a well-publicized federal inquiry into the his political fund-raising methods.)

With that the President lowered his head as if he were studying his knees. I don't think Carter ever raised his head during the whole hour-and-a-half ride back to Chicago—nor did he ever raise his voice much above a mumble. It was clear that he was upset with the media coverage given to this investigation, the costs to him personally for all the auditors he had to hire, and the hours of questioning that Rosalyn

Breakfast reception given at our home in 1979 for President Jimmy Carter, shown here with Jay, myself, and Kathy.

had gone through. "I knew," he said, "Rosalyn kept very accurate books. She used to sit in the barn every night making her fund-raising phone calls and recording every commitment faithfully—and yet we had to be put through all this." He kept shaking his head from side to side, as if to say, "What can you do?" After a brief reference to the way the press portrayed his brother Billy as a "buffoon," he dejectedly shook his head again.

Finally, Carter switched gears. With his head still down, he mentioned that his aides Jody Powell and Ham Jordan had been accused of using cocaine. "Rosalyn and I were aboard the *Delta Queen* when we heard about these accusations. Jane, I love those boys. Those boys have been with me from early on. Why, next to Rosalyn and Amy, I love those boys the most. I knew those boys weren't about to do anything to hurt me. As soon as I could get to the phone, I called Ben Civiletti"—the Attorney General of the United States. "I told him, 'Ben, I haven't talked to the boys about this cocaine sniffing, but what should I do?' Ben said, 'You did the right thing, Mr. President, coming to me. Don't talk to the boys. I'll just turn the whole matter over to the FBI.' "

I thought we'd *never* get back to Chicago. Carter's phrase "I love those boys" kept ringing in my ears. He loved them, trusted them, and yet turned them over to the FBI without so much as hearing their side. Tapping my arm, Carter asked, "What can we do? What can we do? If I had my way, I'd want the Justice Department investigating drugs and organized crime, but what can we do?"

My thoughts wandered. This man was President of the United States. Inflation ran rampant. The cost of borrowing money was incredible. Housing starts were at zero. And what preoccupied him? His peanut farm and his allegedly coke-sniffing assistants. He tapped my arm again, I suppose seeking some sort of answer. "It sounds like a leadership problem, Mr. President," I replied. Had these words actually come out of my mouth? My stomach churned as I glanced at him, hoping he'd missed my implication. To my amazement, Carter was nodding his head in agreement. I had a fleeting impression that Jimmy Carter had forgotten he was the leader of the country.

I reached City Hall in time to put in an afternoon's work, though drained from the depressing car ride. Several weeks later, I discussed my observations about Carter with George Dunne, who said, "We still don't even get so much as the courtesy of an informative letter out of Carter in regard to federal job openings. I don't care if they judge our candidates unqualified, we should at least be given the courtesy of applying. I discussed this with Carter a year ago when Bilandic had him here for a dinner. My suggestions fell on deaf ears. We are the bottom of the barrel to him and his crowd. You ought to think about that in regard to your own position of leadership. Carter can't win in 1980. Kennedy could win. You ought to think about it, but this time we should be first to come out." While George was never a stirring leader and I hadn't forgotten his history with me and the Democratic women, I tried to work with him rather than go through a divisive party fight for a new chairman.

Usually a pacifier, he was very combative on this issue. I was surprised by his assurance that if I was ready to announce for Kennedy, he was too. He had no doubts. Through Steve Smith, Kennedy's brother-in-law, and the Senator himself, plans were made to endorse Ted Kennedy for President. George, as chairman of the party, planned to hold a joint press conference with me in late October and start the ball rolling. He phoned the Sunday before the press conference to say he'd taken some polls of his precinct captains over the weekend and wasn't picking up good vibes about the Kennedy endorsement.

In this Dunne was less than candid. I lived in his ward, and there were no polls—I'd have known about them. Actually, according to Mike Brady, Danny Rostenkowski had flown in from Washington on behalf of Carter and persuaded Dunne not to endorse Kennedy. George owed me for allowing him to remain on as county chairman, but he'd spent a lot of years with Rostenkowski in the Springfield legislature. They were political friends, part of the old-boy network. Not being an old boy, I was left holding the bag.

I phoned President Carter to let him know I was going to endorse Teddy. "I understand," he said. "You go way back in politics with the name of Kennedy. But will you help me with my fund-raising?"

"Mr. President," I said, "fund-raising goes with the endorsement. I'll be doing that for Kennedy."

"I understand, but will you help me raise funds?"

I was puzzled. "If you mean will I help you by not stopping others from fund-raising for you, I will cooperate. But I myself will be raising funds for Kennedy. Mr. President, I'm sorry; this is a personal matter with me. I will be endorsing Kennedy personally—not as mayor and not as a member of the Democratic Central Committee."

There was always something slightly bizarre about most of my contacts with President Reagan, but there was always something else as well—a professionalism, even in the smallest things, that was a welcome relief after the aimlessness of the Carter people. With the Republicans, we weren't going to get big money for the cities, but when we made a phone call, we got an answer. Nothing was allowed to hang in the air. I began to suspect the Reagan White House operated according to two watchwords: imagery, efficiency.

Not long after the President was shot in an assassination attempt, he and Nancy were going to make a brief stop at a Republican fund-raiser in Chicago on their way to their Santa Barbara ranch. When Jay, Kathy, and I got out to Meigs, the gleaming red carpet was already laid out, and Air Force One taxied up to us, exactly as scheduled. Obviously, the Reagans had been told that some woman was mayor of Chicago, but they had no idea who. As they came down the ramp and went through the receiving line, things became very confused. Kathy swore that they thought she was mayor, and we had a good laugh about the snafu on the way home. After a six-week vacation, the Reagans came back to Chicago on the way to Washington, and we went out to the airport again. As we took our assigned places, I looked down. Taped on the carpet at my feet was a card with large letters reading, "Mayor Byrne," facing away from me. I peered down the line. There was a card for everyone in the welcoming committee. This time, when Reagan came down the ramp, he glanced briefly at my feet and said warmly, "Oh, hello, Mayor Byrne." He made it sound as if we were old and trusted friends. Cameras caught him genially calling everyone by name. His people knew the first arrival had been messy. They didn't let it happen that way again.

On that visit, we were to have a private half-hour chat at the Palmer House, but I have stronger memories of our staged encounter the following September. For an entire weekend, I had been involved in round-the-clock negotiations with the school board. I was exhausted from the tension and lack of sleep. Once it was clear that the schools could open by Labor Day, Jay and I decided to go off to Palm Springs and recuperate. By this time, I was succumbing to a virus, along with everything else. Never had I needed a vacation so much. Of course, that's when the phone rang with the news that the President was coming through town that evening. "Damn it," I said to my bodyguard, "there's no way I can cover this puffiness and the deep circles under my eyes. You watch television tonight. The man's practically thirty years older than I am, but I'm going to look his age and he'll look mine." (The days when looking good was considered feminine vanity have long gone, of course, at least in political life. Every political professional knows how important it is to look self-assured and rested to retain public confidence; otherwise, you run the danger of looking overwhelmed by the job, as Carter did toward the end.)

Well, this could not be avoided. Off I went to the Palmer House again for the photo ops the White House wanted. The suite was Hollywood perfection. A bowl of the famous jelly beans Reagan liked was posed on the coffee table. The President and I were seated together on the couch, just so, while various staff members hovered silently in the background. We just talked casually about my experiences in Cabrini Green, about the crime rate, about drugs in the inner city. There was no agenda, and Reagan could go on like that for hours. Suddenly, an aide announced that it was time for the press to come in, and I felt like a sheep about to be shorn. The suite was large, but I knew the hot TV lights would come right up to us, revealing every sign of fatigue. The President, heavily made up and rouged, would look fine. Then I noticed a red velvet rope quickly being stretched across the room about ten or twelve feet away.

As the photographers and videographers came in, an aide standing by a drape in the corner ordered, "No lights." This is Chicago, I thought: they're going to do what they want to do. Every light went off. As each succeeding wave of photographers came in, we were filmed only in the soft lighting that had been carefully set up by the White House staff. The President and I would converse for the cameras, which was slightly unsettling.

I have always made it a habit to look people directly in the eye when engaged in conversation. In fact, I try to read people by their eyes. His confused me. I seemed to be looking at two slightly different-colored eyes—one seemed to have a bit more brown than the other. I thought for certain he was wearing two different-colored contact lenses. He wore one shaded brown and one blue. When he wanted to be taped making a serious point, he would cock his chin at me, raise his eyebrows, and fix me with the deeper eye. I don't know what cosmetic effect this had, although I did learn he always wore lenses of different strengths when he made a speech—one to focus on the teleprompter, one to look into the crowd—and perhaps that was it. Even more unnerving was Reagan's breathing that night. As he spoke, he paused every few words and took two quick gasps. It was done so skillfully, though, that the mikes didn't pick it up, and the overall level of his conversation remained on an even plane. (Later, a Deaver aide would explain that this was a lingering effect of the gunshot wound and later disappeared. I wondered whether the President's odd, almost stumbling gait was another aftereffect, but apparently not. The aide claimed that staffers were told throughout Reagan's Presidency to avoid lengthy shots of him walking. I don't know why, but it was a peculiar walk.)

That night, I was to appreciate anew the theatrical genius of the Reaganites. On the evening news, we both looked as if we were glowing with good health and vigor, ready to take on Richie Daley and Mikhail Gorbachev and all the rest.

The White House obsession with imagery tended to give some people the impression that Reagan was never in control. Certainly this impression was reinforced in most conversations with him, at least in my experience, for he could ramble on and on about being governor of California without ever making a discernible point. He also seemed to say whatever came into his head, without editing it. After he and Nancy took a tour through the Caribbean, he confided to me that he had feared the worst, particularly wondering what they could possibly eat. To his astonishment, the food was good, the accommodations pleasant, and the people hospitable and sophisticated. "You know, they can be quite wonderful in their own countries," he said, to the mayor of racially uneasy Chicago. "It's when they come here that the problems start."

Nonetheless, there was a competent side to Reagan. On one occasion, Rich Williamson, then White House liaison to the big-city mayors, called to warn me that David Stockman's budget people intended to take a big whack out of revenue-sharing funds headed our way. He thought it a good idea for some of us to meet with the President and explain what such a move would do to our budgets. About ten mayors assembled at the White House. The President argued that the cuts would ease the nation's problem with high inflation. As we went around the table, other mayors rebutted with pretty much the same predictable arguments, over and over.

When it was my turn, I thought, This is my one opportunity and I'm not going to waste it saying what everyone else has. "Mr. President," I said, "I agree that we have to get inflation down. The country's borrowing terrific amounts of money just to exist. But when I left Chicago today, the unemployment rate was nine percent, and we've had projects waiting for federal approval from your people that could, as a matter of fact, put people to work. I send my projects here, and we have to wait a long time to get them okayed." I sat back.

Ronald Reagan looked at me and said simply, "Mayor Byrne, it's our fault." Then he turned to George Bush, the Vice President, and snapped, "George, I thought I told you to be the one to cut out all the ifs, ands, buts, and curlicues in these federal regulations." Bush responded that the task was half way completed. "Believe me, Mayor Byrne," Reagan went on, "The technocrats, the bureaucrats, they don't care who the President is. The President is a prisoner in his own White House. Give me a list of the projects you want done, and I'll get them for you." He was really steaming. "I understand what goes on in your cities. You've got abandoned buildings, then drugs, then gang rapes. It's all due to this bureaucracy and red tape. You'll get your projects, Mayor Byrne."

I was startled at this outburst. If I'd blown up like that at City Hall and called myself a prisoner, the word would be "There she goes again . . . how neurotic . . . there goes the mouth." Even as Reagan left the room and we rose, he turned back again, pointed to an aide, nodded to me and said, "You'll see, Mayor Byrne, you'll get your projects."

Meeting in the White House—President Ronald Reagan, Vice President George Bush, Secretary of the Treasury Donald Regan, and several mayors from across the country.

Don Regan, Treasury Secretary at the time, poked my arm and said, "You hit the most sensitive nerve in the President's being. He cannot stand bureaucracy."

I laughed, but glanced at the Vice President. Boy, I thought, I hope that's the position he stays in, because after being dressed down by the President because of me, he's going to remember.

That afternoon, when I got off the plane in Chicago, I was astonished to find three commissioners waiting to see me, each asking what I had done at the White House, for they had all received calls from the appropriate federal agencies. Their projects had been approved or were in the final stages of approval.

Reagan would one day fire air traffic controllers to signal a hardball attitude toward strikers. This was not my attitude, however, and in 1980 I was determined to make progress on the Chicago labor front. The city's firemen were growling about lack of a contract. I suppose they'd expected my election to secure collective bargaining immediately. The local's president, Frank Muscare, whom I liked personally, was posturing. He set up a wooden "bargaining" table in the Bismarck Hotel, directly across the street from City Hall, demanding that the city come to negotiate.

In early November a long ordinance, a dozen pages or so, was prepared. When it became a statute, it would enable the city to enter into collective bargaining. The director of personnel, the fire commissioner, and an advisory attorney on labor matters suggested that to show the city's good faith, they take a copy of the proposed ordinance along with the accompanying press release across the street to the Bismarck and give it to Muscare. Maybe that would cool him off. At 9:30 A.M., the group left my office on that mission. Then Donald Haider briefed me on the shaky financial fourth quarter. He felt that with the layoffs and belt-tightening, we might squeak through to the end of the year. He also briefed me on the budget he was preparing for 1980. Unfortunately, the budget included an increase in real estate taxes plus a sewer tax and water tax, but there was no other way out of Daley's last years of accumulated debt.

Toward the end of the day—an unusually difficult day—I buzzed Corporation Counsel Bill Quinlan to ask about the outcome of the delegation's visit to Muscare. He offered to check into it, then called back quite agitated: "Mayor, you aren't going to believe this, but they have entered negotiations."

The bullet was out of the gun! I asked Quinlan how we could possibly be negotiating without the legal right to do so. I was extremely angry. I had two unattractive options: to call a halt to talks and explain the problem, an action that would enrage the rank and file; or to allow the bargaining to continue and push the city council to pass a law they didn't want. I chose the latter and set to work on it.

To me, the firemen weren't the issue; governmental process was the issue. I had always intended to give the firemen a contract, but by virtue of law. Pent-up frustration is a terrible force, however, and Chicago firemen were frustrated.

Firefighters in Chicago don't work an eight-hour day; they work a twenty-four-hour shift. The firehouse is the fire fighter's second home. The firehouse kitchen is the center of this home away from home, and the best coffee served anywhere in Chicago is brewed there. The union set up a firehouse hotline to keep the members informed on the day-to-day negotiations, which were stalemated on only one point. The firemen, being a closely knit group, wanted all the officers as well as the sworn personnel to belong to the union. Management, from captains and battalion chiefs all the way up to the commissioner, would, in that case, be included. There would be no chain of command under this system. The union was intractable on the issue, but so was I. I directed the commissioners to go to the firehouses and explain the city's position.

Quite probably, I should have become personally involved, but on November 15 I had to present the 1980 budget to the city council. Of course, any new tax draws fire, but I vowed the real estate increases would be eliminated as soon as the city's finances were in order. On the whole, the reception was as good as I could have expected.

Compared to what I heard later in the day, it was positively good news. That evening, Joe Hannon, the superintendent of schools, called me at home: "I have to see you, Mayor, It's urgent." I returned to City Hall about six-thirty with Jay, and Hannon showed up with John Perkins, president of the Continental Bank. Several of my aides were around, too, and sat in on the meeting.

What rolled out of Hannon's mouth was the worst news I would hear in my four years as mayor. According to the superintendent, the Board of Education had an immediate shortfall. The interest payment on its debt could not be made. John Perkins detailed the consequences of a default. Once again, I heard predictions of a snowball effect: nonpayment could produce a bankruptcy for the schools, leading in turn to their immediate closing. Perkins and Hannon suggested that the solution was to have the city cosign a loan to make the payment.

Obviously, the schools couldn't close, and my first reaction was to avoid such a catastrophe at all cost. Yet I couldn't allow the city to swallow additional debt, since our own debt at the end of the year was still being projected at $50 million to $70 million. I was firm, stating that the city was in no financial condition to take on the debt of the schools.

My aides seconded my opinion. Griffin felt it was the state's constitutional responsibility to fund the schools and that the state should bail the Board of Education out. Then Don Haider calmly remarked that we could do nothing on this at the moment and that we would have to look at the board's books.

John Perkins suddenly asked, "What about us?" Perkins was hot. It was apparent to me that the banks had put together the syndicate that sold the board's paper and backed those bonds with their full faith and credit. Their names were on the line. Perkins clearly felt the city should do something about it. Perkins was running on, particularly disturbed and visibly shaken, saying that the board had used segregated accounts for operation. His tone was intimidating, too nasty for my taste.

I thought Perkins was too upset to ask him at that time what I would later ask him in private: with one of his own senior vice presidents sitting on the board, why didn't he know?

I had been mayor only seven months. This was years of rolled-over debt. I had had nothing to do with this, but I knew that Mayor Daley had left me a difficult legacy. His habit of always bailing out the schools, always settling the strikes, had given the public a feeling of enormous confidence in the power of the mayor's office. Griffin was correct that the State of Illinois had a constitutional responsibility, but the parents wouldn't care. They expected the mayor to handle such matters, and they expected school doors to stay open. I would be blamed. We agreed to meet later in the week after the city's Budget Department analyzed the board's books.

The city's audit produced an even gloomier picture. School board record-keeping was so inefficient that it was difficult to get a handle on an accurate total, but Haider estimated that the debt would range from $150 million to $300 million. We met again on Sunday. At my request, a top businessman in Chicago, Patrick O'Malley, president of Canteen Corporation, attended the meeting. He agreed that the city could not assume any of the board's debt.

Joe Hannon was strangely silent through it all, never offering any explanation or justification. Not until the crisis blew publicly did I learn that none of it was his fault. Joe Hannon's career was over even so, and he resigned. Bill Griffin showed me correspondence dug out of the mayor's office, letters from Hannon to Mayor Daley, Mayor Bilandic, and Tom Donovan. Year after year he had insisted that the schools would collapse without an increase in school taxes. Lacking that increased revenue, Hannon had in the end done what the city had done—rolled over school debt and borrowed from other internal accounts. Even taxes withheld from teachers' paychecks had been used to keep the schools running. Finally, it all had come crashing down—on me.

A summit meeting in Springfield pulled the fat out of the fire. In the ensuing agreement, the state legislature fired the entire Board of Education and established a state-guaranteed funding source as well as an oversight committee to monitor the board's budgeting process.

Then Governor Thompson advanced state money to pay the teachers while the financial mechanisms were put into place. On January 28, however, before the painfully slow process could be completed, Chicago's teachers walked out, not to return until February 11, 1980. Despite my best efforts, our schools closed.

Meanwhile, during the budget period from November 15 to the end of the year, Richie Daley made his move—but not to take over the office of chairman of the party, as Mike Royko had predicted he would do as a first step toward the mayoralty.[2] He instead announced he would run for state's attorney. When asked if he would seek the support of the Democratic organization and Jane Byrne, he replied, "No."

A resentment of another kind was building. I wanted underprivileged children to wake up Christmas morning to a Christmas tree. I had taken over $200,000 from my political war chest to fund most of the cost of holiday partys and tree-giving events at all public housing units. I couldn't forget those two mothers at the Jewel supermarket on Division Street during my "outsiders campaign." "We live in Cabrini Green. Santa doesn't come there." They were words of hopelessness, spoken in front of the next generation. I wanted to show that child and many children that society does care. The tree was only a symbol to adults, but to a child its lights might bring hope.

There *was* some resentment in City Hall because I requested voluntary contributions to help with the cost of the trees. Many of the complainers from Bridgeport and Beverly blamed the increase in black voter turnout for my primary victory. Of course, public housing was mostly black. What a holiday spirit was building around me. Meanwhile, Richie was creating a public relations image of himself as a victim: he had proved he was for the people, he had tried to end the sales tax taken off food and drugs, while Jane Byrne wasn't for the people, she'd kept the sales tax. Also, I was picking on him because I was afraid he'd run for mayor.

Fortunately, the public was not fooled. In a *Chicago Sun-Times* poll on February 8, 1980, asking whom the public held responsible for the city's financial woes, the mass transit strike, and the schools' difficulties, over 42 percent of the respondents pointed the finger at Mayor Daley, less than 15 percent accused Bilandic, and less than 9 percent blamed me.[3] I was certainly relieved. When questioned about the poll at a press conference, I said I agreed with it, but privately I didn't blame Mayor Daley, for two reasons—first, the financial problems accumulated after his second stroke, when his health was obvi-

Christmas party at Lathrop Homes, a Chicago housing project, 1980.
COURTESY OF DOM NAJOLIA, *Chicago Sun-Times.*

ously deteriorating, and second, he wasn't around to defend himself. Three years earlier, a tax increase plus moderation of teacher demands could have prevented this incredible debt. Richie intentionally prevented my response, charging that I spoke ill of the dead and of the man responsible for my political career, and that I was trying to destroy his family. Richie's posturing gave Bridgeport a chance to mourn again and to dream of the day the heir would seek revenge and regain his father's office in City Hall.

In 1989, Richie did move into the mayor's chair, defeating Mayor Eugene Sawyer. Sitting on the anchor desk as a political consultant for CBS-TV, I watched Bridgeporters celebrating Richie's victory at Schaller's Pub, a neighborhood tavern. The interviewer asked a middle-aged couple who had retired to Florida what had brought them back to town. They replied that on that dark night of 1979, they had vowed they'd be here for every election till the son of the mayor took his rightful place in his father's chair where he belonged. They had been there in 1983 when he tried and thought it a terrible night, but tonight they had done it.

CHAPTER 19

A Time of Affluence

As Robert Kennedy once said, "The world yields painfully to change." I had learned that lesson the hard way during a year in the mayor's chair. At times, I felt whipsawed and all but helpless in my effort to shake Chicago out of its inertial patterns. Much of the turmoil could be attributed to the defeat of the machine. The old-boy network felt threatened. Cozy relationships between City Hall and the press were strained, as sources dried up. I was advised Chicago would seem unstable if I didn't reach out to the machine.

Meanwhile, the north side Establishment of my youth seemed terribly detached from the real problems facing Chicago. During the first days of my administration, for example, leaders of the business community under the aegis of the Central Area Committee had handed me a list of their priorities. At the top of the list was a new international air terminal; a system of skywalks connecting the major downtown buildings was a close second. The list made no mention of the needs of the decaying minority neighborhoods, nor was there talk of making jobs available for trained minorities.

One powerful businessman who I hoped would commit to summer jobs for minority youth replied candidly, "If you quote me on this, I will of course deny it, but I could probably handle two per shift—any more than that would mean trouble that I don't need." I met with board members of the city's Economic Development Committee and advised them that I was going to push a law for the city similar to the federal government's requiring that 20 percent of all federally funded projects be granted to minority contractors. I wanted the same provision for municipal contractors. It was not difficult for the EDC to reach consensus: I would destroy Chicago's workplace. "Business wouldn't locate here if there was such a law. . . . Business hates regulation. . . . It isn't prejudice; it's just that the suburbs don't have any such regulation and business would go there." I never succeeded in sponsoring the law, but the city staff of the Economic Development Department spurred development in the black community. I am happy to say that a report in *Crain's Chicago Business*, September 17, 1990, noted that "Chicago led the nation in 1982 in gross receipts of black-owned firms." How long it always takes for facts to be established!

Once the banks committed to bailout loans for Chicago's schools, they moved in to review the city's books. In late December 1979, John Perkins asked me to meet with him, his staff members, and their counterparts from the 1st National Bank of Chicago at Continental's corporate suite in the Ritz Carlton. I was to come alone, without any press attention. The matter was delicate, he thought. An infuriated group of bankers confronted me: "We have been lied to. The city is broke." They yammered on with that high-handed self-righteousness peculiar to bankers. Their discovery was not news to anyone else. For months, I had been trumpeting the financial woes of the city and the Board of Education to the world.

I felt some of these crises would have been avoided had I not been a woman. There is always a testing of the new kid on the block in politics; I was certain the testing was a bit tougher because of my sex.

One test gave me a good laugh. During Chicago's Marathon of 1979, Jay and I sat having coffee in the kitchen waiting to hear from my guards when we should leave to be at the finish line to greet the winner. I glanced out the window and saw the terrible traffic jam caused by the Marathon on Michigan Avenue. Worse, I noticed there was an ambulance trying to get through, but it was clearly stalled. There wasn't a traffic policeman in sight. I picked up the phone and dialed 911. Without identifying myself, I described the situation and suggested they assist it. Jay and I went on talking. About ten minutes later I noticed the ambulance had moved only about a half a block. I politely called 911 again. I told the dispatcher it was my second call and I really thought there should be a policeman there to help direct the traffic. The dispatcher sounded annoyed and asked my name. I told him.

Almost immediately thereafter, my guard Rory O'Connor called to say they were on their way to pick me up. Shortly after getting into the limo, I heard the dispatcher for the police radio communications ask, "How is the situation at Michigan Avenue and Ohio? We had a beef on that."

From somewhere out there in police-radioland a voice replied, "We're moving it. The mayor was the beef. If she's so worried about it, why doesn't she come down and move the traffic herself?"

This conversation was beamed over citywide radio communications, which were always turned on in the limo. Rory's face turned purple. I could only see the neck of the driver, Officer Jack Higgins, but it matched Rory's color.

Finally, Rory asked, "Did you beef, Mayor? You should have called us—we would have handled it."

I said, "Rory, give me the mike and patch me into citywide."

He said, "Oh, please, Mayor, don't do that."

I said, "Give it to me now."

Rory called in, "This is car one, patch us in to citywide." In the minute it took to patch us in, Rory again said, "Please, Mayor, don't do it."

I signaled him to hand me the mike. I pushed the button and barked, "This is the mayor. Who said that?"

There was a sudden deafening absence of sound on the normally hectic radio. No one spoke—no one. We arrived at the finish line. There were many police standing around for crowd control. As we walked past them, I smiled to one sheepish-looking face after another.

Perceptions of power can backfire, too. One night I was coming down from the dais of a public dinner given by the Chicago Board of Trade when a bodyguard met me with a very serious face. "Don't get excited," he said. "Kathy's been burglarized." He was being kind, but I could hardly keep from getting excited. I felt a sudden lump of fear in my throat. "She's all right," he went on. "She did the smart thing, called the police and didn't go in herself."

We got into the limo and shot over to Kathy's condo. Her door had been ripped off its hinges; her things were scattered all over the place. It was a violent invasion, I felt. Inside, to my amazement, three police commanders, several detectives, and other officers were talking with my daughter, who was calmly explaining that so far as she could tell, only a television set was missing. Outside, blue lights were flashing up and down the street as cruisers gathered. The apartment was so

Marching with "Chicago's Finest" at the St. Jude League Parade, 1980. COURTESY TONY SUAU, *Chicago Sun-Times*.

crowded with the forces of the law that you could hardly move, and Kathy was soon making pots of coffee in her kitchen. Suddenly, a detective rushed up the stairs. "We've caught him, Mayor!" he announced breathlessly. I don't think I'd been there ten minutes. I was stunned, to say the least, and the police commanders looked very pleased with themselves.

Later, I'd learn that Kathy's intruder was about the dumbest criminal in Chicago. He'd walked across the street, carrying the stolen TV set, and asked a grocer to use his phone to call a cab. He'd given his name and home address to the dispatcher, taken the cab, and gone home. Worse, he was on parole for a prior conviction. He might as well have left a map on the floor. We all had a good laugh about this bizarre event, but I knew that many a taxpayer in my city was going to get an exaggerated notion of the power of the mayor's office. "See?" they would say. "When it's the mayor's daughter, they can catch the thief in ten minutes, but when it's just Joe Blow . . ." This was just another case in which perception would not necessarily catch up with reality.

Not everything was a test, however. New York's New Year's Eve celebrations have always attracted massive crowds, but Chicago was lucky if a hundred people showed up in the Loop on December 31. We decided to sponsor a New Year's Eve celebration and advertised a fireworks display for midnight. As Jay and I drove over, I wondered if the Bridgeporters would show up. They and the disgruntled firemen made a practice of appearing at every major public event so their loud booing could be heard over the airwaves. When I arrived, the police told me they hadn't expected such an enormous crowd. I was pleased to see tens of thousands of Chicagoans—and no demonstrating firemen—in the downtown area.

I also wanted to revivify the Loop after business hours and on weekends. For too long in many of the older, larger American cities, residents fled at dusk to the suburbs or the safety of their neighborhoods, abandoning downtown. Chicago was not immune. One never saw crowds strolling along State Street at night, window-shopping or making their way to the Blue Note. The marches, demonstrations, and gang riots of the 1960s had ended that era. I vowed to bring back the crowds, to make Chicago so lively that the people would return to the heart of the city and to its abandoned parks.

Attracting moviemaking to Chicago would encourage that spirit, and one of my funniest mayoral experiences flowed from that effort. A nervous John Belushi came to see me in the spring of 1979 to discuss the shooting of *The Blues Brothers*. Prior administrations had discouraged the movie industry. Mayor Daley felt sure that Chicago would be portrayed unkindly. Permits were delayed; streets would not be closed off for film crews and equipment. Belushi, who had begun his career at Chicago's famed Second City, knew the problem well and arrived in the mayor's office hat in hand. I assumed the straight and stoic Daley face as well as I could. Belushi blurted out, "We really want to shoot our film here. We need permission to drive a car through the plate-glass window of Daley Plaza in the chase scene. It's crucial to the film. We'll fix the window at once; no one will even know it happened. We'll even contribute fifty thousand dollars to your favorite children's charity if we can do it." Belushi was actually stammering.

I almost laughed aloud. Drive a car through the plate-glass window of Daley Center? Good idea. Let it symbolize an open city, a city

Rebirth of the movie industry in the city in 1979 when John Belushi and Dan Akroyd asked permission to film *Blues Brothers* in Chicago.
COURTESY TONY SUAU, *Chicago Sun-Times.*

not afraid to show itself. The film industry was born here, after all. "Be my guest," I said simply. Thus was filmmaking reborn in Chicago, and the number of locally made films soared, including *Dr. Detroit* and *The Thief*, and provided thousands of jobs.

Outdoor cafés also flourished across the city for the first time. As a commissioner I had encouraged cafés, but only in a limited way, owing to city council opposition urged by the Restaurant Association. And we did restore horse-drawn touring carriages. Their route began at the old Water Tower and Pumping Station and clip-clopped along the side streets of Streeterville and the Gold Coast. The formula was basic: the more attractions, the more people, the more life for the city.

During 1980, Chicago had in fact been two cities—one doing well, even prospering, and the other a struggling giant trapped in financial quicksand. At last, government had a bit more money, thanks to the sale of tax anticipation notes, and we learned to exist frugally on the first Byrne budget.

That first year had aspects of a Saturday movie serial—tune in next week. Will the train run over the mayor, or will she be pulled off the tracks in time? We became so preoccupied with city finances and the schools that Frank Muscare and his firemen's union received scant attention. I'd dug in my heels on the strict separation between officers and men in the ranks. My collective bargaining ordinance had been bottled up in committee for three months. At midnight on February 14, 1981, four months after bargaining had begun, a message went out on the union's hotline: "Happy Valentine's Day, Mayor Byrne. We are on strike."

Bill Griffin called me at 2:00 A.M. The firemen were walking out of every firehouse in the city. Those who didn't want to walk were physically chased out. It was and still is a sad comment on my term; not so much that it happened—fire departments all over the country had been calling strikes—but that I had not been able to deliver immediately on my collective bargaining pledge. Understandably, the union regarded the delay as another City Hall stall, but even so, in light of the many financial crises, I thought Fire Department leadership should have restrained its membership a few weeks longer.

I was saddened to see these proud men rip themselves apart, for it was a bitter strike, pitting brother against brother, father against son, as they individually wrestled with the decision to strike or remain on the job. It lasted three grueling weeks. The major leaders of organized labor in Chicago reasoned with the officers of the union, but the fire fighters viewed them with suspicion and vacillated on agreements.

The strike turned political. Aides reported to me that Richie Daley's alderman, Patrick Huels, was down on the strike line blithely passing out "Daley for State's Attorney" buttons. Privately, however, the union offered to endorse Kennedy over Carter in the March presidential primary along with Daley's opponent locally if the city would cave in. An alderman got into the act, sensing opportunity in turmoil, and came to my office just before the strike. If I would transfer a particular police commander, he claimed, Muscare would be grateful and there would be no strike. This emissary alleged that the union leader was deep in gambling debt and "juice loans." (Juice loans carry an exorbitant rate of interest; street lore ties the mob to such loans made to gamblers.) Supposedly, those owed would cancel the debt in return for this one transfer.

If one transfer could prevent a strike, so be it. I spoke to the superintendent of police about transferring the commander, and he agreed. A few minutes later, I learned from an assistant that gambling apparatus had been found in the back room of a tavern in that district on a police raid.

If it was the mob that wanted the commander gone, forget it. It took less than a minute to countermand my own order. The commander was not transferred.

This alderman was not known to front for the mob. Was Muscare in fact in debt at all? Who could know? I felt sorry for the firemen out on the line, for in much of what was happening behind the scenes, they were pawns.

The city was getting nowhere in negotiations, and we were further angering the striking fire fighters by supplying food to the non-strikers still working at the stations. Men from Streets and Sanitation and the Department of Sewers assisted the working firemen on their calls. We were accused of trying to break the strike, but we were simply determined to save lives. No serious fires, thank God, broke out during the three-week strike, and no lives were lost.

But it was only a matter of time before some disaster would bring this strike down on my head. I had to reach a settlement, and my negotiating team was exhausted. I checked with Judge John Powers Crowley, whose opinion I respected, about a replacement for our labor negotiator. Crowley recommended William B. Hanley, a labor attorney. I also replaced the other negotiators, including Fire Commissioner Richard Albrecht, who had vowed right up until the moment the firefighters walked out that "my men will never strike." Within two days, Hanley produced a workable solution. The one sticky issue—whether the union would include the higher-ranking officers—would go to arbitration. We'd done it.

As the negotiating team was leaving my office, Jesse Jackson appeared with his entourage of eight or ten advisers and admirers. I knew what this was about. Jesse fancied himself a peacemaker, a crisis manager; whether freeing hostages or settling strikes, it was all the same to him. Jesse had materialized to save us. Indeed, he offered to mediate the strike and, not incidentally, demanded more affirmative-action hiring.

We were waiting only for the final papers and signatures. I didn't tell Jesse this, because we had been close to settling on four occasions, and the union's bargaining unit had reneged each time. The strike was technically over, but even a mayor with all his or her power can be upstaged by the power of the TV camera and a word called "perception." At that time three million people in Chicago had been without adequate fire protection for three weeks. Jesse had enough sources within the department to know that the strike was settled, but he had hit the target perfectly. Had I refused his offer, would many blacks feel slighted and angered? Yes, indeed. And the firemen would suspect me of stonewalling, refusing help because I didn't really want to give a contract.

At any rate, Jesse knew what media buttons to push. He set up an elaborate press conference outside my door—lights, cameras, reporters—then visited the firemen's union leaders. I don't know what they discussed, but at the rank-and-file ratification meeting that night at McCormick Place, Jesse walked onstage to a cheering Fire Department—the same Fire Department judged by a federal court to be the most racist department in city government! Jesse took over the union meeting, phoning us to ask if he could send over the document for my signature; Muscare would sign it at McCormick Place after I signed. Again, I could have chosen to say to Jesse that we would sign it as previously agreed in my office the following morning in the presence of all those who helped settle the strike. But I might be perceived as an arrogant mayor who was trying to keep the strike going.

I signed the agreement, sent it back with one of my guards, and watched Jesse Jackson announce the settlement of the firemen's strike. I was so tired after three weeks of sleepless nights and so happy the strike was over I didn't care who grandstanded. I knew the truth: I had pushed through the first collective bargaining legislation in Chicago, and I had signed the first union contract in the history of Chicago city government.

The strikers returned to work, angry with nonstrikers, angry at their loss of respect among Chicagoans for participating in an illegal strike, and angry with me as the supposed cause of it all. I was no less furious at them for breaking the law. On the other hand, I was also enormously grateful to the other city departments that had supported the city. This had been an unnecessary, even silly, strike. The firemen, like the police, would eventually have got their contract, strike or not.

One minor mystery of my term involved six thousand of Holland's finest tulip bulbs. As part of my ongoing campaign to have Chicago selected for the 1992 World's Fair, we had invited Queen Beatrix of the Netherlands to a state dinner. Well beforehand, her very well organized representatives came by City Hall frequently to ensure that everything would go smoothly. When the consul-general asked what state gift might be appropriate, I thought of the obvious: spring bulbs for the spring visit. Soon, six thousand huge tulip bulbs arrived, undoubtedly the finest in the land, and I envisioned a patchwork of color lining State Street for the Queen's arrival.

They were sent over to the Department of Streets and Sanitation, which reported that it was not then the season for planting spring bulbs on the shores of Lake Michigan. The Bureau of Forestry put them into cold storage until the proper time, and everyone agreed that they would be in full bloom right on schedule. The bulbs were planted in due course, and I forgot all about them.

Three weeks before the state visit, a very worried commissioner of streets and sanitation came into my office. "Bad news, Mayor," he said glumly. He was of the old school that never liked to tell me anything disturbing because he expected people always to blame the messenger for his news. This was not my way, but I was momentarily alarmed. Quite a few disasters, natural and otherwise, could occur in the huge and vulnerable system administered by his department.

"What is it?" I asked.

"They're all dead," he mumbled. "The tulips aren't going to bloom."

Frankly, it took me a moment to remember what he was talking about, and I went on to other things. Pressure was building from the local representatives of her majesty's government, though, and my protocol aide became very worried. She shared her concern with Kathy, who claims no direct knowledge of what happened next.

On the day of the Queen's procession down State Street, tulips in glorious full bloom nodded their heads in the breeze, reminding everyone in the crowd of Holland's famous horticultural achievements. All had been cadged practically overnight from the Park District Conservatory and other parts of the city and replanted in time for the occasion. Diplomatic relations between Chicago and the Netherlands remained cordial.

Chicago is always beautiful in the spring, but never more so than in 1980, for Chicago was moving again. Ground had been broken for the extension of the rapid transit out to O'Hare. Spring's softer ground eased the laying of desperately needed sewers and water mains throughout the city. Intersections were being torn up for new water mains and sewers; newly constructed streets would close over them before fall. Decaying, rusted bridges were being repaired or put out of service for construction of new bridges. Wabash Avenue was an open trench from one end of the Loop to the other. To lay new sewer lines there, workers dug up old streetcar tracks probably laid by Yerkes in the early 1880s; it made no sense to encourage the downtown building boom if skyscrapers emptied their waste into century-old sewers. Construction began on a new bridge to connect Illinois Center, the eastern most section of the stem of the Chicago River, with the Dock and Canal property over the river. When finished, it would be the largest bascule bridge built in the country in the last fifty years. (A bascule bridge is one built in the fashion of a seesaw, one end counterbalanced by weights on the other.)

Thanks to the Crosstown Expressway money, an increase in the water tax, and the new sewer tax, Chicago was also experiencing a boom in private construction that would generate very welcome income from real estate taxes. In the summer of 1985 I was pleased to read a report released by the Northwestern Center for Urban Affairs and Policy Research: "Downtown Chicago has experienced perhaps its greatest building boom since the fire of 1871. $4.5 billion had been invested in a 'Downtown Renaissance' from January 1979 to December 1984." The study cited 160 completed projects plus forty-five under construction and fifty still on the drawing boards.[2]

At the suggestion of several restaurateurs, we established "Taste of Chicago," a three-day neighborhood festival in the Gold Coast, beginning July 4. A million people attended. On Memorial Day that year, we introduced another event that became annual—the appearance of the famous Barraboo Wisconsin Antique Circus. Navy Pier had always been a popular attraction, but, like so many other structures, it had seen better days. Its infrastructure needs alone were estimated to be over $100 million. It was safe enough for ChicagoFest, and its main ballroom had been redone, but it couldn't be used very heavily without being rebuilt. To that end, we began negotiations with the Rouse Company, the real estate organization that developed Quincy Market in Boston and Harbor Place in Baltimore. We were also negotiating with the major airlines at O'Hare regarding construction of a new international terminal.

Politics never takes a holiday in Chicago. After Richie Daley won the election for state's attorney, he immediately swung into an investigation of my administration. Richie had been observant, noting how

Adamowski tormented Mayor Daley throughout the 1950s with the power of the state's attorney's office. Suddenly the papers announced that Richie was investigating ChicagoFest to determine if food vendors had forked over payoffs to gain concession booths. Next a separate investigation was announced into the awarding of the *street sweeping* contract. Then the government's investigatory powers were trained upon the awarding of the *junk car* contract. As a matter of fact, it was becoming a joke in the corporation counsel's office that he could wallpaper his walls with subpoenas. Daley did his utmost to get someone sent to jail, but there were never any convictions of members of my cabinet. Each thrust, however, produced headlines, as every investigation does. They can do harm. Has anyone ever seen a headline proclaiming that all was found to be ethical? Even after all these years, I remember vividly how hurt I was by this continuing harassment. It felt like something more than political hardball.

In the meantime, I was finding out some things on my own that shocked me. I had assumed, and I think the public does, too, that once a story breaks exposing some alleged wrongdoing in government the practice is stopped. Incredibly, that is not always the case. I discovered that quite a bit of the city's insurance was still being handled by Johnny Daley. I would later learn that the law firm of Richard and Michael Daley was still retained at $50,000 a year by Gulf & Western. The firm had made well over $400,000.[3] The people and the press had forgotten all the old headlines regarding racetrack scandals and why O'Hare has only one hotel on its grounds.

The one glitch in the building boom was the north Loop, stalled in a political holding pattern. Democratic County Assessor Thomas Hynes vacillated for three years over whether to grant a tax break to the north Loop developers, the Hilton Corporation. It seemed to him bad form to give a tax break during the depths of recession, but this was backward thinking. Every other major city in America was granting tax breaks to spur economic development, while Hynes sat on his hands. According to the north Loop plan, which I inherited, the Hilton flagship hotel would stimulate the entire north Loop—an area from the river at Wacker Drive to Madison Street. All the old theaters—the Selwyn, United Artists, and the Chicago Theatre—were to be renovated, and residents would again stream into the north Loop to live theater. The development had much in common with parts of the old Daniel Burnham plan of the late 1800s, which had called for a section of downtown Chicago buildings connected with government to be located in one governmental area. The new State of Illinois Building was already under construction at Randolph and LaSalle, across from City Hall; the Daley Center stood splendidly nearby at Clark Street.

I made up my mind—if Hynes waffled on, the city would launch the north Loop on its own, and eventually we did just that. We constructed new subway stations and new underground pedestrian walkways, and repaired the landmark "Loop El structure," badly rusted and in need of paint.

We finally broke the Loop logjam when developers moved forward without a Hilton resolution. We broke ground for the skyscraper transportation building and launched the first of what would become the glittering facade of Wacker Drive and the Chicago River.

Throughout these efforts, I did not ever forget an element that has always played an essential role in political life: good politicians stay in the game because they love the interaction with the people. No matter how rough things got when I was mayor, it was the support of the public that kept me going. The first eight months of my term, for example, were really brutal: transit strike, firemen's strike, collapsing schools. I was getting banged up pretty good.

When Wally Phillips, a top radio talk show host, and I wound up together in a Walkathon down Michigan Avenue one day, he said, "Well, you're certainly going through a baptism of fire."

I could only look at him and half-smile.

"Mayor," he went on, "half the people who are giving you a hard time were never with you anyway. Look over there." Beside us, a bus had stopped at the light. ' 'Those are your people."

I looked, and it was wonderful—everyone was waving from the windows, smiling from ear to ear, giving me the thumbs-up or V-for-victory sign. That's what it's all about. You get recharged and are ready to do battle twice as hard for what you believe in.

Early one morning in mid-March of 1981, I woke up to a news report: "And there was another shooting at Cabrini Green last night." Two mornings later: "There were two more shootings at Cabrini Green last night."

I looked out my bedroom window toward Cabrini, the sprawling public housing project due west. From such a remove, Cabrini Green looked calm, which it obviously was not. I asked for a copy of Ca-

Cabrini Green. Our apartment for a short time in 1981 was on the fourth floor of this building. COURTESY OF LEE BALTERMAN.

brini's police log right away. The statistics detailed ten deaths and over thirty shootings in less than three months. I was shocked not only by the violence but also by the lack of media attention. Had those murders occurred in another neighborhood, the media would be clamoring for my head. Why weren't they? I sent for the superintendent of police, Richard Brzeczek, and the chairman of public housing, Charles Swibel, to learn more, but they didn't know much about Cabrini Green. I asked them to get answers and told Brzeczek to increase manpower at Cabrini if he didn't have enough.

About three days later, after presiding at the opening of the rehabbed Knickerbocker Hotel, I asked my driver to swing over to Cabrini. From the Gold Coast to Cabrini was scarcely a ten-minute drive. As we approached the huge campuslike setting of high rises, low rises, and townhouses nestled together, I noticed a starkness. No one was out enjoying the balmy spring weather. It was the lunch hour, yet the playgrounds and parks were virtually empty. Where were the children? And where were the police? No sign of them, either.

As we headed back to City Hall, I called ahead, ordering that the mayor's second car—a station wagon—be ready to go. Then I sent for Swibel and Brzeczek and asked if they had inspected Cabrini yet.

They had not, so I suggested that we all go together and see it for ourselves. "That's a good idea, Mayor. We'll call our offices and let them know where we are in case of an emergency. And we'll be all set to go." I quickly suggested they call from my car, knowing full well that there was no phone in the station wagon. Had I allowed them to phone their offices, the entire scene would have changed within minutes. We'd have been greeted by a cadre of enthusiastic CHA workers, happily mowing and raking and hauling. And there would have been police on every corner, tipping their hats to the superintendent and the mayor.

When we pulled into Cabrini Green, I suggested we chat with the few residents who were about. Simply strolling around the grounds was drawing a big *no* from my guards, but we were the symbols of government authority. If we couldn't move freely here, how could any resident? Half a dozen residents we encountered vociferously confirmed my worst fears; they seldom if ever saw the police.

A unit assigned specifically to Cabrini, a so-called vertical patrol, was supposed to be visible in each building and make routine rounds of all of them. The lieutenant in charge of that unit soon joined the superintendent, the commissioner, and me on the Cabrini sidewalks. He suggested we talk in his office; it would be safer inside.

I cringed. "Lieutenant," I said, "we'll talk out here. What *is* going on?"

He looked around and regarded me blankly. "Well, Mayor, it's relatively calm."

"Lieutenant, it's also calm in the cemetery. If you believe ten dead and thirty shot in a six-week period is relatively calm, you don't belong here."

Eventually, we did walk to his office to look at the vertical unit's attendance sheets, which indicated an absentee rate of over 40 percent that day. I asked the lieutenant if he ever requested additional help from the district. "No. We try to keep a lid on things from within." Keep a lid on it—that was the thinking of the sixties! It wasn't the lieutenant's fault—he was telling me what he thought I wanted to hear. About ten years before, snipers at Cabrini had shot two police officers. Once the murders were prosecuted, an invisible wall seemed to go up at Cabrini Green. It was just written off.

I spoke directly to the lieutenant: "If you think I'm going to drive by these projects and look at gangbangers guarding the entrances to the buildings as they openly puff marijuana, forget it. These doorways don't belong to them. Perhaps you'd better start thinking of the constitutional rights of the twenty-five thousand people holed up in here because of them." ("Gangbangers" is an apt street and police term—so casually did the gangs resort to shooting, and so incessant had the sounds of gunfire become in many public housing areas.)

After the usual yes-ma'ams and promises, our little group walked somberly back to the station wagon and drove on to City Hall.

But I couldn't shake what I had seen at Cabrini Green, and it proved hard to get the action I wanted. Bureaucracy, chains of command, the whole system was slow. The following Saturday, I again asked the guards to drive me through Cabrini, where we came upon a police foot chase. Some young men were in custody, others were scattering like quail. There were certainly enough police. Several dozen, I judged. As an unmarked squad car approached us heading east on Division Street, we signaled it to stop. The sergeant driving pointed to the backseat of his car, where a teenage girl lay curled up in a fetal position. The sergeant said, "Gang rape, Mayor." I was so distressed I could barely look at the girl. "We got the offenders."

If the police attended to their duty, Cabrini would obviously be a safer place to live. Now with the police around, many tenants were outside. This horrible place obviously required constant attention.

How could I put Cabrini on a bigger map? Suddenly I knew—I could move in there. Jay liked the idea and agreed we should try it. I said, "Jay, let's write a release. You give it to the City News Bureau for dissemination. Just state that because of the rash of serious crime, we are taking up residence at Cabrini Green."

Next, I had my guards to contend with—if we lived there, so would they! All of my personal guards were exceptionally fine men and women. We also had uniformed police officers at the high rise. Jay and I were especially close to the personal guards, who are by your side so continually they become almost as close as family. Sixteen personal guards might seem like a lot, but actually they compose two shifts, each starting the day at six-thirty and ending it whenever I ended. Since a mayor works usually as much at night as by day—what with community meetings, ribbon cuttings, and benefits—a mayor's guards average a twelve-to-fourteen-hour day.

The personal detail consisted of three cars. An advance car checked everything out before the arrival of the mayor's car, which was followed by a tail car. While the third car does serve as a form of protection, it is primarily there in case the mayor's car becomes disabled, or to aid in crowd control and safety if the mayor's care is going at great speed to the scene of a disaster. They were with me through sad events such as the crash of a DC-10 at O'Hare in May 1979, and at hospitals after the fall of a brother in the Police or Fire Department, and during the good scenes as well. The one experience that none of them had ever shared, however, was life in public housing, and the prospect was a bit much for them.

My laughter at their horrified reactions turned to tears the following week as letters arrived from a third-grade class near Cabrini. The students thanked me for thinking of them, but each one offered the same advice: "Don't come here, Mayor Byrne. You'll be killed." Eight- and nine-year-old children living in my city did not think their mayor could survive in their home neighborhood! I was going to be in a very special situation, of course, and never really worried about being killed. My personal police detail were caring, street-smart, FBI-trained guards and friends. They chose an apartment for Jay and me and one for themselves, took care of the security, and prepared to move in when we did.

A district superintendent of schools, Marge Harrigan, phoned my office several days after the announcement. She was crying, but had called to thank me for announcing the plan. It seemed she had been in meetings about Cabrini with the 18th District police. "I didn't know what to do. Our enrollment was down to zero. Every mother was refusing to let her children out of the apartment to attend school. They're so frightened that their children could be killed in gun crossfire."

At last, information came across my desk throwing light on the cause of the violence. Two gangs, the Disciples and the Stones, were engaged in a turf war over control of drug sales. Their activities were not limited to public housing; for they and not the mob, according to the police, controlled drug traffic in much of Chicago. Once I realized that, I was smoldering all over again. Chicago is a big city, but every neighborhood is patrolled and individual unto itself. What was going on?

I sent for Alderman Fred Roti of the 1st Ward. Our conversation sticks in my memory.

"Alderman," I said, "I am no fool. I am not moving into Cabrini Green to get caught in the crossfire between two gangs. These gangs," I went on, eager to make my point clear, "are not just fighting and shooting guns off at random; they're shooting over who will control the sale of drugs in the projects."

Alderman Roti was emphatic about not knowing anything about that, about drugs in the projects or anywhere else.

"Well," I went on, "somebody is letting it in. I want it to stop, and I'm warning you, if so much as a blade of grass moves while I clean that place out, there will be trouble like you've never known."

"But Mayor, why are you telling me?"

I replied that perhaps somebody in the alderman's crowd might know somebody who knew somebody who *did* push drugs.

"Everybody is on vacation," the alderman said.

"Then, Alderman," I finished up, "you reach somebody and let them know how I feel. I'm not going to tell anyone *when* I'm moving in, but you had better be back here by the end of the week to tell me someone has made the proper connection."

There was a short silence, then a sort of low groan, before Roti left, saying words something like "Mayor, I've taken more Gelusil since you got into office than I took with Daley and Bilandic combined."

The week passed—it was now March 1981—and Alderman Roti didn't call. Various newspaper accounts had mentioned that Tony Spilotro might be running the Chicago mob or was at least in its hierarchy. (A few years later, in 1984, he and his brother were found murdered gangland-style in Indiana.) I'd had enough—I would take direct action. I dialed a hotel in Palm Springs mentioned often as a wintering spot for Chicago mobsters and asked for Mr. Spilotro. I was told Spilotro was in California and was given his hotel number.

Perhaps because of the unnecessary Capone image about Chicago, mob stories are frequently elaborated on in the press—just as they often are in City Hall. One such story is that they don't like to talk on the phone for fear their lines are bugged by the FBI. If that was true, I was certain Spilotro would not feel warmly toward the chap in Palm Springs who gave me his number.

I dialed Spilotro. It was 4:30 A.M. in California; I hoped to catch him sleeping and off guard. To my amazement, the operator put my call right through. I had never before talked to a kingpin of the mob, and again the memory is vivid.

"Yah," a gravelly voice answered at the other end of the line.

"Good morning," I said. "Is this Mr. Spilotro?"

"Who wants to know?"

"Jane Byrne, the mayor of Chicago."

I felt I had his attention now.

"I'm sorry, your honor," the voice began, and went on to say that

I was "the talk of Vegas," that I had balls—"what balls," he actually said—to move into the housing project. "Why, I hear they even have hand grenades in those apartments."

I said I was glad he'd raised the subject.

"Yeah? What's up?"

"I understand, Mr. Spilotro, that the shootings at Cabrini are caused by gang wars over the control of drug turf."

"We aren't into that," the voice said firmly.

I told him I hadn't said he was, and the voice repeated the denial, heatedly.

Here was my moment. "I believe, Mr. Spilotro," I said, "you are in an area of the country where you meet many types of people from various walks of life. Perhaps you can make it your business to bump into someone who might bump into someone who is involved with pushing drugs."

"I dunno. We never touch drugs."

"Mr. Spilotro, let me put it this way," I said slowly, with as much steel in my voice as I could muster. "As I look out of my kitchen window, I view Holy Name Cathedral at Chicago and State. If I walk into my den, I can see where State Street and Rush Street merge." (Some of the Rush Street restaurants and smart pubs have over time been accused of being fronts for mob interests.) "If you don't bump into someone who might know someone who is into drug pushing, I guarantee by the time you return to Chicago, you will think that Rush Street is an extension of Holy Name Cathedral."

"I'll see what I can do," the voice said. "I can't promise nothin'."

The following Monday morning, a badly shaken Roti came into my office. "Why were you talking to him on the telephone?"

I said, "Alderman, I told you to get back to me. I told you I meant it. You didn't get back to me. I hope the FBI was on the phone. Don't think I'm kidding. I will shut Rush Street down."

Again, Alderman Roti left my office, both hands holding his head.

On a windy March evening, date and time unannounced, Jay and I took up residence at Cabrini Green. Our new address was 1160 Sedgewick, Apartment 402. The elevators were broken, which is not unusual in public housing, so Jay and I walked the four flights past the graffiti-laden walls up a narrow stairwell to our apartment. It was clear that maintenance had just scrubbed down the stairwell, for the smell of Lysol hung heavily in the air. The two-bedroom apartment wasn't terrible and could easily have been made comfortable for a family of four. I used the second bedroom as an office.

Right away I realized from the constant hubbub that the children used the hallways and not the playground for recreation. I also surmised, to judge from the tremendous numbers of children on the loose, that many families were too large for their assigned apartments. There was certainly not enough room for so many children to study or play in their own homes. There was no place even to think alone. What chances did they have?

Bulletproof glass panels had been installed behind all the windows. I quickly removed them. Otherwise, there was no way for fresh air to enter, and I couldn't hear what was going on outside. A uniformed policeman from the house detail was stationed near my door. Two personal guards, partners since their rookie days, stayed in the apartment next door.

Living in Cabrini was not uncomfortable, but all in all it was a sobering experience. The first night, a group of elementary school youngsters came to my door. They wanted to know what it was like to be mayor and whether I'd be staying for a while. (The answer was yes.) As we chatted in my doorway, I glanced to the left, down the darkened hallway. Someone was down there, standing casually on watch. I invited the children to stop by every evening. Our talks would become a ritual. The next knock at the door that first night came from two teenage girls, Lilli and Tina. I invited them in to discuss my goals for Cabrini. They, too, visited every night.

Jay, always the enthusiast for trying something new, had set certain rules for our residence there. First and foremost, we were to set up housekeeping as if we were still at home on Chestnut Street. Jay is very nutrition-minded and quite a chef. He intended to continue doing the marketing and cooking in our Cabrini digs. That required a daily trek to the supermarket and eternal vigilance regarding the roaches. Any stored food had to be well secured. Baby roaches, grandfather roaches—the whole family was entrenched. These were absolutely the healthiest roaches imaginable. They would crawl out of wall sockets in a steady stream, or come up and out of the bathtub drain even with the hand shower going full-blast.

Jay's cooking went well save for one embarrassing moment. When I came in quite late from work one evening, I noticed he had prepared a great-looking salad and was getting ready to broil steaks. (We did eat red meat once a week.) I went into the bedroom to change into more comfortable clothes. I was out of one outfit but not yet into the next one when all sorts of sirens and bells went off. My guards came running into the apartment, guns drawn. I stood frozen in my room, then grabbed my robe and ran to the living area, where I viewed a somewhat shaken Jay saying over and over, "But I was only broiling steaks." Smoke from the stove had triggered the very efficient smoke devices installed by my protectors.

As I climbed into bed each night, I could look out the window that faced east toward my own home on Chestnut not so far away. What a difference a few blocks makes! Why has this place always been Little Hell? That's how my grandfather Burke knew it, and it is hell for the children living here now. The Black Hand may have been replaced by the Stones and Disciples, but my grandfather and these young Chicagoans endured the same fear. Often, when we first moved in, a pickup truck appeared, circled the parking lot, with gangbangers standing in back, arms folded military-style, shouting, "Stones, Stones, Stones!" Cabrini Green was at war. I slept poorly some nights, and not only because I was in a strange bed.

Gangs had long been a cancer in Chicago. The city couldn't stop them from forming, but they could be controlled, I thought, with good police work. To that end, I created a new division in the Police Department—the Gang Crimes Suppression Division—and appointed Joe McCarthy deputy superintendent of the division. I pushed for a thousand-member Gang Crimes Unit to work in all public housing units and on buses and transit lines where gang crimes were rampant.

To have the mayor living at 1160 Sedgwick had indeed put Cabrini Green "on the map." City government was falling all over itself to provide extra services to Cabrini. The maintenance men on the CHA payroll were both embarrassed by the state of things and frightened that they might get fired. I relied upon the Departments of Sewers, Streets and Sanitation, and Public Works to clean up the project. The Department of Human Services provided paint, and tenant volunteers gathered to paint over the graffiti. Consumer Affairs set up food co-ops for bulk and even cheaper purchasing.

The public also experienced a newfound awareness. According to a citywide poll, 82 percent supported my move into the project. From the private sector, money was donated to the "One Chicago Fund" to create baseball fields and basketball courts at Cabrini. Jay became the baseball coach. Cabrini had lights for night games before the Cubs did. In a short time, the Gang Crimes Unit had the gangs under control. Perhaps the phone call to Spilotro had been helpful. At any rate, after three weeks of intensive police pressure and vigilance, my guards reported that the gangbangers were pleading, "Just get her out of here, man, please. There'll be no more shooting, no more killing. Please, man, we got no action, man. We got no action at all, man."

Every night, as the children visited, I finally realized that the man flattening himself against the wall was a gangbanger spying on them. "Who is your friend over there in the corner?" I asked.

Without even turning around, they said, "That's Benny, and he's real, real bad."

By now, I knew there was a Benny on every floor. In every building, children were watched as a form of intimidation to keep them in line. I hated it. But overtly the crime at Cabrini had stopped. The once sterile empty play lots were full of children; attendance in school was back to normal; there was a free and open feeling about the place. People walked across the plazas between the high rises without fear. Cabrini seemed like any other neighborhood now, not like a prison. It was time to leave.

I wanted to have a party, with an awards ceremony for the children who had worked on the cleanup and tutoring programs. Human Services decided on a kite-flying and roller-skating event to be followed by refreshments and the awards. That evening, when teenage Tina and Lilli arrived, I asked if they were coming to the party. After much prodding, Lilli finally said, "Please, Mayor Byrne, don't tell on us and don't get mad. We can't come."

"What do you mean? Are you too grown-up for that kind of thing?"

"No. See, Mayor Byrne"—it was pouring out of Lilli now—"you don't know this. We aren't Stones, and you aren't a Stone. But everyone who lives in the red buildings are Stones because they live in the red buildings. All the gray buildings across Division Street are the Disciples' buildings. You put the party across the street, so we can't go."

Stunned, I said, "Is that all? Don't be silly. You will be perfectly safe there. I'll be there. The police will be there. You have nothing to be afraid of."

They said, "No, Mayor Byrne. One day you'll be gone from here, and the gangs will remember. We can't go, and nobody else in the red buildings can go."

I was furious. Just as Benny was out there every night, so the gangs were biding their time, waiting for me to leave.

I was going to win this one. We scrubbed the kite and roller skating idea and came up with CabriniFest, a celebration that would shut down Division Street throughout the projects. There would be a midway: ponies, merry-go-rounds, Ferris wheels, popcorn, hot dogs, cotton candy, music, bingo. Most of the rides and the food would be donated. Top players from the Bears, White Sox, and Cubs agreed to appear. They *would* cross that street.

On Holy Saturday at 10:00 A.M., we were ready. It was time to begin. There was only one problem. No children appeared, from *either* side of the street. One hour passed, then another half hour. The midway stood virtually empty.

Around noon, my personal guards John Parilli and Mike Plovanich came over. "If we all hang on a little longer, Mayor, you'll win. Holy hell is going on inside. The kids are screaming they want to go. The gangs will have to cave in."

Minutes later, a young man sauntered out of a gray building and made his way down Division Street, boogying through the rides and food stands. A Gang Crimes officer told me he was head of the Disciples, top dog of all the gray buildings. He was letting the children know he would see them if they ventured out on that street.

Livid, I walked down the street to confront him. Barely controlling myself, I asked him if he cared to go on a ride. He smirked. "I haven't made up my mind yet."

Losing it, I spit out, "I don't like your earring, and I don't like any of your other gang insignia. I don't like you, either, and I don't like what you stand for. You're a bully. You terrorize children. Listen to me. I'll give you three minutes to go back in that building and tell your goddam Bennies on every floor to let those children out here, or you won't be making up your mind if you are going on a ride, because you will be going for a ride in one of those blue-and-white squad cars right over there. I'll go, too, and I'll sign the complaint against you as a tenant here. I'll also testify against you. I swear to you, the last person you'll see when they lock you up is me. And if you ever come up for parole, I'll come back and testify to the holy hell you put these children through. Go on now. You've got three minutes!"

He turned slowly and ambled toward one of the gray buildings, saying, "I'll let you know." I hoped he wouldn't call my bluff.

It wasn't much more than two minutes before children from both sides of Division Street swarmed out into the street. The Cabrini Fest came to life. Around 2:00 P.M. a group of "protesters" recruited by

Bennies appeared, hoping to make deadline for the evening news. When they raised the familiar cry "police brutality," mothers of the joyous children chased them away, shouting, "Go on. Get out of here. We *want* the police."

My twenty-five-day stay at Cabrini had made a mark, but I was not glad to be going, for I had made those children at Cabrini my friends. None of them knew I was going. On my last night, they left me a basket of brightly colored Easter eggs. Their chances, I reflected, were nearly that fragile. Beyond the El tracks I could see the new Olympia Center, the powerful John Hancock, and, just beginning to soar, the One Magnificent Mile Building. Over there was an affluent world. Over here was hell.

Suddenly, the large bond issue that the city desperately needed didn't seem all that important. What did it matter that much of Chicago glittered and boomed when so many children lived trapped in places like Cabrini? Had we made any difference? Certainly, security and the recreational programs improved at Cabrini, and indeed at all the public housing complexes in Chicago. In the end, one statistic pleased me most—not one murder occurred at Cabrini Green until after I left the mayor's office more than two years later.

Another brush with Cabrini Green gave me a humorous lesson in the ways of power. After Jay and I had moved out, word came that gangs had set up shop just across Division Street at Sedgwick Street, not all that far from where we'd lived. I decided I'd just have to drive through as a signal that they would have to move on. Sooner or later, I hoped, they'd get the message that I intended to make them join the normal people of Chicago and stop terrorizing their neighbors.

As we drove down the street, I said, "No wonder they come here to hide out. It's darker than anyplace else." Some of the trees had not been trimmed, and the streetlights were dirty. My guards agreed that it was dreary and threatening.

The next morning, I made sure the Bureau of Electricity and the Department of Streets and Sanitation were put on the job. At around 5:00 P.M., I got a report that five hundred streetlights had been washed or replaced and trees had been trimmed for six straight blocks. I felt good about that. Sometimes you really can get things done, I thought.

A little later that evening, as the limo turned onto Michigan Avenue, I was puzzled. "Now *this* area looks dark and dreary, doesn't it?" My guards agreed. We speculated that there was some sort of power problem weakening the lights. Concerned, I pushed the button on the

The pride and beauty of Chicago's skyline, its people, Lake Michigan, and its warmth. COURTESY OF LEE BALTERMAN.

power window to get a better look. As the glass slid down, all the lights of the avenue suddenly burned more brightly.

I roared with laughter. The limo was brand-new, and, as I now realized, its windows were slightly tinted. For the last two evenings, we had been getting an unusually dark view of Chicago. "Well," I said. "The taxpayers' money has been properly spent. Trees have been trimmed, and lights have been brightened." But the people of Sedgwick Street owed it all, this time, to tinted windows.

CHAPTER 20

Madame Ex-Mayor

n 1982, the Daleyites still hanging on within my administration continued to throw sand into the works, but they couldn't stop our momentum. They busied themselves with anonymous phone calls to investigative reporters alleging irregularities in this department or that. None were found. Richie was forever sniffing around. Eventually, he had five grand juries going at one time, but he was out of his league. He or someone on his staff, realizing that ChicagoFest and all the other big festivals brought me enormous public approval, constantly went after these events. Badly advised or something else, Richie threatened to shut down ChicagoFest because mustard and other condiments were supposedly spilling off Navy Pier. In carcinogenic quantities? Of course, vendors should have been more careful, and we instituted tighter sanitation cleanup. With great fanfare he also announced a suit against Commonwealth Edison for a rate increase granted by the Illinois Commerce Commission and pledged to bring the citizens a rebate. Rates *were* high, but they weren't regulated by *my* government. A public weary of recession was understandably inclined to buy into the criticism. Richie's suit was quietly settled after the 1983 election—so quietly that few realized the absence of benefits.

As the fiscal year ended, we pitched our plans for a large Chicago bond issue to the rating agencies in New York—more than $190 million. The money would buy half a fleet of garbage trucks for Streets and Sanitation, new squad cars for the police, miles of paving, additional police and fire stations, new libraries, and more ambulances. Chicago was credit-worthy once more.

The city seemed back on course, and I allowed myself to believe that little could possibly go wrong—a mistake. One fine morning, Donald Hovde, an Under Secretary at HUD, the federal funding source for all public housing, called on me. After preliminary niceties, he handed me a letter, gravely saying he wanted to deliver it personally. HUD, according to this missive, was not satisfied with the work of the board members at the Chicago Housing Authority. They had decided to follow the recommendation of an outside management study that the entire board be removed. The decision was final. HUD wanted me to agree to let a New York management team take over the CHA and run it while they and I jointly engaged in a national search for new board members.

Public housing is never luxurious, but ours, particularly since the pressure at Cabrini, was deemed vastly improved by most tenants. Was this a ploy for HUD to seize control through its handpicked management team? CHA is a big business. Maintenance contracts, building and construction contracts, elevator repair contracts, exterminating contracts—they could add up to quite a bit of patronage. Was this move political? Why? Reagan's federal cutbacks had made it hard enough to run CHA. To turn the whole operation over to outsiders was out of the question, and I had no intention of complying. This "management study" of CHA smelled fishy to me. (In fact, in view of the disclosures from 1988 on regarding the scandalous behavior of Samuel Pierce at HUD, Hovde's visit was certainly highly suspicious.)

I phoned CHA Chairman Swibel to ask him about it. He claimed the investigatory team had spent a mere three days studying our public housing. Swibel stopped by my office to read the HUD letter. He wondered how it, and Hovde's visit, tied in with the agency's "Request for Proposal" solicitations, which were mailed to real estate companies. They proclaimed that the federal government no longer wished to manage public housing and would like advice on what should or could be done with it: should the federal government attempt to convert it to condos, should it be sold to private contractors for the private sector to manage for profit, or should much of it be demolished and the land turned over to the private sector for whatever use it choose? I was puzzled. If the feds wanted out, why did the White House insist on its own supervisory team for Chicago?

Hovde had told me his visit was personal, out of respect, and confidential so as to assist in making a smooth transition from the old board to the new. To my utter surprise, within a few days the *Chicago*

Sun-Times headlined Washington's demand as "Swibel Must Go! HUD," not pointing out that the feds had called for dismissal of the entire board. For the next three months, the *Sun-Times* went after Swibel only, then the focus broadened to include Byrne, who presumably wouldn't fire him because he was her chief fund-raiser. The coverage put my "obscene political war chest" at $10 million, though it was in fact half that. If the *Sun-Times* wanted to get Swibel, it had chosen an unpromising target, for he had served without pay as CHA head for over twenty years. Moreover, Swibel was a battle-hardened veteran who had been dissected by many *Sun-Times* investigations during Mayor Daley's tenure. Nothing amiss had ever turned up.

I thought the campaign against Swibel terribly unfair, marked by innuendo and generalized statements regarding management style. The real culprits in public housing are discrimination and poverty, aided by the workings of the machine. In my view, the machine had built the high-rise ghettos in order to contain the controllable black votes and to secure white neighborhoods. But who could say such things aloud? This was too emotional an issue to be brought rationally out into the open at that time.

Thousands of residents live in Chicago's public housing. They are poor, very poor. They can't get work, they subsist on food stamps, they are unhappy. Now, twenty years of frustration, of broken elevators, of crowded living conditions, of crime and unemployment, had found a target: Swibel. Soon, militant black leaders took up the cry, picketing my office and my home. Not long after Chicagoans had rallied to the aid of Cabrini residents, these demonstrations began to stir old fears in other neighborhoods.

Before HUD intervened, I had planned to make changes at CHA, but such reform, including making the chairmanship a full-time paid position, required rewriting the state legislation that created the CHA board. Governor Thompson could change the board's composition by fiat. I phoned Jim and asked if he planned to remove the board and, in particular, Swibel. He said he used Swibel as much as I did, but thought that the newspapers, didn't like Swibel and that I had allowed him to become too upfront.

Swibel, who had contacts on both sides of the legislative aisle, had always been known as a behind-the-scenes operator. If he could get the job done, why make it something mysterious and hide him? He could be effective, and, frankly, I didn't know many other people who wanted to run public housing without financial compensation.

In confidence, I asked the leader of the Illinois house to make the chairman's position a well-paying, full-time job, but the change took several weeks to accomplish. Every day, meanwhile, the *Sun-Times* more or less changed, "Swibel must go," continuing to link him to my fund-raising. I met with the *Tribune* editorial staff to tell them what they already knew—that there would be legislative changes regarding the board of the CHA. They took a milder position than the *Sun-Times*, stating they had lived with Swibel as chairman for twenty years, and waiting a few more weeks wasn't going to bother them.

The *Sun-Times* pressure, really an all-out attack, was frightening even HUD's Mr. Hovde, who called to ask if I had resolved the situation. I advised him that when the legislature concluded its session, Swibel would be replaced by the executive director, Andrew Mooney, as full-time chairman, and Elmer Beard, a black deputy commissioner of the city's Housing Department, would transfer over to CHA as executive director. Two vacancies would open on the board, Swibel's seat and that of Darryl Grisham, a black businessman who had also served many years. Grisham was the only board member willing to resign; the others felt that to resign would tarnish their reputations. I informed Hovde that no outsiders were taking over Chicago's public housing. Reminding him of his own words to me, "Everyone is pleased with the wonderful progress you have made personally, Mayor, with the CHA," I also asked, again, for specific charges against the board. I had not been shown the actual report—a two-page summary of mismanagement charges and recommendations for take-over. Hovde weakly reiterated that the New York consulting agency had found "a poor management style."

This was a chaotic situation. Not even Hovde seemed to understand what was at play here, and he seemed genuinely sorry about it: "Just following orders" was his line. He warily requested a copy of my legislative plan for his records, in case he was questioned, so I forwarded a confidential copy of the plan, still pending legislative approval in Springfield. The next day, the *Sun-Times* featured a copy of my letter. I called Hovde; how in God's name had the contents of my confidential letter landed on page one? Claiming ignorance, he offered to find out, then phoned back to tell me that Congressman Harold Washington and Senator Charles Percy had both requested copies of the CHA file under the Freedom of Information Act. He didn't know which of the two had fed the *Sun-Times*, nor even if they had. He could not explain how it had happened so quickly.

Swibel was not the reason that I refused to accept an outside board. I disliked intensely the notion of a newspaper publisher turning someone into a scapegoat. To me, that is governing with two sets of values. One might have thought the issue was settling down, but it wasn't, as I found when I appointed two women, both white, to fill the vacancies: Estelle Holzer, an insurance executive, and the former acting superintendent of schools, Dr. Angeline Caruso. I had learned one thing from my weeks in public housing: it is a matriarchal society. Also, the children desperately needed education. Dr. Caruso, a Harvard graduate, could be very useful in establishing tutoring classes in the projects and in developing an environment more receptive to education.

Black militants again charged me with "arrogance," for in announcing the appointments, I hadn't hidden my reasons for choosing these women and had spoken about the matriarchal society in public housing. The protesters reacted to this and to the race of the women, especially Dr. Caruso, citing a supposedly racial incident some ten years earlier when she was a school principal. New protests blared. I thought I had struck a fairly even racial balance. The five-member board now included three whites—Holzer, Dr. Caruso, and Patrick Nash—along with two black board members, Renault Robinson and Letitia Nevil. Beard had become the CHA's first ever black executive director. The angry voices of black militant leaders like Dorothy Tillman and Lu Palmer virtually monopolized black radio stations in condemnation of the appointments. The Swibel issue faded, taking a backseat to Dr. Caruso, even though absolutely no anger had surfaced three years earlier when she became acting superintendent of schools. The demonstrations were renewed at my home and at City Hall. Not three months earlier, I had been a champion of public housing. Now, suddenly, I was a villain. This CHA hassle would cause me trouble right through to the end of my administration.

One of my greatest difficulties personally was how people perceived me, Jane Byrne. Some of the misperception was my fault, but not all of it. First of all, it was natural that someone who beat an entrenched machine would be labeled "feisty," "a fighter," "tough." Few realized that the Goliath I slew was more like a paper tiger, in some ways. The machine was indeed powerful and could make the difference in many different situations, but it was not all-powerful. Only five wards could be delivered lockstep every time; the other forty-five were considered "soft" by insiders, and fewer of the spoils of patronage were distributed to them. When I was elected, the five wards, representing only about 200,000 to 250,000 people, were in charge of all of the important city departments. The taproot of the machine ran deep, and the old guard didn't like having it cut off. When I tried to break this stranglehold by moving in people from other wards, I was portrayed as "vindictive" and "petty." I was a threat to a well-functioning system that earned tax breaks and lowered assessments for the real estate crowd and diverted huge amounts of business to the "right" bankers and insurers. It's like that old saying: I was the baby that wasn't supposed to be.

Sexism was another factor behind the most unfair attacks on me. When I made a strong move, I was called "a gutsy blonde." In exactly the same situation, any man would have been considered "brave" or "independent." Some of the sexist remarks were too frivolous to take seriously; sad to say, most women who go out and work for something in politics have to deal with them, even today. Others, I admit, hurt me very much.

But the charge that I was a "sellout" was the most damaging of all. Some of my supporters wanted radical changes that the city council could not afford to make. Others wanted me to bang away at all of the old committee chairman for the sake of banging, but I knew that that kind of bloodbath would be counterproductive to our aims. I had been in politics long enough to appreciate a very basic fact: all of those aldermen who did not originally support me had been elected by voters who apparently liked them. They were representatives of their neighborhoods, and I had to deal with them fairly. I disappointed some of my supporters by not warring constantly with the city council, but I knew that I could make no progress without that twenty-six-vote majority. I did not "side with the evil cabal," as some people charged, but I practiced the art of compromise, without ever making improper or underhanded deals. It's harder to walk a tightrope than to engage in a slugfest, but it gets you somewhere.

I want to make clear that the mayoralty is not simply one crisis after another. There were antic moments, and many a humorous or touching glimpse of the famous. When the legendary Italian tenor Luciano Pavarotti came to town to raise funds for earthquake relief in his native country, he generously sang virtually nonstop in a benefit concert for perhaps three hours. That very night, about fifteen thou-

Luciano Pavarotti, an unexpected treat at a fundraiser, thrilled the audience, especially my daughter, Kathy. COURTESY OF DAVE SCHEUSSLER.

sand guests were coming to a fund-raising dinner for my reelection campaign, and he offered to stop by late in the evening. Kathy, who was in charge of the dinner arrangements, had a swanky limo with a police car escort waiting for him at the concert hall, as befit a celebrated classical artist. "So nice, so lovely of you," Pavarotti said when he saw the limo, "but I would prefer to go in that"—pointing to the squad car, and whirling his finger in the air—"and make the siren go." To get the star to the mayor's fund-raiser, the poor officers had to let him ride in the front seat, working the sirens furiously during the entire ride. This was not by the book, but the world's greatest tenor has the great gift of getting his way on charm alone.

Actually, a kind of directness, even simplicity, characterizes many accomplished people. When Pope John Paul II visited Chicago, he inadvertently reminded me of my uncles and their friends, who always came to Sunday dinner in casual clothes without their Roman collars. When the Pope arrived at O'Hare, I was struck by the perfect skin of his face—no lines or wrinkles, pinkish-cream like a baby's—and his clear, alert blue eyes. When he bowed his head to pray, I noticed that he would also peek at the crowd every now and then, just to check their reactions to the show, with all of its splendor. In his white robes and gold sash, he was dressed as formally as the highest-ranking member of the Catholic Church could possibly be, but when he sat down and crossed his feet, I saw that he was wearing a pair of brown loafers and white socks. I recalled how my uncles always wore nothing but black with their robes—black shoes, socks, pants—but that was the "Old Church." John Paul looked like a regular guy, a Sunday athlete who'd just come in from a day of golf and thrown his papal robes over his casual clothes. A small thing, maybe, but it suggested that he was truly a Pope for the modern day.

In fact, few public occasions are actually as stiff and formal as they seem from the perspective of the audience. Some dignitaries restrict themselves to polite chitchat, but many are relaxed and natural. To them, public life has become normal life. When we gave a dinner in Chicago to honor Jihan Sadat, first lady of Egypt at the time, she and I were soon talking quite intimately, even though hundreds of people were sitting in front of us in the banquet room. A remarkably beautiful woman with dark shining brown eyes, she spoke in an arresting deep voice and had a presence that suggested that she understood much about many things. We discussed the condition of women in her country and her fight for expanded rights. Her husband, Anwar, did not always agree with her on that issue, but tears came to her eyes when she told me a story about his generosity to the deposed Shah of Iran, who was dying of cancer.

The Shah's wife, a close friend from Jihan's childhood, had begged her for help in a "pitiful" telephone call. "What are we going to do?" she had asked. "He is so very sick, and no one will have us."

Jihan had gone to her husband, who was working in his library. He listened to her account of the call and quickly said, "Well, there is no problem. You tell her to bring the Shah here. They will be welcome. I am strong; my people are strong."

Perhaps Mrs. Sadat and I looked as if we were having some sparkling, idle conversation, but she was deeply moved by the recollection. "Isn't he a fine man?" she said. "He was very kind to them. I'm so glad he helped them." She loved her husband very much, she admired him, and they were obviously very close. I recalled this wonderfully loving conversation with great sadness almost exactly a year later. It was the morning I woke up to the news that President Sadat had been shot to death by Islamic fundamentalists, as Jihan looked on.

In July 1982, only seven months until the Democratic primary for mayor, Bill Griffin wanted to start interviewing political consultants for my reelection campaign. He recommended either of two choices— David Sawyer of New York or Robert Squires of Washington. Squires, though very successful, might not be a wise pick; he had put together commercials for Richie Daley's state's attorney campaign. When I met him five years later in New York, he told me that my feud with Daley was in his opinion inevitable. He generally viewed it as not just a fight with Richie but something that the whole family was involved in; he thought they had disliked seeing me at the late mayor's side, but when I actually took his chair their feelings became much more intense. There was nothing he felt, that could have been done to stop it.

Shades of Earl Bush. I recalled how he had said over and over that the boys had shoved him out, envious of the mayor's "alter ego." How sick I thought that was! I didn't know the extent of their resentment in 1982, but my hunch then was that if Richie Daley decided to run against me, I would beat him.

I hired David Sawyer to orchestrate my campaign. If any political consultant ever walked into a firestorm, he did. The ink had barely dried on his contract when a woman in Indiana called a black radio talk show to ask why Jesse Jackson hadn't done something about my arrogant behavior in appointing the two white women. The host asked her what she thought Jesse could do. "Boycott ChicagoFest," she replied.

The idea caught fire, and Jesse did indeed call a boycott, extending it to performers. Stevie Wonder and Kool and the Gang had signed for that year, but Wonder pulled out. Kool and the Gang said they would perform wearing black armbands. The black food vendors, who'd had no contracts when I became mayor but now held 30 percent of all the ChicagoFest concessions, were pressured to pull out. Attendance, normally a million or so, dropped 20 percent. When Frank Sinatra showed up to perform, crowds swelled again, but some in the audience paraded around wearing T-shirts reading "White Honkie." As I sat under the stars, listening to the thousands cheering Sinatra's deft interpretation of "Chicago," I was anything but happy.

David Sawyer, not surprisingly, predicted a tough campaign. He was certain Richie would enter and his family name would draw votes. He was also certain that the black community would field a candidate. Sawyer's strategy was to ignore Daley, let him say and do what he wanted, and continue with the theme of solid government.

In August, we broke ground on the Delta Terminal at O'Hare and launched the airport's ten-year expansion. While our credit rating at Moody's slipped from Aa to A between 1979 and 1980 and at Standard and Poor's from A+ to A-, Chicago nonetheless held the highest bond rating of any major city east of the Mississippi. The 1983 budget reduced real estate taxes, as I had promised. We also moved to take $1 off the head tax on private sector employees. (The head tax, a $3 annual tax on all employees in companies or corporations with fifteen employees or more, pained the business community, created extra paperwork, and put us at an economic disadvantage with the competing suburbs. It was repressive to business and not in keeping with sound economic development.) We also pledged to eliminate the remaining $2 in the next two years. In spite of these tax reductions, Moody's was able to state in January 1983 that Chicago had "turned the corner in its financial difficulties."

Our announcement of reduced taxes was of course received favorably by voters weary of inflation. One of the biggest boosts to the city occurred came when the U.S. Conference of Mayors voted Chicago "The Most Livable City in America," an award based on our many cultural events and pleasant environment. This was my overriding goal—a city *alive* for its people. Most gratifying of all, the Bureau of International Expositions voted us the World's Fair city of its choice for 1992, with a sister fair in Spain. The world would be coming to see Chicago in just ten years, I thought.

My polls were encouraging. Nevertheless, Daley entered the race in November, and some blacks, as Sawyer had foreseen, sought a candidate of their own. Congressman Harold Washington had at first refused to run, but by late November 1982 he had been persuaded to change his mind. The media accorded him little chance to win; he had no money to speak of and no organization. The media's four years of gearing up for the Byrne-Daley contest was finally coming to a head. Our poll results held; late in 1982 we were 22 to 24 points ahead of both Daley and Washington.

On December 7, Sawyer informed me that judging by the polls,

Daley was technically out of the race. That's what I had expected, but I was wary of Washington, a man of imposing presence who made an impressive campaigner. Washington was tarring me with a Ronald Reagan brush at every turn. Times were hard in the nation, so this was a smart move.

The holidays approached. Still hoping to develop the north Loop right at the river, I directed that all the trees along Wacker Drive be lit with holiday lights. Every bridgetender house was adorned with huge wreaths bearing red bows. I thought again of the family story about my great-great-grandfather Crane boarding the Christmas ship to choose the family tree. I put the city's Christmas tree at State and Wacker Drive—right there at the river, joining the north and south sides. The fountains would be illuminated, and for the first time we lit the river bridges from below. My intent was that all of Chicago's traditions be united by the lights from State to Wacker Drive down through the curve at Wacker to the turn and then to the beautiful lights on the Magnificent Mile. But Chicago's Christmas tree had previously stood in the Daley Center, so I had handed the Daleyites another grievance.

Richie was running an ugly campaign, hurling charges of misconduct and kickbacks. Simultaneously, the Better Government Association sued me personally for $10 million as well as Festivals, Inc., over a technicality about funding for the Fest. A Daley supporter instigated the investigation leading to both suits. My administration had followed the precedent of funding established by Bilandic at the very first Fest; rather than seek city council approval of funding, we had awarded the contract as a *personal service* contract, requiring no council action. The BGA, which had not attracted many headlines since its media heyday of the 1960s and 1970s, implied to reporters that there was some kind of dirty dealing going on. This seemed a stupid ploy to me, for if anything my administration did was an open book, it was ChicagoFest. A million people were involved in one way or another. The suits did earn the BGA new headlines, and I suppose it could hope that if good luck struck, the personal suit against me would give them access to that mythical $10 million alleged to be in my war chest. For six years, from 1982 to 1988, this nuisance litigation festered, going all the way to the supreme court of Illinois, which in the end ruled in my favor.

Matters heated up on other fronts. Daley workers, principally from Bridgeport and Beverly, including many angry firemen, unmerci-

Chicago Christmas scene, 1982, showing the tree at State and Wacker Drive, and the softly-lit bridges spanning the river. COURTESY OF PETER J. SCHULTZ.

fully attacked me and my family, particularly Jay and our marriage. At one point in the heat of the campaign, my corporation counsel told me that a legal associate had asked him if it was true the mayor and her husband didn't live in the same apartment. He laughingly said, ''I told him I had called your home at six-thirty that morning and it was Jay who answered the phone.'' Rumors of divorce were bandied about. My Italian-American cabinet members were especially victimized. Two of my finest executives, Anthony Fratto and Al Boumenot, were linked by innuendo to the mob. All was grist for the *Sun-Times* mill.

One of the worst press distortions, building upon charges by State's Attorney Daley, involved a tracklaying contract for the rapid transit to O'Hare. During construction, two strikes had been called. The first was statewide, called by the operating engineers, and caused a shutdown of all construction. The second strike was back East at the plant that made automatic signal switches. The tracklaying contract had been awarded to the Deprizio Company, an old Chicago company that had laid track at Navy Pier over a quarter of a century ago. One of only two bidders, Deprizio won the contract fair and square. The strikes made it impossible for the company to lay its tracks. No work, no money from the federal government. An official in Public Works explained to me in the spring of 1982 that the Deprizio Company was out of money; he recommended an advance. It was worked out in my office that the city would grant a $1 million advance (federal money) only on condition that Deprizio's bonding company would fully insure the sum. An ironclad contract to that effect between the bonding company and the city was attached to the contract regarding the advance. Within a week it got political. A bold headline blared, "CITY LOANS ONE MILLION DOLLARS TO DEPRIZIO." The reporter never printed the facts that (1) the money was federal money, not city money, and (2) the city was fully insured for the advance. At no time was taxpayer money in jeopardy, and the city had done nothing improper. I don't think the taxpayers ever learned that the loan was insured.

Throughout January and the first two weeks of February 1983, the polls by all three networks remained about the same: Jane Byrne ahead of both candidates by over 20 points. The thrust of my campaign was to highlight the achievements of my administration. The television commercials were designed to show me as a strong politician. Attired in drab business suits and blouses with little bows at the neck, I portrayed the cool chief executive above the fray. (If anyone thinks for a second that it was easy to march around in my pinstripe suit smiling while Daley and Washington were ripping my programs and me apart, he or she is vastly mistaken; this took constant discipline.) Many times I wanted the bows and the gloves to come off. I had long regarded Harold Washington as a real threat. In Washington's race against Bilandic, he had carried five black non-machine wards and racked up good numbers in the black machine-controlled wards.

On January 3 my advisers suggested a change in our strategy. They advised me to go on the offensive against Daley, although he was still a poor third in the polls. They feared he would attract a loyal constituency for old times' sake. "Go for the throat, bury him," my pollster urged.

I didn't like the sound of this, and Sawyer caught that in my face. "If you don't want to do it, Mayor," he said, "we can do it with negative TV spots."

I thought about the whole thing. At the beginning of the campaign, the Daley family was walking on water, but every time Richie opened his mouth, he lost support. Richie Daley was not important to me personally; he was simply a pest. I didn't like him, but that was not important. I realized that I was feeling sadness—not for him, but for his father. In a hardball campaign, going with that emotion is a dangerous luxury, but I did so. I imagined the Bridgeport reaction to Richie's coming in third. I knew their language well: I was the "bitch" or the "broad," Harold was the "nig." Why, I wondered, was Richie doing this to his father's name? His pollster knew where he stood. Why didn't he get out?

My advisers were right, and I was wrong. I lost sight of the fact that I was in a three-way race. Taking Daley down 10 points would allow me plenty of room in case Washington's numbers improved.

The campaign dragged on, and then came the televised debates. While political writers felt I "won" them, I sensed a mere short-run advantage, for the exposure gave Washington credibility, along with an opportunity to tell off the mayor of Chicago. We had each been given the same amount of tickets for supporters. The Washington supporters paid no attention to that; they came early and took all the seats. Washington clearly spoke for the hurt and disaffected. At times, as I looked out at his fervent audience screaming for my blood, I half expected to see Madame Defarge in the audience clicking her knitting needles.

Yet, with two weeks to go, and in spite of the fact that Richie received the endorsements of the *Sun-Times* and *Tribune*, the polls showed me still 20 to 25 points ahead, with 35 to 40 percent of the black vote sticking with me. Blacks in the projects, in particular, seemed solidly behind me. When the Democratic organization held a massive rally for me at the Hilton, ten thousand supporters showed. Very impressive, but I wasn't fooled. The machine could turn them out for Donald Duck, remember? I had the machine endorsement, but I didn't have all the hearts and minds. Although I didn't want to owe the machine and detested the notion of sitting there as it voted, I had sought its endorsement. As my advisers put it, "If you don't go and ask for it, the Daley forces will say you didn't ask for it because you knew you couldn't get it." I also won the endorsement at CBS, at that time the number one opinion-maker.

When Washington's staff held a rally at the University of Illinois Circle Campus on February 3, better than ten thousand showed up. At a meeting of Jesse Jackson's Operation Push, a minister declared, "No white candidate should be welcome to speak in a black church. Woe to the minister who invites a white candidate." Immediately thereafter, scores of black churches canceled invitations issued to me. To enter any that hadn't canceled was to risk a nasty encounter, with crowds of Washington supporters chanting, "Harold, Harold, Harold!" and brandishing signs with a cruel pun, *"Byrne the Bitch."* The Hispanic community did not follow suit—my supporters there remained loyal and helped me tremendously—but the black votes were slipping away. The press never tumbled to the reality, that this fight was not between Daley and Byrne.

On Saturday morning, three days before the February 22 primary, a weary political staff again met in the mayor's office. I was tired and sick with the flu. A pollster reported that after Washington's Circle Campus rally, we'd begun to slip a point and a half a day in the black community. Eighteen points had slipped away. This was not a campaign, my advisers felt, but a religion. It's hard to argue with a religious movement.

It all came to a head at a rally scheduled at Cabrini Green. Washington supporters lay in wait for me as the car pulled up. Our advance man came over and warned me that this so-called Byrne rally was actually a setup. With the Washington workers there in such force, the tenants probably wouldn't come out of their apartments, much less attend a rally. "Fine," I said, "We'll go door to door." I knocked on doors amid chants of "Harold, Harold, Harold!" The tenants didn't seem to be involved in this display, yet the number of demonstrators grew steadily. Soon the atmosphere had turned so abusive a riot threatened. Plastic bags of excrement came flying from windows, as the gangbangers finally had their day.

Deep inside, I longed to know one thing. Had those I knew within, those with whom I had worked, joined in this? What of the children—what were they thinking? They had to be confused. I felt a deep sense of anger. This racial hate-mongering was not needed anywhere in Chicago. Joe McCarthy, deputy superintendent of the police in charge of gang crime suppression, approached our party. Joe was certainly not afraid of gangs or worried for our safety, but he suggested it was time to leave before a serious riot broke out. And I did. The machine had labeled this campaign racist. So it had become.

Election day arrived at last. I kept my 20-point lead in the TV polls until the very end, but our own polling was more accurate. That morning we projected a 6-to-7-point lead. As the long day wore on, NBC planned to name me the winner early in the evening. Jay and I ate a quiet dinner in our suite at the Ambassador West Hotel. Around 6:45 P.M., NBC decided the race was too close to call. That did it for me. I no longer thought I'd make it. Daley conceded early; he had, as expected, polled a poor third. Downstairs, a large crowd of Byrne workers and well-wishers waited, not knowing what we knew. The television returns they watched had me in the lead, but the south side vote not yet turned in would push Harold Washington over the top. I begrudged him nothing and wished him well.

Kathy and I had exchanged looks several times as the results came in throughout the night; we didn't need to speak. We had often been on the seesaw of triumph and disappointment. When the time came to leave, she whispered, "Bye, Mom. I'm sorry." She couldn't hide a tear, but she summoned up a broad smile for me.

Jay and I reached home around midnight. None of us—my guards, Jay—had spoken a single word. Pulling into the driveway, I looked across the street at the Tremont Hotel. Parts of it had been saved from the original Tremont, the first major building to be moved, and without so much as a broken windowpane, when the city raised its streets in the 1850s. I thought of my great-great-grandfather Crane's amazement at the parade of houses rolling past him to higher ground. My family and I had had a long love affair with Chicago. Now I wouldn't be taking care of her anymore. And she was divided, terribly polarized.

Defeat is a complete thing. You feel it in every part of you. It is depressing, demoralizing, exhausting. Back in our apartment, staring out at the great city below, I thought of how defeated I was as a young girl when my first husband was killed. I took time to heal, but I did. The memory gave me some strength—I was tired and defeated, but in time I would heal *again*. I would because I had to.

Jay came into the living room and put his arm around my shoulder. He looked at the sprawling city just as I was doing. With a lump in his throat, he said, "I know how much you love it out there. I am so sorry. But we'll be all right, honey. We'll be all right."

I thought again of how tired I was. It was time to go to sleep—sleep heals. Would I ever try again? I really did not know.

Suddenly my thoughts came back to reality. Spring was around the corner. Easter would soon be here. A thought raced through me. Somewhere out there a little girl is already asleep. In the early morning she will awake and rise for Mass. I bet she peeks out the window to see if the tulips have sent up their green shoots yet, tulips that represent rebirth, renaissance, and hope.

AFTERWORD

When I dragged into my office the morning after defeat, my secretary had lost control of the situation. People who would never have dared come in without appointments were milling around, walking all over the place. "Don't be hard on Wanda," a guard whispered to me. "She wasn't able to get out of here since yesterday." Unknown to me, the phones had been ringing constantly all night long. "Burn Baby Byrne!" the angry callers had shouted. "No one's going to take the election away from Harold!" Wanda had been besieged with warnings, threats, and racist insults.

This brushfire was inadvertently sparked by CBS commentator Walter Jacobson. Making the standard Chicago joke after the votes were in, he'd said, "Chicago's Chicago. A lot can happen while we sleep. It's not all over." The city was tense, and some of Harold's supporters were primed for drastic action. Now, it seemed to me, the most important thing was to make sure that everyone believed in the fairness of the process. Chicago had its first black mayor, and that was that. By state law, any candidate within 3 percent of the winner could ask for a recount. By recount, Jim Thompson had just reversed his apparent loss to Adlai Stevenson and won the governorship. But a recount that made me winner, should that happen, would only fuel the racial fire. Many blacks would feel that the fix was in, just as in the old days, and I did not think it possible to govern a town with 43 percent of the people alienated from my administration. I wanted to see my city go forward peacefully. I told the press there would be no recount. I had publicly conceded already, and I wished Harold well.

That very afternoon, along with two bodyguards, Jay, Kathy, and I flew off to Palm Springs for an attempt at recuperation after the grueling campaign. We were all very, very tired and demoralized. When we deplaned at the small airport in the desert, I was amazed to see a crowd of about 250 shouting, "Go back, Mayor Byrne, go back! Fight for your city!" I stopped dead in my tracks, and tears welled up in Kathy's eyes. I knew I would start crying myself if we did not get out of there fast. My overwhelming feeling was impotence. There was no way I could respond. I had lost the night before. When we got out into the warm desert air and felt the southern California sun on our faces, I thought, This will be a time of healing and repair. That night it began to rain, and it rained for the rest of our stay. The creamy stucco Mediterranean-style buildings became dark and dank.

No sun, and no rest, either. Phones rang constantly, sending one message over and over: go for a write-in. The emotion in the calls was disturbing. Peace had not been restored at all. Daley was being booed as a spoiler everywhere he went and didn't dare try again. There was suspicion on all sides. When we flew back home after five days of being holed up in our rooms, about four hundred Chicagoans were waiting at O'Hare chanting, "Write-in, Write-in!" Again, I was moved by this response, but I did not think there was anything I could do.

The general election was in full swing. The Republican nominee, Bernard Epton, had received a mere 11,397 votes in the primary, as would be expected in Chicago. Bowing to the inevitable, he had sat out the entire primary contest in Florida. Now, when I snapped on the TV news, Bernie had miraculously gained hundreds and hundreds of supporters willing to follow him everywhere he went. An awkward, inexperienced candidate, he hadn't become Kennedyesque overnight, but he was performing with great zeal. Usually, the Democratic nominee's campaign need only be perfunctory, but Harold, too, was out on the hustings exhibiting great bravado and gusto. What I was seeing on the nightly reports, of course, was not political support but cheering and jeering. It was ghastly. At white rallies, the mikes picked up chants like "Get rid of the nigger in the woodpile." At black rallies rose the cry "It's *ours* now!" As a lifetime Chicagoan and sitting mayor, I ached inside as I watched my city tear itself apart.

Only a week before, I could have said, "Knock it off . . . we're not going to do this." But now I was the lame duck. The campaign grew even uglier. Somehow, hospital reports of Epton's two hospitalizations for psychiatric care were leaked to the TV stations, and the streets were filled with crude rumors about Washington's past. Racial hate notched up visibly every day. I finally decided I'd had enough. I wanted all of this divisiveness stopped. Would a write-in help? One of my pollsters had been sampling the mood of the city all along and thought I should try, because my numbers were well into the mid-60s in percentage. Bob Dituri, one of my best volunteer coordinators, had found the same feeling among the volunteers who had worked so hard for me in the primary. This was a difficult decision, and I dallied over it, perhaps fatally. When I decided to go for it, a new element had entered: many white committeemen of the Democratic machine endorsed Republican Epton. I was a write-in candidate for all of thirty-six hours. I did not want to be a part of this increasing ugliness.

By now, Epton's rallies had an aura of the Second Coming, so palpably religious was the fervor. Meanwhile, in the nation's one surviving Democratic machine town of any size, the two-party system had experienced an amazing renaissance. After only six weeks of primary campaigning, Republican Epton, political neophyte, scored 619,-926 votes. Democrat Washington beat him with 668,176 votes, a plurality of about 50,000. Chicago was exhausted, and I was sickened. We had been forced to gaze too long at the raw underbelly of the city. I couldn't wait for Harold's inauguration to take place. Two days after he took the oath of office, I gratefully took off on a speaking tour.

When I returned, the city's politics had entered a new phase, dubbed "the council wars" by the pundits of the press. The white majority of twenty-nine councilmen stymied the new mayor at every turn, suggesting to their frightened white constituents that they were protecting the store from the black intruder and his twenty-one councilmen. The truth was very different. As program after program was canceled or forestalled, supposedly to ensure that tax dollars were wisely used, "the twenty-nine" were actually scheming to retain all control of pinstripe patronage. It was the old story; they wanted their share of the spoils. The first major victim was the Navy Pier project, a total rehabilitation and development requiring not one red cent from the taxpayer. I'd arranged the contract, signed it, and left it on Harold's desk. When he sent it to the council, it got shot down in committee. The loss of projected revenue from amusement, sales, and hotel-motel taxes was enormous, quite apart from the fun and good spirit of a reawakened pier. Our hopes for another World's Fair were dashed, too, along with an estimated 65,000 jobs over a ten-year period. The expansion of O'Hare was delayed for over a year, losing an entire construction season. Washington wanted to authorize a bond sale to finance the project, but the white majority wanted to control the pinstripe patronage to the underwriters, bond salesmen, bankers, and financial advisers who would benefit from such a huge offering. The mayor would make no commitments in this regard, so the council would not approve the sale. Voters didn't seem to care, but I knew that the loss of these plans for revenue enhancement could have only one outcome, as the cost of government kept rising . . . and, indeed, taxes soon went up. Through it all, the shouts of recrimination and name-calling in council chambers grew even louder. The Democratic troops were in fighting form. I was in and out of town quite a bit, speaking all over the country at universities and public affairs events. Each time I returned, there seemed to be yet another new fight. To the *Wall Street Journal*, Chicago was now "Beirut on the Lake." This was quite a progression from 1982, when we had won the award for Most Livable City in America.

If Harold had compromised, some of the projects would have been authorized, but he told me later that he couldn't risk the label of "sellout." I didn't agree, because no matter what he did, he seemed to have a solid ethnic base of 43 to 44 percent of the electorate and only needed 6 more points to win reelection. He stuck by his decision and made himself something of a martyr. It seemed to me that a mayor has to learn to compromise judiciously in order to move a divided city forward.

After a while, many of the old Byrne supporters began urging me to prepare to run again. I was not enthusiastic. The rapid, unexpected political defeat in the 1983 race had shocked me, and it hurt. There would have to be a compelling reason for me to try a comeback.

Meanwhile, the political stalemate endured. Taxes were rising, and the tax base was shrinking as many left the city. No planned economic development was in harness, so far as I could see, and there was little concerted effort from government to encourage business to relocate here. Chicago was no longer a happy, optimistic community. Urged to meet with political consultants in New York and Washington, I heard advice that suited my personality. Get in there first, they said, because it will be very, very close—perhaps as slim a margin overall as 2 percent. After the previous election, I knew that the white candidate who did not enter first would be called a spoiler, as Richie had been dubbed, so racial had the political strategizing of Chicago become. In any case, a campaign wouldn't be easy. Some basic rules of machine politics don't change, despite council wars, and therefore

Washington could count on contributions from contractors, developers, real estate speculators, and other well-heeled special interest
groups. He was in position to raise $6 million to $7 million; as it
turned out, we would raise about $1.2 million. I was amazed that we
were able to raise that much in what was so obviously an uphill
campaign, and will always be grateful to Tom Ward, my chief fund-
raiser and true friend for pulling off such a feat.

My announcement was handled in a novel way right before the
July 4 weekend of 1985. The night before my official press conference
throwing my hat in the ring, we ran TV spots making the announcement on the local and national news programs of all the Chicago
stations. With this ploy, my campaign commandeered local news coverage for about forty-eight hours. The Daley wing of the machine was
angry.

I was determined to avoid both the "old politics" and this
wretched new racial divisiveness. My speeches concentrated strictly
on economic issues. A few Democratic regulars, most notably Park
Superintendent Ed Kelly, gave me strong and early support. By December 1986, the polls showed Harold and me jockeying within 1 or 2
percentage points of each other, just as my advisers had predicted.
Suddenly, new political parties began forming. Tom Hynes, county
assessor, created the Chicago First Party so he could run against us,
and Vrdolyak, the Democratic Party chairman, announced he would
become the candidate of the Solidarity Party. Technically, therefore,
neither man could be called a spoiler, because neither would be listed
in the Democratic primary. To most Chicagoans, however, this tech-
nicality was meaningless. It looked as if three white candidates were
vying in a single race.

In a mailer to all Daley supporters, Bill Daley in general terms
advised that they should register in time for the "real election," the
general election in April. This could be taken as a subtle message to
skip the primary. The word went out in the Daley/Hynes strong-
holds: "Wait for Tommy." To add to the confusion, Vrdolyak's
twenty-eight councilmen were not bowing to him; they were throwing their support to me in the primary. At my rallies, voters would say
to me, "We're going to vote for you, Jane, but how can you beat three
men?" I'd try to explain that only Harold and I would be in the
primary, but they'd go home that night and see an ad for Hynes playing on television. For over a year, I had been going house to house
trying to fight the disinformation put out by southwest side politicians during the '83 race. I had made headway. Now with Hynes in

the race, my workers, when canvassing were being told, "We're waiting for Tom."

My supporters and consultants felt that the Hynes race was being mounted by the Daley camp for one reason only—to stop me. On one level, I couldn't think about it. I was working night and day to shake that one last hand, get that one last wink implying support at the ballot box. At another level, though, I felt that I was facing a replay of 1983.

On election night, Harold and I attracted the highest total number ever recorded in a Democratic primary in the city. Each of us broke over 500,000 votes, but he surpassed me by to 60,000. The sobering truth, I realized, was that I had been able to change nothing on the racial front. Epton, Daley, or the biggest dummy on earth, if white, would have earned my totals, and any black candidate that year would have matched Harold's. I don't say this to deny his special qualities, only to note that voters of both races were not seeing beyond skin color.

The day after the primary results, I was moved to find that Harold had truly been touched by the magic of Room 507. He phoned me to say that we had to help bring the city together, and I could not agree more. "We both got a champion's vote," he said, "and we have to meet." When we did, we frankly discussed our political differences, but Harold was a shrewd politician and understood there had been nothing personal in my campaign. Afterward, I publicly endorsed him and cut a TV commercial for his campaign.

Meanwhile, the white candidates made their moves. Daley, surprising no one, endorsed his stalking horse, Hynes. The assessor's name recognition was 14 percent at the beginning of the primary. After $750,000 was reportedly spent to air TV and radio spots in the final week of that contest, it rose only to 17 percent. There would be no waiting for Tommy; he sensibly withdrew. Vrdolyak, obviously pushing the racial buttons, offended a sizable number of white voters. In the general election against Harold he earned only a little over 450,000 votes, a good sign that Chicagoans had at last been turned off by the racial divisiveness.

After the race, I worked with the mayor on a couple of projects, particularly the World's Fair. Even though the leader of the international site committee thought Chicago could pull it off in time, Harold was afraid that the project had been delayed too long to be made successful.

Once, he inadvertently got me in a little trouble. Immediately after the election, he asked me to run for clerk of the circuit court. I wasn't interested, but Harold wanted to head off Vrdolyak, now a Republican, who planned to run for the post. "I can't have him around," said the mayor. "He isn't good for Chicago. You have to do this. You're the only one who can beat him." I was still uncertain. At slate-making, seven or eight people would always show up to compete for each spot, and I knew many of them would have strong reasons and credentials specific to the job. I also knew that George Dunne, named Democratic chairman again, would be likely to oppose me. "No, my mind's made up," Harold said. "I'll have to put out a few brushfires, because you and George aren't on the same wavelength, but I want you."

That November, I went before the slate-makers in open session, something I abhorred, and duly presented my credentials. The next day, in executive session, the slate-making committee locked horns for almost three hours, all because of Jane Byrne. Dunne, apparently still angry because I had not backed him in his third attempt to be county chairman, would absolutely not have me, and the nod went to someone else. This was extremely unpleasant. I was perched out on a limb, running for a spot I didn't want, and Washington was nowhere to be found. The next thing I heard, he had endorsed the committee's ticket from top to bottom. Jackie Grimshaw, his political aide and strategist, called to explain that the pressure had just been too much and he had had to cave in at the last moment. He was sorry. That can happen in politics, of course, and I was curious to see where all of this would lead.

Five days later, Harold was dead. He had suffered a massive coronary in his office and never recovered.

Even as doctors at Northwestern tried to save the stricken mayor, the long knives were out. The scrambling made the raw grabs for power after Daley's death look like a church picnic. Again, the struggle was to name an acting mayor. "The twenty-nine" had many good allies and golfing buddies among the old guard black leaders, so the machine truly was back and able to build a coalition behind the black alderman Eugene Sawyer, a very nice human being who was not cut out for this sort of thing. The progressives found him too weak and conservative for their aims and united behind Alderman Timothy Evans. Numbers in the council favored the machine, of course, and they were prepared to ram through their decision. As the council met, at least ten thousand Washington supporters showed up at City Hall, having been bused from a memorial tribute to the late mayor at the

Circle Campus auditorium. The crowd swelled the council chamber, the lobby, and the hallways and spilled out to LaSalle Street, loudly jeering and shouting over and over, "Judas! Judas!" This show, televised live, went on into the wee hours of the morning. Gene was elected acting mayor to fill out the term, but the Washington troops went to court and were able to have a special election scheduled for 1989.

Gene had no peace at all. Once they had outmaneuvered the progressives, the machine whites dropped him like a hot potato. Old guard blacks stayed behind him, progressives backed Evans . . . and Richie Daley stepped back onstage. After he announced, my phone began ringing, and the pressure mounted to run, but I didn't see the benefit to me or to Chicago. I was working on this book, Jay was really enjoying his retirement, and Kathy, now an attorney, was doing well. Besides, my campaign would only add to the divisiveness of a political situation that had come to be defined almost entirely by race.

In the Democratic primary between Gene and Richie, the Evans supporters stayed home, and Daley won. The general election between Daley and Evans was an exact reversal; the disgruntled Sawyer supporters stayed away, and Richie became at last his father's successor in Room 507. As a consultant for CBS-TV during the races, I watched from the sidelines with some surprise. No longer did the streets thunder with emotion, as they had in 1979 or in Harold's 1983 race. There were no sparks in any of the three campaigns, and I supposed that Chicagoans were just tired of the incessant wrangling.

Bridgeport breathed a deep sigh of relief. With a white mayor in office, they apparently felt they would have a lock on the office for another fifty years. It seemed unlikely that any other white would run against Daley, because she or he would risk earning the label of "spoiler."

Richie himself began to put on a puzzling show. In one of his first public statements after the election, he said he was disgusted about nonpayment of water bills and was going to do something about it. He would start by releasing the names of the biggest debtors to the city. One, it turned out, was the Public Housing Authority. Naturally, the press said, "That's a governmental agency. Why don't you make it pay its bills?" He bristled and fired back, "They ought to put meters on the showers of people in public housing." He also suggested that the bills would be lower if residents cut down on the number of six-packs they drank.

Not long afterward, Richie began privatizing some of the city's medical services. Privatization can be a useful, legitimate tool for cutting government expense, but there can be a downside. In this case, a fine alcoholic and drug treatment center founded in the 1950s was privatized, thus becoming unavailable to the poor who have dependency problems. Richie announced that the homeless would be ejected from O'Hare, where many slept at night, because they were unsightly. There was some negative reaction, but the order went through on January 1, 1990. When several people were found dead of exposure during the following week, it turned out some of them had been staying nights in O'Hare.

Back in the Reagan recession, I had been unable to get work going on a third Chicago airport, though studies made clear that one would be essential in the near future. Daley had discounted this idea during his campaign, forever praising O'Hare as "the gem of Chicago." Suddenly he announced without warning that a southeast side neighborhood was going to be razed for a new field. This was a well-established, hardworking community of ten thousand homes. When they solidly opposed the plan in a referendum, Richie retorted that he didn't govern by referendum.

City Hall was getting stronger and the citizens of Chicago were getting weaker, but I had other things to think about. In March, out of the blue, we learned that Jay had cancer. When he hadn't been able to shake a bout of pneumonia, doctors found a large tumor blocking a main tube in his lung. This life-threatening illness required five harrowing months of very aggressive, experimental treatment. Every sixteen days, Jay had to spend five days in the hospital, undergoing radiation treatment and submitting to three different intravenous chemotherapies around the clock. The oncologists had pulled no punches; this was a very serious case. The treatment was exhausting for Jay, and for me, but he never complained. By July, though he was physically weakened, the cancer had gone into remission. By September, he was feeling quite well again.

I surfaced and looked around me. To my astonishment, the budget announced for 1991 was based on a projected rise in the state income tax and a predicted increase in sales tax revenues—both at the height of a recession. They were doing it again, just as the city had rolled over its debt and fallen into the financial woes I inherited in 1979. The school budget was to be balanced on the projected income tax increase as well as invasions of the teachers' pension fund and the building fund.

Meanwhile, I noticed from the papers that the murder rate in Chicago was beating all previous records. When someone asked Daley to comment, he blamed drugs and said the problem was bad all over the country. No one pointed out that he had assigned only sixty officers out of twelve thousand to the Narcotics Division.

The cab companies wanted a rate increase. Even drivers were opposed, because the companies would have increased leasing fees and the drivers might make less in tips. The companies promised not to raise fees, and the rate increase went through. Four months later, the leasing fees were raised.

To help balance the budget, the city intended to ax the hospital benefits that were included with retiree pensions—a terrible thing to do to people on fixed incomes. Jay and I had just been reminded of the extremely high cost of hospitalization and treatment. At one point in council, Alderman Timothy Evans suggested an alternative to a specific proposal in the budget. "Do we ever think of doing it this way?" he asked. Richie, perched on the rostrum, replied, "No—no. That's why I'm up here and you're down there."

I was disturbed by all of these things, and more of the same. Policemen would come up to me on the street and say, "Mayor, do you know what they're doing to us?" Cabbies would stop and urge me to run. One-on-one with Daley, I believed I could win, but I knew that a three-way race would be to his advantage.

When I announced, still having friends in City Hall, I was advised by them that after Daley had done some polling, he and his advisers expressed amazement at the strength of my numbers in the polls, but others must have been startled as well. Soon, Congressman Gus Savage was calling around the black community, encouraging the alderman and the more progressive activists to unite behind a consensus black candidate. Suddenly, Alderman Danny Davis, an independent until the previous October, when he had been slated by the machine for county commissioner, was in the race. Was he Richie's candidate, as the press surmised? Rarely can you find the truth behind these things. A respected columnist wrote that Daley insiders told him that Davis had been promised a congressional seat if he made the run, but the alderman denied it. If it was a Daley ploy, he'd never tell, and Davis himself might not know he was being used. About a month later, as I was campaigning at a nightclub in a black neighborhood, Savage happened by. "Hi, Gus," I said. He stepped back. "You still speaking to me after what I did to you?"

My 1991 campaign focused on issues—crime, drug sales and usage, economic development, tax increases, phony budgeting—but my numbers began slipping. The white community did not want to lose a white mayor, and black voters were being prevailed upon to vote for "one of our own." At least I could put my criticisms and my proposals on the record, and as I predicted, by the summer of 1991 the Chicago school board revealed it faced a $300 million deficit for the coming school term. Chicago slipped down in the national ratings of cities, and mediocrity seems to have a stranglehold on government.

The election of February 26, 1991, pulled the lowest voter turnout since the 1930s—in other words, since the days of Ed Kelly, the first mayor from Bridgeport. The winner, Richie Daley, was approved by 27 percent of Chicago's registered voters, a total lower than he'd gained when he first won the mayor's chair. The machine had stayed behind him. Byrne voters stayed home, (I came in third, as I expected.) fearing that Danny could win, but his black constituency didn't come out strongly, either; he got about 30 percent of the registered black vote. Off in the Middle East at that time, Americans of all racial backgrounds were fighting together to show the world the meaning of democracy, but more than half of Chicago didn't bother to vote.

How much things change, and how much they stay the same. . . . The same families are powerful in the Chicago establishment as a century ago, the newspapers carry on the same wars, and the descendants of the Cranes and Nolans and Burkes are still eagerly in the thick of my inimitable city's struggles and triumphs.

It was a great privilege to be mayor of Chicago. We were able to build mammoth projects during a recession, and we were often able to bring people together. When I look out my window on the forty-third floor, I can see my hand in the growth of the city. But the two achievements that mean most to me are not at all the most mammoth projects.

One is the Vietnam Veterans Fountain, the first memorial to those soldiers built anywhere in the nation. I wanted to be the first to thank them publicly. It was dedicated on a gray, rainy, chilly day that suited the somber mood following that controversial, troubling war. The Chicago cold went right into our bones, and the rain poured down, and when I looked at the faces of the vets standing in front and

Vietnam Veterans Memorial Fountain—the first official monument in America dedicated to the men and women who served in Vietnam. The monument was meant to ease memories of the violence of the 1968 Democratic convention over the Vietnam war. COURTESY OF PETER J. SCHULTZ.

looking up sadly at the fountain, I saw that many were still beaten men. Yet in their eyes was the beginning of relief from the pain, I truly believed. When the fountain was turned on and began to spray, the tears began streaming down their faces as they stood there shaking in the cold and rain, and no one made a sound.

Then there is the Children's Fountain, a lovely creation with cherubs and their harps. When we dedicated it, children came from every ethnic group in the city, many in ethnic dress. It stands on Wacker Drive, not far from the river gateway that brought generation after generation here, and always reminds me of all the magical children who were born here and built this great city. Jay is a great walker, averaging eight to ten miles a day, and he would get me walking around the city after my loss in 1983. But it was months before I could

Children's fountain—dedicated in 1982 to all the children of Chicago.
COURTESY OF PETER J. SCHULTZ.

walk with him to stand beside the Children's Fountain. It was my favorite project, a work of the heart, and I could not look at it for a long, long time.

Yes, it was a privilege to be mayor of Chicago, but it is a privilege just to live and work and play every day in the city of my ancestors and my future. What that will be, no one can say, but I will try to keep to the pathway laid down with so much love and hard work by those long-ago immigrants who came here with little but hope and grit.

REFERENCES

CHAPTER 1 A Magic of Its Own

1. Alfred T. Andreas, *A History of Chicago: From Earliest to Present Times* (Chicago: A.T. Andreas Co., 1884–86; reprint. New York: Arno Press, 1975), Vol. 1, pp. 78–9.
2. Ibid., pp. 198–99.
3. Ibid., p. 193.
4. Ibid., pp. 75–99, 129–33.
5. Stephen Longstreet, *Chicago: 1860–1919* (New York: David McKay, 1952), p. 51.
6. Gregg Wolper, *The Chicago Dock and Canal Trust: 1857–1987* (Chicago: Chicago Dock and Canal Trust, 1988), pp. 11–13.
7. Richard Wilson Renner, "In a Perfect Ferment: Chicago, 'The Know-Nothings' and the Riot for Lager Beer," *Chicago History* 5:3 (Fall 1976), pp. 161–70.
8. *Old Chicago Watertower District* by the Commission on Chicago Historical and Architectural Landmarks (Chicago: 1984), pp. 1–16.

CHAPTER 2 The Spirit of Chicago

1. Harold M. Mayer and Richard C. Wade, *Chicago: Growth of a Metropolis* (Chicago: University of Chicago Press, 1969), pp. 117–18.
2. Josiah Seymour Currey, *Chicago: Its History and Its Builders* (Chicago: S. J. Clark, 1912), Vol. 2, p. 26.
3. Ibid., pp. 97–98.
4. Ibid., p. 161.
5. Jay Robert Nash, *Makers and Breakers of Chicago* (Chicago: Academy Chicago, 1985), pp. 11–15.
6. Bessie Louise Pierce, *A History of Chicago* (New York: Knopf, 1937–57); Vol. 2, p. 253.
7. Ibid., p. 275.
8. Ellen Skerrett and Dominic Pacyga, *Chicago, City of Neighborhoods* (Chicago: Loyola University Press, 1986), pp. 371–74; Currey, Vol. 2, pp. 152–59.
9. David L. Protess, "Joseph Medill: Chicago's First Modern Mayor," in Melvin Holli and Paul M. Green, eds., *The Mayors: The Chicago Political Tradition* (Carbondale: Southern Illinois University Press, 1987), p. 10.
10. Ibid., pp. 13–15.

CHAPTER 3 Haymarket Violence

1. Edward R. Kantowicz, "Carter Harrison II: The Politics of Balance," in Holli and Green, eds., *The Mayors*, pp. 16–18.
2. Stephen Becker, *Marshall Field III* (New York: Simon & Schuster, 1964), p. 36.; Lloyd Wendt, *Chicago Tribune: The Rise of a Great American Newspaper* (Chicago: Rand McNally, 1979), pp. 281–87.
3. "Haymarket, 1886!" *Chicago History* 15:2 (Summer 1986), pp. 23–33; "Chicago Historical Society Haymarket Centennial Exhibit Highlights" in same issue.
4. Becker, pp. 40–41.

CHAPTER 4 The White City

1. Louise de Koven Bowen, *Growing Up with a City* (New York: Macmillan, 1926), pp. 90–91, 120–21; Skerrett and Pacyga, pp. 47–49.
2. Ellen Skerrett, "The Catholic Dimension," in Lawrence McCaffrey and Ellen Skerrett, eds., *The Irish in Chicago* (Urbana and Chicago: University of Illinois Press, 1987), p. 39.
3. Allen Spears, *Black Chicago: The Making of a Negro Ghetto, 1880–1920* (Chicago: University of Chicago Press, 1967).
4. Currey, Vol. 3, pp. 123–62; Daphne Christianson, ed., *Chicago Public Works: A History* (Chicago: Rand McNally, 1973), pp. 35–40; "On the River," *Chicago Public Works Quarterly*, n.p., n.d.; John Clayton, "How They Tinkered With the River," *Chicago History* 1:1 (Spring 1970), pp. 32–46.; Louis P. Cain, "Creation of Chicago's Sanitary District and Construction of the Sanitary and Ship Canal," *Chicago History* 8:2 (Summer 1979), pp. 98–110.
5. R. Reid Badger, *The Great American Fair* (Chicago: Nelson-Hall, 1979), p. 48; *Chicago Tribune*, June 28, 1889.
6. Badger, p. 84.; Jeanne Weimann, *The Fair Woman: Story of the Woman's Building and Worlds Columbia Exposition* (Chicago: Academy Chicago, 1981), p. 242.
7. Weimann, p. 106.

CHAPTER 5 Coming of Age

1. John Hogan, *A Spirit Capable: A Story of Commonwealth Edison* (Chicago: Mobium Press, 1986), p. 52.
2. Skerrett and Pacyga, pp. 431–32.
3. Currey, Vol. 2, p. 7–9.
4. William Tuttle, Jr., *Race Riot: Chicago in the Red Summer of 1919* (New York: Atheneum, 1970), pp. 108–120.
5. K.C. Tessendorf, "Captain Streeter's District of Lake Michigan," *Chicago History* 5:3 (Fall 1976), p. 157; Robin L. Einhorn, "A Taxing Dilemma: Lake Shore Protection," *Chicago History* 18:3 (Fall 1989), pp. 34–51.
6. Harold Henderson, "Dirty Water," *The Reader* 13:2 (October 7, 1983), p. 5.
7. Nash, p. 131.
8. Becker, p. 55–57.
9. Skerrett, in McCaffrey and Skerrett, eds., *Irish in Chicago*, p. 49.

CHAPTER 6 Modern Chicago

1. Tuttle, pp. 120–23.
2. John D. Buenker, "Edward F. Dunne: The Limits of Municipal Reform," in Holli and Green, eds., *The Mayors*, pp. 40–48.

3. Nash, pp. 77–78.
4. Ibid., p. 29.
5. Douglas Bukowski, "Big Bill Thompson: 1915–1923; 1927–1931," in Holli and Green, eds., *The Mayors*, pp. 61–63.
6. Skerrett, in McCaffrey and Skerrett, eds., *Irish in Chicago*, p. 49.
7. Tuttle, pp. 4–10, 42–64.
8. Nash, p. 80.

CHAPTER 7   The Roaring Twenties

1. Robert I. Goler, "Black Sox," *Chicago History* 17:3,4 (Fall–Winter 1988–89), pp. 42–69.; Photographic Essay of Chicago Historical Society Exhibit, Spring 1989.
2. Tessendorf, pp. 152–60.
3. Hogan, pp. 52–53.
4. Douglas Bukowski, "William Dever and Prohibition," *Chicago History* 7:2 (Summer 1978), p. 110.
5. Ibid., p. 113.
6. Milton Fairman, "The 28th International Eucharistic Congress," *Chicago History* 5:4 (Winter 1976–77), pp. 202–7.
7. Bukowski, "Big Bill Thompson," p. 76.

CHAPTER 8   Buddy, Can You Spare a Dime?

1. Joseph Sander, "Magic Moments," *Chicago Tribune*, August 14, 1983, pp. 16–27.

CHAPTER 9   The Dark Shadow of War

1. Roger Biles, "Big Red in Bronzeville," *Chicago History* 10 Summer 1981, p. 104.
2. Nathan Miller, *FDR: An Intimate Portrait* (New York: New American Library, 1983), p. 450.
3. Ibid., p. 480.
4. Ellen Williams, "Harriet Monroe and Poetry Magazine," *Chicago History* 4:4 (Winter 1975–76), p. 212.

CHAPTER 10   Postwar Prosperity

1. Roger Biles, *Big City Boss in Depression and War: Mayor Edward J. Kelly of Chicago* (DeKalb, Ill.: Northern Illinois University Press, 1984), pp. 135–36.
2. Ibid., p. 138.

CHAPTER 11   The King Maker

1. *Chicago Tribune*, March 25, 1955, p. 2; Mike Royko, *Boss* (New York: New American Library, 1976), p. 89.
2. John M. Allswang, "Richard J. Daley: America's Last Boss," in Holli and Green, eds., *The Mayors*, p. 148.

CHAPTER 12   The Challenge to the Machine

1. Dempsey J. Travis, *An Autobiography of Black Politics* (Chicago: Chicago Urban Research Press, 1987), p. 262.

CHAPTER 13   The City That Wasn't Working

1. *Who's Who in America*, 39th ed. (Chicago: Marquis, 1976–77), Vol. 1, p. 725; *University of Chicago Magazine*, November 1964, p. 5.
2. Charles Nicodemus, "For Governor," *Chicago Daily News*, February 21, 1968, p. 11.
3. Peter Lisagor, "I'm in It: Bobby" *Chicago Daily News*, March 16, 1968, p. 1.
4. Lyndon Baines Johnson, "Lyndon Baines Johnson: Withdrawal Speech, Delivered on March 31, 1968, to the Nation," *Annals of America* 18:1961–68, ed. William Benton, (Chicago: Encyclopedia Britannica, 1968), p. 615.
5. Frank Sullivan, *Legend* (Chicago: Bonus Books, 1989), p. 262.
6. Dan Corditz, ed., "Mayor Daley's Mouthpiece: Excerpts from Interviews," *New Republic*, September 21, 1968, pp. 17–18.

CHAPTER 14   It Can't Happen Here

1. Royko, *Boss*, p. 179.
2. Sullivan, p. 38.
3. Royko, *Boss*, p. 189.
4. Travis, p. 407.

CHAPTER 15   The Tumultuous Seventies

1. Travis, pp. 425–58. For a sampling of press coverage of the Black Panthers, see listings in the Bibliography for journalists William Braden, Henry DeZutter, John Klemer, L.F. Palmer, Jr., Clarence Page, and D. Zochert.
2. Racetrack-related newspaper stories include Robert Glass and Sy Adelman, "Kerner Loses a Winner: Sold Stocks Too Soon," *Chicago Today*, August 1, 1971, p. 1; Charles Nicodemus and William Clements, "Marj Everett's Role in Kerner Deal Told," *Chicago Daily News*, September 16, 1971, p. 1; Charles Nicodemus, "Rostenkowski Future Periled by Track Deal," *Chicago Daily News*, October 21, 1971, p. 1; Ronald Koziol and Thomas Powers, "Report Marj Everett Gave Stock Deals for Race Dates," *Chicago Tribune*, September 16, 1971, p. 1; Mike Royko, "Taking Stock of That Stock," *Chicago Daily News*, September 21, 1971, p. 3; Charles Nicodemus and William Clements, "Tell Kerner Profits on Track Stock," *Chicago Daily News*, September 16, 1971, p. 1. See also "Hoellen Hints Daley Deal in Plan for Hotel at O'Hare," *American*, June 5, 1969.
3. Robert Glass, "Race Stock Exclusive, How Lynch Hid Deals of 5 Pols," *Chicago Today*, September 17, 1971, pp. 1, 3; Edward T. Pound and Joel Weisman, "How Judge Lynch Turned Over $2.3 Million in Track Shares," *Chicago Today*, September 21, 1971, pp. 3–18; Glass, "New Race Stock Deal Revealed: $163,400 Profit for Judge Lynch," *Chicago Today*, November 21, 1971, pp. 1, 3; Len O'Connor, *Clout* (Chicago: Avon Books, 1976), p. 250.
4. Edward T. Pound and Joel Weisman, "Disclosure Near, So Dunne Told of Holdings," *Chicago Today*, September 15, 1971, pp. 4–5.
5. Edward T. Pound and Joel Weisman, "Rostenkowski Deal: $500 Track Stock—$42,000 Profit, Congressman's Secret Holdings," *Chicago Today*, September 29, 1971, p. 1; Pound and Weisman, "Bare Rostenkowski Secret Stock Windfall!" *Chicago Today*, September 29, 1971, p. 3; Betty Washington, "Didn't Discuss Rostenkowski's Stock: Daley," *Chicago Daily News*, October 4, 1971, p. 10.
6. John O'Brien and Peter Negronida, "Daley Insurance Deal Told: Sends City Business to Firm Tied to Son," *Chicago Tribune*, February 9, 1973, pp. 1–4; Neil Mehler, "Public Missing Point in Daley's Aid to Sons," *Chicago Tribune*, May 12, 1973, Political Editor's Column; Charles Nicodemus, "Daley and Honest Graft," *Chicago Daily News*,

February 17, 1973, Political Editor's Column; "The Fabled Kingdom of Clout" [editorial], *Chicago Daily News*, February 16, 1973; "All in the Family" [editorial], *Chicago Today*, February 12, 1973.

7. John O'Brien and Peter Negronida, "Daley's Son's Firm Acted Without State OK on City Policies," *Chicago Tribune*, February 10, 1973, pp. 1, 7.

8. Thomas Powers, "Wigoda Found Guilty," *Chicago Tribune*, October 11, 1974, pp. 1, 15.

9. Danaher-related newspaper stories include Richard Phillips, "Indict Daley Pol Danaher: U.S. Names 3 in Bribe Plot," *Chicago Tribune*, April 11, 1974, p. 1; "List of Top Democrats Indicted Here Grows," *Chicago Tribune*," April 11, 1974, p. 16; "This Indictment Hurt Daley Most," *Chicago Tribune*, April 11, 1974, p. 16.

10. Keane-related newspaper stories include Dennis Fisher, "Keane Gets Five Years, Fine of $27,000," *Chicago Sun-Times*, November 19, 1974, p. 3; Rob Warden, "Keane Guilty: 18 Counts of Fraud & Conspiracy," *Chicago Daily News*, October 9, 1974, pp. 1, 13–14, 16–17; Daniel Young and Edward Schreiber, "City Council Faces a Power Vacuum in Convictions' Wake," *Chicago Tribune*, October 13, 1974, pp. 2, 3.

11. Bush-related newspaper stories include Jay Braneman, "Bush Did Night Work for Daley Told," *Chicago Today*, August 23, 1974, p. 13; Thomas Powers, "Bush Innocent on 9 Counts; Mistrial on 11 Charges," *Chicago Tribune*, August 31, 1974, pp. 1–4; Frank Zahour, "More Troubles Ahead for Bush—Carey Eyes $202,000 Suit," *Chicago Tribune*, October 13, 1974, p. 2; Richard Phillips, "Bush Shifts Answers in Fraud Trial," *Chicago Tribune*, October 11, 1974, p. 2; David Gilbert and Ron Koziol, "Bush Quits Daley Staff; Was Top Aide," *Chicago Tribune*, August 2, 1973, p. 6; Gilbert and Koziol, "Ex-City Aide Owns Stock in O'Hare Ad Firm," *Chicago Tribune*, April 3, 1973, p. 2; Edward Schreiber, "Mayor Demotes Bush from Press Aide Post," *Chicago Tribune*, March 30, 1973, p. 3. See also O'Connor, *Clout*, p. 257.

12. William Juneau, "Daley's Sons' Realty Tests Fixed, 3 Say," *Chicago Tribune*, March 8, 1974, pp. 1–10.

13. Thomas Powers and Jack Fuller, "Daley Son in O'Hare Deal: Represented Avis Auto Firm in Pact Talks," *Chicago Tribune*, May 4, 1974, p. 1; Phillip J. O'Connor, "U.S. Joins Probe of Korshak and Daley Son Deal," *Chicago Daily News*, May 4, 1974; Harry Golden, Jr., "Daley Son Aided Avis at O'Hare," *Chicago Sun-Times*, November 5, 1974, p. 5; Jay McMullen and Phillip J. O'Connor, "City Denies 'Sweetheart' Rent-Car Pact at O'Hare," *Chicago Daily News*, May 6, 1974, p. 1.

14. Ronald Koziol and Thomas Powers, "Daley OK'd Contract to Firm Paying Son Fees: $747,000 in School Cabinets," *Chicago Tribune*, January 27, 1974, p. 1; Thomas J. Moore and Edward T. Pound, "Daley Son Paid Retainer by Voting-Machine Firm," *Chicago Sun-Times*, January 21, 1974, p. 1; "Daley Son Still on Job for Vote Machine Maker," *Chicago Today*, January 22, 1974, p. 5.

CHAPTER 16   Daley's Last Hurrah

1. Sullivan, p. 188.
2. Len O'Connor, *Requiem* (Chicago: Contemporary Books, 1977), p. 32.
3. Jay Braneman, "Bush 'Night Work' for Daley Told," *Chicago Today*, August 23, 1974, p. 10.
4. Sullivan, p. 179.
5. O'Connor, *Requiem*, pp. 154–55.

CHAPTER 17   The New Mayor of Chicago

1. Robert F. Kennedy, *To Seek a Newer World* (New York: Doubleday, 1968), p. 233.

CHAPTER 18   Great Dreams for Chicago

1. *Illinois Revised Statutes, 1989.* Chapter 24: Sec. III; 14.3; State Bar Association Edition, St. Paul, Minnesota: West Publishing Co., 1989: 1212.
2. Mike Royko, "Divine Right of Bridgeport? Target for '83: Daley," *Chicago Sun-Times*, March 9, 1979, p. 2.
3. Brian J. Kelly and Pat Winegart, "Voters Don't Blame Byrne for City's Financial Woes," *Chicago Sun-Times*, February 8, 1980, p. 6.

CHAPTER 19   A Time of Affluence

1. Robert F. Kennedy, p. 234.
2. Mary Ludgin and Louis Masotti, *Downtown Development: Chicago 1979–1984*, cited in *Urban Affairs News* [newsletter], ed. Audrey Chambers, (Evanston: Northwestern University Center for Urban Affairs and Policy Research), Fall 1985, pp. 1–2.; John McCarron, "Loop Rides Fast Track in Growth," *Chicago Tribune*, August 20, 1985, pp. 16–17.
3. Art Petacque and Charles Nicodemus, "Big Racetrack Fees to Daley Firm Bared," *Chicago Sun-Times*, October 24, 1980, p. 1; Bob Secter, "Charge Senator Daley 2 Dems Dodged Report," *Chicago Daily News*, April 14, 1977, p. 5.

BIBLIOGRAPHY

Note: This listing includes some newspaper accounts and editorials; many others are cited in the References section in support of passages in the text.

Abbott, Grace. *The Immigrant and the Community.* New York: n.p., 1917.

Abbott, W.J. "Makers of the Fair." *Outlook* 48, November 18, 1893, pp. 884–85.

Addams, Jane. *Twenty Years at Hull House.* New York: Macmillan, 1910.

———. "Why the Ward Boss Rules," *Outlook*, april 2, 1898, pp. 879–82.

"Aldermen Are Split on Daley Riot Orders." *Chicago Tribune*, April 16, 1968, Sec. 1, p. 2.

Alkalimat, Abdul, and Doug Gills. *Harold Washington and the Crises of Black Power in Chicago.* Chicago: Twenty-First Century Publications, 1989.

Allen, David. "Jane Addams vs. the Ward Boss." *Journal of Illinois State Historical Society* LIII, Autumn 1960, pp. 247–65.

Allen, F. L. *Only Yesterday.* New York: Simon & Schuster, 1939.

Allswang, John M. "Richard J. Daley: America's Last Boss," in Holli and Green, eds., *The Mayors: The Chicago Political Tradition.*

Alter, Sharon Z. "A Woman for Mayor?" *Chicago History* 15:3 (Fall 1986), pp. 52–68.

Andreas, Alfred T. *A History of Chicago: From Earliest to Present Times.* 3 vols. Chicago: A. T. Andreas Co., 1884–86. Reprint New York: Arno Press, 1975.

Angle, Paul. "Raising the Grade." *Chicago History* 3:4 (Fall 1953), pp. 263–70.

———. "Chicago and the First World War." *Chicago History* 7:15 (Fall 1964), pp. 129–44.

———, and McCelland, eds. *The Great Chicago Fire, October 8–10, 1871, Described in Seven Letters by Men and Women Who Experienced Its Horrors and Now Published in Commemoration of the Seventy-fifth Anniversary of the Catastrophe.* Chicago: Chicago Historical Society, 1946.

"Annual Report of Chicago Dock & Canal Company." Reckitt, Benington and Le-Cleak, Certified Public Accountants. Chicago: May 17, 1927.

"Attempt to Block Mr. Kennedy Fails." [Editorial.] *London Times*, April 16, 1968, p. 7.

"Autopsy on Chicago." Nation 207, September 16, 1968.

Avrich, Paul. *The Haymarket Tragedy*. Princeton, N.J.: Princeton University Press, 1984.

Bach, Ira. "A Reconsideration of the 1909 Plan of Chicago," *Chicago History* 2:3 (Spring-Summer 1973), p. 132.

Badger, R. Reid. *The Great American Fair*. Chicago: Nelson-Hall, 1979.

Baker, Ray S. "Hull House and the Ward Boss." *Outlook* LVIII, March 28, 1898, pp. 769–70.

Barnard, Harry. *Eagle Forgotten: Life of J. P. Altgeld*. New York: Duell, Sloan and Pearce, 1938.

Barry, William J. "The Once and Future Pier." *Chicago Public Works Quarterly*. Spring 1974, pp. 1–5.

Becker, Stephen. *Marshall Field III*. New York: Simon & Schuster, 1964.

Biles, Roger. *Big City Boss in Depression and War: Mayor Edward J. Kelly of Chicago*. De Kalb, Ill.: Northern Illinois University Press, 1984.

———. "Big Red in Bronzeville: Mayor Ed Kelly Reels in Black Vote." *Chicago History* 10 (Summer 1981), pp. 99–111.

Blakesly, Richard. "How War Came to Chicago 40 Years Ago." *Chicago Tribune*, June 27, 1954, pp. 14, 17.

Blatchford, Paul. *Memories of the Chicago Fire*. Chicago: Chicago Historical Society, 1921.

Boorstin, Daniel J. "A Montgomery Ward's Mail Order Business." Chicago History 2:3 (Spring-Summer 1973), pp. 142–52.

"Boss Daley's Fatherly Fist." *Newsweek*, September 9, 1968, pp. 40–41.

Bowen, Ezra, ed. *This Fabulous Century, 1920–30; This Fabulous Century, 1930–40; This Fabulous Century, 1940–50*. New York: Time-Life Books, 1969; reprint 1975.

Bowen, Louise de Koven. Growing Up with a City. New York: Macmillan, 1926.

Braden, William. "Hampton Interviewed." *Chicago Sun-Times*, May 25, 1969, p. 7.

Bragdon, Henry, et al. *History of a Free People*. New York: Macmillan, 1961.

Brown, Edward O. *The Shore of Lake Michigan*. [Legal brief read before the Law Club of the City of Chicago.] Chicago: Chicago Law Club, 1902.

Buder, Stanley. *Pullman: An Experiment in Industrial Order and Community Planning 1880–1930*. New York: Oxford University Press, 1967.

Buenker, John D. "Chicago Ethnics and the Politics of Accommodation." *Chicago History* 3:2 (Fall 1974), pp. 101–10.

———. "Edward F. Dunne: The Limits of Political Reform." In Holli and Green, eds., *The Mayors: The Chicago Political Tradition*.

Buettinger, Craig. "The Rise and Fall of Hiram Pearson: Mobility on the Urban Frontier." *Chicago History* 9:2 (Summer 1980), pp. 112–17.

Bukowski, Douglas. "William Dever and Prohibition: The Mayoral Elections of 1923–1927." *Chicago History* 7:2 (Summer 1978), pp. 109–18.

———. "Big Bill Thompson: 1915–1923; 1927–1931." In Holli and Green, eds., *The Mayors: The Chicago Political Tradition*.

Buley, R. Carlyle. *The Equitable Life Assurance Society of the United States*. 2 vols. New York: Appleton-Century-Crofts, 1967.

Burns, J.M. *Roosevelt: The Lion and the Fox*. New York: Harcourt Brace, 1956.

"Byrne Foresees Losing Party Post." *Chicago Tribune*, December 31, 1976.

Byrne, Harlan. "Extraordinary REIT: That's Chicago Dock and Canal on More Grounds Than One." *Barron's*, November 3, 1986, pp. 16–18.

Cahan, Cathy, and Richard Cahan. "The Lost City of the Depression." *Chicago History* 5:4 (Winter 1976–77), pp. 233–42.

Cain, Louis P. "The Creation of Chicago's Sanitary District and Construction of the Sanitary and Ship Canal." *Chicago History* 8:2 (Summer 1979), pp. 98–110.

Carson, Herbert N. *Cyrus Hall McCormick: His Life and Work*. Chicago: A. C. McClurg, 1909.

Casey, Robert J. "Crowd Jams Fair Opening: A Pageant of Color." *Chicago Daily News*, May 27, 1933, pp. 1,4.

Chappell, Sally Anderson. *The Chicago World's Fair of 1893–The Columbian Exposition*. [Filmstrip Presentation Grant to De Paul University from Illinois Bicentennial Commission.] Chicago: George W. Colburn Laboratory, 1976.

Chicago 1992: Goals and Policies and Ten Year Capital Development Strategies. Miles Burger, Chairman. Chicago: City of Chicago Plan Commission and Department of Planning, 1982.

"Chicago: Daley's Defense." *Time* September 20, 1968, pp. 27–28.

"Chicago Dock and Canal Vote Expected on City Front Center." *Crain's Chicago Business*, February 16, 1987, p. 1.

Chicago Dock and Canal [Appellant] vs. *Chicago Dredging & Dock Co.* #7368. In Appellate Court of Illinois: First District. [Abstract of Record.] Ino N. Jewett & Jewett Bros. [Solicitors for Complaintant]. Chicago: Barnard & Gunther, 1886.

Chicago Dock and Canal [Appellant] vs. *Gwintit Lean H. Kinzie*. #5426. Supreme Court of Illinois, Northern Grand Division. [Abstract of Record for Appellee.] Caulfield, Patton & Honore & Geo. C. Christian [Solicitors for Appellee.] Chicago: Chicago Legal News Co., 1879.

Chicago Dock—Equitable Venture . . . Guidelines. Chicago Department of Planning. Elizabeth Hollender, Commissioner. September 1985.

Chicago Historical Society Staff. *Summary of Information on the Site of Fort Dearborn: Wacker Drive and Michigan Avenue*. Chicago: 1971.

"Chicago: The King Richard Version." Newsweek, September 23, 1968, p. 35.

"Chicago Protest Called Off, Fear of Further Violence." *Overseas News*, April 15, 1968, p. 4.

"Chicago: The Reassessment." Time, September 13, 1968, pp. 16–21.

"Chicago River Reversed." *Chicago American*, January 2, 1968.

"The Chicago Tribune's 'Money Market.' " *Inter-Ocean*, October 6, 1872, p. 6.

"Chicago's Reconstruction: Auditor's Report—Insurance Fire Losses and Payments." *Inter-Ocean*, October 18, 1872, p. 3.

Chlereth, Thomas J. "A Robin's Egg Renaissance: Chicago Culture 1890–1933." *Chicago History* 8 (Fall 1979), pp. 144–54.

Christianson, Daphne, ed. *Chicago Public Works: A History*. Chicago: Rand McNally, 1973.

Citizens Association of Chicago. "*Holding That the Chicago Dock and Canal Company Had No Legal Title to the Land for Which the City Is Now Asked to Pay $300,000.00*." [Pamphlet.] Chicago: 1913.

———. *The Outer Harbor Land Purchase*. [Citizens opposed to Chicago subsidizing Chicago Dock and Canal.] Chicago: 1913.

City Council of the City of Chicago. *Journal of the Proceedings of the City Council, 1967–1968*. Vol. April 20, 1967, to March 26, 1968. Chicago: Office of John Marcin, Chicago City Clerk, 1968. [March 6, 1968], p. 2293; [March 20, 1968], p. 2373.

"City Front Dock & Canal: How City Front Rose from Conflict." *Crain's Chicago Business*, April 24, 1989, pp. 3–4.

"City Improvements." *Chicago Weekly Democrat*, September 15, 1848, p. 2.

"City in a Bind: The Anger and Ferment of Black Chicago." *Look*, August 6, 1968, pp. 28–33.

"A City Run by a Machine." *U.S. News & World Report*, February 12, 1968, p. 47.

Clifton, James A. "Caldwell's Exile in Early Chicago." *Chicago History* 6:4 (Winter 1977–78), pp. 218–28.

———. "Chicago, September 14, 1833: The Last Great Indian Treaty in the Old Northwest." *Chicago History* 9:2 (Summer 1980).

Coffey, Raymond R. "Dossier on Daley." *Nation* 207, October 7, 1968, pp. 328–30.

Condit, Carl. *The Chicago School of Architecture: A History of Commercial and Public Buildings in Chicago 1875–1925*. Chicago: University of Chicago Press, 1964.

———. *Chicago, 1910–29: Building, Planning, and Urban Technology*. Chicago: University of Chicago Press, 1973.

———. *Chicago, 1930–70: Building, Planning, and Urban Technology*. Chicago: University of Chicago Press, 1974.

"Conolisk Acts Quickly on Daley Riot Order." *Chicago Tribune*, April 16, 1968, p. 2.

Conwell, Russell H. *Acres of Diamonds*. New York: Jove Books, 1978.

Corditz, D., ed. "Mayor Daley's Mouthpiece: Excerpts from Interviews." *New Republic* 159, September 21, 1968, pp. 17–18.

Currey, Josiah Seymour. *Chicago: Its History and Its Builders*. 3 Vols. Chicago: S. J. Clark, 1912.

"Daley City Under Seige." Time, August 30, 1968, pp. 15–19.

Darling, Sharon S. "Arts & Crafts Shops in the Fine Arts Building." *Chicago History* 6:2 (Summer 1977), pp. 79–85.

Davis, Charles A. "A Chicago Love Affair." *Chicago Defender*, June 19, 1985, p. 10.

"Delays Hit North Loop." *Crain's Chicago Business*, June 6, 1988, p. 83.

"Dementia in the Second City." *Time*, April 26, 1968, pp. 10–11, 18–19.

"The Democrats After Chicago: Survival at the Stockyards." *Time*, September 20, 1968, pp. 27–31.

Deuel, Wallace. "Nazis Bomb Warsaw: Hitler Challenge to World." *Chicago Daily News*, September 1, 1939, p. 1.

DeZutter, Henry. "Panthers Try to Cool Violence." *Chicago Daily News*, September 25, 1969, p. 1.

Dornfeld, A. A. "Chicago Age of Sail." *Chicago History* 2:3 (Spring-Summer 1973), pp. 156–66.

Drury, John. *Old Chicago Houses*. Chicago: University of Chicago Press, 1975.

Ducato, Theresa. "Pulling for Pullman." *Inland Architect*, March–April, 1982, pp. 7–19.

Duis, Perry R. *Chicago: Creating New Traditions*. Chicago: Chicago Historical Society, 1975.

————. "Where Is Athens Now?" *Chicago History* 6:2 (Summer 1977), pp. 66–78.

————, and Glen E. Holt. "The Importance of Being Best." *Chicago Magazine*, January 1979, pp. 194–96.

————. "One Hundred Years of Smoke: Before Ozone-Laden Smog, Black Clouds Shrouded the City." *Chicago Magazine* 28 (September 1979).

Dumas, Malone. "Charles Wacker." In *Who's Who in Midwestern American Biography*, Vol. 10. New York: Scribner & Sons, 1936.

Duncan, David Douglas. "War Photographer on Michigan Avenue." *Newsweek*, September 9, 1968, pp. 42–46.

"Durable Dick Daley." *Look*, August 18, 1968, pp. 20–23.

Dytch, Meridith M. "Remember Ellsworth—Chicago's First Hero of the Civil War." *Chicago History* 9:1 (Spring 1982), pp. 14–25.

"Eight of White Sox Indicted." The *Chicago Daily News*, September 28, 1920, p. 1.

"Equitable–City Front Breaks Goal." *Crain's Chicago Business*, October 24, 1988, p. 8.

"Extremists: The Panther Bite." *Time*, September 20, 1968, p. 32.

"Fair Housing Is Now The Law of the Land." *Chicago Daily Defender*, January 13, 1969, Sec. I, p. 3.

"The Fair Is Worth the Risk." [Editorial.] *Chicago Tribune*, June 12, 1985, Sec. 1, p. 14.

Fairman, Milton. "The 28th International Eucharistic Congress." *Chicago History* 5:4 (Winter), pp. 202–10.

Farber, David. *Chicago '68*. Chicago and London: University of Chicago Press, 1987.

Farwell, Abby Ferry. *Reminiscences of John V. Farwell by His Elder Daughter*. 2 vols. Chicago: Ralph Fletcher Seymour, 1926.

"Fear of Violence." *Nation* 207, September 16, 1968, pp. 227–28.

Foner, Philip S., ed. *The Haymarket Autobiographies*. New York: Humanities Press, 1969.

————. *The Factory Girls*. Champaigne and Urbana, Ill.: University of Illinois Press, 1977.

Frazier, Arthur H. "The Military Frontier: Fort Dearborn." *Chicago History* 9:2 (Summer 1980), pp. 81–85.

Freeman, David. "The Least Known Mayor of Chicago." [Mayor Dever.] *New City*, March 28, 1990, pp. 5, 10.

From Lake Michigan to You: A Description of the Chicago Water System. Chicago Department of Water, n.d.

Furer, Howard B., ed. *Chicago, A Chronological and Documentary History: 1784–1970*. New York: Oceana, 1974.

"Galena & Chicago Railroads . . . Michigan Central Merge." *Chicago Weekly Democrat*, January 4, 1851, p. 4.

Gardner, Virginia. "A Literary Editor Reminisces: Henry Blackman Sell." *Chicago History*. 3:2 (Fall 1974), pp. 101–10.

Garraghan, Gilbert S. J., *Chapters in Frontier History*. Milwaukee: Bruce, 1934.

Geoghegan, Thomas. "America's Greatest City: Chicago Pride of the Rustbelt." *New Republic*, March 25, 1984.

Gilbert, Paul, and Charles Lee. *From Chicago and Its Makers: A Narrative of Events from the First Day of the White Man to the Inception of the First World War*. Chicago: Felix Mendelsohn, 1929.

Goff, Lisa. "Chicago Dock Seeks City Help for Huge Project." *Crain's Chicago Business*, March 4, 1985, pp. 1, 45.

———. "Chicago Dock Developers May Face Landmark Hurdle." *Crain's Chicago Business*, August 5, 1985, p. 34.

"Goldblatt Site Praised as First-Rate by Officials." *Chicago Sun-Times*, February 23, 1986, Sec. 1, p. 7.

Golden, Harry, Jr. "Office Plan Hits as 'Manhattan' in Loop." *Chicago Sun-Times*, February 26, 1986, Sec. 1, p. 12.

———. "Primary Vote Rolls Pegged at 1.4 Million." *Chicago Sun-Times*, February 26, 1986, Sec. 1, p. 18.

Goldston, Robert. *The Great Depression: U.S. in the Thirties.* Greenwich, Conn.: Fawcett, 1968.

Goler, Robert I. "Black Sox." *Chicago History* 17:3–4 (Fall–Winter 1988–89), pp. 42–69.

Gompers, Samuel. *Seventy Years of Life and Labor.* New York: Dutton, 1925.

Gondey, Michel. "A European Looks at America." *Look*, August 6, 1968, pp. 25–27.

Gordon, Ann D. "Investigating the Eastland Accident." *Chicago History* 10:2 (Summer 1981).

Gordon, Beverly. "A Furor of Benevolence." *Chicago History* 15:4 (Winter 1986), pp. 48–65.

Gottfried, Alex. *Boss Cermak of Chicago: A Study in Political Leadership.* Seattle: University of Washington Press, 1962.

"Gov. Roosevelt Elected—Horner Seen As Victor." *Chicago Daily News*, November 8, 1932, p. 1.

"Governor Kerner Appointed Head of Presidential Commission on Violence in America." *Chicago Today*, February 12, 1973, p. 2.

Graham, Bruce J. "A City in Need of a Vision." [Editorial.] *Chicago Tribune*, April 1, 1985, Sec. 1, p. 11.

Granger, Alfred. *Chicago Welcomes You: A Century of Progress.* Chicago: A. Kroch, 1933.

Green, Paul. "Anton J. Cermak: The Man and His Machine." In Holli and Green, eds., *The Mayors: The Chicago Political Tradition.*

Greene, Hurley. "Only in Chicago." *Chicago Independent Bulletin*, February 24, 1983, p. 4.

———. "Slammin the Slate." *Chicago Independent Bulletin*, November 21, 1984, p. 4.

Griffin, Al. "The Ups and Downs of Riverview Park." *Chicago History* 4:1 (Spring 1975), pp. 14–22.

Grimshaw, William J. *Black Politics in Chicago.* In Urban Insight Series. Chicago: Center for Urban Policy of Loyola University, 1980.

Grosch, Anthony. "H. L. Mencken and Literary Chicago." *Chicago History* 14:2 (Summer 1985), pp. 4–25.

———. "Social Issues in Early Chicago Novels." *Chicago History* 4:2 (Summer 1975), pp. 68–77.

Haeger, John Denis. *The Investment Frontier: New York Businessmen and the Economic Development of the Old Northwest.* Albany: State University of New York Press, 1981.

————. "Eastern Money and the Urban Frontier: Chicago, 1833–1842." *Journal of the Illinois State Historical Society* 64, Autumn 1971, pp. 267–84.

Halas, George S. *Halas: An Autobiography*. Chicago: Bonus Books, 1986.

————. *Halas by Halas*. New York: McGraw-Hill, 1979.

Hamilton, Henry Raymond. *The Epic of Chicago*. New York: Willett, Clark, 1932.

Handlin, Oscar. *The American People in the Twentieth Century*. Cambridge: Harvard University Press, 1954.

Harrington, Michael. *The Other America*. New York: Macmillan, 1962.

Harrison, Carter H. *Stormy Years*. Indianapolis: Bobbs-Merrill, 1935.

————. *Growing Up with Chicago*. Chicago: Robert Fletcher Seymour, 1944.

Harrison, F., Jr. "Map of Mouth of Chicago River: For the Purpose of Showing Proposed Harbor Improvements." In A. T. Andreas, *A History of Chicago*, Vol. 1, p. 112.

"Haymarket, 1886!" *Chicago History* 15:2 (Summer 1986), pp. 20–35.

Hayner, Don, and Tom Mcnamee. *Streetwise Chicago: A History of Chicago Street Names*. Chicago: Loyola University Press, 1988.

Heise, Kenan. *The Chicagoization of America: 1893–1917*. Evanston, Ill: Chicago Historical Bookworks, 1990.

Henderson, Harold. "Dirty Water: The Sullied Past and Murky Future of a City and Its River." *The Reader* 13:2 (October 7, 1983), pp. 1–3.

Hogan, John. *A Spirit Capable: A Story of Commonwealth Edison*. Chicago: Mobium Press, 1986.

Holli, Melvin, and d'A. Jones, eds. *Ethnic Chicago*. Grand Rapids, Mich.: W. B. Eerdmans, 1984.

Holli, Melvin, and Paul M. Green, eds. *The Making of the Mayor*. Chicago: 1983. Grand Rapids, Mich.: W. B. Eerdmans, 1984.

————. *The Mayors: The Chicago Political Tradition*. Carbondale: Southern University Illinois Press, 1987.

————. *Bashing Chicago Traditions*. Grand Rapids, Mich.: W. B. Eerdmans, 1989.

Hoyt, Homer. *One Hundred Years of Land Values in Chicago, 1830–1933*. Chicago: University of Chicago Press, 1933.

Hurt, Jethro, ed. *The House at 1800 Prairie Avenue*. Chicago: Chicago Architecture Foundation, 1978.

Hutchinson, William T. *Cyrus Hall McCormick: Seed Time, 1809–1856*. New York and London: Century, 1930.

————. *Cyrus Hall McCormick: Harvest Time, 1856–1884*. New York: D. Appleton–Century, 1935.

"International Harvester Company: IH Facts." Novistar International Corporation, 455 N. Cityfront Plaza Drive, March 11, 1990.

Insull, Samuel. "Illinois in the War." Address to Commercial Club of Chicago, January 18, 1919.

"Investigations: Refighting Chicago." Time, September 20, 1968, p. 19.

"Investor Opinion Divided over Chicago Dock Pace." *Crain's Chicago Business*, September 21, 1987, p. 54.

Jahant, Charles A. "Chicago: Center of the Silent Film Industry." *Chicago History* 3:1 (Spring-Summer 1974), pp. 45–53.

Johnson, Lyndon Baines. Text of Resignation Speech, delivered March 31, 1968, to the nation. *Annals of America 18:1961–68*, ed. William Benton. Chicago: Encyclopedia Britannica, 1968.

Johnson, Mary Ann, ed. *The Many Faces of Hull House: The Photographs of Wallace Kirkland.* Chicago: University of Illinois Press, 1989.

Julian, Ralph. *Chicago and the World's Fair.* New York: Harper and Brothers, 1893.

Kantowicz, Edward, R. "Carter Harrison II: The Politics of Balance." In Holli and Green, *The Mayors: The Chicago Political Tradition.*

Kearney, John. "Mayor Daley: Decision-Maker in Chicago." *Commonwealth* 88, August 9, 1968, pp. 518–19.

Kennedy, John F. "The Negro and the American Promise." [TV address.] *Congressional Record*, 88th Congress, 1 Sess., pp. 10965–66.

Kennedy, Robert F. *To Seek a Newer World.* New York: Doubleday, 1967.

Kenton, Edna, ed. *The Jesuit Relations and Allied Documents.* New York: Albert & Charles Boni, 1925.

Kerch, Steve. "Tracking the Future: Once Again, Railroads Become Chicago's Engine of Development." *Chicago Tribune*, September 26, 1990, pp. 4–9.

———. "Collision Course: City Planners, Largest Landholders Differ . . . Goose Island. Chicago Tribune, September 26, 1990, pp. 19–20.

Kerner, Otto. *Kerner Report: Supplemental Studies for the National Advisory Commission on Civil Disorder.* New York: Praeger, 1968.

"Kerner Report . . . Urban Riots Result of White Racism." *Chicago Sun-Times*, May 10, 1976, p. 3.

Kiemer, John. "Police in Chicago Slay Two Panthers." *New York Times*, December 4, 1969, pp. 1, 34.

Killian, Thomas Fletcher, et al. *Who Runs Chicago.* New York: St. Martin's Press, 1979.

King, Martin Luther, Jr. *Where Do We Go from Here: Chaos or Community?* Boston, Beacon Press, 1968.

———. "Letter from a Birmingham Jail." Reprinted, *Christian Century*, June 12, 1963.

Kinsley, Philip. *The Chicago Tribune: Its First Hundred Years.* 3 vols. Chicago: Chicago Tribune Press, 1865–1900.

Kirkland, Joseph. *The Story of Chicago.* 3 vols. Chicago: Dibble, 1892–94.

———. "The Poor in Great Cities." In *Among the Poor of Chicago.* New York: Charles Scribner's Sons, 1895.

Kling, William. "Why, What, When of Riots: Kerner Commission Tells Findings." *Chicago Tribune*, March 1, 1968, pp. 1–3.

Koenig, Msgr. Harry C., ed. *A History of the Parishes of the Archdiocese of Chicago.* 2 vols. Chicago: New World, 1980.

Kogan, Bernard. "Chicago's Pier." *Chicago History* 5:1 (Spring 1976), pp. 28–38.

Kogen, Herman. *Give the Lady What She Wants.* [A story of Marshall Field Company policy.] Chicago: Rand McNally, 1952.

Koziol, R. "Carey Probe of Bush Bared." *Chicago Tribune*, August 8, 1973, p. 8.

———. "Park District Probed . . . Links to Bush." *Chicago Tribune*, August 11, 1974, p. 5.

Lamb, John M. "Early Days on the Illinois and Michigan Canal." *Chicago History* 3:3 (Winter 1974–75), pp. 168–76.

The Landowner: Journal of Real Estate. First Anniversary Issue of Chicago Fire, October 1872; Second Anniversary Issue, October 1873.

Leach, Paul M. "Mayoral Race . . . Cermak Repeats Pledge . . . Elimination Waste and Graft." *Chicago Daily News*, March 31, 1931, pp. 1, 8.

Leighton, I. *The Aspirin Age.* New York: Simon & Schuster, 1949.

Leonard, Jonathon Norton. *Three Years Down.* New York: Lippincott, 1944.

Lindsey, Almont. *The Pullman Strike.* Chicago: Chicago University Press, 1942.

Longstreet, Stephen. *Chicago: 1860–1919.* New York: David McKay, 1952.

Looby, Dave. "Hynes Speculates on '87 Mayor's Race." *Southwest Sentinel*, May 17, 1985, pp. 5, 7.

"Lots of Law, Little Order." *Newsweek*, September 9, 1968, pp. 38–41.

Lowe, David, ed. *The Great Chicago Fire.* New York: Dover, 1979.

———. *Lost Chicago.* Boston: Houghton Mifflin, 1975.

"Lyndon Tells Nation He Will Not Seek Reelection." *Chicago Tribune*, April 1, 1968, p. 1.

Marquette, Jacques, S. J. "Departure of Father Jacques Marquette for the Discovery of the Great River . . ." In Edna Kenton, ed., *The Jesuit Relations and Allied Documents*, pp. 333–65.

Marsh, Barabara, and Sally Saville. "International Harvester: How a Great Company Lost its Way." *Crain's Chicago Business*, November 8, 1982, pp. 21–43.

———. "A McCormick's Mission: The Sleeping Giant." *Crain's Chicago Business*, November 5, 1982, pp. 19–41.

"The Marvels of a Year." [Editorial.] *Landowner*, October 4, 1872, p. 166.

Massa, Anna. "Chicago's Martyrs: A Parable for the People." *Chicago History* 15:2 (Summer 1986), pp. 54–57.

May, Henry F. *The End of American Innocence: The First Years of Our Times: 1912–1917.* New York: Knopf, 1969.

Mayer, Harold M., and Richard C. Wade. *Chicago: Growth of a Metropolis.* Chicago: University of Chicago Press, 1969.

Mayer, Harold M. "Launching of Chicago: The Situation and the Site." *Chicago History* 9:2 (Summer 1980) pp. 68–79.

The Mayors of Chicago . . . a Chronological List. 1987 Ed. Elizabeth Levine. Chicago: Municipal Reference Library, 1987.

McCaffrey, Lawrence, and Ellen Skerrett, eds. *The Irish in Chicago.* Urbana and Chicago: University of Illinois Press, 1987.

McCarthy, Michael P. "The Short Unhappy Life of the Illinois Progressive Party." *Chicago History* 6:1 (Spring 1977), pp. 2–11.

McCormick, Cyrus. *The Century of the Reaper.* Boston: Houghton Mifflin Company, 1931.

"McCormick's Factory." Chicago Weekly Democrat, March 29, 1851, p. 3.

"McCormick's Reaper." *Gem of the Prairie* 6:21 (December 1, 1849), p. 4.

McElvaine, Robert S. *The Great Depression: America, 1929–1941.* New York: Times Books, Random House, 1984.

McGibney, Ruth Thompson. "The Iroquois Theatre Fire." *Chicago History* 3:3 (Winter 1974–75), pp. 177–80.

McGrath, Paul. "The Consigliere: Under Two Mayors from the 11th Ward, Tom Donovan Has Quietly and Efficiently Controlled all City Jobs." *Chicago Magazine*, March 1979, pp. 126–28, 174–79.

———. "Jane Byrne's Strategy." *Chicago Magazine*, January 1980, p. 20.

———. "The She Decade." Chicago Magazine, January 1980, pp. 143–60.

———. "The Masotti Documents." *Chicago Magazine*, May 1980, pp. 166–69.

———. "Has Byrne's Revolution Stalled?" *Chicago Magazine*, November 11, 1979, p. 22.

McIlvaine, Mabel, ed. *Reminiscences of Chicago During the Forties and Fifties*. Chicago: Lakeside Press, R. R. Donnelley & Sons, 1913.

———. *Reminiscences of Early Chicago*. 3 vols. Lakeside Classic Series. Chicago: Lakeside Press, R. R. Donnelly and Sons, 1902.

Meeker, Arthur. *Chicago with Love*. New York: Knopf, 1955.

———. *Prairie Avenue*. New York: Knopf, 1949.

Metcalfe, Ralph. "The Blues, Chicago Style." *Chicago History* 3:1 (Special, Summer 1974), pp. 4–13.

Michuda, Stephen J. "Growth of the Great Chicago Bridge System." [Monograph.] Chicago Department of Engineering, 1949.

Mikva, Abner J. "The Shame of Chicago." *Nation* 207, September 16, 1968, p. 229.

Miller, Nathan. *FDR—an Intimate History*. New York: Doubleday, 1983.

Mitchell, Steven. *Elm Street Politics*. New York: Oceana Publications, 1959.

Monroe, Cockrell F. *Banking in Chicago, 1929–1935: Deep Depression Years*. Chicago: privately published, 1948.

"Movable Bridges of Chicago." Department of Public Works, *Bureau of Engineering*, Chicago, 1983.

Mumford, Lewis. "The Chicago Fairs." *New Republic* 65, January 21, 1931, p. 272.

Murphy, H. Lee. "Investors' Opinions Divided over Chicago Dock's Pace." *Crain's Chicago Business*, September 2, 1987, p. 1.

Murray, George. "Chicago's Famous Bridges." *Chicago American*, reprint November 3, 1958.

Murrow, Edward R., and Fred Friendly. *I Can Hear It Now:* [Recordings.] I, *1919–1932*, Ml. 4076; II, *1933–1945*; Ml. 4261; III, *1945–1949*; Ml. 4261. New York: Columbia Masterworks, n.d.

Nash, Jay Robert. *Makers and Breakers of Chicago*. Chicago: Academy Chicago Publishers, 1985.

Nelli, Humbert. *Italians in Chicago, 1888–1930: A Study in Ethnic Mobility*. New York: Oxford University Press, 1979.

Nelson, Bruce. "The Movement Behind the Martyrs." *Chicago History* 15:1 (Summer 1986), pp. 4–20.

Newfield, Jack. *Robert Kennedy: A Memoir*. New York: New American Library, 1988.

Newman, Mark. "On the Air with Jack L. Cooper: The Beginnings of Black Radio Appeal." *Chicago History* 2:2 (Summer 1983), pp. 51–58.

Charles Nicodemus. "New City Library: White Elephant or Crown Jewel?" *Chicago Sun-Times*, February 23, 1986, Sec. 1, p. 1.

Niles, H. [Military Governor of Streeterville]. *A Brief History and the Legal Standing of the District of Lake Michigan*. Chicago: C. Swanberg, 1900.

Norris' City Directory for Chicago 1847–48. Chicago: J. H. Kedzie, 1847.

"North Shore Docks." *Chicago Tribune*, June 21, 1870, p. 3.

O'Connor, Len. *Requiem*. Chicago: Contemporary Books, 1977.

———. *Clout*. Chicago: Avon, 1976.

O'Malley, Peter J. *Mayor Martin H. Kennelly of Chicago: A Potential Biography*. Chicago: University of Illinois, 1980.

Opportunities for World's Fair Residuals. Chicago: World's Fair Planning Unit, Department of Planning, 1984.

"The Outer Harbor Land Purchase." Corporation Counsel City of Chicago. Chicago: Opinion Rendered July 1, 1912.

Page, Clarence. "Black Panthers." *Chicago Tribune*, September 18, 1969, p. 14.

Palmer, L.F., Jr. "Black Panther–Sketch." *Chicago Sun-Times*, May 25, 1969, p. 7.

———. "The No-Choice Bag." *Nation*, 207, October 21, 1968, pp. 394–95.

"Partial Reconstruction of McCormick's Reaper Manufacturing." *Gem of the Prairie* 7:44 (March 29, 1851), p. 2.

"Payoff from City Front Center, a Distant Goal for Chicago Dock & Canal Co." *Crain's Chicago Business*, September 25, 1989, pp. 62–63.

Peretti, Burton W. "White Hot Jazz." *Chicago History* 12:3–4 (Fall–Winter 1988–89), pp. 26–41.

Peterson, Jacqueline. "Good-bye Madame Beaubien: The Americanization of Early Chicago Society." *Chicago History* 9:2 (Summer 1980), pp. 98–111.

Piehl, Frank J. "Shall We Gather at the River." *Chicago History* 2:4 (Fall–Winter 1973), pp. 196–205.

———. Chicago's Early Fight to Save Our Lake." *Chicago History* 5:4 (Winter 1975–76), pp. 223–32.

Pierce, Bessie Louise. *A History of Chicago*. 3 vols. New York: Knopf, 1937–57.

Platt, Harold. "Samuel Insull and the Electric City." *Chicago History* 15:1 (Spring 1986), pp. 20–35.

"Preservationists Score a Victory." *Crain's Chicago Business*, August 12, 1985, p. 80.

Protess, David L. "Joseph Medill: Chicago's First Modern Mayor." In Holli and Green, eds., *The Mayors: The Chicago Political Tradition*.

"The Protest Syndrome." [Editorial.] London Times, April 15, 1968, p. 11.

Rakove, Milton. "A Transfer of Power: The Machine is Dead. Long Live the Machine." *Chicago Magazine*, May 28, 1979, pp. 186, 188.

Ralph, Julian. *Harper's Chicago and the World's Fair*. New York: Harper & Brothers, 1893.

Randall, Frank A. *History of the Development of Building Construction in Chicago*. New York: Arno Press, 1972.

Ranney, G.A., Jr. "Reports, Washington, United Nations, Illinois, Hungary." *Atlantic* 221, May 1968, p. 22.

Regnery, Henry. "Stone, Kimball and *The Chap Book*." *Chicago History* 4:2 (Summer, 1974), pp. 87–95.

Reich, Peter. "How We Went War 50 Years Ago." *American*. April 3, 1967, p. 12.

Reidy, James L. *Chicago Sculpture*. Urbana, Ill.: University of Illinois Press, 1981.

"Rejected and Unequal." [Editorial.] *London Times*, April 18, 1968, p. 14.

Renner, Richard Wilson. "In a Perfect Ferment: Chicago, 'The Know-Nothings' and the Riot for Lager Beer." *Chicago History* 5:3 (Fall 1976), pp. 161–70.

Rettenberg, Dan. "About that Urban Renaissance." *Chicago Magazine,* May 29, 1980, pp. 152–58.

Riis, Jacob A. *How the Other Half Lives.* New York: Wang, 1957.

Roberts, Sidney L. "The Municipal Voter's League and Chicago's Boodler's." *Journal of the Illinois State Historical Society* 53:2 (Summer 1960), pp. 117–48.

Roderick, Stella Virginia. *Nettie Fowler McCormick.* Rindge, N.H.: Richard M. Smith Publishers, 1956.

Rooney, Edmond J. "Troops Enforce an Uneasy Calm." *Chicago Daily News,* April 4, 1968.

"A Rose by Another Name." [Editorial.] *Chicago Tribune,* April 16, 1968, Sec. I, p. 16.

Royko, Mike. *Boss.* New York: New American Library, 1976.

Sachs, Benjamin. "The First Years of the New Century." In H. L. Meites, ed., *History of Jews in Chicago.* Chicago: Jewish Historical Society, 1924.

Sanborn Fire Insurance. Map of Cook County. "River and Lake Front." Plate 13. New York: D.A. Sanborn, 1868–69. n.p.

Schlereth, Thomas J. "A Robin's Egg Renaissance: Chicago Culture, 1893–1933." *Chicago History* 8:3 (Fall 1979), pp. 144–55.

Schlesinger, A. M., Jr. *The Coming of the New Deal.* Boston: Houghton Mifflin, 1959.

———, ed. Robert Kennedy in His Own Words. New York: Bantam Books, 1989.

Schmidt, E. "William E. Devers: A Chicago Political Fable." In Holli and Green, eds., *The Mayors: The Chicago Political Tradition.*

Schmidt, John R. *The Mayor Who Cleaned Up Chicago.* DeKalb, Ill.: Northern Illinois University Press, 1990.

Schneidman, Dave, and Monroe Anderson. "Byrne, Cuts in Schools Hit at King Rally." *Chicago Tribune,* January 16, 1980, Sec. 2, p. 2.

Schnell, Christopher J. "Mary Livermore and the Great Northwestern Fair." *Chicago History* 4:1 (Spring 1975), pp. 343–49.

———. "Shoot Arsonists: Daley Appoints Committee to Investigate Riots." *Chicago Tribune,* April 16, 1968, Sec. 1, pp. 1–2.

Scott, Anne Furor. "Saint Jane and the Ward Boss." *American Heritage* 12:1 (December 1960), pp. 12–17, 94–99.

"Second Phase of Housing Law Bows." *Chicago Daily Defender,* April 11, 1968, pp. 3, 24.

"Sensible Views . . . Frederick Douglass at the National Convention of Colored People in Cleveland." *Gem of the Prairie* 5:20 (October 7, 1848), p. 3.

Shales, Jared. "Storefronts for Life." *Inland Architect,* March-April 1983, pp. 3, 4.

"Should Lookers Be Shot?" Time, April 26, 1968, p. 18.

"Site of Camp Douglas." Chicago: Commission on Chicago Historical and Architectural Landmarks, 1976.

"Site of the DuSable/Kinzie House." Chicago: Commission on Chicago Historical and Architectural Landmarks, 1977.

"Site of the Marquette Camp." Chicago: Commission on Chicago Historical and Architectural Landmarks, 1976.

"Site of the Sauganash Hotel and the Wigwam." Chicago: Commission on Chicago Historical and Architectural Landmarks, 1975.

"Site of Wolf Point Settlement." Chicago: Commission on Chicago Historical and Architectural Landmarks, 1975.

Skerrett, Ellen, and Dominic Pacyga. *Chicago, City of Neighborhoods*. Chicago: Loyola University Press, 1986.

Sklar, Katheryn Kish. "Hull House in the 1890s: A Community of Women Reformers." *Signs* 10:4 (1985), pp. 658–77.

Smith, Carl S. "Cataclysm & Cultural Consciousness: Chicago and the Haymarket Trial." Chicago History 15:2 (Summer 1986), pp. 36–53.

Smith, Henry Justin. *Chicago's Great Century, 1833–1933*. Chicago: Consolidated Publishers, 1933.

Smith, M.J.P. "No Little Deals." [North Loop redevelopment, citizens denied process, preservation, and fair purchase price.] *Inland Architect*, November-December 1987, pp. 13, 16, 19.

Sorenen, Charles E. *My Forty Years with Ford*. New York: W. W. Norton, 1956.

"Space-Squeezed NWU Eyes Plot." *Crain's Chicago Business*, October 26, 1987, p. 11.

Spalding, Albert G. "America's National Game (1911)." In Paul Angle, ed., *The American Reader*. Chicago: Rand Mcnally, 1958.

Spears, Allen. *Black Chicago: The Making of a Negro Ghetto, 1880–1920*. Chicago: University of Chicago Press, 1967.

Steffens, Lincoln. *The Autobiography of Lincoln Steffens*. New York: Harcourt, Brace, 1931.

Stern, Frederick C. "Eleven Hours in Chicago." *Nation* 21, April 22, 1968, pp. 533–35.

Strahler, Steven R. "Why Chicago Dock, Equitable Scrapped Cityfront Pact." *Crain's Chicago Business*, December 2, 1985, pp. 3, 89.

Strickland, A. E. *History of the Chicago Urban League*. Urbana and London: University of Illinois Press, 1966.

Sullivan, Frank. *Legend*. Chicago: Bonus Books, 1989.

"Summary of Information on Site of Fort Dearborn." Chicago Historical Society Compilation. Chicago: Chicago Historical Society, 1971.

Talbott, Basil. "Dunne Hints Mrs. Byrne Ouster." Chicago *Sun-Times*, December 31, 1974, p. 2.

Tarbell, Ida M. "How Chicago Is Finding Herself." *American Magazine* 67, November–December 1908, p. 33.

Tebbel, John. *An American Dynasty: The Story of the McCormicks, Medills and Pattersons*. New York: Greenwood Press, 1968.

Terry, Clifford. "The Many Faces of Hull House." *Chicago Tribune*, October 8, 1989, pp. 20–21.

Tessendorf, K. C. "Captain Streeters' District of Lake Michigan." *Chicago History* 5:3 (Fall 1976), pp. 152–60.

"The Thing in Spring." Time, April 26, 1968, pp. 17–18.

Thompson, James. "Map of the Town of Chicago, 1830." In A. T. Andreas, *History of Chicago*, Vol. 1, p. 112.

Thompson, Robert E., and Hortense Myers. *Robert F. Kennedy: The Brother Within*. New York: Dell, 1962.

"Three Voices from the West Side." *Look*, August 6, 1968, p. 34.

Toner, Philip S., ed. *The Haymarket Autobiographies*. New York: Humanities Press, 1969.

Travis, Dempsey J. *An Autobiography of Black Chicago*. Chicago: Chicago Urban Research Institute, 1981.

————. *An Autobiography of Black Politics*. Chicago: Chicago Urban Research Institute, 1987.

Troy, Edwards, and Tom W. Pew, Jr. "The Hilton Hotel Incident." Nation 207, September 16, 1968, p. 229.

Tuttle, William, Jr. *Race Riot: Chicago in the Red Summer of 1919*. New York: Atheneum, 1970.

"Two U. of C. Professors Give Views on Sit-Ins." *Chicago Daily Defender*, February 5, 1969, p. 5.

"The U.S.'s Toughest Customer." *Time*, December 12, 1968, pp. 89–95.

Van Brunt, Henry. "The Columbian Expedition and American Civilization." Atlantic Monthly 71, May 1893, pp. 577–88.

Vinci, John. "Carson Pirie Scott: 125 Years of Business." Chicago History 8:2 (Summer 1979), pp. 92–97.

Viorst, Milton. "Mayor Daley's Convention: Can the Ring Master Keep the Show Going?" Saturday Evening Post, August 24, 1968, pp. 26–27, 70.

Wade, Louise Carroll. "Graham Taylor: Pioneer for Social Justice: 1851–1938." In Paul Angle, ed., *American Reader*. Chicago: Rand McNally, 1958.

————. "Something More Than Packers." Chicago History 2:4 (Fall–Winter 1973), pp. 224–31.

————. *Chicago's Pride: Stock Yards, Packing Town, and Environs in 19th Century*. Urbana, Ill.: University of Illinois Press, 1987.

"Walker Appointed to Head Federal Study of Chicago's Convention Week Disorders." *Chicago Tribune*, December 2, 1986.

Walker, Daniel. *Rights in Conflict: Convention Week in Chicago August 25–29, 1968: A Report*. New York: Dutton, 1968.

Walsh, Timothy. "Catholic Education in Chicago: The Formative Years: 1840–1890." Chicago History 8:2 (Summer 1978), pp. 87–97.

Washington, Sam. "Black Panthers." *Chicago Sun-Times*, September 6, 1969, p. 3.

Weimann, Jeanne Madeline. *The Fair Woman: Story of the Woman's Building and World's Columbia Exposition*. Chicago: 1893. Reprint Chicago: Academy Chicago Publishers, 1981.

————. "A Temple to Women's Genius. The Woman's Building of 1893." *Chicago History* 6:1, (Spring 1977), pp. 23–33.

Weingartner, Fannia, Gail T. Casterlina, and Rober Casey, eds. "James Thompson's Plot of Chicago: A 150 Year Perspective." Chicago History 9:2 (Summer 1980), pp. 66–67.

Weinrott, Lester A. "Chicago Radio: The Glory Days." Chicago History 3:1 (Spring–Summer, 1974), pp. 14–22.

Wells, Sarajane. "My Life in Radio: Reminisces About Her Experiences on Jack Armstrong . . . Other Serials." Chicago History 7:3 (Fall 1978), pp. 179–82.

Wendt, Lloyd. Chicago Tribune: The Rise of a Great American Newspaper. Chicago: Rand McNally, 1979.

Wertheimer, Barbara M. "Union Is Power: Sketches from Women's Labor History." In Jo Freeman, ed., *Women, a Feminist Perspective*. Palo Alto, Calif.: Mayfield Publishers, 1984.

Whitehead, Ralph, Jr. "What Daley Needs, Daley Gets." *Nation* 207, November 11, 1968, pp. 468–87.

Whitney, Sharon, and Raynor Thomas. *Women in Politics.* New York: Franklin Watts, 1986.

Williams, Ellen. "Harriet Monroe and Poetry Magazine." Chicago History 4:4 (Winter 1975–76), pp. 204–12.

Wing, J.M. "Rebuilt Chicago—Buildings Erected Since the Fire by Honorable Cyrus H. McCormick, Leander J. McCormick et al." *Landowner:* 4:10 (October 1872).

Wolper, Gregg. *The Chicago Dock and Canal Trust: 1857–1987.* Chicago: Chicago Dock and Canal Trust, 1988.

Wright, Amos W. "World Fair Progress." Harper's, August 31, 1889, p. 707.

———. "World's Fair of 1889–1892." Harper's, August 10, 1889, p. 652.

Zimberoff, Aleen. "Venture Partner Split Won't Hurt Cityfront." *Crain's Chicago Business,* August 5, 1985, p. 34.

Zimmerman, G. "Chicago's Mayor: Durable Dick Daley." Look, September 3, 1968, pp. 16–20.

Zochert, D., and Edmund J. Rooney. "Black Panthers Target of Justice Department." Chicago Daily News, June 11, 1969, p. 7.

INDEX